FOREIGN DIRECT INVESTMENT AND THE GLOBAL ECONOMY

CORPORATE AND INSTITUTIONAL DYNAMICS OF GLOBAL-LOCALISATION

REGIONS, CITIES AND PUBLIC POLICY SERIES

Series Editor: Ron Martin, Department of Geography, University of Cambridge

Throughout the industrialised world, economic transformation, rapid technological change and increasing globalisation are giving greater prominence to the nature and performance of individual regional and urban economies. The patterns and processes of regional and urban development are being fundamentally redrawn. At the same time, regions and cities are assuming an increased importance as arenas of public policy innovation and implementation and as new loci of social and economic intervention and regulation. *Regions, Cities and Public Policy* is an international series which aims to provide authoritative analyses of the new significance of regions and cities for economic development and public policy. It aims to combine fresh theoretical and empirical insights with constructive policy evaluation and debate, to provide a definitive set of conceptual, practical and topical studies in the field of regional and urban public policy analysis.

FOREIGN DIRECT INVESTMENT AND THE GLOBAL ECONOMY

CORPORATE AND INSTITUTIONAL DYNAMICS OF GLOBAL-LOCALISATION

edited by

Nicholas A Phelps and
Jeremy Alden

CRC Press
Taylor & Francis Group
Boca Raton London New York

CRC Press is an imprint of the
Taylor & Francis Group, an **informa** business

First published 1999 by Stationery Office

Published 2021 CRC Press
Taylor & Francis Group
6000 Broken Sound Parkway NW, Suite 300
Boca Raton, FL 33487-2742

CRC Press is an imprint of Taylor & Francis Group, an Informa business
No claim to original U.S. Government works

ISBN 13: 978-0-11-702378-9 (pbk)

Visit the Taylor & Francis Web site at
http://www.taylorandfrancis.com
and the CRC Press Web site at
http://www.crcpress.com

A CIP catalogue record for this book is available from the British Library
A Library of Congress CIP catalogue has been applied for

CONTENTS

LIST OF TABLES

LIST OF FIGURES

CONTRIBUTORS

JEREMY ALDEN is a professor in the Department of City and Regional Planning at Cardiff University. His research interests are in labour market issues associated with urban and regional economic development (both in the United Kingdom and overseas), and the interface between economic development and the statutory planning system.

YUKO AOYAMA received her PhD in City and Regional Planning from the University of California at Berkeley; she is currently an associate professor in the Department of Geography at Clark University.

NIGEL BERKELEY is a lecturer with the Centre for Local Economic Development at Coventry University. His main research interests are in the role of foreign direct investment in local and regional economies and restructuring in the UK retail industry.

THOMAS BREWER is a professor at the Georgetown University School of Business, Washington DC and editor of the *Journal of International Business Studies.* His research specialisms include international investment agreements and political risk.

KEITH CHAPMAN is Head of the Department of Geography at the University of Aberdeen. His research interests are concerned with problems of industrial location and regional development with particular reference to the oil and chemical industries.

CLIVE COLLIS is Director of the Centre for Local Economic Development at Coventry University. His main research interests are the role of foreign direct investment in local and regional economies, third age labour markets and small town regeneration.

JOHN DUNNING is Professor of International Business, Rutgers University, New Jersey, USA, and Emeritus Professor of Economics, University of Reading, UK. He has published extensively on many aspects of multinational enterprise.

JONATHAN DURNIN is Research Assistant at the Centre for Regional Economic Development at the University of Northumbria, Carlisle Campus. Current research includes work on inward investment and the regional impacts of the purchasing strategies of large firms.

ROBERT HINE is Senior Lecturer in Economics at the University of Nottingham and since 1987 a visiting professor at the College of Europe in Bruges. His journal articles are in the fields of international trade, European integration and agricultural policy. Recent co-edited books include *Agriculture in the Uruguay Round* (Macmillan, 1994), *The Reform of the Common Agricultural Policy* (Macmillan, 1998) and *Intra-Industry Trade and Adjustment* (Macmillan, forthcoming).

SUNG-HOON JUNG is a doctoral candidate in the Geography Graduate Division at the Sussex European Institute at the University of Sussex, Brighton. His research interests are in the restructuring of Korean industrial complexes.

JOCHEN LEGEWIE is a research associate at the German Institute for Japanese Studies in Tokyo. His main research interest is in the political economy of East and South-east Asia, particularly in industrial relations between Japan and other Asian countries with a focus on Japanese production networks in the Asian-Pacific region.

MAX MUNDAY is a member of the Welsh Economy Research Unit at Cardiff Business School. His main research interests are in regional economic development, the economics of multinational enterprise, and Japanese foreign direct investment in the United Kingdom.

DAVID NOON is Associate Dean of Coventry Business School and Deputy Director of the Centre for Local Economic Development at Coventry University. His main research interests are in the area of urban and regional economic development with a particular focus upon regeneration, labour market analysis and inward investment.

FRANK PECK is Research Director at the Centre for Regional Economic Development at the University of Northumbria, Carlisle Campus. Research interests include the regional effects of corporate restructuring, in particular the impacts of inward investment, reinvestment and investor development strategies for local economies.

MICHAEL PEEL is a Distinguished Senior Research Fellow at the Cardiff Business School, Cardiff University. His main research interest is corporate performance evaluation, particularly with respect to the relative financial performance of foreign-owned subsidiaries.

NICHOLAS PHELPS is a lecturer in the Department of City and Regional Planning, Cardiff University. He is author of *Multinationals and European*

Integration (Jessica Kingsley) and has written on the problems of economic development in older industrial regions of the United Kingdom.

ANDY PIKE is a lecturer and researcher in the Centre for Urban and Regional Development Studies (CURDS), University of Newcastle upon Tyne. He works on the political economy of local and regional development, institutions and policy in Europe.

PHILIP RAINES is a research fellow at the European Policies Research Centre at the University of Strathclyde in Glasgow. His research has principally been on the impact of national and EC policies on foreign direct investment, particularly with regard to labour standards and employment legislation.

LORNA WALLACE is a doctoral candidate in the Faculty of Management at Rutgers University of New Jersey. Her doctoral research has focused on the implications of globalisation and FDI for the state of New Jersey.

FIONA WISHLADE is a senior research fellow in the European Policies Research Centre at the University of Strathclyde in Glasgow. Her main research interests are in the regional policies of the EC member states as well as the regional and competition policies of the European Community.

STEPHEN YOUNG is Professor and Co-Director of Strathclyde International Business Unit at the University of Strathclyde, Glasgow. He has a range of research interests in the areas of international business and multinational enterprises, with an emphasis on public policy.

[illegible] Kingdom and has written on the [illegible] of economic development in older industrial regions of the United Kingdom.

ANDY PIKE is a lecturer and researcher in the Centre for Urban and Regional Development Studies (CURDS), University of Newcastle upon Tyne. [illegible]

[illegible]

[illegible]

[illegible]

PREFACE

The idea for this book first arose around Easter of 1997 when we considered the possibility of editing a book based loosely around some of the proposed contributions to the 'Regional Frontiers' conference organised by the Regional Studies Association and held at Frankfurt-on-Oder, Germany, in September of that year. Here we were encouraged by the success of Jeremy Alden and Phil Boland's edited collection from the Regional Studies Association 'Regional Futures: Past and Present, East and West' conference in Gothenburg two years earlier which was published by Jessica Kingsley.

In the course of our own work, we have been struck by the vast, and yet often separate, bodies of literature dealing with the activities of multinationals at several geographical scales. Three features of this vast body of work seemed particularly interesting to us. First, there is the remarkable convergence of interest across different academic disciplines – for example, economics, political science, geography and planning – in the actions and regulation of multinationals at these various scales. Second, much of this interest has centred on an apparent global–local paradox – the more economic processes have become globalised the more economic activities remain tied to particular places. Finally, both the economic processes orchestrated by multinationals and the regulatory environments orchestrated by institutions tend to have spillover effects or span different territorial scales.

More specifically, then, this book is an attempt to capture some of the complexities of, and connections between, the actions and regulation (in its broadest sense) of multinational companies at these various geographical scales. To this end we have tried to include an international spread of contributions from a range of academic disciplines to provide illustrations of these processes.

In actual fact, the book draws in more or less equal measure on selected papers from the Regional Frontiers conference together with a number of invited contributions. In doing so we have attempted to create a degree of coherence centred on the idea of there being patterns of multinational restructuring and firm–institution interactions at several spatial scales. The spatial scales we have concentrated on here are the global, trade bloc, national and subnational scales; though as a number of contributions make apparent, territorial scale is something which is actively defined through the actions of multinational companies and institutions. We hope this book will be a useful addition to an understanding of the contribution of multinational companies to the global-localisation of economic activity.

We are grateful to Sally Hardy at the Regional Studies Association, Kerensa Todd at The Stationery Office and Ron Martin the Regions, Cities and Public Policy series editor, and we thank the contributors – especially those who worked to produce chapters from scratch – for bearing with us in our editorial deliberations and in ensuring timely delivery of the final manuscript. Thanks also to Geraldine Bousie, Janice Cole, Sean White and Adri Stoffaneller for their invaluable work in preparing figures, tables and text for the book. Above all, we wish to thank Diane Tustin for her patience in formatting and assembling the final manuscript and liaising with contributors.

NICHOLAS PHELPS AND JEREMY ALDEN, CARDIFF, JULY 1999

1 Introduction: The Corporate and Institutional Dynamics of FDI in the Global Economy

INTRODUCTION

There has been a convergence of interest among geographers, planners, economists and political scientists in understanding an apparent tension between the way in which the world economy has become ever more closely integrated, yet economic activities remain tied to places as centres of production, consumption and political and cultural organisation. This tension has found expression in geographical literature in the use of terms such as 'global-localisation' (for example Cooke 1993) and 'glocalisation' (for example Swyngedouw 1992). The subtitle of this book makes use of one of these terms – 'global-localisation' – as a shorthand for a range of political and economic interactions at numerous spatial scales.

In the 1960s and 1970s economists directed much of their attention to analysing, to use Dunning's (1979) terminology, the ownership and internalisation advantages of multinationals, largely ignoring the location-specific advantages which play a role both in the origin and destination of foreign direct investment (FDI). More recently, economists have begun to pay greater attention not only to these location-specific advantages upon which multinationals draw but also to the way in which these also feed into the ownership advantages of firms (for example Dunning 1997c).

After a period in the 1970s and 1980s in which the dissolution of many traditional regional industrial specialisations was documented and the domination of localities by large, multinational companies was given prominent attention, geographers have once again returned to analysing the distinctiveness of places. In the first instance, much of this work was abstract and theoretical, falling under the rubric of locality studies in the UK (for example Cooke 1989) and agglomeration and industrial districts in the US

(Scott 1983, 1986, 1988a; Piore and Sabel 1984). Subsequent empirical and theoretical work has diverged into strands dealing with: the socio-cultural and technological (Storper 1995) basis of successful industrial agglomerations and local systems of governance (Evans and Harding 1997; Painter and Goodwin 1996; Teague 1994) or 'institutional thickness' (Amin and Thrift 1995). It is here that the interests of geographers coincide most closely with those of planners who have sought to integrate consideration of the land-use planning system within broader local systems of governance (Healey 1997). Their specific intent has been to promote the role of collaborative methods of planning practice in the building of local institutional capacity.

Traditionally, political science has concentrated on analysing central–local state relations and the sovereignty of the nation state in relation to international inter-governmental affairs. However, some tendencies towards increasing political and administrative autonomy of subnational territories (for example Keating 1997) and increasing powers and competencies of supranational bodies have rendered the traditional nation-state-centred analysis of political scientists less appropriate. These shifts in the powers and competencies of agents of governance at the subnational, national and supranational scales have been captured in the notion of multiple levels of governance (Marks *et al.* 1996).

This book is intended as a contribution to debates about the global-localisation of economic activity. We hope it will be of interest to scholars from a wide range of disciplines: notably economics, geography and planning. The contributions included here provide some important illustrations of the multiple levels of firm–institution interactions from which global economic integration is constructed. In the remainder of this chapter I explore some of the connections between corporate and institutional dynamics at various geographical scales. I begin by discussing the tensions between global and regional economic integration, and I then go on to discuss more specifically the manner in which there are important interactions between multinational firms and other agents of governance at supranational, national and subnational scales.

GLOBAL AND REGIONAL ECONOMIC INTEGRATION: SOME TENSIONS

The concepts of regionalisation and globalisation are both partial in their emphasis. The former concentrates on the political bases (or institutional dynamics) of economic integration. The latter tends to focus on the possibilities of the internal organisation of production within multinational companies and as a result has tended to overstate the mobility of investment and the sophistication of corporate organisation. However, there is now some momentum behind the thought that regionalisation and globalisation should not be talked of or analysed separately (Dent 1997; Oman 1997; Wyatt-Walker 1995). As Oman notes:

> Globalisation and regionalisation are opposites only in the sense that one can usefully be understood as a centrifugal process and the other as a centripetal process and in the sense that one is driven by microeconomic forces and the other is often a political phenomenon. In practice, globalisation and regionalisation tend to be mutually reinforcing but only insofar as regionalisation stimulates internal competition. (Oman 1997, p. 51).

There are a number of implications arising from this which I shall explore in a little more detail in the remainder of this section.

First, the actual extent of economic globalisation and regionalisation depends on the referents or indicators one considers (Allen and Thompson 1997). Labour remains the most immobile factor of production. Correspondingly, movements of labour have played no significant part in promoting regional integration in, for example, the EU (Findlay 1995), let alone global integration. At the other extreme, finance capital has become globally hypermobile. It is the globalisation of financial markets not aspects of the 'real' economy which has undermined the sovereignty of nation-states (Oman 1997) since the global financial system has become ostensibly 'a privatised system beyond the realm of political–institutional control' (Tickell and Peck 1995). The main impact of capital movements has been to reinforce inter-regional integration rather than intra-regional integration. Even when one examines indicators of integration of the 'real' economies of nations, processes of globalisation, including inter-regional linkages in the form of trade and investment, are at least as important as intra-regional linkages (Wyatt-Walker 1995). Indeed, trade has not been a particularly strong element in regionalisation. The trade diversion effects of European integration, for example, have been sufficiently small to have resulted in an increasing integration of the European countries into patterns of world trade (Jacquemin and Sapir 1988). Arguably, direct investment flows have become more important in promoting regionalisation, but again Wyatt-Walker (1995) suggests that FDI flows have been at least as important in engendering inter-regional integration. At present, then, forms of globalisation and regionalisation are both apparent, being more symbiotic than contradictory – a point which emerges from Robert Hine's chapter in this book.

Second, the close connections between processes of globalisation and regionalisation become apparent in geographical terms. Naturally much depends upon the geographical scale in question. While processes of industrial restructuring associated with global and regional economic integration may have a very uneven impact at a subnational level, patterns of economic activity remain quite stable across nations and very stable indeed across larger geographical areas such as groupings of countries. Both trade and investment are characterised by friction – friction of distance, of culture and language, etc. Most trade and investment in the world economy takes place between advanced economies and then again between geographically or culturally proximate advanced economies. Viewed in this way, the regionalisation of the world economy is nothing more than this phenomenon writ large with Japan, the EU and North America representing the largest advanced economies. Gittelman (1997) has suggested that 'selected developing countries, far from being marginalised, are playing an integral role in intra-Triad competitive gamesmanship. In this respect each Triad member may be seen as a high-technology, high-cost island surrounded by a sea of less-developed, low-cost countries, which collectively form the basis for regional blocs' (Gittelman 1997, p. 76). Jochen Legewie reflects in his chapter on aspects of economic integration between core and peripheral countries in South-East Asia as a product of the divisions of labour being created by Japanese multinationals. Similarly, Clive Collis, Nigel Berkeley and David Noon's chapter looks at peripheral European host economies which have been integrated with higher cost production locations through FDI.

Third, the connections between global and regional economic integration are apparent over time and have been mutually reinforcing. 'Regionalisation increases the necessity for large firms to become "insiders" in other regions, promoting globalisation. In turn, increased foreign competition across a broad range of industries has prompted the USA and EU to pursue regional alternatives in an effort to alleviate problems of adjustment and to promote non-economic regional objectives' (Wyatt-Walker 1995, p. 77). Thus, over the last twenty-five years international trade has increased by a factor of twelve and trade among regional groupings by a factor of seventeen (Dent 1997, p. 12). The consensus of opinion appears to be that inter-regional economic integration has been driven by the international capital movements needed to underpin state financing but that the very success of GATT in liberalising world trade has prompted an element of regionalisation. In this respect a number of authors have pointed to the importance of structural transformations in the sphere of production, orchestrated by multinationals, which have in turn driven regulatory responses (Strange 1996; Wyatt-Walker 1995). Gibb and Michalak (1996) have gone the furthest in associating what have been widely interpreted as new flexible forms of production with regional economic integration. For them, 'the economies of flexibility at the individual enterprise or national state are extended into the international sphere in the search for greater flexibility on a continental scale' (Gibb and Michalak 1996, p. 55). However, there are clearly identifiable limits to the phenomenon of regionalisation when taking a longer-term perspective in global patterns of trade, investment and capital movements. Thus, 'The 1950s represent … an important watershed because it was then that the opening up of national economies and their reintegration into the world economy began. As this process is still in progress in the early 1990s, it means that it has gone further, lasted longer and involved more countries than anything else experienced before 1914' (Panic and Vacic 1995, p. 4). The roots of the current regionalisation are in longer-term global economic integration under the auspices of multinationals.

MULTIPLE LEVELS OF CORPORATE AND INSTITUTIONAL DYNAMICS

Both the political and economic bases of market integration need to be considered together. As Julius (1997) has observed, 'Globalisation makes stakeholder groups more diverse, it enhances the claims of some groups, and erodes those of others. In so doing, globalisation sharpens conflicts among stakeholders, making the task of management more difficult, and slowing the globalisation process itself' (Julius 1997, p. 454). Indeed, following Sklair (1997), we can consider that an emerging Transnational Capitalist Class (TCC) plays an important role in orchestrating economic globalisation. Sklair sees the TCC as a group composed of the executives of multinational corporations, politicians, professionals and bureaucrats involved with globalisation and 'consumerist elites' (Sklair 1997, p. 521). This is not to say that such a class is already fully formed but rather that 'in the struggles within ruling class structures at all levels the balance of power is swinging decisively from the localisers (inner-oriented economic nationalists) to the globalisers (outward-oriented neoliberals)' (Sklair 1997, p. 523). This TCC does not simply exist at a transnational (global) level but forms an important element within supranational, national and subnational systems of governance. The remainder of this section offers some observations regarding firm–institutional dynamics at supranational, national and subnational scales.

The project of European integration is also closely associated with the idea of 'Euro-champion' firms able to dominate in European markets and be significant players at a global level. Yet while there are some limited trends toward the formation of such Euro-champions, 'Europeanisation is not replacing a national approach to concentration and rationalisation' (Cox and Watson 1995, p. 330). There is evidence to attest to important EU-wide forms of restructuring associated with the likes of merger and acquisition activity as Keith Chapman details in his chapter. There is a complex relationship between concentration and multinationality of business within the EU. On the one hand, then, while leading firms in member states undertake important shares of production in other host EU countries, the vast bulk of their production remains concentrated in the home economy (Davies and Lyons 1996). On the other hand, 'the single market may be encouraging rationalisation, but this may not be leading inexorably to the creation of Eurochampions so much as the further global concentration of ownership by major multinational companies and financial institutions ... at the expense of marginalised and sub-optimal former national champions within EU member states. (Cox and Watson 1995, p. 331).

Moreover, it would be equally misleading to assume that European integration has involved the inevitable ascendancy of supranational regulation of industry over regulation at a national scale. Instead, as Whitley has observed, 'the institution of relatively free movement of goods and services through the European Community will not, in itself, lead to a pan European business system' (Whitley 1992, p. 278). There is no necessary connection between convergence of the social and institutional bases of national systems of production and economic integration in Europe (Rubery 1992). The limitations of current supranational regulation of industry are nowhere more apparent than when one considers the powers at EU-level over the actions of multinationals. There is really very little in the way of formal regulation of the actions of multinationals at EU-level whether one thinks in terms of competition policy, labour relations, investment rules or incentives packages (Brewer and Young 1995) – a point which is amplified by Phil Raines and Fiona Wishlade in their chapter contribution. Instead, industry–institution relations at the EU-level are more accurately characterised as being informally orchestrated (Middlemas 1995). This informal orchestration itself appears to have evolved in response to increasing pressures of globalisation. Thus 'while the European system failed to usurp the national authorities' position as the primary political locus for industrial representation, the nation state/business relationship gradually came under pressure from industrial globalisation ... In the late 1970s, the existence of dual European and national systems presented business with the opportunity to resist national corporatism, while avoiding the collective action overtures of the EC institutions.'

According to Marks *et al.*, 'European integration is a polity creating process in which authority and policy-making influence are shared across multiple levels of governance' (Marks *et al.* 1996). And at a global level there may well be a greater impetus to, and prospect of, regulation of multinationals than at a regional level, mirroring the influence of global corporate restructuring on European and national patterns of restructuring. Certainly, the attention of international organisations has now turned toward the creation of multilateral investment rules. It is such multilateral investment rules which may yet have the most profound effect on the organisation of multinationals and the scope of institutional interventions at narrower – regional, national and subnational – scales as Stephen Young and Tom Brewer's contribution illustrates. For the time being and,

> unless or until supranational political organisation acquires not only governmental powers but also some measure of popular-democratic legitimacy, the national state will remain a key political factor as the highest instance of democratic political accountability. How it fulfils this role will depend not only on the institutional matrix and shifts in the balance of forces of globalisation, triadisation, regionalisation and the resurgence of local governance proceed apace. (Jessop 1997, p. 23).

Most commentators see this continued role for the nation state as a regulator of multinational activity as particularly pertinent in the sphere of human capital formation: the state's direction of the education and training systems which provide the supply-side conditions crucial to the creation of ownership and locational advantages drawn on by multinationals (for example Amin *et al.* 1994; Campbell 1994; Reich 1990). Here then the dominance of multinationals in a nation's economy is of less relevance than the type of activities carried out by these firms and their demands upon, and reproduction of, labour skills. In this respect 'the international competition for jobs, originating within the strategy-making of the giant, transnational companies of the advanced industrial countries, is moving up the production and occupational hierarchy' so that 'heavy investment in education and training is a necessary condition of rapid economic development and a move toward full employment ... but it is not a sufficient condition for development in the present context' (Cowling and Sugden 1996, pp. 297–298).

Arguably, the initiatives of subnational institutions – such as local authorities or development agencies – have assumed increasing importance in influencing the actions of multinationals. At the subnational scale an increased potential embeddedness of multinationals can be seen as the product of a degree of convergence between the initiatives of subnational institutions and the proclivities of recent investment conceived and undertaken by multinationals. As Safarian notes, 'A regional and, at times, global strategy of production by MNEs is being gradually met by a regional and, at times, global strategy of national policies on trade and investment' (Safarian 1993, p. 474). One might also add that policies directed at increasing the integrity of subnational and national economies are, at times, being met by the desire of MNEs to tap into local sources of competitive advantage.

There has been a growing interest in the possibilities for, and efficacy of, subnational systems of governance and the contribution of such systems of governance to local economic development. The emergence of distinctive systems of subnational governance appear to be one by-product of both autonomous institutional capacity-building in the face of the globalisation of economic activity and the decomposition of the nation-state and the emergence of systems of multilevel governance (Jessop 1997; Marks *et al.* 1996). Here the creation of institutional capacity or 'thickness' is considered vital if economic activity, much of which is globally mobile, is to be tied down locally (Amin and Thrift 1995; Healey 1997). Subnational systems of governance would include the entire range of local institutions and service-providing organisations, not simply those traditionally concerned with economic development and the provision of business services (for example, see Painter and Goodwin 1995). In his chapter, Jeremy Alden touches on the contribution of the planning system and its institutions to the participation of overseas firms in Wales. In this broader sense there appear to be differences in subnational systems of governance across the UK regions which may in turn have a systematic effect on economic development. As Evans and Harding observe, 'there is considerable evidence that "regional" institutions in Scotland and Wales are better able to understand, articulate and engage with and act upon regional problems and opportunities than their counterparts in England' (Evans and Harding 1997, p. 24). Indeed, there may be important variations in institutional capacity within subnational territories as Frank Peck and Jon Durnin illustrate with reference to Cumbria. The resources and remit of organisations concerned with economic development in general and the attraction and development of inward investment in particular do vary across EU and UK regions (Halkier and Danson 1997) and indeed across US states as illustrated by John Dunning and Lorna Wallace in their chapter on FDI in New Jersey. Yet there is little evidence to suggest that such strategies have a determinant bearing on the character of inward investment in a given region. General supply-side factors such as labour skills and costs rather than variations in institutional capacity appear more important in determining regional variations in the quality of mobile investment attracted to EU regions (Amin *et al.* 1994).

The assumption behind much national and subnational policy aimed at attracting and developing inward investment is that the embeddedness of industry is largely complementary to industry competitiveness. However, as Safarian notes, 'A conflict arises between a government's attempt to "internalise" production nationally and the firm's attempts to internalise the same activities within the MNE internationally.' (Safarian 1993, p. 36). This observation is grounded in the established view of multinationals' desire to economise on transaction costs when exploiting ownership advantages internationally. According to this view the most appropriate policy role for national and subnational government revolves around reducing the transaction costs facing multinationals in their territories. This is an approach in which the UK government and its regions have been highly successful (Hood and Young 1997). Yet it is also an approach which has attracted inward investment of a particular nature: namely that centred on relatively low-technology, labour intensive manufacturing operations (De Smidt 1992). In their contributions, Sung-Hoon Jung, Max Munday and Mike Peel highlight this when identifying the locational determinants and organisational characteristics of Korean and Japanese FDI in the UK.

Multinationals are increasingly willing to shoulder the burden of increased transaction costs of a local presence when there are significant opportunities for the creation and re-creation of ownership advantages. Creation of such local advantages may raise the transaction costs facing multinationals in terms of, for example, engaging more fully with a larger set of local institutions, but there is much evidence to suggest that this does not deter multinationals and may have had a positive effect on the quality of foreign investment across regions and nations of the EU (Dunford 1996). Yuko Aoyama, for instance, highlights the importance of relatively high-cost host European country contexts to generating important market-related externalities for Japanese multinationals.

If question marks remain over the precise contribution of subnational systems of governance to the attraction and development of FDI in host economies, then equally there is debate over the precise nature of recent waves of FDI. Many economists and geographers, as Andy Pike describes in his contribution, have been attracted to the proposition that FDI is now much more favourably disposed toward local host environments. This has led some to talk of multinationals' increasing desire to tap into host economies as sources of competitive advantage (Cantwell 1995), although it should be remembered that such trends are, as yet, extremely limited in extent (Allen and Thompson 1997) and centre on only the largest multinationals (Dunning 1997). Furthermore, one implication of the United Nations' studies of multinationals (UNCTAD 1994) is that increased plant status and autonomy can also bring with it tighter integration within parent company organisations, a point which both Andrew Pike and I address in later chapters.

STRUCTURE OF THE BOOK

In this chapter I have considered the way in which global economic integration has implications at a number of geographical scales. The chapters of this book are organised according to geographical scales: at the global, the regional (or trade bloc), the national and subnational levels. As this introductory chapter has tried to illustrate, there are important interconnections between patterns of multinational investment and regulation at these different spatial scales. Consideration of the actions of multinationals at these four scales does make for ease of presentation; the intention is that some of the interconnections alluded to in this introduction will be apparent in the individual chapter contributions.

Part I focuses on the actions of multinationals and institutions concerned with the regulation of multinationals at the global scale. To begin with, Stephen Young and Tom Brewer consider recent developments in multilateral regulation of investment and as such help set the scene for considering corporate and institutional dynamics surrounding multinationals at the broadest geographical scale. Robert Hine then further examines the tensions between global and regional economic integration and the complementarity of the trade and investment orchestrated by multinationals. I also pursue some of these ideas when exploring the implications of global and regional corporate integration at the subnational scale when examining multinational restructuring in the chemicals industry in Wales.

In part II the emphasis is on considering the organisation and regulation of multinationals at the regional (trade bloc) level. Again, the scene is set by Phil Raines and Fiona Wishlade who consider the extent to which supranational policies of the European Commission have an impact on the organisation of multinationals. We then have a number of empirical studies which to varying degrees examine the organisation of multinational investments in the EU as these interact with the policy context. To date little has been written about Korean FDI in Europe. Sung-Hoon Jung identifies the main aspects of Korean FDI in Europe, focusing on the different strategies of global-localistion adopted among Korean multinationals. Discussion of multinational manufacturing strategies tends to concentrate on production-side considerations. Yuko Aoyama's discussion of Japanese manufacturing investment in the EU concentrates on the market-oriented nature of Japanese FDI. Finally, Keith Chapman examines patterns of merger and acquisition activity in the EU. Drawing upon established sources and his own unique data set on the chemicals industry, he identifies the distinctive south to north transfer of ownership which appears to be one result of EU-wide merger and acquisition activity.

In Part III the analysis of FDI is at a yet narrower geographical scale – the nation-state – and draws upon more diverse examples. Clive Collis, Nigel Berkeley, David Noon, Max Munday and Mike Peel examine the nature of Japanese investment in the UK. There has been concern over the nature of Japanese investment attracted to the UK. Munday and Peel's evidence suggests that concerns are indeed warranted. At various times and with varying degrees of validity, concern has been raised over the 'hollowing out' of domestic industry by way of outward FDI (for example see Fröbel *et al.* 1980; Williams *et al.* 1991). Jochen Legewie considers current fears surrounding the 'hollowing out' of the Japanese economy. In some respects this process is the mirror image of that considered in the previous chapter by Munday and Peel. His analysis of aggregate data suggests that, to date, overseas direct investment has been integral to a process of 'natural' adjustment of, and industrial specialisation within, the domestic economy. Clive Collis, Nigel Berkeley, and David Noon consider the main dimensions of FDI in the East European economies. They point to the relevance of policy developments in the UK to the East European context.

The fourth part of the book considers the actions of multinationals and agents of governance at the narrowest geographical scale – subnational territories. Jeremy Alden examines the investment figures relating to Wales, considering some of the main impacts of recent FDI and focusing in particular on the relationship between major investors and institutions of the land-use planning system. Andy Pike's chapter looks at the process by which individual investments of multinationals can become upgraded and the way in which local circumstances, including the actions of local institutions, can have a bearing on broader corporate strategies. Frank Peck and Jon Durnin's account of the difficulties of attracting inward investment to Cumbria provides an important reminder that not only does institutional capacity differ between subnational territories but that there can be significant economic and institutional marginalisation *within* subnational territories. In the final chapter of the section, Lorna Wallace and John Dunning situate the US state of New Jersey within the context of the global economy when considering its performance in attracting and retaining FDI.

Finally, in our conclusion Jeremy Alden and I briefly draw out some of the most important themes to have emerged across the various sections and individual chapter contributions in the book.

PART I:

FDI AND THE GLOBAL ECONOMY

2 Multilateral Investment Rules, Multinationals and the Global Economy[1]

INTRODUCTION

The multinational enterprise (MNE) has had a pervasive influence on economics, politics and social affairs in the world economy for many decades. Its ubiquitous effects derive from its involvement in trade, technological development and technology transfer, global financial flows and managerial innovation. While the global reach (and potential monopoly power) of the MNE was recognised many years ago (Barnet and Müller 1974), global strategies – meaning the multinational coordinating and integrating its resources on a worldwide basis behind global objectives – are much more recent. Global strategies strengthen both the possible positive and negative impacts of the MNE on economic development at worldwide, regional, country and local levels.

The need for a policy framework to encompass MNE activity has long been recognised (Goldberg and Kindleberger 1970; Bergsten and Graham 1992; Graham 1996). Such a framework should focus upon the MNE as an international business organisation rather than only FDI *per se* and upon both the removal of impediments to international business and upon constraining the anti-competitive impacts of international oligopolies. Similarly, there is an awareness that this regulatory framework for investment should be *multilateral* to ensure equivalence with the domain of the *multinational enterprises.* Yet the reality has been a patchwork of overlapping and conflicting rules at different levels, promoted by different bodies and focusing upon different issues.[2] The purpose of this chapter therefore is to present the case for multilateral investment rules for a global economy; to assess the progress in multilateral rule-making and the impacts to date; and to identify the challenges for the future.

THE SIGNIFICANCE OF THE MULTINATIONAL ENTERPRISE

Foreign direct investment has played an important role in the international economy since the latter part of the nineteenth century. However, much of this investment capital was lost as a result of two world wars, and it is the last half-century that has seen the most favourable conditions for multinational expansion. As at 1995, 39,000 parent MNEs owned or controlled 270,000 foreign affiliates and invested $2.7 trillion abroad (UNCTAD 1996a). The sales of foreign affiliates have now surpassed exports as the principal means of servicing foreign markets and globalisation at the enterprise level has led to (UNCTAD 1994):

- global manufacturing and service activities, global sourcing and global customers;
- the emergence of international production and distribution systems;
- new forms of corporate governance. Decision making units in research and development (R&D), procurement, marketing, finance etc. may be widely spread geographically, with integrated flows of technology, skills and finance as well as goods and services. Hierarchical relationships between headquarters and subsidiaries may be partially replaced by heterarchical and network relations;
- strategic alliances and external networks linking the MNE to customers, competitors, suppliers and the non-business infrastructure (universities, research institutions, governments, etc.).

For the debate on multilateral investment agreements, there are a number of highly significant implications of the above. First, the MNE has a major involvement in international trade as an exporter (and importer) of final goods and services from its home base and its subsidiary companies. Integrated companies also organise and coordinate the flows of intermediate products and services across national boundaries. Given its multinational status, the enterprise internalises these cross-border markets, with internal transfer pricing mechanisms replacing arm's length trade. At the global level, total worldwide intra-firm trade was estimated at $1.6 trillion in 1993, representing one-third of world trade and one-half of the total trade of MNEs (UNCTAD 1995). Trade and foreign direct investment are as complementary as they are competitive. There are obvious difficulties, therefore, in trying to separate out multilateral trade and multilateral investment agreements.

Second, the multinational enterprise is a principal source of innovation in the world economy. The desire to appropriate fully the returns from its R&D investment in proprietary assets is a major reason for the internalisation of know-how within the enterprise and hence for the very existence of the multinational corporation. MNEs will patent some know-how, and in certain cases formally license this within the firm as well as externally. Therefore, the MNE has an overwhelming interest in a strengthened international legal system to ensure the protection of intellectual property rights (IPR). This issue is a major source of contention between developed and developing nations, essentially over the public goods nature of technology. As a public good, the conditions for optimality would require know-how to be openly available without charge, apart perhaps from a price to cover the costs of circulating it (as developing countries would like). But to do this could discourage new investment in information creation.

A third and linked issue concerns the MNE and technology transfer. There is again a conflict between the goals of host nations (mainly but not solely developing countries) which emphasise the technology transfer potential of multinationals and those of the firm which stress internalisation as the route to profitability. The tradition of joint ventures in developing countries from the 1960s and 1970s has its roots in the attempt to capture some of the potential technology transfer benefits of MNEs. Translated into an issue for multilateral investment agreements, it draws attention to the debate over the relative rights and obligations of enterprises and nation states in such agreements.

Fourth and more conventionally, the MNE has a major role in global financial flows through its initial and sequential investments, through remittances of profits, dividends, royalties, management fees, etc., and through foreign exchange exposure and management measures. From an international policy perspective, there are important issues concerning capital controls and foreign exchange controls which historically have been maintained by national governments for balance of payments, exchange rate and national security reasons but which may severely hamper market access through FDI.

Fifth, many MNEs are large firms operating in oligopolistic markets. Major issues arise for international competition policy, which ultimately must represent a constituent of a comprehensive trade and investment agreement. But these issues are highly problematic in an era of strategic alliances, networking, and other forms of what has been referred to as quasi-internalisation (Dunning 1993b). Related problems arise in respect of defining the country of origin of enterprises.

THE CASE FOR MULTILATERAL INVESTMENT RULES

Economic analysis suggests that, as with trade, increased international flows of FDI should be encouraged since they generate both global and national benefits. Growth would be stimulated by more efficient production and prices lowered through stronger competition (Caves 1996; Graham 1996). The general assumption is, however, that MNE operations are hampered by a variety of government-created obstacles.

Wholesale embargoes on FDI are increasingly rare, and those which exist even in developed countries are argued (probably unjustifiably) on national security grounds. On the other hand, on the inward investment side there are still restrictions in most countries as well as a lack of clear public guidelines on who can invest and under what conditions. The implication for public policy is that government policy should be liberalised, thereby guaranteeing a secure and stable environment for investors.

The second line of analysis emphasises the potentially anti-competitive behaviour of large MNEs operating in oligopolistic industries. The implication for public policy is that government policy should be devised to facilitate competition and deter restrictive business practices. Policies are also necessary to remedy market failure in areas such as environmental protection and, to curb beggar-thy-neighbour investment incentive schemes which favour rich countries with deep pockets.

Consideration needs, in addition, to be given to policy interactions and conflicts. It has been shown that the gains from a multilateral policy could best be achieved in a policy environment of neutrality or non-discrimination. A third implication for public policy is, therefore, that non-discriminatory treatment of foreign and indigenous firms in the domestic market and non-discrimination between trade and investment as market servicing methods are important principles.

Finally, as implied above, the application of national or regional policies may generate some net advantages for particular countries or firms but in the process generate inefficiencies and lead to a misallocation of resources on a worldwide basis. Hence, there is a case for developing multilateral rules and institutions for investment on the grounds that they will lead to greater efficiencies.

At present the overall investment policy scene is characterised by fragmentation, confusion and conflict, with a wide range of FDI policies existing at national, bilateral, regional and multilateral levels. National level policies are implemented by host or home nations and are designed to encourage or to regulate FDI flows and projects on the basis of diverse criteria. A feature of much of the 1990s was a sweeping tide in favour of liberalisation at the national level, although many barriers still exist. Bilateral Investment Treaties (BITs) concerned exclusively with investment have been in existence since the late 1950s; their numbers grew rapidly in the 1980s and 1990s and totalled 1,630 in 1997 (OECD 1997). For the capital-exporting country, the major objective is to obtain legal protection under international law; for the capital-importing nation, BITs are used as one means of attracting inward FDI and they provide important signals concerning a country's investment climate.

From 1947 to 1994, 109 regional integration agreements (RIAs) were notified to the General Agreement on Tariffs and Trade (GATT), and while not all these agreements include FDI rules, many do (WTO 1995). This expansion of regionalisation is highly controversial, and with much of the discussion being 'framed in terms of "building blocks" or "stumbling blocks", will regional economic agreements … facilitate the development of an open and liberal international economy, or do they portend the devolution of the world economy into closed, competing economic areas' (Kobrin 1995, p. 15)? Essentially, at present, the European Union (EU) and the North American Free Trade Agreement (NAFTA) are the two most significant blocs incorporating FDI rules of one form or another; they are a reality and, to date, have been a driving force for multilateral trade and investment liberalisation. However, there is in such agreements the potential for discrimination and distortion, and the mere fact of their existence hampers the global integration of the multinational. For multilateral investment policy the lesson is to try to include RIA-specific FDI rules into wider multilateral agreements; at present the rules of the GATT provide legitimacy for regional integration agreements, but they are trade-oriented, weak and actually create dangers of protectionism.

PROGRESS IN MULTILATERAL INVESTMENT RULE-MAKING

For most of the post-war period, trade liberalisation was a major driver of growth in the world economy. The creation of the GATT led to a series of rounds of tariff cutting involving an increasing number of countries. The Kennedy Round negotiations (1963–7) also began to recognise an issue of growing importance, namely that of non-tariff barriers (NTBs), in particular through the conclusion of an anti-dumping code. And the Uruguay Round (1986–94) included not only trade and goods, but also measures affecting FDI, trade in services, and intellectual property. This was a belated recognition of the interrelatedness of trade and FDI in the global economy, for as early as the 1960s and 1970s a variety of studies (reported in Hood and Young 1979) showed complementaries between trade and foreign investment as well as substitution effects. At the same time trade liberalisation stimulated FDI in a variety of ways: most obviously trade-oriented FDI was encouraged, enabling MNEs to establish production and service operations in low-cost sites from which their output could be exported; by allowing MNEs to outsource inputs; and by facilitating the formation of regional and global networks and hence integrated international production. At the same time the GATT framework was a factor in generating a stable investment climate at a multilateral level and thereby encouraging FDI.

While tariff levels fell sharply, the period from the 1970s saw the rise of the so-called 'new protectionism', with the growth of NTBs designed to restrict imports and shelter domestic industries. Such NTBs, allied to threats of other trade restrictions, have encouraged Japanese and other Asia-Pacific producers to undertake FDI designed to preserve market access. In these circumstances FDI has had the beneficial effect of circumventing trade restrictive measures. On the other hand the induced FDI might be oriented towards host country markets only, thus reducing the beneficial effects associated with trade-oriented FDI; when NTBs have been linked to local content requirements, moreover, resources are misallocated through the replacement of efficient overseas sourcing by less efficient host country sourcing.

It was in this context that the World Trade Organisation (WTO) was formed in 1995 with a much wider remit than the GATT it replaced. It would be incorrect to suggest, however, that the issue of multilateral investment rules suddenly appeared on the international policy agenda in the mid-1990s. As will be shown, interest in the development of a multilateral framework for investment has ebbed and flowed over a period of fifty years, as indeed has the focus on liberalisation as opposed to regulation in rule-making efforts. Table 2.1 charts these stumbling attempts to establish multilateral investment rules over the period since the visionary Havana Charter for an International Trade Organisation (ITO) was published in 1948.

Investment was only one among a cluster of issues that were tackled in the context of the International Trade Organisation initiative. Others were tariffs, quotas, export subsidies, restrictive business practices, employment, exchange controls and commodity agreements; and investment itself was considered within the context of economic development matters, including post-war reconstruction in Europe. The ITO initiative foundered when the US Congress failed to ratify it; it was perceived as a threat to US sovereignty and to the interests of US corporations, especially with regard to its mandate on international cartels. Its partial reincarnation in the form of the GATT focused only on trade issues, with investment and related matters such as competition policy effectively dropped from the agenda.

This early period did see the establishment of the Organisation for Economic Cooperation and Development (OECD). Although its membership is limited to the industrialised countries, the OECD has maintained a sustained interest in investment matters, initially through its Codes of Liberalisation of Capital Movements and of Current Invisible Operations introduced in 1964. Yet it is still the case that MNEs may be hampered by controls over capital movements, in developed as well as developing countries; for example, it was not until April 1998 that Japan planned to abolish its remaining exchange controls.

During the early post-war 'honeymoon' period, there was neither much concern about regulating MNEs nor much sense of urgency of liberalising government FDI policies. All this changed dramatically at the start of the 1970s as both developing and developed host nations expressed fears about the economic power of multinationals. In developing countries these concerns were related to broader questions concerning the establishment of a New International Economic Order (NIEO). They led, through the United Nations (UN), to the formation of a Centre on Transnational Corporations (CTC) with a remit *inter alia* to formulate a binding code of conduct to curb MNE power. The strong bargaining position of Third World nations was in truth a transitory phenomenon, and the developing countries themselves became increasingly less of a unified bloc. In consequence, while discussions on a voluntary UN code continued intermittently until 1990, its contents were not approved by UN members. In retrospect the UN Code of Conduct is mainly of interest in illustrating an orientation towards MNEs, focusing upon the obligations of firms and the rights of countries, as the following extracts (UNCTAD 1996b) reveal: 'Transnational corporations should/shall respect human rights and fundamental freedoms in the countries in which they operate'; 'Transnational corporations should contribute to a strengthening of the scientific and technological capacities of developing countries'.

The main impact of the UN code was probably to encourage the industrialised nations to produce in 1976 a set of voluntary *Guidelines for Multinational Enterprises* (OECD 1976) laying down standards on a range of

TABLE 2.1: THE EVOLUTION OF MULTILATERAL INVESTMENT AGREEMENTS

Period	Features of period	Main developments
Mid-1940s –late 1960s	*Inauguration* Honeymoon period: little concern about regulating MNEs or about liberalising government FDI policies.	• Havana Charter for International Trade Organisation published in 1998 but not ratified. Post-war international economic order constructed around establishment of the International Monetary Fund/World Bank and the General Agreement on Tariffs and Trade.
Late 1960s–early 1980s	*Control* Negative attitudes towards MNEs, especially in developing countries.	• Binding OECD Codes on Liberalisation of Capital Movements and Current Invisible Operations introduced in 1963. Former required liberalisation of policies on inward and outward capital flows over long term. • Discussions commenced on binding United Nations Code of Conduct on Transnational Corporations in mid-1970s with aim of controlling MNEs. Draft of voluntary code finally submitted in 1990, but not ratified. • Voluntary OECD Guidelines for Multinational Enterprises published in 1976: set standards on employment and industrial relations, information disclosure, financing, taxation etc. Little evidence of implementation by MNEs.
Early 1980s–mid-1990s	*Liberalisation* Liberalisation of government policies, including FDI policies at national, bilateral, regional and multilateral levels.	• Completion of GATT Uruguay Round negotiations, and establishment of the World Trade Organisation in 1995. Mainly trade agreement but some investment powers in respect of services, local content rules and intellectual property rights.
Late 1990s	*Expansion* Liberalisation trend continued, but increasing concerns of developing countries and conflicts between developed nations. Other issues include multiplicity of agreements at different levels and overlapping relationships.	• WTO's enhanced dispute settlement procedures begin to be implemented, including some investment cases. Agreements reached in 1997 on liberalising telecommunications, information technology and financial services industries worldwide. • Negotiations commenced on OECD Multilateral Agreement on Investment in 1995 but were suspended without agreement in 1998. Aim to achieve comprehensive agreement, mainly emphasising liberalisation issues and protection of investments and investors.

topics from information disclosure to science and technology. To quote, 'The common aim ... is to encourage the positive contribution which multinational enterprises can make to economic and social progress' (OECD 1976, Annex 1). MNEs' adherence to the OECD guidelines seems to have been very limited, but there have been a series of reviews subsequently concerning improvements in implementation and follow-up procedures and in clarifying the guidelines.

In any event, the policy emphasis on regulation and the obligations of firms has switched fundamentally since this period. The era of the 1980s and 1990s has been characterised by government FDI policy liberalisation at all levels, from national to multilateral, linked to wider programmes of deregulation, privatisation and market reform throughout the world. Yet multinationals are still faced with many barriers at every level.

At multilateral level, a major step forward was taken with the inclusion of a number of investment-related issues on the GATT Uruguay Round agenda. Under pressure from US MNEs, the American government had been trying to get investment issues on the GATT agenda for many years; the aim was to liberalise other countries' investment policies and ensure market access for highly competitive US firms in service industries. The ten-year Uruguay Round negotiations that led to establishment of the WTO in 1995, however, made only limited headway on investment matters. Table 2.2 summarises the position, revealing restricted progress on a patchwork of issues. The Uruguay Round negotiations were predominately about tariffs and non-tariff barriers to trade, and about changes in institutional structures and procedures concerning trade.

Despite its inauspicious beginnings with regard to investment matters, the Uruguay Round agreements do provide for subsequent negotiations and reviews of the General Agreement on Trade and Services (GATS) and the agreement on Trade Related Investment Measures (TRIMs). These and other negotiations scheduled for the early years of the WTO (see Brewer and Young 1998, table 6.1) suggest the potential for a significant expansion of the WTO's coverage of investment issues. Already new sectoral agreements in basic telecommunications, information technology and financial services, that include investment as well as trade provisions, were agreed in 1997.

Maintaining this momentum in multilateral rule-making, the OECD undertook a major initiative by beginning formal negotiations on a Multilateral Agreement on Investment (MAI) in 1995. It was designed to be a comprehensive investment agreement covering all economic sectors, with negotiations due for completion in mid-1998. However, while a draft consolidated text was made available in April 1998, no agreement was reached and negotiations ended. At the OECD Ministerial Council meeting in 1998, member countries expressed support for the work programme on investment in the WTO and resolved to seek the support of their partners for the creation of investment rules in the WTO.

TABLE 2.2: URUGUAY ROUND AGREEMENTS

Agreement with explicit investment content
Trade Related Investment Measures (TRIMs) – limits FDI performance requirements
General Agreement on Trade in Services (GATS) – includes FDI in services
Agreements with continuous and direct relevance to investment
Trade Related Intellectual Property Rights (TRIPs) – establishes standards and enforcement procedures
Subsidies and Counterveiling Measures (SCMs) – limits subsidies and retaliatory actions
Dispute Settlement Understanding (DSU) – includes government-to-government disputes on investment issues
Trade Policy Review Mechanism (TPRM) – includes review of countries' investment policies
Other agreements with some relevance to investment
Agriculture – GATT 1994 Agreement on Tariffs and Other Trade Issues (for example Anti-dumping) – Import Licensing Procedures – Pre-shipment inspection – Rules of Origin – Safeguards – Sanitary and Phytosanitary Measures – Textiles – Technical Barriers – Plurilateral Agreements (civil aircraft, government procurement, dairy, bovine meat)

Source: Brewer and Young 1998, table 5.4

Although the focus of this chapter is upon multilateral investment issues, the 1990s were a period of intense activity for investment issues at the regional level, especially in the Western hemisphere. Gestrin and Rugman (1996, p. 63) assert that 'no other multilateral or bilateral investment agreement goes as far as the NAFTA in terms of the scope of the coverage, the depth of coverage or the enforcement of rules'. This is true in respect of FDI rules *per se* (the EU does not formally have an FDI policy; see Brewer and Young 1995) and also in its consideration of the interrelatedness of investment, trade, intellectual property protection and services. Yet, the NAFTA investment rules are also in some respects limited: for example, NAFTA ignores investment subsidies (reflecting the US position, which has prevailed in other forums) and is weak on anti-dumping rules and competition policy. Furthermore, the NAFTA rules – especially on rules of origin – are in some respects discriminatory.

A REVIEW OF MULTILATERAL INVESTMENT RULES IN THE LATE 1990s

As the brief summary above has shown, there have been significant shifts in the mix of liberalisation–regulation tendencies and in the prevailing attitudes and policies towards MNEs and FDI. These shifts were integrally bound up with the more general economic policy philosophy prevailing at particular periods. In the 1980s and into the 1990s the pendulum swung to an almost exclusive focus on liberalisation. This was a reflection of the general economic climate, but also of the high degree of understanding of the economic benefits associated with multinational activity and by extensive experience among both companies and countries in handling relationships with MNEs.

The major multilateral (and regional) investment agreements in effect at the end of the 1990s are summarised in table 2.3. A number of conclusions may be reached.

First, the critical importance of the core liberalisation principles of investment agreements: national treatment, most favoured nation (MFN) treatment, freedom of entry and investment protection are generally accepted. National treatment means that countries agree to treat foreign investors no less favourably than they treat their own investors. National treatment does not mean treatment for foreign investors that is necessarily equal to, or the same as, the treatment for domestic investors; the treatment of foreign investors can actually be more favourable. According to the principal of most favoured nation treatment, once a country has granted a given level of treatment to a foreign investor or a foreign investment, it cannot grant less favourable treatment to any other investor or investment from a different country. These seemingly simple principles are far from being realised in existing agreements (for example, the OECD's National Treatment Instrument contains many sectoral exceptions), but are recognised as core building blocks upon which future agreements can build. The Energy Charter Treaty (ECT) and NAFTA provide state-of-the-art provisions on these issues.

Second, it is beginning to be understood that many FDI policy matters are interrelated, and also that there are interrelationships among, for instance, trade, FDI, technology licensing and competition rules. Concepts of market contestability and modal neutrality recognise that firms can service ('contest') markets through a variety of modes such as trade, FDI and licensing, and that there should be no discrimination in favour of one mode over another. Where modal neutrality exists, policies leave to the firm the decisions as to how the market should be serviced. However, the existing frameworks of rules, as shown in table 2.3, fail to deliver on these principles. Emerging from the GATT, the WTO has a much stronger trade than FDI orientation, both in terms of emphasis of rules and in expertise. Thus the TRIMs agreement in the Uruguay Round dealt only with investment matters related to trade and goods, and the GATS is focused primarily on trade. While progress is being made (for example, a WTO Working Group on the Relationship between Trade and Investment started work in June 1997 (WTO 1997), the patchwork problem has been exacerbated at the same time, both in terms of issue coverage and sectoral coverage. And yet the development of semi-autonomous industry-specific agreements may make it easier to address investment policy–trade policy–technology policy linkages: for example, the linkages between trade performance requirements and trade subsidies, on the one hand, and investment incentives on the other, are central issues in the automotive industry but not in financial services.

Third, the agreements in force differ not only in their country coverage but also in their enforcement possibilities (legally binding versus non-binding rules). The argument in favour of voluntary guidelines which are in some sense an 'ideal' is that they are helpful in setting aspiration levels, provided

TABLE 2.3: SUMMARY CHARACTERISTICS OF MAJOR MULTILATERAL AND REGIONAL INVESTMENT AGREEMENTS IN EFFECT IN LATE 1990s[a]

	Multilateral							Regional/sectoral		
									Regional	
	WTO[b]			OECD[c]						
Characteristics	GATS	TRIMs	TRIPs	Cap	Cur	NTI	MNE	ECT[d]	NAFTA[e]	APEC[f]
Binding	yes	yes	yes	yes	yes	no	no	yes	yes	no
Year	1994	1994	1994	1963	1963	1976	1976	1994	1993	1994
Country coverage (number)	124[g]	124[g]	124[g]	26	26	26	26	51	3	18
Objectives	Establish services trade and investment framework	Limit performance requirements in manufacturing	Protect intellectual property rights	Liberalise restrictions on capital transactions	Liberalise restrictions on capital transactions	Establish national treatment principles	Establish guidelines for firms' behaviour	Liberalise energy trade and investment in Central and Eastern Europe	Liberalise regional trade and investment	Liberalise regional trade and investment
Features	Complex architecture	Narrowly focused	Includes technology protection and technology transfer	Covers many types of capital transfers	Focused on balance of payments current account transactions	Many sectoral exceptions	Brief statements on selected issues	Detailed sector-specific and region-specific coverage	Detailed coverage of numerous issues	General principles to follow in establishing national rules

Notes:

a Strictly agreements which include investment provisions since they may also relate to trade, technology etc. The European Union has been excluded from this table, because it does not formally include an investment agreement; but the EU is far ahead of other organisations in terms of its degree of integration, and the inclusion of elements such as competition policy which would be included in a comprehensive investment agreement.

b WTO agreements are: GATS – General Agreement on Trade in Services; TRIMs – Trade Related Investment Measures; TRIPs – Trade Related Intellectual Property Rights. TRIPs is not an investment agreement *per se* but has major, direct implications for MNEs and FDI.

c OECD Agreements are: Cap – Code of Liberalisation of Capital Movements; Cur – Code of Liberalisation of Current Invisible Operations; NTI – National Treatment Instrument; MNE – Guidelines for Multinational Enterprises. As at the time of writing a Multilateral Agreement on Investment (MAI) was being negotiated.

d Energy Charter Treaty

e North American Free Trade Agreement

f Asia Pacific Economic Cooperation (APEC) Non-Binding Investment Principles

g Number of countries increased in early years of WTO

Source: Adapted from Brewer and Young 1998, table 11.1

they are complementary to existing sets of rules. However, there is a danger of non-binding agreements being ignored or sidelined. Self-evidently, binding agreements have greater status, and while the standards of rules may reflect the lowest common denominator, they do 'lock-in' the liberalisation which has been achieved. The latter argument is extremely important given swings in the policy pendulum.

As the above suggests, the future of multilateral investment rules will be integrally bound up with the international political situation, and in particular with the position of the United States government and the US Congress. Despite the alleged decline of US hegemony, the American position on nearly every investment policy issue is still of great significance. Thus US Congressional opposition killed off the ITO initiative in the 1940s. During the 1970s the USA actively opposed the development of a (control-oriented) multilateral agreement on investment at the UN, and successfully sought a non-binding code among more like minded developed countries of the OECD. During the 1980s, after having been rebuffed in earlier efforts to include investment issues on the GATT agenda, the USA was successful in getting investment into the Uruguay Round. By the last years of the millennium, the frequent use of the new WTO dispute settlement procedures, particularly by developing countries, led to a more legalistic and public approach to conflicts over investment as well as trade issues; and conflicts between the EU and the USA over investment became sharper. The result has been a decline in US support for multilateralism, with a shift in policy preferences towards regional agreements. Thus active US support led to the NAFTA, the APEC Forum, the Free Trade for the Americas initiative and even a Trans-Atlantic Dialogue; although their emphasis was on trade liberalisation, investment issues were also included on their agendas. Alongside this regional approach were continued efforts to extend the network of BITs and occasional surges of unilateralism (commonly industry specific, as in the numerous US–Japanese agreements); the decision by the US Congress in autumn 1997 to deny the President 'fast-track authority' to negotiate new trade agreements was an example of the latter. At the multilateral level, US efforts have recently focused on sectoral agreements – particularly telecommunications, financial services and information technology at the WTO.

There are other reasons to suggest that major developments in investment rules will occur at regional rather than multilateral level into the twenty-first century. Economic ties encourage regional integration agreements; enforcement possibilities are easier, especially when there is a regional hegemon (the USA in NAFTA) or hegemonic axis (Germany and France in the EU); and agreements are less complex. By contrast despite stronger settlement mechanisms in the WTO, its complex patchwork of rules creates problems for enforcement, and further progress is similarly difficult. A rise of regionalism may in turn be allied to greater protectionism, if economic recession hits the world economy; such a scenario is entirely feasible if the Asian financial crisis of 1997–8 initiates a global economic downturn and sparks off a massive increase in exports from the depreciated currency Asia–Pacific economies.

CONCLUSIONS AND DISCUSSION

In synthesising the material in this chapter, it is appropriate to address four questions:

1. Why are multilateral investment rules desirable?
2. Do the existing multilateral investment agreements meet the requirements for improved market efficiency and world welfare in an era of global multinational strategies?
3. Linked to 2, have the existing multilateral agreements stimulated foreign direct investment flows?
4. Linked to 2 and 3, have existing multilateral rules enhanced economic development at a host and home country level?

The Desirability of Multilateral Investment Rules

The arguments for free international direct capital movements are similar to those for free trade. To facilitate investment projects investors need long-term stability of rules and procedures, access to markets and non-discriminatory treatment in comparison with domestic investors. They also require protection of existing investments and an international dispute settlement mechanism. There has been a growing recognition among host country governments that a liberal investment regime is critical to attracting FDI, and an appreciation that restrictions and discriminatory measures distort investment flows with a detrimental effect on efficiency and economic development.

At the same time, there is evidence (Caves 1996) that MNEs (commonly large firms operating in oligopolistic industries) could have adverse effects upon the home or host countries through their monopoly powers and restrictive business practices. An effective competition policy (at multilateral level) is essential. Rules to protect the environment and to prevent wasteful competitive bidding on investment incentives within and between countries are also desirable. More controversially, the rights of countries and obligations of firms (as set out, for example, in the 1976 OECD guidelines should be reflected in appropriate standards of behaviour in the conduct of business abroad.

Bilateral investment treaties and regional agreements do not match the global domain of the multinational, impede the free flow of capital and hamper MNEs' global strategies while at the same time allowing the firm to play off countries and, potentially, regions against one another.

Progress with Existing Multilateral Agreements

With an accord on a number of investment related matters in the GATT/WTO system during and after the Uruguay Round, more progress has been made on multilateral rules in the past five years than in the previous fifty. There have been some achievements therefore in implementing the liberalisation conditions necessary for market efficiency. However, widespread distortions exist, with a patchwork of policies operating at different levels, involving different organisations and applying to different sectors.

Furthermore, the conditions for market contestability do not exist with discrimination between different methods of market servicing. One of the best illustrations in this respect concerns the continued existence of anti-dumping rules. In an EU context these have not only discriminated against foreign firms but have encouraged cartel behaviour within the Union. Anti-dumping rules have encouraged FDI from Japan and other Asia-Pacific countries as a means of circumventing actual or potential duties. Other distortions arise where EU MNEs locate production in Asia-Pacific locations or enter into joint ventures with producers in the Asia-Pacific region for subsequent export to Europe; anti-dumping actions against such imports may for obvious reasons be impossible (for a full discussion, see Brewer and Young 1998, chapter 9).

The approach to liberalisation has, moreover, been unbalanced, with virtually no progress being made in introducing the necessary governance (for example, competition policy) rules for market efficiency. Anti-competitive behaviour by firms is of major concern in an era of global MNE strategies and yet is extremely difficult to identify, for a number of reasons. First, regional and global integration is associated with higher levels of intermediate and intra-firm trade. This means that it is more problematic both to measure concentration levels meaningfully at national level and to identify anti-competitive practices. Second, and linked because of globalisation, competition problems increasingly transcend national boundaries. Examples include international cartels, export cartels, restrictive practices in international services such as air or sea transport, world-scale mergers and the abuse of a dominant position in several major markets (European Commission 1995). Third, the increasing range and complexity of relationships between and within firms is difficult to establish and investigate, let alone judge the pro-competitive versus anti-competitive effects. And fourth, MNEs can play off one jurisdiction against another in competition policy (as in other) matters. An extremely complex case, which highlights many of the problems associated with international acquisitions is that of Gillette's takeover of Wilkinson Sword (see Brewer and Young 1998, box 9.1).

A number of proposals have been made for an international competition policy (see, for example, Scherer 1994; European Commission 1995; Graham and Richardson 1997). However, little progress has been made, and this issue represents probably the biggest challenge for the multilateral investment policy agenda for the future.

Investment incentives represent another area where very few initiatives have been taken to date in any policy forum. Yet there are important liberalisation questions, given that many investment incentives represent inefficient and inequitable government intervention and lead to wasteful, beggar-thy-neighbour bidding within and between nations. An interesting recent case concerned the political furore within the UK over competitive bidding between Scotland, Wales and the English regions. The UK government, represented by the Department of Trade and Industry, was forced to climb down over its proposal to reclaim central control over inward investment subsidies throughout the UK; instead a 'concordat' was agreed, designed to prevent bidding battles (*Financial Times* 14 November 1997).

Aside from the waste and misallocation of resources from subsidy wars, competition may be distorted, especially when large-scale, capital-intensive projects are aided in oligopolistic markets (European Commission 1996). To date the distortions created have primarily been intra-country or intra-regional. However in an era of globalisation, it would be expected that certain types of projects, at least, would become globally, as opposed to simply regionally, mobile. Worldwide competition for such projects could lead to greater incentive bidding because of fewer constraints (the very limited scope of international rules at present) and the more widely varying types and levels of incentives (Brewer and Young 1997). As an illustration of this competition, Seagate Technology of the USA announced the closure of its factory in the Republic of Ireland in December 1997 with the loss of 1,400 jobs; production was to be transferred to the Asia-Pacific region, illustrating the vulnerability of assembly plants to price competition (*Financial Times* 15 December 1997).

Multilateral Investment Rules and the Growth of Foreign Direct Investment

It is extremely difficult to isolate the effects of multilateral investment rules *per se* on flows of FDI. Rates of economic growth have a major influence on both domestic and foreign investment; and hence it is possible to associate, for example, the relatively slow growth of FDI flows in the 1970s with the oil crisis and follow-on repercussions which included world recession, high rates of inflation, trade protection and debt service problems in developing countries. But factors other than economic growth are important too, as shown in the period from the mid-1980s when an exceptional concurrence of events supported FDI growth. These included trade liberalisation through the Uruguay Round, accompanied by extensive investment liberalisation (particularly at national level and relating to both outward and inward FDI) and sectoral liberalisation agreements affecting telecommunications and other services. Liberalisation in turn was driven by and also drove globalisation; while in the FDI area, progress in regionalisation, especially through the EU's Single Market programme and the formation of NAFTA, operated positively in support of globalisation trends.

Progress in liberalising investment policies at all levels has thus been influential in providing a stable and supportive environment for FDI. However, the existing patchwork of investment policies is undoubtedly a deterrent to MNEs' global integration strategies; and the suggestions above, regarding a focus on regionalism rather than multilateralism into the future, will similarly inhibit global strategies. The massive strides which have been taken in trade liberalisation encourage worldwide MNE-based trade, but investment policy barriers, overlaps and conflicts do not permit the full exploitation of the international division of labour.

Multilateral Investment Rules and the Impacts on Economic Development

There is a long standing debate about the equity consequences of policies designed to achieve market efficiency. In respect of FDI, the gains from multinational activity may not be distributed evenly among countries. It is such concerns which explain the hesitancy of some developing nations to participate fully in investment policy liberalisation. In securing future progress on multilateral investment rules through a world organisation like the WTO, at least two issues must be resolved. First, there needs to be a greater recognition of the interests of developing countries in negotiations in respect, for example, of trade-related investment measures (especially local content, trade balancing and export requirements). Developed countries are mostly agreed that these TRIMs cause distortions in patterns of trade and development, whereas developing nations regard them as important tools to promote development objectives and strengthen trade balances. By contrast, developing states have sought control over investment incentives, while the industrialised world has been unwilling or unable to agree on such controls. A second and related issue concerns the need to incorporate a developmental component into multilateral investment instruments (see the extended discussion in Brewer and Young 1998, chapter 10).

Aside from these exceptions, the encouragement of general country policy trends towards liberalisation of FDI are desirable from the perspective of both national and global efficiency and growth. Throughout the world, nevertheless, investment policies are only one constituent of a package which should include measures to ensure macroeconomic stability, plus investment in human capital, research and technological development and other public goods. It is in this latter respect that interest has grown in local development initiatives in industrialised countries, designed to build and support technological clusters, promote MNE plant upgrading and capitalise upon multinational strategy trends towards heterarchical structures.

NOTES

1. This chapter draws extensively on Brewer, TL and Young, S (1998) *The Multilateral Investment System and Multinational Enterprises.* Oxford: Oxford University Press.

2. The following tangible examples are suggestive of the inadequacies of present arrangements at all levels:

- At the bilateral level, the standard US bilateral investment treaty (BIT) includes provisions concerning rights of establishment as well as post-establishment operations, but the typical European BIT concerns only post-establishment issues.
- At the regional level within Europe, although the EC Commission – rather than the individual national governments – has formal authority to represent community interests on many issues at the WTO, it does not have the authority on all issues in the WTO or on any issues in the OECD.
- At the regional level in the Western Hemisphere, the investment-diverting effects of the NAFTA are a source of tensions between NAFTA members, on the one hand, and Caribbean countries that are involved with the USA in the Caribbean Basin Initiative.
- At the inter-regional regional level, the negotiations within the OECD on a Multilateral Agreement on Investment (MAI) creates tension within the Asia-Pacific Economic Cooperation (APEC) forum between those APEC economies that are members of the OECD and those that are not.
- At the multilateral level, the Uruguay Round agreement on trade-related investment measures (TRIMs) did little more about such policies – and perhaps even less – than already existing provisions of the GATT.
- More recently at the multilateral level, the 1997 sectoral Information Technology Agreement (ITA) covers only tariffs and investment-specific issues.

In view of these and other issues concerning existing international arrangements affecting multinational enterprises' activities, including their foreign direct investments, it is desirable to give continuing and detailed attention to the international framework for investment.

ROBERT HINE

3 Globalisation versus regionalism? Trade, Investment and Multinationals

INTRODUCTION

Two powerful forces have been reshaping the world economy in recent years. One is known loosely as 'globalisation' and refers to the increasing integration of the world economy through an intensification of international trade and foreign direct investment. The other major force is regionalism, the promotion by governments of closer economic links between neighbouring countries. The most developed example of regionalism is the European Union, but regional trade arrangements have proliferated elsewhere in recent years. To some extent regionalism and globalisation drive economies in the same direction of increased cross-border interaction. However, there are also potentially opposing forces to the extent that regionalism encourages closer integration among neighbouring economies at the expense of links with the rest of the world. This raises important issues about the nature of and motivation for regionalism, and the effectiveness of international economic cooperation through multilateral institutions such as the World Trade Organisation (WTO).

This chapter examines first the factors that are driving increased integration of the world economy, and in particular trade intensification, increased foreign direct investment (FDI) and the growing influence of multinational companies. The second part addresses regionalism, considering its nature, extent and motivation. It also considers the spread of regionalism: is there a dynamic to regionalism, a 'domino' effect that, once initiated, draws in a growing membership? Has there been a movement towards increased regionalisation of trade, and how does regionalism affect FDI? The third section explores the mutual compatibility of regionalism and globalisation: are regional trade arrangements stepping stones or stumbling blocks to greater international economic integration? A final section concludes.

TOWARDS A MORE INTEGRATED GLOBAL ECONOMY

'Globalisation' has become a dominant economic motif of the late twentieth century, articulating the view that fundamental forces are driving the world's economies towards increasing interdependence. One major channel for this process is international trade. As the volume and variety of cross-border transactions in both goods and services expand, national economies become increasingly integrated into international markets. A second major channel is through the activities of multinational companies. Foreign direct investment, joint ventures and strategic alliances create international linkages in production, research and development and marketing and distribution. Furthermore, a high degree of integration has been reached in financial markets, allowing large-scale and rapid financial flows among the world's major capital markets. Trade, FDI and financial market integration, together with strategic alliances, networks and licensing arrangements allow developments in technology to be rapidly diffused around the globe. In this section we focus especially on trade and FDI as vehicles for globalisation.

Trade Intensification

Over recent decades, the growth of world trade has been swift and sustained. The WTO (1995) estimate that, in real terms, trade multiplied fourteen-fold between 1950 and 1994, corresponding to an annual volume growth of 6 per cent. This compares with an annual expansion in world merchandise production of 2.5 per cent. Hence, the trade to GDP ratio more than doubled from 7 per cent in 1950 to 15 per cent in 1974. The macroeconomic disorder of the late 1970s and early 1980s temporarily slowed the international integration process down, but by 1994 the ratio had reached 22.5 per cent. Not all regions shared equally in this trend. The demise of central planning in Eastern Europe, the turbulence of oil markets in the Middle East and the debt crisis in Latin America were all associated with undynamic performances in these regions, whereas the 'economic miracle' in East Asia – at least until 1997 – was strongly based on foreign trade. But, though there have been variations over time and among regions, the role of trade in the world economy has shown a progressive expansion.

There have also been important changes in the nature of trade. In particular, the colonial pattern of an exchange of manufactured goods for raw materials has been supplanted by the two-way exchange of finely differentiated industrial goods. This 'intra-industry trade' (IIT) now accounts for some 80 per cent of trade in manufactures. Theory and some empirical evidence suggest that IIT is driven by the suppliers' attempts to offer consumers a wide range of choice while simultaneously achieving economies of scale in production. Producers draw on specialised intermediate goods from a global network of suppliers, and trade in these goods accounts for the bulk of intra-industry trade. An emerging and potentially important development in world trade is that the individual firm's production is increasingly dispersed around the globe.

Different locations are used for each stage of production in what Krugman (1995) describes as 'slicing up the value added chain'. This helps to explain the dynamic nature of world trade, since the trade data measure gross sales and a product may cross international boundaries several times in the course of manufacture. In the established industrial countries, it is now feasible to subdivide the production process of goods conventionally thought of as human-capital intensive or technology intensive. Consequently, labour-intensive activities such as assembly can profitably be transferred to low-wage economies. In this way, the East Asian countries have been able to move beyond their initial specialisation in labour-intensive manufactures such as clothes and toys.

The advantages of international specialisation have long been recognised. But why has the expansion of trade been so marked in recent years? The most obvious answer is the improvement in transport and communications.[1] Yet, as Krugman (1995) points out, even a century ago technology permitted global trade through the combination of steamships, railways and the telegraph. What is new is that computers and sophisticated telecommunications equipment make it possible to coordinate a complex, globally dispersed production process. This relies on a massive exchange of information as well as ease of personal contact. The speed of airfreight is also critical to international production in industries such as electronics.

Improvements in technology have undoubtedly been an important enabling factor. But the critical issue for trade expansion has been the trade policy environment. Whereas in the inter-war period beggar-thy-neighbour policies of raising protection held back the growth of world trade, since the creation of the GATT in 1948 trade has been increasingly liberalised. This is most striking for tariffs: on manufactured goods these have come down from an average of over 40 per cent to 4 per cent (post Uruguay Round) in the industrial countries. In addition, other barriers such as exchange controls, quotas and voluntary export restraints have been progressively dismantled. Liberalisation has also spread to developing countries often through the unilateral reduction of tariffs.

Foreign Direct Investment

As a means of supplying foreign consumers, international trade has been surpassed in recent years by overseas production (UNCTAD 1995). Along with trade, foreign direct investment is therefore a key element in globalisation. FDI may be defined as occurring 'when an investor in one country (the home country) acquires an asset in another country (the host country) with the intent to manage that asset' (WTO 1996, p. 46). FDI flows have risen dramatically in the last decade. From a position of relative stability in real terms during the 1970s and the first half of the 1980s, flows of FDI grew from around \$60 billion in 1985 to \$315 billion in 1995; in real terms, they tripled over this period. Consequently, the growth of FDI has exceeded that of trade over the last twenty years by a comfortable margin.[2]

FDI outflows have mainly come from, and been destined to, high-income countries, the biggest recipients being the USA, the UK and France. However, over the period 1985–95, seven of the top twenty host countries were developing economies, China being the leading recipient with an inflow of $130 billion. Much of the investment in developing Asian countries has come from Japan. Overall, manufacturing and services dominate in FDI, and have been of roughly equal importance. There is some variation in the sectoral pattern of FDI among source countries with Japan having a strong concentration in services.

The process of FDI creates or expands multinational enterprises (MNE),[3] defined as enterprises that own and control production or services facilities in two or more countries. This involves the parent company of an MNE based in one country having management control over one or more affiliates in another country or countries. This factor raises a fundamental issue for analysts of globalisation: why are affiliates established when firms could alternatively supply foreign markets directly by exports from the home country or by licensing their technology to foreign companies? In his 'eclectic paradigm', Dunning (1981) brought together three major considerations: ownership-specific advantages, location-specific variables and internalisation incentive advantages. Together they help to explain why firms choose to become MNEs. Among the ownership advantages which firms can profitably exploit on a comparatively large scale as MNEs are intellectual property (such as technology and brand names), organisational and managerial skills and marketing networks.

Locational factors help to explain why firms exploit their ownership advantages internationally through overseas production rather than exports. For service industries, the issue is straightforward: to be competitive a firm must generally have a local presence in foreign markets since much service activity requires contact between supplier and consumer. For manufacturing, locational factors can favour multinational operations in two ways. First, where there is multistage production, through vertical FDI a firm can choose to locate different stages of production in different countries, as observed earlier. Hence, for example, labour-intensive activities can be located in a country with low labour costs, while parts of the production process which require a high input of human capital can be established where skilled labour is relatively abundant. In this way, the firm attempts to minimise production costs by utilising several production sites linked by trade in intermediate products. Second, multinational operations can also confer advantages where similar types of production activities take place in different countries through horizontal FDI. Thus, for example, for products with high weight/value ratios local production may save significantly on transport costs. Similarly, it may be important to produce close to customers, as with component suppliers under just-in-time delivery systems. Local production may also be advantageous in adjusting to local standards or assessing local rivals. A further motivation for horizontal FDI may be the aim of escaping trade barriers, as with 'tariff-jumping' FDI or 'quid pro quo' FDI (where the objective is to reduce the probability of future protectionist actions). Taken together, ownership-specific advantages and locational factors may help to explain why foreign production is the preferred method of supplying the foreign market.

Dunning's third element, internalisation advantages, focuses on why production is carried out within the MNE rather than under licence by foreign companies. Many benefits from internalisation have been identified (see, for example WTO 1996). They include the avoidance of transaction costs associated with arm's length market transactions (for example, costs of contracting and dealing with quality assurance). The legal environment for protecting property rights in a foreign country may give a firm less control under licensing than where production is within the firm. Similarly, the external market may undervalue a firm's technology, perhaps because it demands other complementary technologies or persons with specific knowledge and skills not readily available outside the firm concerned. For various reasons, therefore, multinational operations may offer decisive advantages over licensing.

Early multinational enterprises were largely European-owned, but post-World War II, US companies have dominated. Their own expansion into Europe was motivated both by the significant advantages derived from their presence in the large and affluent American market and by the prospect of breaking through European trade barriers. US manufacturers now sell six times as much from their European affiliates as is exported from the USA across the Atlantic. And similarly for European firms, the bulk of their supplies for the US market comes from their US affiliates. Japanese FDI in Europe developed later than that of the US, taking off in the 1970s. The output of Japanese factories in Europe now matches in value to Japanese–EU exports. But unlike transatlantic FDI, the FDI relationship is asymmetric: by the early 1990s Japanese FDI in Europe was eleven times that of European FDI in Japan (Mason 1994).

An important issue arising from these developments is whether production from affiliates acts as a substitute for, or stimulus to, trade. This could have significant implications, for example, for labour market adjustment both in the home and the host countries. The traditional view, following the work of Mundell (1957), has been that trade and factor movements are substitutes, given standard Heckscher–Ohlin assumptions. Thus, in a two-country world, the free movement of factors of production leads to goods price equalisation. Since comparative advantages are neutralised, trade in goods is eliminated. However, relaxing the assumption of identical technology in the two countries could lead to the opposite result – factor movements and trade are complementary (Ethier 1996; Lloyd 1998). Consequently, the theoretical literature suggests that the complexity of FDI arrangements defies simple generalisations about the relationship between trade and factor movements.

Consider first the case of the *home* country. Even if foreign production replaces exports of final products, it is not clear that total exports will decline. For one thing, the foreign affiliate may import parts and components from the parent. The scale of this trade may even exceed the previous exports of final products if the affiliate succeeds in capturing a bigger share of its local market. Similarly there is uncertainty as to how the home country's imports will be affected. The fall in exports of final products may result in reduced imports of intermediate products. Possibly offsetting this, though, there might be imports of finished products from the affiliate. For the home country, then, no simple substitution or complementary relationship can be posited between trade and FDI. The outcome is similarly unclear for the *host* country. As noted above, reduced host country imports of final products have to be offset against possible increases in intermediate product imports.

Empirical evidence on trade and FDI relationships is limited, but US data suggest a generally complementary pattern (WTO 1997). Thus Hufbauer *et al.* (1994) find that US exports were positively and significantly related to US FDI stocks in 1980, 1985 and 1990. Similar results have been observed for Sweden, Germany, Austria and Japan. Less empirical work has been done in relation to home country imports, but there is some indication that FDI has a positive but weak impact. The link between trade and FDI is also underlined by the extent of intra-firm trade: about one-third of world trade involves transactions between parts of the same MNE. In some instances, the majority of trade is intra-firm – for example 60 per cent of Japanese exports to Europe take this form.

In addition to the expansion of international trade and FDI, integration of the world economy has other important dimensions. There has, for example, been a massive expansion in foreign portfolio investment (FPI): foreign equity holdings that do not confer management control. By 1992, the stock of FPI exceeded that of FDI. The growth of FPI reflects in part the offensive and defensive competitive strategies of firms. Through international equity holdings firms are able to diversify their profit sources, spread risks and undertake collaborative cross-border ventures. Similarly, strategic alliances are a growing and potentially highly significant aspect of globalisation and take a number of forms from loose-knit informal cooperation to arrangements such as joint ventures and consortia involving joint equity holdings. They can be seen as devices to spread the costs and reduce the risks associated with large-scale international operations.

Taken together, the developments mentioned provide evidence of a powerful expansion in the globalisation of economic activities, particularly over the last decade. The economic forces that are driving this process are strong and are likely to intensify. However, international economic integration depends also on a favourable political environment. Through such bodies as the WTO, a high level of mutually advantageous international cooperation has been achieved over the last fifty years. There is no guarantee that this will be maintained – the problems in reaching agreement in the Uruguay Round of trade negotiations illustrate the fragility of the system. Furthermore, the history of the first half of the twentieth century shows that international economic integration can be undermined: protectionism in the inter-war period sharply reduced both trade to GDP ratios and international capital flows. Currently, the growth of regionalism is widely seen as the most potent threat to further global economic integration. The 'nightmare scenario' is the development of large, mutually antagonistic trade blocs. The nature and spread of regionalism, and its effects on trade and FDI, are explored in the next section.

REGIONALISM IN THE WORLD ECONOMY

Regional Integration Arrangements

Regional integration arrangements (RIAs) were established earliest and have progressed furthest in Europe. From its foundation as the European Economic Community (EEC) in 1958,[4] the European Union (EU) has increased both its membership – from six to fifteen countries – and its scope. The EEC created a customs union in which trade among the member countries is free of tariffs and quotas and there is a common external tariff on imports from non-members. This laid the basis for the establishment of the Single European Market (SEM) in 1993 with the removal of internal border controls and the free movement within the SEM of goods, services, labour and capital. In addition, policies in certain areas such as agricultural support and competition have been harmonised, and most of the member countries adopted a single currency from 1999. The EU has a network of trade agreements with neighbouring countries and has opened negotiations to extend membership to a further six countries within the next decade.

The development of the EU is underpinned by the political ambition to unite a continent which was the scene of devastating military conflicts twice in the twentieth century. By contrast, regional integration in North America is driven by more limited, largely economic, considerations. It began in 1989 with a free trade agreement between the US and Canada which was extended to include Mexico in 1994 through the formation of the North American Free Trade Area (NAFTA). Within the free trade area, goods originating in the area are traded tariff-free; there is no requirement on the members to harmonise their external tariffs. Nor, unlike the EU, do members commit themselves to the free movement of labour within NAFTA, indeed the extension of free trade to Mexico was seen as a means of reducing pressure for migration. Elsewhere in the Americas the progress of regionalism has been erratic. Efforts to establish regional groupings in the 1970s made little real progress. More recently there has been a resurgence of interest, notably in the launch in 1991 of Mercosur. This is intended to create a common market among Argentina, Brazil, Paraguay and Uruguay. In 1995, a Free Trade Area for the Americas was proposed to extend free trade in principle to all countries in North, Central and South America by 2005.

The spread of regionalism has been much less marked in Asia, the principal exception being the Association of South East Asian Nations (ASEAN) which in 1991 pledged to complete a free trade area over fifteen years. However, strong regional trade and investment links exist, centred on the dominant trading economy in the region, Japan. Regional trade among the Pacific Rim countries could be stimulated by APEC (Asia Pacific Economic Cooperation) which includes three of the world's largest economies: the US, China and Japan. APEC aims to achieve an 'open market' among the developed country members by 2010 and to extend this to the rest of the group by 2020. 'Open regionalism' aims to reduce barriers among members without discriminating against non-members. Initially this could be achieved by eliminating tariffs on products of most interest to APEC countries, but ultimately it implies that APEC countries would eliminate tariffs without demanding reciprocity from outsiders (mainly the EU). The significance of this would depend on progress made in the meantime through the WTO in dismantling tariffs multilaterally.

It is important to recognise that the growth in RIAs encompasses a wide diversity of forms and content. This goes far beyond the traditional distinction between free trade areas and customs unions. Arrangements differ, for example, in relation to free movement of labour, capital and services, in industrialisation provisions (including production sharing agreements) and payment terms. The potential impact of RIAs on international economic integration thus varies widely.

RIAs: Motivation and Spread

The diversity of RIAs reflects differences in motivation and aims. Whalley (1998) suggests six main reasons why regional arrangements have been established:

- *Traditional trade gains.* The removal of trade barriers allows low-cost suppliers in one country to displace higher-cost local producers in the market of another member country (trade creation); customs union theory, however, suggests that a net gain may not be achieved since trade may also be diverted to higher-cost suppliers within the union, and these trade-diversion losses could outweigh trade creation gains.
- *Strengthening domestic policy reform.* A regional trade treaty can help to prevent domestic policy reforms from being reversed: the international legal commitment helps to 'lock-in' the domestic measures.
- *Increased multilateral bargaining power.* By combining together in a regional group, countries may be able to exercise more leverage in international negotiations, insofar as they share common interests.

- *Guarantees of access.* Small countries may be motivated to seek a preferential trade agreement with a larger neighbour in order to obtain greater security of market access. In the US–Canada case, for example, Canadian producers obtained partial exemption from anti-dumping and countervailing duty actions.
- *Strategic linkage.* A regional trade agreement can help to underpin security arrangements among the member countries. The aim of preventing further military confrontation between France and Germany was the primary motivation for regional arrangements in Europe.
- *Multilateral and regional interplay.* The actual or potential implementation of regional agreements can be used as a tactical device in securing multilateral negotiating objectives. Thus the possibility that the USA might have recourse to increased regional agreements helped bring pressure on negotiating partners to conclude a Uruguay Round agreement.

The latter argument suggests one possible reason for the growth in US interest in RIAs: as a tactical device to support multilateralism. A different view is that the USA, the erstwhile champion of non-discrimination in the GATT, has become a convert to regionalism (Bhagwati 1993). However, as Whalley (1993) and others have pointed out, the pressure for NAFTA and other western hemisphere trade links has not come from the USA but from its trade partners. In any case, US conversion to regionalism could not be seen as an explanation for the spread of regional integration arrangements elsewhere, notably in Europe, which took place earlier.

Another view is that the spread of RIAs reflects frustration with the multilateral GATT approach to trade issues. Countries may have turned to regionalism as a politically easier route. Certainly, the increasing number of participants in multilateral negotiations – over a hundred in the Uruguay Round – adds to complexity, but it is not clear that this has made GATT negotiations politically more difficult (Krugman 1993). This depends on the nature of the issues. With the decline in industrial tariffs, negotiations have had to refocus on less tractable non-tariff issues. This may tilt the balance towards regional negotiations where the participants are more likely to share similar views. However, outside Europe this argument is not persuasive since most RIAs are shallow in scope and have made limited progress on non-tariff issues. A further aspect of 'frustration with the GATT' argument is that countries might have turned to regionalism in recent years because of discontent with the slow progress of the Uruguay Round negotiations. But this seems implausible for reasons of timing. First, the launch of the Single Market programme in Europe preceded even the start of the Uruguay Round negotiations; and, second, US involvement in regional preferences dates back to its 1965 auto pact with Canada.

Baldwin (1993, 1997) has suggested an alternative explanation, a 'domino theory' of spreading regionalism. The domino effect is triggered by an initial event that alters the pattern of trade preferences. Then, the formation of a regional group or the accession of a new member country leads to trade diversion against excluded countries. This upsets the political equilibrium in each excluded country, and could shift the balance in favour of joining the regional group since membership would enable the country to recoup its lost trade. But enlargement of the regional group would then exert a trade diverting effect on remaining non-members whose trade is oriented towards the preference group. Hence, a further round of enlargement could follow. As more countries join, the pressure on the remaining ones to follow suit intensifies and the domino effect spreads.

This explanation requires an initial trigger – an idiosyncratic event which upsets the political equilibrium. In North America, Baldwin suggests that it was the unilateral reforms undertaken by Mexico in the 1980s which led to NAFTA as a device for locking in the reforms. Mexico's favourable access to the US market then upset the established balance of advantages of other western hemisphere countries. On the other side of the Atlantic, the effort to revive the fortunes of the EU through the Single European Market provided the trigger event. Sapir (1997) shows in particular how the EFTA countries' trade position deteriorated after 1985, leading most of them to apply for full EU membership.

Is World Trade Becoming More Regionalised?

The 'regionalisation' of trade implies that trade between countries in the same regional group has developed more strongly than trade between countries in different regional groups. This could refer to the intensity of trade already achieved or to the relative growth rate of inter- and intra-regional trade flows. Similarly, the definition of regions could vary according to the purpose of the analysis. Lloyd (1992), for example considers the three Triad blocs based around the EU, the US and Japan, as well as specific RIAs such as the EU. In this section, some empirical evidence will be reviewed and consideration will also be given to factors that might drive the regionalisation of trade.

Anderson and Norheim (1993) have analysed the direction of trade of seven regions from 1928 to 1990. The seven regions are Western Europe, Eastern Europe and the Soviet Union, North America, Latin America, Asia, Africa, and the Middle East. Over the period as a whole there was a tendency for countries to conduct a growing share of their international trade with members of the same region. Thus, summed over all regions, the intra-regional share of trade increased from 39 per cent in 1928 to 52 per cent in 1990. The regionalisation of trade varied over time, with setbacks during the World War II period and during the late 1970s and early 1980s.

Simple measures of trade regionalisation such as those just referred to are a useful starting point but can be misleading. In particular, their magnitudes depend on how regions are defined and specifically on the size and number of countries. To abstract from this, Brown (1949) and Kojima (1964) developed an intensity of trade index:

$$I_{ij} = \frac{X_{ij} / X_i}{M_j / (M_w - M_i)}$$

where X_{ij} is country *i*'s exports to country *j*
X_i is *i*'s total exports
M_j is *j*'s total exports
M_i is *i*'s total imports and
M_w is total world imports.

Using this measure Anderson and Norheim examine intra-regional and extra-regional trade intensities. They find evidence of a growth in the intensity of intra-regional trade until about 1958, but thereafter relative stability (table 3.1). This reflects different trends across regions. The upward trend persisted in Western Europe and North America after 1958, but not in Asia. Intra-Asian trade did grow rapidly, but this simply reflected the dynamic trade performance of the economies in the region. Trade between Asia and other regions grew more impressively, taking account of the generally slower growth in the trade of Asia's partners. A similar methodology can be applied to *extra*-regional trade. The average for the seven regions shows a progressive decline over the period as a whole, with the lowest value reached in 1990. Thus the trade intensity index in general supports the view that trade has become more regionalised, taking account of the (trade) size of countries but with the notable exception of the Asian region.

TABLE 3.1: THE REGIONALISATION OF WORLD TRADE, 1928–90

Year	Intra-regional trade as % total trade	Trade intensity index intra-regional	Trade intensity index extra-regional	Propensity-to-trade index intra-regional	Propensity-to-trade index extra-regional
1928	39	1.85	0.86	0.45	0.21
1938	37	2.16	0.75	0.43	0.15
1948	33	2.43	0.83	0.54	0.19
1958	40	2.65	0.75	0.57	0.16
1963	44	2.84	0.68	0.60	0.14
1968	47	2.81	0.67	0.61	0.15
1973	49	2.62	0.64	0.73	0.18
1979	46	2.64	0.68	0.91	0.23
1983	45	2.68	0.66	0.82	0.20
1990	52	2.62	0.62*	0.88	0.21

Source: Anderson and Norheim (1993)

The analysis of regionalisation in trade can be usefully extended by taking into account also the relationship between trade and GDP. As noted earlier, the openness of economies has increased over time. This raises the possibility that although extra-regional trade may have been undynamic relative to intra-regional trade, when scaled against GDP the performance could be more impressive. For this purpose Anderson and Norheim use a 'propensity to trade' index, again applied to intra- and extra-regional trade. This index is defined as:

$$P_{ij} = t_{ij} / m_{ij}$$
$$= t_{ij} \cdot I_{ij}$$

where

t_{ij} = *i*'s exports to *j* divided by *i*'s GDP, and
t_i = the ratio of *i*'s total exports to *i*'s GDP.

Anderson and Norheim find that the propensity to trade intra-regionally has approximately doubled over the sixty-year period, and an important part of this change has taken place since the late 1960s (table 3.1). The *extra*-regional propensity shows a remarkable stability: the expansion of extra-regional trade has kept pace with the growth of GDP over the period as a whole. Compared with the 1960s, the ratio has increased by about a third. North American and Western European trends approximate to the world trends, although by 1990 the propensity to trade index for extra-regional trade was higher than in 1928 in North America but lower in Western Europe. Asian trends are different, mainly because of developments in Japan. After World War II, the Japanese economy became much less open (trade as a percentage of GDP fell from 35 per cent in 1928 to 8 per cent in 1948), and Japan's trade shifted away from its Asian neighbours towards extra-regional partners.

In general, the empirical analysis of Anderson and Norheim supports the view that at the continental/subcontinental level there has been an increasing regionalisation of trade. What has driven this regionalisation process? Four possible influences can be suggested:

- *Changes in the commodity structure of world trade.* Traditional trade patterns – particularly the exchange of manufactures for primary products – were driven primarily by differences in factor endowments (Heckscher–Ohlin trade). Since factor endowments are more likely to differ between regions than among neighbouring countries, this favoured extra-regional trade flows. By contrast, modern trade consists predominantly of an exchange of differentiated manufactures with similar factor intensities in production between countries with similar income patterns and tastes. Such intra-industry trade is less likely to be biased towards inter-regional exchanges.
- *Changes in transport and communications costs.* The relative importance of transport modes differs between intra- and extra-regional trade, hence differential cost changes between modes, could influence

trade patterns. For example, in North America and western Europe short-distance (intra-regional) trade is more likely to involve road transport whereas long-distance (extra-regional) trade depends more heavily on sea transport. Thus, if road haulage charges have increased more slowly than sea freight rates (for example through deregulation of road freight, improvements in vehicle performance, etc.) this would favour intra-regional trade. In addition, transport costs reflect both handling/loading charges and distance covered. A relative decline in handling/loading costs (for example through containerisation and bulk handling) would favour short-distance traffic.

- *International production as a substitute for trade.* The relationship between trade and FDI was discussed earlier. Foreign production from an affiliate is more likely to substitute for trade where the distances between home and host countries are large, since the saving in transport costs would be more compelling. Furthermore to the extent that affiliate production serves a regional market, this would generate intra-regional trade.
- *The growth of regional trade preferences.* The economic rationale for the formation of RIAs is to expand trade between the member countries in order to raise national incomes. Most RIAs are located entirely within one continent or subcontinent. Hence, to the extent that RIAs have been successful in promoting trade between the member countries through eliminating tariff and non-tariff barriers, they contribute to an expansion of intra-regional trade as shown in table 3.1. Furthermore, to the extent that there is trade diversion against non-member countries, this would have a negative impact on extra-regional trade.

Although there have been numerous attempts to measure the trade and welfare effects generated by the formation of particular RIAs, especially in Europe and North America, the evidence remains largely inconclusive. Examining trends in European trade, Lloyd (1992) found an increasing intra-regional trade share for the EC six and EFTA until 1973, and for the EC twelve after 1973. But the latter reflected the upward trend in non-manufactures, especially food. For manufactures, a declining intra-EC share was found. Other factors such as multilateral tariff reductions and changes in comparative advantage may have outweighed the regional preference effect. In a survey of *ex post* studies and counterfactual analyses of RIAs, Srinivasan *et al.* (1993) conclude that apart from a consistent finding that European integration in the 1960s generated trade creation, little can be said with confidence about how RIAs have impacted on trade and welfare.

Recent *ex-post* analysis of RIAs has focused on the use of the gravity model, whose theoretical underpinnings have been re-examined by Deardorff (1998). The model argues that the amount of trade between two countries is proportionate to the product of their GDPs and is inversely related to the distance and other trade restrictions between them. Gravity models have a fairly long history and appear to fit bilateral trade data well. The results of a recent application by Frankel *et al.* (1998), using pooled time-series and cross-section data for 1970–90, can be considered representative of current work. They find that distance has a powerful inhibiting effect on trade: when the distance between two non-adjacent countries increases by 1 per cent, the trade between them falls by 0.5 per cent. This led Grossman (1998) to remark that the distance factor in gravity models is empirically too important to be reflecting only transport costs. It must be driven by imperfect information where familiarity declines rapidly with distance, by localised tastes and by the nature of distribution networks. Frankel *et al.* also find that adjacent countries trade with each other more heavily than their economic size and distance apart would suggest. They try to test for the impact of RIAs by including dummy variables for membership, and conclude from this that joint membership of the Western European, Western Hemisphere or East Asian blocs had a positive and significant effect on bilateral trade. Interestingly, the most powerful effect was in East Asia where no formal bloc-wide trade preferences exist. Furthermore, in this study, as in other gravity model estimations, membership of the regional group appears to have an effect in advance of its formal inauguration. This may reflect earlier but more limited collaboration between countries or anticipation by economic agents of forthcoming arrangements, but it may also be that the dummy variable for membership of a regional group is picking up other, unexplained, influences.[5]

Regionalism and FDI

The establishment of RIAs is likely to have conflicting effects on FDI both within and between regions. Within regions, the existence of national trade barriers may previously have raised the costs of exports, encouraging firms to supply markets by local production from affiliates. The establishment of an RIA which reduces trade barriers between member countries could switch the balance of advantage in favour of supplying markets within the RIA by exports. However, the negative effect of this on intra-regional FDI is potentially offset by the possibility of shifting production to low-cost regions that are now better able to exploit their comparative advantage (Krugman and Venables 1990). In this way, Spain and Portugal were able to attract a large inflow of FDI following their accession to the EU.

Inward and outward FDI with non-member countries is also affected by the establishment of an RIA. Outward FDI may be discouraged if it is designed in part to supply goods or services to members of the RIA. Instead the FDI may be diverted to an RIA member. Baldwin *et al* (1996) suggest that the EFTA countries, for instance, may have lost FDI from EU-based firms in 1987–8 after the launch of the Single European Market (SEM). This investment diversion effect ended when negotiations were announced that led eventually to the European Economic Area. This extended to the EFTA countries many of the advantages of SEM membership.

Inward FDI from non-member countries is likely to be stimulated by the formation of an RIA. In particular, the more integrated regional market is likely to be more attractive to MNEs through greater scale economies. In Europe, the initial moves towards integration in the 1950s and 1960s attracted an inflow of FDI by US MNEs who were better positioned to take advantage of the wider market opportunities than many European firms. Some FDI may have been an attempt at pre-emptive action against local firms in relation to the bigger European market. The acceleration of Japanese FDI in Europe in the late 1980s was influenced by (misplaced) fears that the reduction of internal barriers in the SEM might be accompanied by increased external protection – the 'Fortress Europe' scenario.

Over the last decade, European integration has been accompanied by an expansion in inward FDI, in particular following the announcement of the SEM programme. There is evidence that the share of US and Japanese FDI directed to the EU experienced a modest increase. However, it is difficult to disentangle the SEM effect from the upsurge in global FDI that began in the mid-1980s, and econometric studies of FDI flows failed to find convincing evidence of an SEM impact. Thus Clegg (1995) found no significant effect in the period 1987–90. Similarly, Srinivasan and Moody (1997) found no evidence that the share of Japanese or US FDI directed to Europe increased as a result of the SEM, at least until 1992 (Dunning 1997a, b). A cautious conclusion seems justified: the upswing in world FDI flows coincided with further integration in the EU, and the EU participated fully in this aspect of the globalisation process. But it is not clear from the empirical evidence that European integration augmented the FDI inflows from non-member countries. Intra-EU FDI flows have expanded rapidly particularly through mergers and acquisitions. It is possible that much of this activity involves non-European based firms (Commission 1997).

Outside Europe, most RIAs have taken the form of free trade areas. Their impact on external trade and FDI depends on the strictness of rules of origin which determine eligibility for tariff-free treatment on intra-area trade. Strict rules which make it difficult to incorporate non-area inputs may induce foreign firms to establish plants within the area to take advantage of area treatment. As with customs unions, the impact on intra-area FDI is ambiguous: some affiliate plants motivated by tariff-jumping may be closed down, but FDI in low-cost locations could be stimulated by better access to the RIA market.

REGIONALISM VERSUS GLOBALISATION?

At the beginning of the 1990s there was a vigorous debate as to whether the resurgence of regionalism would contribute to, or work against, global economic integration (Lawrence 1991; Hine 1992). In particular, would RIAs represent building blocks or stumbling blocks in the pursuit of multilateral trade liberalisation? Concern was heightened by the delay in reaching agreement in the Uruguay Round of trade negotiations. The fear was that GATT rules on RIAs were too weak to prevent the establishment of inward-looking, protectionist trade blocs which would divert trade away from more efficient third country suppliers. GATT Article 24 might stop countries from using the pretext of customs union formation to raise tariffs against non-member countries, but it could not preclude the discrimination in favour of member country suppliers which is inherent in any RIA. In any case, the GATT rules were very weakly policed – reviews were generally inconclusive, and the compatibility of RIA arrangements with GATT requirements was seldom effectively challenged. Moreover, in the early 1990s there were fears that members of RIAs were too preoccupied with internal matters to give sufficient attention and political priority to GATT activities, and especially to the conclusion of the Uruguay Round. In retrospect, these particular fears seem to have been unwarranted.

Certainly, there are illiberal aspects of the external trade policies of RIAs: in the EU case, anti-dumping measures and voluntary export restraints on manufactures, and import levies and export subsidies on agricultural products could be cited. The crucial issue is whether protectionism is strengthened by the formation of RIAs. From a political economy perspective, the general view has been to the contrary. RIAs are seen as weakening protectionism as they reduce the relative size of national pressure groups which may then lose some of their political influence, and they also expand the size and number of interest groups at the regional level, making them more susceptible to free-riding. Thus the central authority in an RIA will be less responsive to national lobbies than the member governments (de Melo and Panagariya 1993). However, critics (for example Bilal 1998) argue that the trade policy practice of an RIA will depend on the design and evolution of its policy-making institutions, and that these may favour restrictive trade measures. Winters (1994), for example, argues that the efforts of the Commission bureaucracy to capture control over EU trade policy from the member states could have imparted a protectionist bias. However, in practice this is hard to substantiate and, to the contrary, in recent years the Commission has been active in promoting multilateral trade initiatives.

The empirical evidence, despite the limitations noted earlier, supports the judgement that on balance RIAs have had a positive impact on world trade. RIAs among high-income countries have been predominantly trade creating, with the notable exception of agriculture in the EU. Moreover, RIAs have contributed to the elimination of non-tariff barriers (NTBs). Thus the establishment of the SEM was accompanied by the removal of many national quotas on non-EU imports. More importantly, it can be plausibly argued that experience in tackling NTBs regionally has helped to make faster progress multilaterally, for example on technical standards. And, to the extent that

RIAs have succeeded in raising the incomes of their members, this will increase the demand for imports from non-members countries.

There may be a dynamic in RIAs that will cause them to coalesce and eventually will lead to global free trade. In pure theory, Kemp and Wan (1976) envisaged the possibility that, through an appropriate adjustment in the external tariff, customs union formation would involve only trade creation and no trade diversion. The incentive would then exist for a progressive expansion of a customs union resulting in universal membership, and hence global free trade. However, Krugman (1991) showed, also under restrictive assumptions, that if customs unions used their market power to maximise their terms of trade benefits, then the movement towards a world of a few major trade blocs could be welfare-reducing. More recently, the 'domino theory' described earlier suggests that trade diversion by an RIA creates an incentive for progressive RIA expansion. In Europe, this is consistent not only with the expansion in EU membership but also with the proliferation of EU trade preferences towards neighbouring countries. In the Americas, there is also pressure to link up RIAs and to create a hemispheric arrangement under the Free Trade Area of the Americas initiative. Similarly, Asia Pacific Economic Cooperation (APEC), though envisaging a different form of regionalism, would provide free trade links between the Americas and Asia. There are ongoing discussions on the creation of a transatlantic marketplace and for free trade links between the EU and Latin American countries. In addition, the Asia Europe Meeting (ASEM) has established a dialogue between the EU and Asian countries. One outcome of these initiatives would be a plethora of free trade deals. The sheer complexity of this, particularly in relation to rules of origin, could create pressure in the WTO for the worldwide elimination of tariffs. Thus there is a sense in which regionalism could promote globalisation, at least in relation to trade.

The interaction between regionalism and the globalisation of investment has been less controversial. This is mainly because much of the liberalisation of FDI – at least among high-income countries – predated the upsurge in regionalism. By the end of the 1980s two crucial aspects, national treatment and the right of establishment, were in place in virtually every area in the OECD countries. Controls on investment in manufacturing have been largely removed and the role of the RIAs has been more significant in implementation rather than policy design. Investment in services has been more problematic and here EU activities have had a catalytic effect at the global level. For FDI in general, the issue is not whether RIAs have inhibited inward investment but whether their attraction of FDI has been excessive. For small countries outside an RIA there is a danger of investment diversion as MNEs prefer to locate new capacity within the RIA. Thereby they benefit from superior access to their main markets, particularly where imports from the parent firm are subject to trade measures such as anti-dumping duties at the RIA level. A related issue is that where an RIA negotiates free trade agreements with third countries – 'hub and spoke' arrangements – rules of origin may lead FDI to gravitate to the hub at the expense of the spokes. These reservations aside, regionalism and globalisation are mutually reinforcing with regard to FDI. On the one hand, the creation of larger regional markets acts as an attraction to FDI and, on the other hand, FDI has been a principal mechanism for regional integration.

The benefits of increased integration of the world's economies are large and wide-ranging. They include gains from increased international specialisation, the fuller exploitation of economies of scale, consumer access to a greater variety and better quality of products, the competitive stimulus to improved managerial and worker performance and the faster development and diffusion of technological advances. There may, of course, be a downside to this cornucopia. Rodrik (1997) has articulated three particular concerns in asking, 'Has Globalisation Gone Too Far?' First, reduced barriers to trade and investment may accentuate the asymmetry between those who are internationally mobile and those who are not. In high-wage countries the latter include especially the unskilled workers whose wages and/or jobs come under pressure from imports from low-wage countries. Second, globalisation may generate conflicts within and between countries over domestic norms (for example labour standards, environmental regulations) and domestic institutions that embody them. This already forms much of the new agenda for multilateral trade negotiations. Third, growing international economic integration may undermine the welfare state at the same time as arguably making it more necessary as a safety net. A major issue here is the ability of governments to raise taxes as capital becomes more footloose.

Two further concerns over globalisation could be added to Rodrik's list: instability and loss of competition. At first sight, their inclusion may appear odd. The integration of world commodity markets should have a stabilising effect because of the greater absorptive capacity of the world, as compared with national, markets. Disturbances are spread more thinly over a wider market. But instability could be a problem in a wider sense where marketisation is incomplete. The process of institutional change is inevitably slow, and where this is combined with rapid globalisation the effect could be destabilising. The resulting difficulties could be accentuated by the tendency of foreign exchange markets to overshoot. And within a globalised economy, instability in one region will have widespread effects. Competition is the crucial driving force in a market economy. Thus far, globalisation has brought with it intensified competition, but the spread of MNEs is a relatively recent phenomenon. It is developing in new ways through strategic alliances and networking. A major factor behind these is the desire to reduce risk, particularly in relation to the development and introduction of new technology. The danger then is that there will be a concentration of power at the global level which is inimical to consumer interests and which it is beyond the power of nation states to control.The concerns that have been articulated here over globalisation are certainly not an argument that the process should be stopped or reversed, even supposing that that were possible. Rather, they may suggest another relationship between globalisation and regionalism. What may be beyond the reach of the nation state may be possible at the regional level. Labour standards are a case in point. Thus the EU countries can agree collectively on standards which, acting alone, individual countries would be too weak to enforce in a world of mobile FDI. There may be circumstances in which countervailing power is needed in relation to the activities of MNEs, or collective action is needed on globalisation issues. In the absence of global institutions with sufficient sanctions, regionalism may have an important role to play.

CONCLUSIONS

There has been an upsurge in regionalism over the last decade and an increasingly complex web of trade preferences is in prospect. RIAs, however, vary greatly in their nature and motivation: the EU is not only the biggest but also the most ambitious. Elsewhere the emphasis is on limited trade arrangements. Alongside the growth of regionalism has been an intensification of trade and foreign investment – globalisation – with MNEs playing an increasingly prominent part in the world economy. To the extent that RIAs are inward-looking and protectionist, they would be on a collision course with globalisation. However, the evidence points generally in the opposite direction: regionalism and globalisation have been mutually reinforcing. There has been a long-term tendency towards a concentration of trade within continental regions (except for Asia), but this effect is relatively weak. Globalisation offers important economic gains; but there are also risks, particularly of growing social disintegration, since the costs and benefits of economic integration are unequally shared. In this respect regionalism could have a significant future role to play in mediating the influence of globalisation.

NOTES

1. Between 1930 and 1990, US air transport charges per mile fell from 68 US cents to 11 cents, in 1990 dollar terms; the cost of a three-minute telephone call between New York and London fell from $244.65 to $3.32; and between 1960 and 1990, the costs of a unit of computing power fell by more than 99 per cent (Wolf 1997, citing IMF *World Economic Outlook1997*).

2. Between 1973 and 1995, the estimated value of annual FDI outflows multiplied more than 12 times, compared with 8.5 times for the value of merchandise exports (WTO 1997).

3. There are currently some 37,000 MNEs, but the majority of these are relatively small. The top 500 MNEs account for about 50 per cent of world GNP, and about 70 per cent of trade and investment.

4. Since 1951, the six EEC countries had cooperated in a more limited way under the European Coal and Steel Community.

5. Matyas (1997) has cautioned that gravity models incorporating regional dummy variables may be misspecified.

4 Global and Regional Integration and Subnational Economic Development

INTRODUCTION

Recently, there has been a questioning of the concept of globalisation including the idea of the global corporation. Most telling here are the findings that the majority of multinational companies remain overwhelmingly oriented to their home economies (Davies and Lyons 1996) while only a small proportion of world output is derived from the overseas operations of multinationals (Lipsey *et al.* 1995, cited in Allen and Thompson 1997). Without doubt truly global corporations and truly global corporate strategies have never existed except as academic and managerial ideas which gained some currency during the 1970s and 1980s. Instead, commentators now perceive a retreat from corporate strategies of global integration to integration centred on major regional markets such as the EU and North America (Hirst and Thompson 1995; Ruigrok and Van Tulder 1996). To an extent, these ideas resonate with those of the Commission for the European Communities which has promoted important ideas regarding European-wide industrial restructuring accompanying the creation of a single European market. These ideas centre on the exploitation of economies of scale and greater integration among plants within multinationals.

However, these ideas, like those earlier on global corporations and corporate strategies, tend to speak to leading edge corporate strategies among larger multinationals. My concern in this chapter is not to deny the validity of these observations but to recast them in a way which: (a) questions whether greater corporate integration either within Europe or globally is at all rational to many multinationals and their affiliates many of which are small and oriented toward their home economy or else a limited number of overseas territories and; (b) stresses the complementarities between elements of global and regional corporate integration across the range of multinational companies within, and the resultant impact on, one subnational economy – Wales.

ELEMENTS OF GLOBAL AND REGIONAL CORPORATE STRATEGIES

There is a tension within multinational companies between the need to engage with localised sources of, to use Dunning's (1979) terminology, ownership advantages through their affiliates and the need to exploit these internally. Here the consensus of recent academic opinion also suggests that the changing nature of investment undertaken, and affiliate roles assigned by, multinationals reflect the increasing premium placed on engaging with localised sources of external economies. As a result there is a new optimism regarding the contribution of multinationals to regional development which stems from perceptions regarding the greater autonomy and status of 'quality' investments (for a review of these ideas see: Amin *et al.* 1994; Young *et al.* 1994). This optimism stands in contrast to the huge academic literature on the poor contribution of the branch plants of large, often multinational, firms to host economies – a major centre-piece of which was that close integration with the parent company limited the contribution of branch plants to local economic development (Watts 1981; Phelps 1993). Notions of subsidiary autonomy have, then, important implications for processes of intra-corporate division of labour and associated rationalisation and investment. In this section I consider two main aspects of the coordination of activity internal to multinationals, namely: plant status and intra-corporate division of labour and corporate integration.

Plant Status, Division of Labour and Investment Switching

Recently there has been some convergence of thought regarding the nature of multinational investment apparent in various strands of research on multinationals. Thought has converged around the idea that the status and contribution of much multinational investment in many host economy contexts is now somewhat greater than in past rounds of investment. At the broadest level, work on the global and regional corporate strategies of multinationals has pointed to shifts in the type of investment accompanying European (Pearce and Papanastassiou 1997; Yannopolous 1990) and North American integration (Rugman and D'Cruz 1995) and more complex forms of global and regional corporate integration (UNCTAD 1994) embodying an element of global-localisation (Ruigrok and Van Tulder 1996). Some of these trends in corporate organisation appear to be manifest in the appearance of qualitatively superior forms of multinational investment in certain local economies (Amin *et al.* 1994). One example of this might be the increasing contribution of larger-scale, repeat investments to employment change in local economies (see Stone and Peck 1996 for an analysis of the foreign-owned manufacturing sector in the UK regions). Certainly, these trends have generated concern over the increasing competition among inward-investment agencies to attract such large-scale flagship investments (Amin *et al.* 1994;

UNCTAD 1996). Finally, research specifically on the changing roles of multinational affiliates has documented a wide range of possible roles in any given host economy, the tendency for plants of greater status and capabilities to be associated with corporate strategies of global and regional integration and the potential for an upgrading of the stock of multinational investment in some host economies (Hood and Young 1988).

While all this tends to suggest that recent vintages of multinational investment are indeed more disposed to engaging with their local environments, the relationship between affiliates and their parent company organisations remains a complex one. As the United Nations' work makes clear (UNCTAD 1994), new forms of multinational investment are, to some extent, associated with more complex forms of corporate integration. Thus, recent work suggests that affiliates possessing world and continental product mandates are closely integrated with other parent company plants – perhaps more so than those plants without mandates (Birkinshaw 1996; Roth and Morrison 1992). Plant status, then, also entails a greater inter-dependence on other company plants through some division of labour within the parent company organisation. This in turn means that changes in plant status involve the diversion of investment, responsibilities and functions to or from elsewhere within a network of parent company plants.

There are relatively few studies of investment diversion or switching within multinationals which can provide a guide as to how regional economic integration might impact on corporate divisions of labour and changes in plant status (see, for example, Owens 1980; Buckley and Artisien 1988). Owens's (1980) study of UK FDI in Ireland makes it apparent that a broad definition of such diversionary effects would need to be adopted if the range of direct and indirect consequences of a given investment on other parent company operations is to be understood. A significant proportion of the manufacturing investments made in Ireland by UK firms involved some direct investment diversion from domestic operations. The investment diversion effects noted by Buckley and Artisien (1988), and which took place in the context of market integration in Europe, appear to be less significant – though this may be expected given that the authors were considering investment in the 'periphery' of the European market.

The available evidence from macroeconomic studies suggests that diversion of investment from the EU as a result of regional integration elsewhere in the world economy will be negligible. The trade and presumably the investment diversion effects of the North American Free Trade Agreement (NAFTA) on the EU are estimated to be negligible (Wilkinson 1995). Similarly, in a recent study of the impact of possible Western Hemispheric economic integration, the investment estimated to be diverted from Western Europe amounted to $10.4bn or just 0.8 per cent of total flows into Western Europe up to 2002 (Hufbauer and Schott 1994).

Intra-corporate Integration

Since the status of individual subsidiaries and their integration with parent organisations are two sides of the same coin, in the remainder of this subsection I consider some of the main evidence on a number of indicators of corporate integration, namely intra-corporate exchanges of finished and semi-finished products, labour and technology, and financing of investment. One point which should become obvious is that the extent and nature of global economic integration, and particularly that portion which takes place within multinational companies, is crucially dependent on the referent or indicator of integration one examines (Allen and Thompson 1997).

During the 1970s the extent of corporate integration through intra-firm trade in finished and semi-finished goods was of interest as part of a wider concern with the global reach of multinational companies and the increasing inclusion of developing countries within international corporate divisions of labour. Certainly the role of developing countries as providers of semi-finished products in vertical divisions of labour within multinationals became of specific concern to academics (Adam 1975; Helleiner 1973). Much of this literature may have overstated the flows of investment into developing countries (Gordon 1990), the sophistication of the way in which developing countries were incorporated into the production networks of multinationals and presumably the importance of intra-corporate trade.

What little evidence that exists derives mainly from US Department of Commerce benchmark surveys of foreign business. Information on the trading patterns of Japanese parent and affiliate companies also exists but provides much less reliable an indicator of intra-firm trade (Boutruri and Fukasaku 1993). In assessing the evidence from both these sources Boutruri and Fukasaku suggest that 'the hypothesis that the trend towards globalisation in the 1980s, characterised by a foreign direct investment boom, would increase significantly the relative importance of intra-firm trade in a country's trade, does not seem to be borne out by the US experience' (Boutruri and Fukasaku 1993, p. 155). The share of intra-firm trade has played a significant role in regional integration, especially in the EU. Between 1957 and 1982 US affiliate sales to other affiliates within the EU increased from 14 per cent of the total trade of affiliates to 46 per cent (Dunning, 1997a). This leads Dunning to suggest that one of the most notable features of mark 1 European integration (up to the mid-1980s) was the increasingly elaborate division of labour instituted by US multinationals, the consequent increase in intra-firm trade and its contribution to increases in intra-EU trade.

Undoubtedly the large share of this intra-firm trade in the EU represents trade in finished goods between a decreasing number of rationalised manufacturing investments and non-manufacturing affiliates in a wider spread of national markets. That is, the majority of the intra-firm trade of US multinationals is distributional (Boutruri and Fukasaku 1993). At least part of the increase in intra-firm trade among US-owned affiliates in the EU will have been in transfers of semi-finished products, but this seems likely to apply to specific industries (such as cars and perhaps electronics). The lack of data simply does not permit any definitive statements in this regard.

A number of scholars have examined the role of internal corporate labour markets upon international migration of key or skilled workers. In theory at least, the growing complexity and degree of integration in the organisation of multilocational and multinational firms would imply a corresponding increase in exchanges of key personnel within such companies. That is, the 'hierarchically organised global system of production has reduced the need and the opportunities for settler migration and has prompted new forms of international labour transfer' (Findlay 1988, p. 408). However, in reality, corporate integration in respect of such flows of skilled labour between individual sites has lagged behind the degree of integration in respect of the likes of transfers of finished products and components. Instead, cultural and language barriers which have also hampered corporate integration in terms of flows of materials and finished goods have had an even greater effect in repressing intra-corporate transfers of labour. Nor do deliberate attempts to facilitate movement of labour as under the single European market initiative appear to have facilitated skilled-labour migration as yet. Thus, while international trade in goods has been progressively liberalised since World War II and has returned to the pre-World War I degree of openness, labour markets remain much more controlled than before 1914 with efforts at regional economic integration hardly affecting the situation (Panic and Vacic 1995).

According to much recent literature the exploitation of localised technological externalities represents one of, if not *the* most important constraint on the mobility of investments by multinationals. The exploration of such technological externalities is seen as an important element in the inertia in corporate organisation and a powerful incentive to the local presence of multinationals (Archibugi and Michie 1995; Cantwell 1995). As such, the manner in which technology is developed and exploited within multinationals has changed. As Cantwell (1995) notes, 'In the past foreign technological activity exploited domestic strengths abroad ... At that time the capacity to develop internationally dispersed innovations derived from a position of technological strength in the firm's home base, and led to similar lines of technological development being established abroad. By contrast, today, foreign technological activity now increasingly aims to tap into local fields of expertise' (Cantwell 1995, p. 172).

Such technological externalities can be extremely localised on a national or subnational basis forcing multinationals to have a presence in particular centres of industry skills and expertise, and to this extent there are limits to the degree of corporate integration in terms of exploitation of technology. There is a tension between the presence needed to exploit technological externalities and the desire for corporate integration to exploit these externally (and other internally) derived innovations and expertise internally among a group of plants. This tension may account for the apparent lack of corporate integration in terms of the movement of skilled labour such as managers and engineers, etc. Furthermore, the need for exchanges of such personnel to support internal corporate transfers of technology and expertise may be offset to some extent by vastly improved information and communication technologies. Information and communications technologies have had an important impact on raising the level of corporate integration across a range of functions including management, financial reporting, etc. They have also had significant application precisely to facilitate global expansion of research and development activity and the exploitation of localised technological externalities (Howells 1990). As such, a growing degree corporate integration at both global and regional scales in terms of intra-corporate exchanges of technology has complemented sustained or increased local presence. Research and development intensity stands out as an important determinant of global corporate integration ahead of scale or division of labour within manufacturing activities (Kobrin 1991). Nevertheless, we should be careful of overstating the extent of globalisation of technology since the majority of innovative activity (as measured for instance in patent registrations) is still overwhelmingly concentrated in the home economies of multinational corporations (Patel and Pavitt 1991; Allen and Thompson 1997)

International integration has proceeded furthest in respect of finance with inter-regional integration being at least as important as intra-regional integration. As such there is considerable corporate integration on a global level in terms of the financing of new investment of multinationals. In one way or another most investment in subsidiaries is financed elsewhere in the parent company organisation and as such one could say there is considerable, albeit asymmetrical, corporate integration in terms of finance. Trends in the changing source of finance for investment by multinationals over time are difficult to come by. One recent report points to a lessening of the degree of asymmetry in intra-corporate financing among Japanese multinationals with an increase in finance being raised locally by overseas affiliates rather than through their parent company (De Jonquieres 1995).

THE MULTINATIONAL-OWNED CHEMICALS INDUSTRY IN WALES

There are a number of observations which can be made regarding the development of the multinational-owned chemicals industry in Wales during the last two to three decades. The detailed evidence available here relates to the foreign-owned manufacturing sector rather than the multinational-owned manufacturing more generally.

First, the chemicals industry has long been one of the most important within the foreign-owned manufacturing sector (and the multinational-owned manu-facturing sector more generally) in Wales. However, its importance within these sectors in Wales has diminished somewhat. The first overseas manu-facturing operation to be established in Wales was a chemicals plant. In 1970 the chemicals industries accounted for 16.5 per cent of all foreign-owned manufacturing employment in Wales and was the second largest sector after the electrical and electronic engineering sector. By 1995, chemicals manufacturing accounted for only 11.3 per cent of foreign- owned manufacturing in Wales and had fallen to third largest sector behind the automotive engineering sector which grew rapidly in the 1980s and 1990s.

Second, the multinational-owned chemicals sector has become markedly more capital-intensive over the last two to three decades. Figure 4.1 shows changes in the numbers of plants and total employment in the foreign-owned chemicals industry in Wales. Apart from the odd year, the numbers of foreign-owned chemical plants has grown steadily from sixteen in 1970 to fifty-five in 1996. Employment in the foreign-owned chemicals manufacturing sector has been more erratic. There was steady growth in employment until 1974. The remainder of the 1970s saw employment stabilise before falling by 28.8 per cent from 1980 to 1985. The mid-1980s witnessed a stabilisation of employment before growth resumed from 1988 onwards. As a consequence, the average size of chemicals plants has fallen quite steadily over the last two to three decades. In 1970 the average number of employees per plant was 418.8; by 1996 it had fallen to 154.5.

FIGURE 4.1: EMPLOYMENT AND NUMBER OF PLANTS IN THE FOREIGN-OWNED CHEMICAL INDUSTRY IN WALES

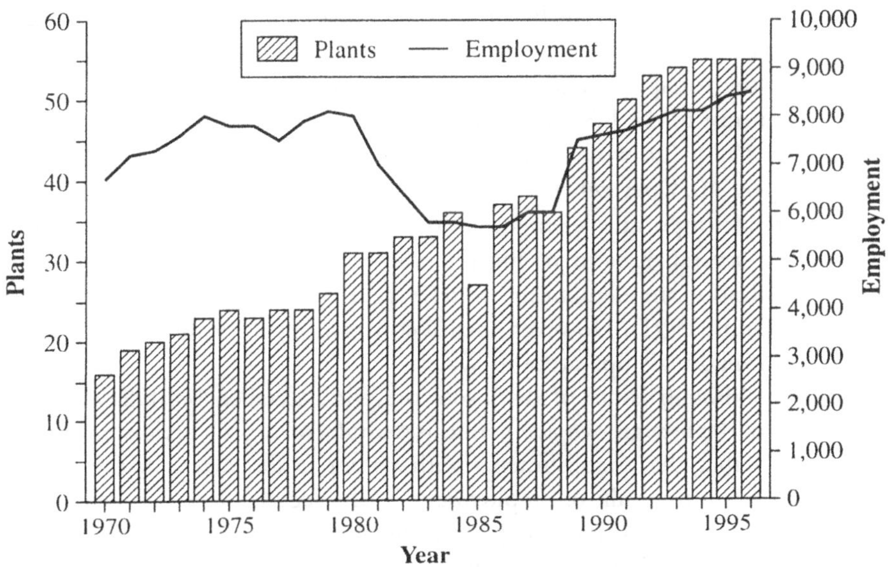

Third, while the foreign-owned chemicals manufacturing sector has become relatively less important within the foreign-owned sector it nevertheless has grown in importance as a part of the chemicals industry as a whole in Wales. In 1970 foreign-owned chemicals plants accounted for 46.9 per cent of total chemicals manufacturing employment in Wales and by 1996 this figure had risen to 67.5 per cent. This growing share of foreign firms in total chemical manufacturing employment in Wales appears to have been a product of the more buoyant fortunes of overseas firms compared to domestic firms during the 1980s and 1990s.

A little more light can be shed on this when referring to the components of employment change in the chemicals industry in Wales (see table 4.1). Data supplied by the Welsh Office do not permit consideration of the contribution of acquisition and divestment upon employment changes, which is unfortunate given their importance to the different dynamics of foreign and 'indigenous' (that is, Welsh and UK) sectors within the chemicals industry in Wales.[1] Between 1970 and 1980 new plant openings amounted to 38.6 per cent of the initial stock of employment in the foreign-owned chemicals sector in Wales. Between 1980 and 1996 the figure had increased to 44.9 per cent. The corresponding figures for the UK/Welsh-owned sector were considerably lower at just 9.8 per cent and 7.4 per cent. The scale of plant closures in the UK/Welsh-owned sector also appears to be greater than that in the foreign-owned sector. Between 1970 and 1980 plant closures amounted to 5.2 per cent of the initial employment stock of the UK/Welsh-owned chemicals sector in Wales. Between 1980 and 1996 this figure had increased to 15.5 per cent. The corresponding figures for the foreign-owned sector were 0.3 per cent and 9.0 per cent respectively. From 1970 to 1980 employment in the foreign-owned sector grew by 20.1 per cent. Between 1980 and 1996 employment growth in the foreign-owned sector had slowed to 6.2 per cent. This is in marked contrast to the UK/Welsh sector, which did not increase employment during the 1970s (growing by just 0.1 per cent) and contracted substantially (declining by 46.3 per cent) during the 1980s and 1990s. Divestment will have been an important element in this as UK multinationals have been involved in several deals involving the wholesale swapping of business portfolios – an important element in the restructuring of the European chemicals industry (Grant 1991). However, in-situ contractions have also been a feature of UK multinationals operating in Wales.

Fourth, although issues of disclosure prevent a detailed breakdown of the ownership of the foreign-owned chemicals manufacturing sector, it is possible to state clearly that the establishments with parent headquarters in the United States constitute the bulk of employment in the sector. Data supplied by the Welsh Office record that some 69 per cent of employment in the foreign-owned chemical manufacturing sector in Wales in 1996 was operated by companies with ultimate headquarters in the USA.

TABLE 4.1: COMPONENTS OF EMPLOYMENT CHANGE IN THE WELSH CHEMICALS INDUSTRY, 1970–96

	1970 Stock	New plant openings	Increased employment	Plant closures	Decreased employment	Net change	
Foreign	6 672	2 575	388	–17	–1 602	1 344	
UK/Wales	7 643	751	1 652	–394	–1 999	10	
Total	14 315	3 326	2 040	–411	–3 601	1 354	
	1980 Stock	**New plant openings**	**Increased employment**	**Plant closures**	**Decreased employment**	**Net change**	**1996 Stock**
Foreign	8 016	3 602	708	–721	–3 089	500	8 516
UK/Wales	7 653	569	1 123	–1 190	–4 047	–2 545	4 108
Total	15 669	4 171	1 831	–1 911	–7 136	–3 045	12 624

Source: Welsh Office unpublished tables

A list of all chemicals manufacturing operations of multinational companies was drawn up using lists supplied from the Welsh Office, the WDA, local business directories and the *Yellow Pages*. Establishments were drawn from the chemicals industries as defined in the Standard Industrial Classification (1980). A wide variety of activities is included under this definition ranging from bulk chemicals through speciality chemicals and pharmaceuticals (which itself includes the likes of medical ligatures and sutures) to films and tapes. The Welsh chemicals industry is indeed represented across this range. Only companies which had manufacturing operations in more than one country were included as multinationals, identified using *Who Owns Whom* and on initial contact. Only those operations which were majority-owned by multinational parent companies were included in the survey. In all, forty-eight establishments were identified.

The total number of establishments identified and contacted is somewhat less than the figure even for foreign multinational chemicals manufacturing operations in Wales as indicated in figure 4.1. When one considers that there is also a small number of establishments owned by UK multinationals there is less correspondence between the numbers of establishments contacted and those suggested by official figures.

From April to September of 1997 managing directors and plant managers of chemicals manufacturing operations of multinational companies were contacted to request their assistance with the research. A flexible approach was adopted which allowed for postal returns of questionnaires as well as telephone and face-to-face interviews. In the event, twenty-eight establishments responded as part of the survey, giving a response rate of 58.3 per cent. These responses included eight face-to-face interviews, five telephone interviews and thirteen postal questionnaire returns. The following discussion draws upon some basic descriptive aggregate information from the survey as well as some illustrative cases drawn from the telephone and face-to-face interview material.

PLANT STATUS, DIVISION OF LABOUR AND INVESTMENT SWITCHING

Exactly one-half of the chemicals manufacturing operations surveyed had either a world or continental product mandate with the other half having no such mandate. In contrast to the idea that there has been some retreat from global to regionally focused strategies (Ruigrok and Van Tulder 1996), the majority of these (ten out of twelve respondents) were world mandates. This implies that an important proportion of plants in the multinational-owned chemicals sector in Wales enjoy significant status within their parent company organisations, and that where they are highly export oriented they are likely to serve more than simply regional (EU) markets. This is confirmed when examining the geography of the markets served by plants responding to the survey (see table 4.2). Table 4.2 shows that over half of the respondents indicated that their plant exported more than half its output. Only one plant was geared solely to the UK market. The figures here are in contrast to other sectors (such as electrical and electronic and automotive engineering) and indeed the multinational-owned manufacturing sector in Wales as a whole in which a sizeable proportion of plants is geared solely to the UK market (see Phelps 1997 for figures). The unweighted average of output exported from respondent plants was 58 per cent. Also, of those plants which exported, on average 20 per cent of output was exported beyond the regional market of the EU, underlining the global orientation of a number of plants noted above.

TABLE 4.2: EXPORT ORIENTATION OF MULTINATIONAL-OWNED CHEMICAL PLANTS IN WALES (NUMBERS AND PERCENTAGES OF PLANTS)

	0%	1–25%	26–50%	51–75%	76–100%	Average
Output exported	1(5.8)	3(15.8)	4(21.1)	4(26.3)	7(36.8)	66.5
Ouput exported outside EU	1(5.8)	12(70.6)	4(26.7)	0(0.0)	0(0.0)	18.4

Note: Percentages may not sum to 100 due to rounding.

The multinational-owned chemicals sector in Wales stands out as one which is clearly more export oriented than the multinational-owned manufacturing sector in Wales as whole. As a result, regional economic integration beyond the EU might be thought to have a negative impact on the export potential and eventually the status of such plants if trade, and consequent investment, diversion is at all significant. However, respondents from all of those operations with such mandates perceived that regional integration in North America and resultant corporate restructuring would not jeopardise the position of the Welsh operation.

Respondents were also asked whether orchestrated attempts to promote regional economic integration within the EU (the Single European Market – SEM) and in North America (NAFTA) had brought about any diversion of investment to or from Welsh operations. Here 'investment' was treated very broadly to include, among other things, investment in new plant and equipment, product or market responsibilities, managerial functions, key personnel etc. At this point it is worth noting that many respondents cited instances of investment diversion but suggested that these were not always the direct product of regional economic integration. Roughly half of all Welsh operations had been affected either positively or negatively (usually both) by the SEM. Only a handful of Welsh operations had been similarly affected by regional economic integration and consequent parent company reorganisation in North America. While the numbers are very small, this nevertheless tempers the findings above regarding the retention of mandates in the face of regional economic integration outside the EU and suggests that there may be minor investment diverting effects associated with North American integration. In the event the three instances of investment diversion following from North American integration embody mixed results. One firm was now making more use of parent company sources of material inputs as a result, one had expanded output but also exchanged product responsibilities with another parent company plant in North America and another had actually gained product responsibilities from a parent company plant in North America.

Examples of changing corporate divisions of labour and investment diversion are informative. Table 4.3 provides brief profiles of a number of case study affiliates referred to in the remainder of this chapter. Affiliates A and B provide contrasting examples of plants assuming central and peripheral roles within their respective parent company groups. Affiliate A has acquired a central position within a worldwide group of parent company plants producing chemical reagents and equipment. In 1990 its parent company launched a global strategy to have a reduced number of centres of excellence. Affiliate A moved quickly to be in the vanguard of new work, management and sourcing practices and became the most technically advanced plant in the group. It gained a central position within its group of plants by aggressively bidding to take on the market and product responsibilities of other plants in the group. The number of plants in the group fell from eight to four with most of the production being transferred to Affiliate A. Affiliate B has effectively been downgraded within its parent company group of pharmaceuticals operations in Europe. In the 1990s Affiliate B's parent company made explicit moves to reorganise itself to better serve emerging regional markets in the world economy, closing and divesting itself of plants in Europe as a result. In the process it designated sites in Ireland, France and Germany its three strategic sites in Europe, transferring production from Affiliate B in Wales and leaving it at the periphery of its European operations. The number of employees at Affiliate B fell from one thousand to three hundred as a result and although it does possess one or two world product mandates, essentially it is geared toward serving the UK market until further notice.

TABLE 4.3: PROFILE OF CASE STUDY CHEMICAL PLANTS

Affiliate	Affiliate employment[a]	Parent company nationality	Parent company employment[b]	Number of plants in group	Number of group plants in EU
A	280	German	142 200	4	3
B	300	US	36 000	7	4
C	80	US	4 000	4	1
D	327	US	3 600	2	1
E	55	US	5 000	2	1
F	120	US	8 000	3	2

[a]As of 1997
[b]As of 1996

Affiliate C has become, through acquisition by its parent company, part of a group of four plants worldwide manufacturing food additives. Affiliate C is the only one of those four in Europe and as a result has acquired some new product responsibilities and functional capabilities without there as yet being any rationalisation within the group. Affiliate D is now one of just two parent company plants producing magnetic tape, the other being in Dallas in the USA. At the end of the 1980s after being acquired by a new parent company, Affiliate D did gain some product responsibilities when a major parent company plant was shut in the USA. Affiliate D is regarded as the technically superior plant of the two and this combined with a deliberate policy following the creation of the single European market has led to an upgrading of its status. All customer service functions, which were previously provided in each member state have now been consolidated at Affiliate D in Wales because of the savings on employment costs. Similarly, products for the entire European market are now distributed from Wales.

GLOBAL AND REGIONAL CORPORATE INTEGRATION

Respondents were asked to indicate whether the degree of integration between parent company operations had increased on a global and EU-wide basis. They were asked to respond with respect to a number of indicators of integration, namely: materials and components, secondments of key personnel (managers, engineers etc.); technical information; research and development activities; financing of new investment; and decision-making. Response rates were more patchy in relation to the latter three indicators. The numbers and percentages of responses are shown in table 4.4. A number of observations can be made from these data.

TABLE 4.4: CHANGES IN CORPORATE INTEGRATION GLOBALLY AND WITHIN THE EU

	Global			EU		
	Increase	Same	Decrease	Increase	Same	Decrease
Materials	11(52.4)	9(42.9)	1(4.8)	11(52.4)	8(38.1)	2(9.6)
Key personnel	12(57.1)	7(33.3)	2(9.6)	11(50.0)	11(50.0)	0(0.0)
Technical information	14(66.7)	6(28.6)	1(4.8)	15(68.2)	6(27.3)	1(4.5)
Research and development	8(44.4)	10(55.6)	0(0.0)	7(36.8)	11(57.9)	1(5.3)
Financing of new investment	11(73.3)	3(20.0)	1(6.7)	12(75.0)	4(25.0)	0(0.0)
Decision-making	8(47.1)	7(41.2)	2(11.8)	10(58.8)	7(41.2)	0(0.0)
Overall	15(71.4)	5(23.8)	1(4.8)	15(68.2)	7(31.8)	0(0.0)

Source: Author's Survey.
Note: Percentages may not sum to 100 due to rounding.

First, the proportions of Welsh operations having become more integrated into their parent company organisations on a global basis are at least as great as the proportions becoming more integrated on an EU-wide basis. This would tend to suggest that global and EU-wide corporate integration are complementary processes if not outcomes of a single process of corporate integration. The findings here resonate with those of Dunning (1997b) who selects the chemicals industry as one important example of where multinationals' efforts at regionalisation and globalisation of corporate structures have gone hand in hand (Dunning 1997b, p. 209). It has been suggested that there has been a retreat by major multinationals away from truly global corporate strategies toward strategies geared to serving specific regional (trade bloc) markets (Ruigrok and Van Tulder 1996). This is perhaps just traceable in the data contained in table 4.2 in as much as there was almost a complete lack of respondents reporting decreased corporate integration on an EU-wide basis. However the trend is sufficiently slight to suggest that greater efforts at regional corporate integration are not at the expense of continued efforts to integrate production on a global level.

Second, then, efforts at global integration of production continue to be made by parent company organisations even in respect of those aspects of business most difficult to integrate over long distances: namely, material and component inputs. Despite greater potential trade barriers and transportation costs associated with inter-regional as opposed to intra-regional intra-corporate transfers of materials and components, Welsh manufacturing operations have become more integrated into their parent organisations with respect to such transfers.

Third, corporate integration varies across aspects of business. There appears to be least effort at integration in respect of decision-making and research and development activities. The former finding is somewhat surprising given that it is probably easier to integrate a group of parent company plants in terms of decision-making than, say, material inputs. However, the low levels of corporate integration here may reflect the genuine difficulties in creating effective corporate divisions of labour within many smaller multinationals and hence the relative isolation of many stand-alone affiliates. The low levels of corporate integration of research and development activity are likely to be a reflection of the highly localised nature of labour skills, the relatively recent attempts of multinationals to internationalise research and development activity and the small size of many of the parent companies of multinationals operating in Wales. Despite labour being the most immobile of factors of production, corporate integration in terms of exchanges of key personnel has been growing on a global and EU-wide basis. The high proportion of Welsh operations exchanging key personnel with other parent company sites on globally could be a reflection of a number of contributory factors including, for example, the large share of non-EU (essentially US) multinationals within the multinational-owned chemical sector in Wales and the growing degree of cross-penetration of operations of EU and North American multinationals with its repercussions for integration of operations between the two blocs.

More detailed material from a number of case studies can shed further light on the processes of corporate integration in which Welsh manufacturing operations are implicated. The case studies tend to suggest that corporate integration, irrespective of whether it is global or regional in scope, tends to be rather unsystematically pursued by multinational parent companies. I have classified multinationals' efforts at corporate integration into three: systematic, partial and *ad hoc*. Systematic integration refers to a growing interdependence among a group of plants resulting from a strategy to create more detailed intra-corporate divisions of labour. Here there are ongoing attempts to integrate a group of operations in terms of one or more of the following: exchanges of materials and components, key personnel, technical information and functional decision-making responsibilities. Partial integration refers to planned but only periodic attempts to integrate operations where there are often important constraints on systematic integration. *Ad hoc* integration refers to very infrequent, unplanned and usually minor attempts to produce greater coordination among a group of plants. Of the thirteen case studies from which detailed information is available, only three Welsh manufacturing operations were involved in systematic corporate integration. Two of these were operated by among the largest of chemicals multinationals in Wales. The remaining ten case study establishments – generally part of smaller multinationals – were involved in markedly less systematic attempts at corporate integration.

At one extreme then we have Affiliates A and B which are part of two of the larger chemicals multinationals with operations in Wales. They present interesting and contrasting examples of Welsh operations being at the centre and at the periphery of strategies of corporate integration. Affiliate A is one of four remaining plants producing chemical reagents and equipment as part of a sector within a division of a large German chemicals multinational. As we saw earlier, it has gained a central position within its sector as the parent company has rationalised simultaneously in Europe and worldwide. In this process, Affiliate A has come to the fore as the most technically advanced of the remaining four operations pioneering corporate experiments in multiple skilling etc., and as such occupies a central position within the parent company's desire to integrate operations primarily in terms of exchanges of key personnel, technical information and best practice. Affiliate B is part of a large US pharmaceuticals and foods multinational and one of four remaining operations in Europe. Affiliate B has lost out to three mainland European plants operated by its parent company and has been left largely unintegrated with them to serve primarily the UK market and one or two specific product markets worldwide until further investment decisions are made. Finally Affiliate C is part of a relatively small US food additives multinational but has become increasingly integrated into its parent company organisation principally by way of backward vertical integration. Affiliate C is one of four food additive plants within a division of its parent company which also has a separate division for yeast products, which are material inputs to food additives. The parent organisation, which has invested heavily in a new yeast plant on mainland Europe, has sought to integrate the yeast products and food additives operations in Europe. In 1995 all of affiliate C's yeast material purchases came from independent firms – mainly brewers – in the UK. By 1997 80 per cent of its yeast material purchases came from the parent company facility on mainland Europe.

At the other extreme are those affiliates which are part of attempts at corporate integration which arise as and when needs or circumstances dictate. Affiliate D provides a good example of where a Welsh operation is largely unintegrated with other parent company plants. Affiliate D produces magnetic tape along with one other parent company plant located in the USA. Both have product development capabilities but in many respects Affiliate D is technically superior to the US plant. Despite a number of plant closures and consolidation of activities at the two sites there remains very little integration between them. Integration where it existed focused on exchanges of technical and commercial information. Even here such exchanges were often, in the words of the respondent, crisis-driven. For example, staff from Affiliate D eventually had to visit the plant in the USA to help implement production process changes after repeated exchanges of advice via telephone, fax etc. Similarly, one US customer preferred to deal with Affiliate D, even though it would be supplied from the US plant, because of previous difficulties in dealing with the parent company's US plant.

The middle ground is composed of a large number of subsidiaries who are party to partial attempts at corporate integration. Such strategies appear to be the product of periodic but unsustainable opportunities for integration among plants. These in turn are the result of variations in capacity utilisation and exchange rates which make the switching of product responsibilities or intra-corporate transfers of material inputs temporarily viable. Affiliate E, for example, is a speciality amine chemicals manufacturer and part of a small US multinational whose major vertically integrated complex is in Port Arthur. Around 10 per cent of Affiliate E's inputs come from this complex, but this can vary according to whether there is surplus output given the parent company's philosophy of maintaining high utilisation of its various chemicals operations.

There is one example of decreasing integration between a Welsh based subsidiary and others within a parent company grouping. However, this is due less to corporate strategy *per se* than technological and market changes which have curtailed established synergies between stages of production and plants within the parent organisation. Affiliate F is part of a large US multinational and produces bromine which, among other things, is an important additive to petrol. It is one of three company plants worldwide: one being in the USA the other, a joint venture run by the partner, in France. Previously Affiliate F enjoyed considerable synergy with parent company oil-refining and chemicals operations in England since bromine products were combined with lead compounds as additives to fuel products. However, with the reduction in lead compounds used in petrol these synergies have decreased (though half of F's output still goes to its parent company's operation in England). Affiliate F's parent company diversified out of lead compound additives, closing plants in England, Germany, Italy and France. Nevertheless the current situation is one in which each of the three bromine plants remain relatively isolated from one another with the only meaningful form of integration being the exchange of technical information between Affiliate F and the US operation.

The chemicals industry is one in which there is likely to be a degree of corporate integration. The industry is one in which there are economies of scale to be derived from vertical integration of activities given the wide range of co-products, intermediates and derivatives of more basic commodity chemical feedstocks. Such economies often can only be internalised internationally within large stand-alone single-company complexes. Alternatively such complexes can be developed around multi-company tie-ups though these tend to dilute the degree of vertical integration possible and desirable (see Chapman 1991 for a typology of such tie-ups in the petrochemical industry). There are several examples of tie-ups to exploit such economies of vertical integration between separate multinationals operating in Wales. However, the nature of the production process largely dictates that opportunities for effective vertical integration cannot easily be internalised across great distances internationally. It is probably this tension between the presence of significant economies of vertical integration and the difficulty of exploiting these internally and internationally simultaneously that results in the mainly partial efforts at corporate integration discussed above.

CONCLUSION

The chemical industry in Wales represents an important part of the multinational involvement in manufacturing industry in Wales. After several decades when the contribution of multinationals to regional and local economic development in Wales, as in other host economies, has been questioned, a more positive role for such firms and their affiliates has recently been depicted (for example see Jenkins in Welsh Affairs Committee 1995; Price *et al.* 1994; Rees and Thomas 1994). These claims have been made with particular reference to the electrical and electronic and automotive engineering sectors. There are signs that the chemicals industry represents a relatively stable picture in terms of the status of affiliates within their parent company organisations despite some important ownership changes.

The survey evidence presented here suggests that attempts at corporate integration by parent company organisations are responsible for gradually bringing Welsh operations into some sort of international division of labour. These efforts at corporate integration have tended to be pursued rather unsystematically by parent company organisations. Nevertheless, these international divisions of labour are not simply ones centred on the European market but also on world markets since the corporate divisions of labour being created at a regional (trade bloc) level are part of much broader attempts at global corporate integration.

Finally, despite the growing integration of Welsh chemicals plants into parent company organisations on a global and regional scale, there appear to be very few negative impacts in terms of investment diversion. Welsh plants have generally retained their status and have tended not to lose product and market responsibilities, investment in new plant and equipment and non-manufacturing functions to other parent company plants as more sophisticated corporate divisions of labour have been created. All this would tend to point to global and regional economic integration having had a neutral effect on subnational economic development in the case of the multinational-owned chemical sector in Wales.

NOTE

1. Components of change tables are available for the whole of the foreign-owned manufacturing sector in Wales, but issues of disclosure dictate that these are not available for the chemicals industry.

PART II:

FDI AND REGIONAL INTEGRATION

PHILIP RAINES AND FIONA WISHLADE

5 EC Policy-making and the Challenges of Foreign Investment[1]

INTRODUCTION

The Treaty of Rome made no mention of foreign direct investment (FDI), but the growth in FDI over the last three decades has been instrumental in the iterative development of two major European Community (EC) policy areas: trade policy and competition policy. The establishment of the EC itself involved a major conceptual change in the approaches to trade and competition policies for the signatories to the Treaty of Rome. Trade between the member states effectively became domestic or internal rather than external, requiring regulation through *competition* policy at the European level, rather than *trade* policy at the national level. These features distinguish European integration; in no other regional trade arrangement have sovereign states so comprehensively pooled their national interests or subjected themselves to a supranational authority to police their respect of the rules. Moreover, community activity in these policy areas has expanded in response to common pressures. Internally, these have included the need to resolve the policy tensions arising from the conflict between and among EC, national and regional interests. Externally, both policies have been shaped by the growing sense of global competition in trade and investment between the EC as a whole and countries such as the USA and Japan. Arguably nowhere are these pressures on EC policy-making more evident than in the policy challenges of FDI.

With the continuing rise of FDI into and within the EC, interest has been growing in the interaction of different government policies and multinational location decisions, affecting both the design of policy instruments and how policy influences FDI flows. At community level, while there have been no *specific* policies for FDI, the importance of adapting existing policies to address mobile investment issues has increasingly been recognised. Most visibly, this is apparent in community participation in the negotiation of a framework of global investment rules, as discussed more fully in Stephen

Young and Thomas Brewer's chapter, but it has become a significant feature in the operation of EC policies not directly related to FDI. Community policies can alter the attractiveness of the EC in the competition for foreign investment worldwide in a way analogous to member state efforts to enhance location advantages at a national level. At the same time, the European Commission has had to react to fierce competition between member states to attract FDI, as more countries have started to perceive inward investment as an important contributor to employment creation and economic development. Incentive programmes – especially fiscal incentives – have increased in western Europe since the mid-1980s, while national economic environments have become more open to foreign investors in terms of liberalised administrative procedures for approving investments and capital controls (Raines and Brown 1998). Further, the agents involved in FDI promotion have proliferated throughout Western Europe, especially at subnational level as local and regional authorities have become more independent and vigorous in their own promotion activities. As a result, anecdotal evidence from investing companies and location consultants suggests that an element of bidding is increasingly present as several countries and regions try to win particularly large projects.

This chapter explores the relationship between FDI and EC policy-making, particularly the use of anti-dumping and trade protection measures in external trade policy and the regulation of financial incentives through competition policy. Using the two policies as case studies, several sets of issues are examined. First, the chapter considers the extent to which EC policy does influence investment decisions and, more specifically, whether such influence is intended by policy-makers or emerged in response to new challenges to the policies' implementation. Second, it examines the reverse side of the relation: how the design and operation of EC policies have changed to accommodate the problems associated with increasing FDI, especially with respect to national competition over investment.

EC TRADE POLICY AND FOREIGN INVESTMENT

When the main EC institutions charged with pursuing a common external trade policy – the European Commission and the European Council – were originally vested with their competencies in the Treaty of Rome, foreign investment was not considered under the definition of policy action. FDI has only become an issue in trade policy with its recent evolution, particularly with the increasingly protectionist stance of EC institutions. Their policies to restrict certain types of trade have not only resulted in higher levels of FDI, but the investment flows have prompted changes in trade policy because of their threat to undermine its key measures.

The link between FDI and trade policy emerged with the more active use of instruments to restrict external competition in certain industries by institutions at EC level, notably the European Council and the commission.

Although EC trade policy originally meant the negotiation of general customs duties, the Treaty of Rome had allowed EC institutions authority in trade agreement and protection measures as well, while allowing member states to retain the power to undertake individual trade actions against countries not otherwise covered by specific EC agreements (Barnes and Barnes 1995). Until the 1980s, trade protection measures did not feature prominently in EC commercial policy, as the freedom to act was limited by the successive rounds of the GATT and the agreed reduction in tariff barriers at a global level. After 1980 though – in line with developments in other countries – the roles of the council and the commission in controlling trade became more prominent, as both the range and frequency of trade barriers grew. Of the measures employed, the most important were:

- *anti-dumping actions*, in which duties were imposed on non-EC importers if their goods were being sold within the EC at less than that deemed to be their 'normal' value;
- *voluntary export restraints*, or VERs, which were effectively the equivalent of sector-specific bilateral quotas with non-EC countries;
- *rules of origin and local content regulations*, by which the EC set minimum levels on the volume and quality of sourcing within the EC by foreign subsidiaries.

By reversing the trend towards greater external trade liberalisation that characterised the previous two decades, the commission was increasingly taking on the protectionist activities that had previously been operated by member states in certain industries and towards specific trading partners (particularly Japan). For example, in the 1970s and 1980s, individual limits had been imposed on Japanese car imports by member states, ranging from Portugal (14 per cent of its domestic market) to Italy and Spain (less than 2 per cent), but these were replaced by common limits for the whole of the EC (Mason 1994). At the same time, following agreement on a series of codes governing the use of non-tariff barriers at the Tokyo Round of the GATT in 1979, such measures were employed more regularly at the EC level. Over the following decade, 315 anti-dumping cases were instigated on products as diverse as hydraulic excavators, ball bearings, photocopiers and semiconductors (Barrell and Pain 1993). Individual member states extended the use of bilateral VERs so that by 1990 they covered imports of most components and units in radio, TV and hi-fi equipment sectors (Moore 1997).

The link between FDI and these trade measures is often not manifest from their design and operation. What seems to have determined growing EC protectionism has been a more vigorous application of its trade powers, in large part to support the competitiveness of certain European industries. It has been argued that these measures have been effectively used as an extension of Community industrial policy, in which external commercial competition has provided shelter for emerging or restructuring EC industries, especially the automotive and certain electronics sectors (Barnes and Barnes 1995). This policy objective is more transparent in the case of trade restraint measures such as VERs, but is also apparent in the way that anti-dumping policies have been implemented. The trade actions have tended to be concentrated in industries in which community companies face intense competitive pressure from non-EC firms, especially Japanese firms. Furthermore, the system for determining anti-dumping charges and penalties in the EC supports its protectionist use. This derives to a large extent from the degree of discretion involved in the decision-making, mainly through the European Council where member state interests have often been exerted effectively in deciding anti-dumping duties (Holmes and Kempton 1996). Nevertheless, the emergence of a more protectionist policy has had a clear, if sometimes indirect, impact on determining FDI flows. This has been prominent in three areas: foreign investment within the EC to circumvent anti-dumping and other trade-related measures; the levels of local sourcing by foreign manufacturing transplants; and levels of production by these transplants exported to other parts of the EC.

First, trade barriers have been linked to forced investment, in which companies are compelled to undertake local production in order to circumvent increasing trade restrictions. As a location determinant, it has helped to explain the surge in Japanese manufacturing investment into the EC, particularly from the mid-1980s onwards. Initial studies were divided on the issue and, until recently, debate lacked sufficient data for empirical analysis. Hence, Heitger and Stehn (1990) argued that EC protectionist measures could be considered a sufficient factor in shaping the foreign investment decisions by Japanese companies in markets they would otherwise prefer to serve by trade. In contrast, Nicolaides and Thomsen (1991) contended that Japanese investment had been determined by wider processes of internationalisation and the product cycle and should not be considered as a form of defensive investment. More recent work has shown strong correlations between circumvention investment and the imposition of new trade restrictions. Examining FDI flows in the 1980s, Barrel and Pain (1993) found that anti-dumping measures appeared to have been a significant factor in Japanese direct investment (in the USA as well as the EC). In an analysis of the electronics sector, Belderbos (1997) concluded that trade barriers were a more significant factor in Japanese FDI decisions than product cycle trends, while Strange (1993) observed the same investment patterns for other industries subject to trade restraints, such as machine tools and ball bearings. Similar findings were made about the link between Japanese 'forced' investment and the use of VERs in certain industries (Flam 1994).

Second, EC trade policy has directly influenced the nature of foreign investment through regulations on local content. Circumvention of anti-dumping actions and VERs had led to several foreign companies 'disguising' the origin of their products through transferring production to a third country, or by supplying community demand through plants located within the EC.

To address this potential loophole in the community's trade policies, a series of measures were introduced after 1987 to restrict the degree of circumvention. The measures were designed not to prevent the location of foreign investment, but effectively to compel companies to maintain a minimum level of local value as defined by the extent of local sourcing undertaken by the firms (Dawkins 1989). The commission's anti-dumping regulation was revised to allow levies on foreign producers within the EC importing more than 60 per cent of the value of components from a country subject to an anti-dumping duty and applied to sectors affected by anti-dumping measures (Vermulst and Waer 1990).

Moreover, the commission tried to define what type of local production would not be subject to anti-dumping duties. Revisions of the anti-dumping regulations restricted the use of 'screwdriver' assembly operations by Japanese companies, as such new production investments were seen as little more than camouflage if they only provided limited value-added functions to product components imported from the original country. The nature of R&D carried out in the EC-based plant was explicitly listed in the revised regulations as a factor in determining how far local production might be subject to anti-dumping duties. At the same time, the commission regarded 'product origin' as being largely determined by the location of the last 'significant' manufacturing process. In the case of semiconductors – where this approach was first used – this resulted in a sharp rise in the number of capital-intensive wafer fabrication plants located within the EC, rising by a fifth between 1987 and 1990 (Jensen-Moran 1996). Indeed, individual companies such as Intel stated that the location of a fabrication facility within the EC was largely the result of local content regulations.

Lastly, and in large part as a corollary of the preceding measures, trade policy has limited exports by Japanese transplants to other parts of the EC. The most notable example of this was the Elements of Consensus, the accord on a time-limited bilateral quota on cars reached between the EC and Japan in 1991 (Mason 1994). The agreement became necessary as member-state trade controls on cars were set to be undermined by the completion of the Single Market Programme (as foreign companies could potentially manufacture cars within the EC and export them without restriction to member states operating VERs on non-EC production). In reaching agreement with Japan, the commission stated that restrictions would not be imposed on Japanese automotive investors in the community nor the movement of their products, while the Japanese authorities would restrain any attempts by Japanese transplants to concentrate sales in specific national markets. In addition, the commission recognised that there was an implicit 'understanding' that a cap would be placed on the volume of Japanese transplant production for the EC market up until 1999 (although the Japanese negotiators did not share the same view).

In general, recent EC trade measures have grappled with a range of challenges arising from FDI which have not only led the regulatory remit of EC institutions to be extended but also to the adoption of common policies that have often supplanted existing member state policies. However, the progressive inclusion of FDI issues within EC trade policy has largely developed as a side effect of the initial policy objectives. In attempting to cope with company efforts to avoid trade restraints, EC policy has been forced to focus on investment issues. FDI issues have been an explicit element of policy in two areas: local content regulations and the resolution of trade conflicts between member states over FDI.

Community local content regulations appear to have been strongly influenced by the aim of encouraging higher value-added investment in the EC. In their development, FDI was initially less of an issue than the need to prevent companies avoiding anti-dumping duties, but a more overt FDI policy goal is evident from the design of the resulting regulations. In the case of screwdriver plants, by specifying the minimum *nature* rather than the *value* of production within the EC – for example, with the stipulation that the diffusion process in semiconductor production must take place in the EC if the product is to be regarded as of community origin – the regulations have clear effects on the level of technology transfer resulting from investments made within the EC. Further, it could also be argued that the commission's treatment of production in third countries has an underlying FDI goal. For example, in the late 1980s, the European Commission argued that exports of photocopiers into the EC from the subsidiaries of Japanese companies located in the United States should be classified of Japanese origin and subject to anti-dumping charges. In combination with existing local content regulations, the measure would have an overall effect of increasing the attractiveness of the community as a location for certain Japanese investments at the expense of the USA.

FDI has also forced EC institutions to act both as a form of intermediary in disputes between member states (often through the commission) as well as a forum for member states to resolve policy differences (mainly through the council). This was seen most prominently in disagreements over local content in the automotive sector that divided member states in the early 1990s. The conflict centred again on Japanese transplants, which at the time had principally located in the UK. France argued that imports from the Nissan plant in the UK should be classified as part of its Japanese car quota unless it could be demonstrated that at least 80 per cent of the vehicles' value had been sourced within the EC (Moore 1997). From the French perspective (shaped largely by a vigorous campaign by Peugeot), the imports represented a strong competitive threat to its indigenous car industry. Recognising the threat to the UK's ability to attract Japanese FDI, the British government contested the French proposals, leading to the intervention of the commission and eventual French acquiescence to the Nissan cars as being of UK origin.

Although the source of the dispute ultimately dissolved as Nissan achieved local content rates of 80 per cent anyway, it remains of interest from a policy perspective for two reasons. First, it highlighted the role of the commission as a mediator between opposing member state attitudes on foreign investment and competition issues. In the case of Japanese transplants, it was not direct competition between member states that was at stake, but the effect that foreign investment in one member state was regarded as having on the industrial competitiveness of another. Second, the differences between the UK and France partly influenced the development of policy at an EC level. The dispute led to the inclusion of Japanese transplant production in the Elements of Consensus negotiations and an agreement addressing the concerns of the different parties (for the UK, by guaranteeing the absence of restrictions on Japanese transplant trade, and for France, by ensuring such trade did not target specific countries with a domestic industry).

EC COMPETITION POLICY AND FOREIGN INVESTMENT

The founding treaty of the EC equipped the European Commission with a formidable array of regulatory and supervisory powers in the sphere of competition; indeed, its autonomy and discretion in this arena are arguably greater than in any other policy field. These powers fall into two broad groups: those that have an impact on the behaviour of firms; and those that govern how member states can intervene in the market. In contrast with the relationship between trade policy and FDI, the operation of competition policy, in so far as it impacts on FDI, is concerned with regulating the behaviour of *governments*, not that of firms.

Competition policy and the behaviour of firms is primarily concerned with the regulation of restrictive practices (Article 85) and the abuse of monopoly positions in the market (Article 86), and, more recently, with mergers that have implications for Community markets. The uniqueness of these provisions lies in the role of the European Commission and in the emphasis on the extent to which firms' behaviour affects competition on European markets. On substance, however, echoes of these provisions are found in national competition and anti-trust policies both within the community and elsewhere.

More distinctive are the provisions that relate to the behaviour of governments. Article 90 of the treaty addresses distortions of competition that arise from public undertakings or undertakings with special or exclusive rights accorded by public authorities. The provisions of Article 90 mainly concern public services and other utilities and have been used with notable effect in liberalising the telecommunications sector in Europe. Further controls on public intervention in the market are provided for in Articles 92 to 94, which are concerned with so-called 'state aids'; the interaction of these provisions with FDI and FDI policy are the focus of this section.

The approach of the 1992 deadline for the completion of the Single Market heightened interest and activity in the field of controlling state aid. This largely reflected the fact that the further dismantling of trade barriers that would take place as part of the Single Market Programme would leave state aid as one of the few measures of protectionism at the disposal of member states. This meant not only that governments were perceived to be more likely to intervene but also that the effects of subsidies would be more keenly felt by competitors in other countries (Cecchini 1988; Padoa-Schioppa *et al.* 1987). Notwithstanding this resurgence of interest in the risks posed by uncontrolled subsidies, it is important to note that provisions for disciplining state aids had been written into the treaty from the start, reflecting early recognition of their potential for distorting trade in the common market.

The essence of community policy under Article 92 is that state aids are banned, subject to certain exceptions defined by the European Commission.[2] The notion of a state aid is, however, rather nebulous. The treaty does not define precisely what types of intervention are targeted (probably intentionally);[3] nevertheless, something approaching a definition has emerged from successive European Court of Justice and European Commission policy decisions.

In broad terms, it is clear that the notion of 'aid' is wider than that of subsidies, so that it includes not just obvious forms such as grants and soft loans, but also tax concessions, equity capital and potentially any intervention by public authorities that is not on strictly market terms; indeed, explicitly, it can be in 'any form whatsoever'. Regarding the definition of 'state', the provisions are designed to cover actions by or on behalf of all levels of government – local, regional and national, including agencies with delegated powers and, on occasion, nationalised firms.

The provision of state aid does not, of itself, contravene the treaty. In order to be caught by Article 92, a measure must distort or threaten to distort competition and must do so by favouring certain undertakings or the production of certain goods. These requirements clearly limit the scope of Article 92; however, in practice, the increasing interdependence of markets within the EC economy has made the finding of a threat to competition almost inevitable. More complicated is the 'selectivity' element. Aid is selective if it applies to a particular type of activity (for example research and development), to a particular sector of the economy, to specified geographical areas or to firms sharing similar characteristics. In this way, a line is drawn between measures of general economic policy, on the one hand, and measures which *directly* or *indirectly* assist specific firms, on the other. However, there remains a significant grey area between state aids and what have come to be termed 'general measures' of government policy (Wishlade 1997). As will be seen, this distinction is of critical importance: the commission has wide-ranging powers *vis-à-vis* state aids, but very limited scope for intervening against other forms of government policy that distort competition. Moreover, the definitional difficulties associated with the distinction between state aids and general measures have led to a degree of creative policy-making in the sphere of FDI attraction.

As far as state aids are concerned, as already mentioned, the ban is not absolute. There are a number of mandatory exclusions from the prohibition, such as social aid and aid related to natural disasters. More important in the present context is the scope for commission discretion to allow aid which addresses certain policy objectives. The treaty allows for this discretion in a number of loosely defined areas. On the basis of these provisions, the commission has drawn up guidelines, codes and frameworks that set out the types of aid that it will authorise and under what conditions.

The are no rules relating specifically to state aids for FDI or mobile investment in the EC. However, since the 1960s, the issue of competition for mobile investment has been the driving force behind the development of commission policy in controlling general investment aid, and, in particular, regional aid.[4] Regional aid was the first policy area in which the commission attempted to introduce a system of coordination of aid policies among the member states and its work in this area has a long and chequered history, the detail of which is outside the scope of this chapter (but see Yuill *et al.* 1997). The main thrust of commission action in authorising or prohibiting general investment aid schemes submitted by the member states for approval has been to restrict the spatial coverage of incentives available to large firms. This has created a *de facto* link between regional policy and FDI attraction in those countries that favour FDI as a mechanism of economic development, and made regional incentives an explicit instrument of FDI attraction in many member states. This is certainly true of the UK, but also of Spain and France, which together accounted for 62.6 per cent of all inward investment flows in the community between 1986 and 1995. In such countries, the potential availability of regional aid to FDI features prominently in inward investment agencies' promotional literature.

A key question is whether this action at community level has had the desired effect of reducing competitive outbidding for mobile projects. The European situation contrasts with that in the USA where there are currently no rules to constrain economic development agencies, states or cities in providing incentives to mobile investment (Donahue 1997).[5] Thomas (1997) notes that simultaneous investments on either side of the Atlantic by Mercedes attracted subsidies of 83–100 per cent of investment costs in the state of Alabama, but only 40 per cent of costs in the European host location in Germany, and attributes this difference to the existence of a system for controlling subsidies in the EC. In practice, there is little empirical evidence that the EC state aid rules impact significantly on competitive outbidding in the community, and this for several reasons.

First, the restriction of general investment aid to designated assisted areas has meant that preventing distortion of competition through state aid has been couched in terms of controlling the coverage of the regional policy map. Reflecting the balancing act between competition and other policy considerations that the commission is required to perform in approving regional aids, higher coverage (as a proportion of national population) will be authorised in the poorer than in the richer countries of the community. This quota approach to area designation has led some countries to focus area designation on those regions that are capable of absorbing large investment projects, sometimes to the exclusion of problem regions not suitable for FDI, arguably undermining the stated purpose of regional development policy.

Second, this over-emphasis on the spatial coverage of regional aids has hitherto largely excluded considerations of award values and regional aid spending. As well as approving assisted areas, the commission also sets maximum values on awards as a percentage of fixed asset investment; in some regions the authorised ceilings are as high as 75 per cent of investment, but 25 per cent is more typical in the richer member states. In practice, however, these ceilings rarely bite as far as regional incentives are concerned. Public expenditure constraints mean that policy-makers are keen to obtain value for money from incentive spending and award no more than is necessary to attract a given project. Related, budgetary pressures are more severe in the poorer countries, and it is precisely in these countries that the higher rates are authorised; in consequence, the poor regions of the poor countries may be unable to do more than match award offers in the poorer regions of rich countries (CEC 1996a; Wishlade *et al.* 1998).

Third, the commission approach to forms of aid has required many member states to amend aid packages on accession to the community or as part of membership negotiations (Wishlade 1998). Perversely, this may have facilitated mobile firms and their advisors in playing off potential locations against one another, since commission pressure has resulted in considerable uniformity in forms of aid and greater comparability of values.

Last, the regional policies of the member states have been subject to considerable and continuous scrutiny by the commission over the last two decades or so. In parallel, however, there has been a growing trend towards the decentralisation of economic development activities and many subnational bodies play a significant role in complementing national aid packages through the provision of land, buildings or company-specific infrastructure, as well as through grants and direct funding. In principle, support of this type does come within the scope of the state aids rules but there is anecdotal evidence that the prior notification and approval rules are often either deliberately flouted or that local policy-makers and politicians are simply unaware of their existence (Raines and Wishlade 1997).

A further policy area which has partially eluded competition policy-maker attention is the use of tax advantages. Ironically, the scrutiny to which regional aid has been subjected may have been counterproductive; a number of countries operate tax schemes which fall outside the definition of a state aid but which are implicitly aimed at attracting FDI. The most high-profile examples are Belgium and Ireland. Belgium offers so-called 'coordination centre' status to headquarter operations of multinational firms which brings a number of tax advantages with it. In Ireland, the corporation tax rate for manufacturing is set at 10 per cent, and is widely regarded as one of the main reasons for Irish success in attracting FDI.

Two recent developments in controlling competition for FDI reflect the extent to which the evolution of policy in this field is a highly iterative process resulting from the interactions of different policies, of different levels of government and the behaviour of firms. First, the emergence of new initiatives with respect to taxation and tax advantages; and second, commission plans to constrain awards to large firms and capital-intensive projects.

For most of the history of EC policy-making, direct taxation has been a dormant issue, in large measure because of its status as a bastion of national sovereignty. Recently, there has been a significant turnaround in this position; rapid progress has apparently been made towards addressing the issue of 'harmful' tax competition, culminating in a code of conduct on business taxation (European Council 1998). Importantly, however, the code is without prejudice to the application of Community law and essentially provides a framework within which member states commit themselves to follow the principles of fair competition. In short, the code is not legally binding but rather in the nature of a 'gentlemen's agreement'.

The motivation for the emergence of the code is essentially twofold. First, some national policy-makers have become increasingly concerned at perceived 'unfair' tax competition and the poaching of mobile investments by allegedly predatory fiscal measures. Second, levels of unemployment across the community have focused attention on an apparent shift in the tax burden from capital to labour, and on the potential negative impact of high employers' welfare contributions on job creation (CEC 1996d). For many EC governments, concerns about the risks of fiscal degradation were heightened by the imminent prospect of a single currency; as EMU approached, the budget deficit targets in the Maastricht convergence criteria increased the pressure to raise revenues from taxation. Spurred into action by the activities of DGXV (internal market) in promoting agreement among the member states in this area, DGIV (competition) is to complement the proposed code by producing a notice on the application of the state aid rules to business taxation measures; it was also planned to review 'one by one' the tax arrangements in force in the member states (RAPID 1997a).

The introduction of the tax code and the development of DGIV policy with respect to fiscal aids is likely to have differential impacts on the member states. Already, the Irish authorities have been under pressure to amend corporation tax provisions for the economy as a whole and the commission has made clear that authorisation of the tax concessions in the International Financial Services Centre will not be extended. DGIV is reported to be reconsidering the Belgian coordination centre tax status in the light of the state aid rules, even though this has hitherto been considered a 'general measure'. Other countries may be relatively untouched by these new developments; the UK, for example, markets itself to potential inward investors as a low tax location but not one in which special benefits or concessions are made to particular firms.

The second development concerns attempts by the commission to control levels of assistance to large projects. Over the last decade a range of options have been considered (Raines and Wishlade 1997), but it was not until the end of 1997 that the commission announced firm plans (RAPID 1997b). The so-called 'multisectoral framework' was applied from September 1998 and aims at reducing aid levels to very large projects;[6] such projects have to be notified to the commission on a case-by-case basis for an assessment of their employment, competition and regional impacts, following which the commission will authorise a maximum rate of award. A further development which is indicative of commission concerns at competition for mobile investment is the requirement in the new regional aid code that investment and jobs in receipt of aid must be maintained in the region for at least five years.[7] This reflects the high media profile of, and growing policy-maker concern at, incidents of relocation apparently in response to offers of financial aid.

FOREIGN INVESTMENT, COMPETITION AND THE EMERGENCE OF EC REGULATION

As at national level, increasing levels of investment have raised issues that have had to be addressed by policy-makers at EC level, especially with respect to influencing the community's competitiveness for FDI in a global context and the control of internal competition for mobile investment projects. Both of the case study policies have impinged on the factors affecting location decisions by multinationals: in the case of trade policy, by raising trade barriers, and in competition policy, by placing limits on the availability and scale of financial incentives. However, the extent to which FDI flows have been directly influenced by the policy actions of EC institutions is not clear. Trade policy measures have had the more identifiable impacts. Although the size of investment creation is difficult to establish, the volume of FDI into the EC has been positively affected by the use of anti-dumping and VER measures, as non-EC companies have sought to circumvent the trade barriers. Moreover, commission local content regulations have also affected the *quality* of foreign investment in some industries by creating incentives for companies to transfer higher value-added parts of production to EC-based transplants. This was seen most clearly in the example of semiconductors where regulations encouraged the location of the wafer diffusion process in European plants.

The impact on FDI has been more difficult to establish in the case of commission regulation of state aids. In large part, a measurement of the effects would require a counterfactual – that is, in the absence of EC-level controls on the use of financial incentives to attract FDI, would unregulated incentive competition for FDI have changed multinational location decisions? Without limits on the use of incentives countries might be prepared to offer large incentive packages to attract investment, both to outbid other member states and possibly (though less frequently) potential locations outside the EC. In theory, countries with the deepest pockets and greatest determination are likely to secure the bulk of investment. By constraining national competition for mobile investment, EC policy would influence mainly the *distribution* of investment within the community – as well as within countries, by limiting the use of investment incentives to specific regions – but not its quality, as in the case of trade policy. While a counterfactual is not easily established, a parallel can be found in the USA, where bidding wars between states for large investment projects have been increasing, resulting in a ratcheting-up of incentive awards made to large mobile investment projects.

Regardless of the actual impact of both policy areas on FDI, competition and trade policies have been significantly shaped by the need to respond to FDI challenges. In both cases, the approach to dealing with FDI has emerged as a side effect of the policies' original focus on other issues. FDI did not feature in the original policy objective of regulating financial incentives, but early in policy development competition for mobile investment became the principal concern of policy-makers, mainly because attracting investment had become the main aim of general investment incentives. Similarly, trade protection measures were not specifically intended to influence FDI flows – arguably apart from local content regulations – but as non-EC companies were able to use investment to circumvent anti-dumping and VER actions, policy-makers at EC level were compelled to adapt trade policy to take account of foreign investment.

In developing a response to FDI issues in the two areas, EC policy-making has been an iterative process, in which policy shortcomings as revealed in their initial application have resulted in subsequent policy reform. Consequently, in trade policy, the avoidance of trade barriers by investments inside the EC led to measures directly regulating those investments. A similar process can be seen in competition policy, where member states have been sufficiently restricted by the existing application of state aids rules to explore other incentive measures for attracting FDI, notably tax incentives. In responding to the potential for competitive bidding, the tax code represents the use of EC policy development channels by member states for collective action, though the extent to which the voluntary agreement will have practical force remains to be seen. Nevertheless, in both areas a degree of policy circumvention – by non-EC firms in trade areas and by member-state governments in competition areas – has led to actions being taken at the EC level resulting in an extension of supranational policy activity.

In addition, the development of policy at EC level has been determined by acute political differences between member states emerging as a result of foreign investment. With trade policy, this has been relatively limited, but the commission has had to intervene as a result of disputes among member states, most notably in the disagreement between France and the United Kingdom over the application of local content rules to Japanese transplants located in the latter, where the commission's actions as an intermediary provided a common framework for dealing with production from Japanese car investments. More explicit links between member state rivalry over FDI and EC policy form the basis for commission controls of state aids. In both cases, competition between countries has been caused by the impact of FDI on industrial competitiveness: for trade policy, it arose because of the perceived threat of Japanese subsidiaries in the UK to the domestic car industries of some of the other member states, whereas in state aids policy the competition was directly for foreign investment projects.

CONCLUSIONS

The parallels between trade and competition policies underline the extent to which the recent growth of global investment flows has shaped international policy-making. However, state aids regulation and trade policy reveal deeper links. At the root of both are issues of competition: both competition in trade and investment globally, as well as between member states over FDI and national industries. In part, the authority of EC institutions – particularly the European Commission – in both policies derives from the responsibility to act against activity distorting trade and investment flows within the EC. Outside of the EC, such distortions include the anti-competitive behaviour associated with 'dumping'; dumping is less likely to occur within the community, so policy has concentrated on the effects of industrial subsidies on competition.

What is interesting in this regard is the way that different policies have implications for other areas of community action. One set of policy initiatives can have potentially conflicting knock-on effects for another. For example, in the case of the car industry, the need to establish a common community approach to limiting Japanese imports and transplant production arose largely because of the undermining of the individual member state car quotas by dismantling trade barriers through the single market programme. Similarly, trade policy's pro-competitive stance is partly compromised by the industrial policy considerations which underlie the community's restriction of imports in certain industries through VERs and the efforts to encourage higher-value investment through local content regulations. Increasing FDI flows present further challenges to EC policy-making as they lead to greater national competition between member states for investment projects and the consequent widening of the range of incentives used to attract FDI. Trade policy also partially comes into conflict with industrial policy goals as non-EC companies locate within the community and raise their market share at the expense of indigenous EC producers, as appears to have taken place in the car industry.

At each stage, policy-making has been influenced by the ripples resulting from changes in other policy areas. The greater attention given to investment issues at EC level proceeds from the fact that FDI occurs at the nexus of different policy responsibilities. It overlaps trade and industrial policies: measures that restrict trade can produce investment as a substitute, but such investment can result in potentially unwelcome competition for local industries. FDI also links together regional and competition policies: as national and local authorities vie with each other to attract mobile investment projects for their economic development benefits, the case for a supranational regulatory authority to supervise the use of incentives is strengthened. It is perhaps the latter issue which demonstrates the most significant aspect of the response of EC institutions to FDI challenges. There has not only been adaptation of EC policies to take account of these challenges but, increasingly, the limits of member state actions are being more carefully delineated in certain policy areas. Through competition policy, by authorising the limited use of regional aids, the policy instruments with which member states compete for investment projects have been defined, just as in trade policy and individual national measures have been replaced with common policies on local content and import quotas.

NOTES

1. In this chapter we use 'EC' as the legal term for referring to the powers of the community in areas of trade and competition policy.

2. For a detailed discussion of the law and policy of state aid control see Evans 1997.

3. Article 92(1) states that: 'Save as otherwise provided in this Treaty, any aid granted by a Member State or through State resources in any form whatsoever which distorts or threatens to distort competition by favouring certain undertakings or the production of certain undertakings or the production of certain goods shall, in so far as it affects trade between Member States, be incompatible with the common market.'

4. 'One of the objectives of the co-ordination and adaptation of general systems of regional aid is to put an end to the outbidding between Member States in order to attract investment to their respective territories' Council Resolution of 20 October 1971 on General Systems of Regional Aid (1977) *Official Journal of the European Communities*. No. C111, 4.11.

5. On occasion, groups of states or cities have entered voluntary agreements not to outbid one another through incentives, but such arrangements have invariably broken down.

6. In practice, the new framework will not apply to all sectors in the first instance; those sectors that are already covered by specific rules (motor vehicles and synthetic fibres, for example) will continue to be so.

7. IP/97/1137 state aid for the regions: focus to be on the poorest regions and the real effect on jobs to be taken into account, Brussels, 17 December 1997.

SUNG-HOON JUNG[1]

6 The Global–Regional Interplay of Korean Foreign Direct Investment in the European Union

INTRODUCTION

The turmoil of South-east Asian economies since 1997 has increased the existing turbulence of the global economy.[2] Compared with the 'South-East Asian Miracle' from the 1970s up to the mid-1990s, the present crisis of capitalism in South-east Asia seems to reduce the 'miracle' to a 'mirage' along with a crisis of national defaults. These countries' crises – particularly that in Korea, which had formerly been regarded as one of the more successful economic models for other South-east Asian countries – have led to confusion over the identity of South-east Asian economic growth. Moreover, the massive outflow of foreign direct investment (FDI) from Korea has been significantly reduced, with current projects often delayed. Indeed, in some cases there has been temporary or complete disinvestment due to the current crisis. Consequently, this turbulent globalisation of Korean industry has caused the regional economies of host countries to become unstable and provides clear evidence of the global –local interplay, although the nature and direction of the interplay differs from country to country.

The aim of this chapter is to identify the character and direction of the global–regional interplay of Korean FDI in the European Union (EU) by considering the trends and motivations from the late 1980s, since when Korean FDI has increased dramatically.[3] To do this, the motivations for Korean FDI are presented by focusing on the relationship between profit-squeezing pressures within the Korean economy and the massive outflow of its FDI.

Second, the motivations and trends of Korean FDI are explored at the level of the EU. Here I concentrate on FDI in the consumer electronics industry, where the main motivations for Korean FDI in the EU centre on trade regulations such as anti-dumping tariffs and quotas imposed by the EU rather than by individual member states. Therefore, this economic interplay between Korea and the EU, namely 'the global–regional interplay', is premised on the global–local interplay of its FDI in particular regions of the member states. In other words, while the motivation for Korean FDI in the EU is concerned with investment decision-making by Korean firms, Korean FDI in the individual member states is related to locational decision-making. Of course, not every motivation for Korean FDI in the EU has arisen from the character of global–regional interplay. Whether its individual FDI is related to the character of global–regional, global–national or global–local interplay depends on the different motivations of particular firms. Nevertheless, this chapter focuses on the global–regional interplay of Korean chaebols' FDI in the consumer electronics industry in the EU, because Korean consumer electronics chaebols have a high share of the FDI in the EU both in terms of investment values and cases.

In a final section, five interrelated trends of Korean FDI in the EU are considered: trade-related, consumer electronics-based and big-Korean-firm-led (the so-called 'chaebol-led') FDI trends, the attraction of Korean FDI into old industrial regions of the EU, and trends and tendencies of vertical integration of Korean production networks within the EU.

MOTIVATIONS FOR KOREAN FOREIGN DIRECT INVESTMENT SINCE THE LATE 1980S

In general, Korean FDI since the late 1980s can be characterised as *profit-defensive* due to the falling domestic profitability of Korean firms. A number of subsidiary characteristics, such as 'trade-related', 'export-substituting', 'market-oriented', 'low wage-pursuing', 'band-wagon-effected', might also be attached to Korean FDI. All of these factors have prompted some Korean chaebols to invest massively or actively pursue acquisitions (The Bank of Korea 1993, 1997; Shin and Lee 1995; Dent and Randerson 1996). According to one Korean daily newspaper, 'they distorted FDI as a means of the ostentatious display of their power rather than investing overseas with the cool-headed logic of capital' (*Digital Chosunilbo* (Website), 9 January 1998).

In other words, the nature of profit-defensive FDI lies behind different patterns of Korean FDI and determines the main source of Korean FDI's competitiveness, namely cost-competitiveness (Dent and Randerson 1997). Since 1988 net outflows of Korean FDI have increased sharply; indeed, the value of its FDI in 1994 was double that of 1993 (although instances of Korean FDI have decreased since 1995 (see figure 6.1)[4] In the context of the Korean economy, the phenomenon of profit-squeezing made the year 1988 an economic turning point for Korean firms, following the economic turbulence at global and national levels in 1987. This mechanism of profit-squeezing has proceeded in different but interconnected directions at global and national levels, and it has been the main motivation for Korean FDI overseas since then (figure 6.2).

FIGURE 6.1: OUTFLOW OF KOREAN FOREIGN DIRECT INVESTMENT

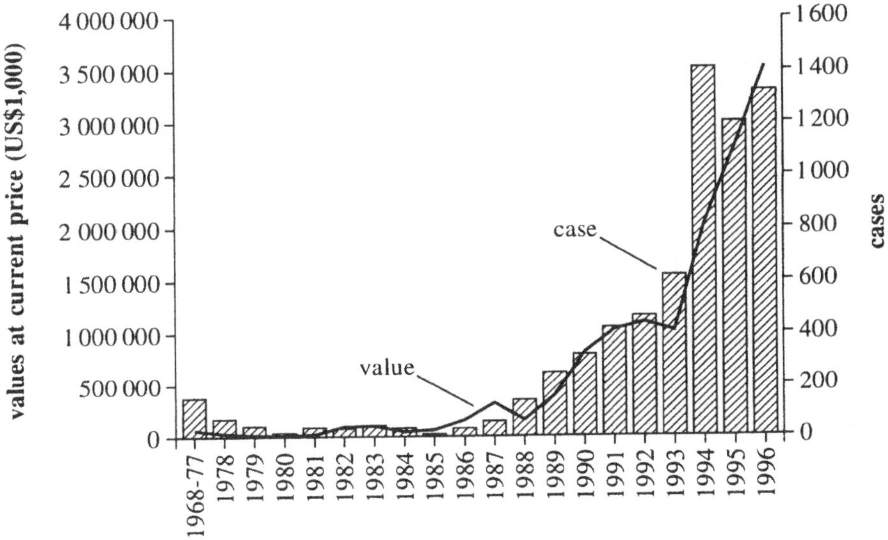

Source: The Bank of Korea, 1997, *Yearbook of Overseas Direct Investment Statistics*

In the late 1980s, along with the revaluation of the Korean currency (the Won) against the US dollar and a sharp increase in the trade surplus during that period, the Korean economy was faced with the pressures of opening domestic markets and of trade friction with developed countries (figure 6.3). This short-term economic boom turned into a trade deficit immediately after 1990, alongside the devaluation of the Won. As the cycle of trade surplus reached its highest point in 1988 and the exchange rate appreciated at a lower point in 1988, the more intensified trade frictions between Korea, the USA and the EU resulted in the vigorous imposition of anti-dumping duties, non-tariff barriers and quotas (Kang 1994). In addition, the main Korean export industries such as textiles, clothing and consumer electronics, based upon the low and middle ranges of cost-competitiveness since the 1970s, were challenged by other South-East Asian countries such as Malaysia, Thailand and Indonesia. These factors produced a profit-squeeze on Korean firms which, at the same time, became the main push factors of Korean FDI at a global level.

Since 1987, the Korean economy suffered from more severe labour disputes than previously. The number of labour disputes increased dramatically from 113 cases in 1984 to 3,749 cases in 1987, and the number of workers involved

FIGURE 6.2: MOTIVATIONS FOR KOREAN FIRMS' FOREIGN DIRECT INVESTMENT ON A GLOBAL SCALE SINCE THE LATE 1980s

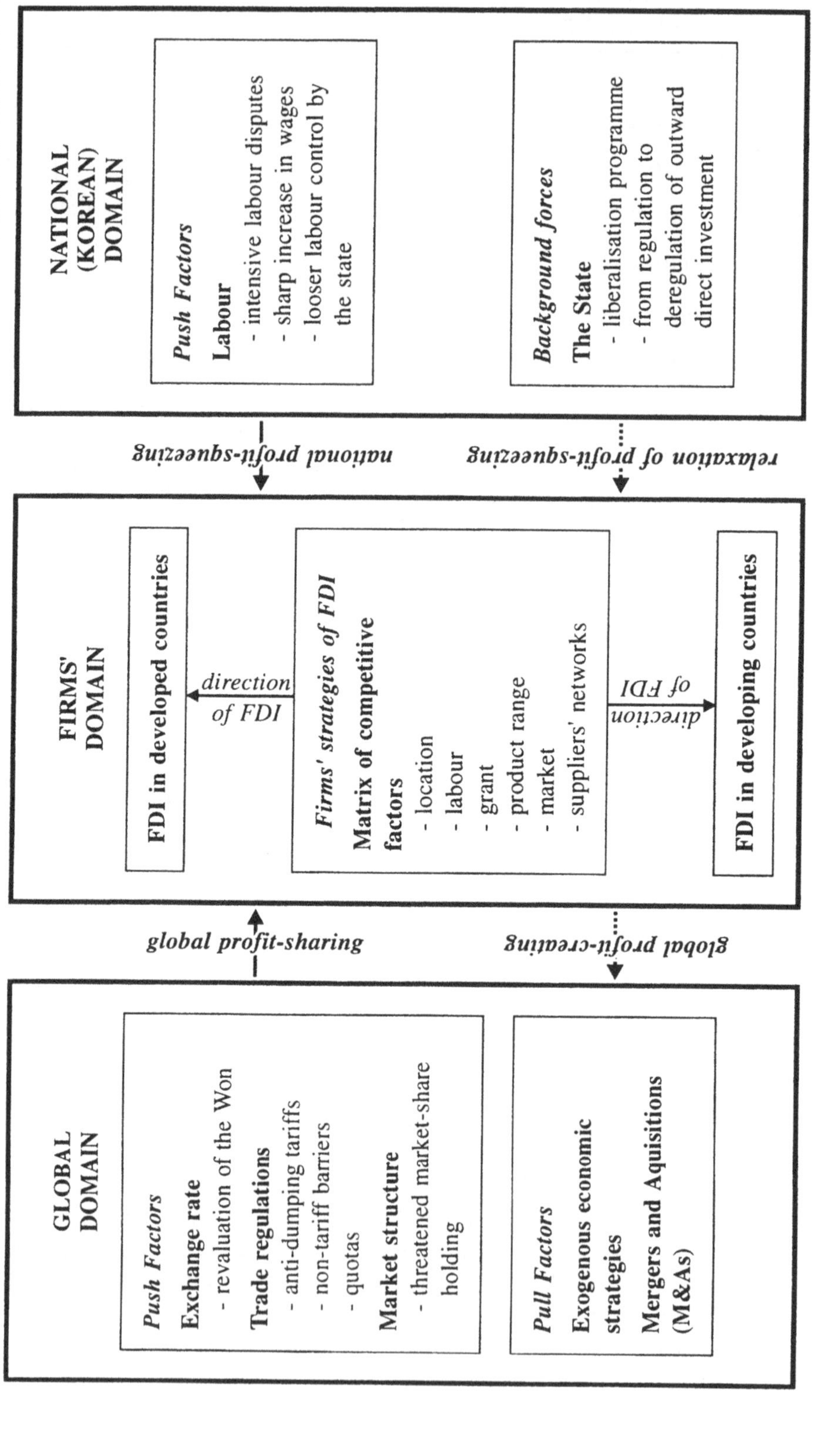

in those disputes also rose sharply from 16,400 in 1984 to 1,262,285 in 1987. The labour disputes were over demands for wage increases and they led to a sharp increase in real and nominal wages in Korea; as a result, the state relaxed its tight control of labour and capital. Higher wage costs subsequently caused a squeeze on firms' profits at a domestic level and pushed Korean labour-intensive industry to low-wage regions such as Indonesia and China (Korean Export and Import Bank 1992; Korean Foreign Trade Association 1993; Shin and Lee 1995; Jung 1996).

FIGURE 6.3: THE EXCHANGE RATE AND TRADE BALANCE IN KOREA

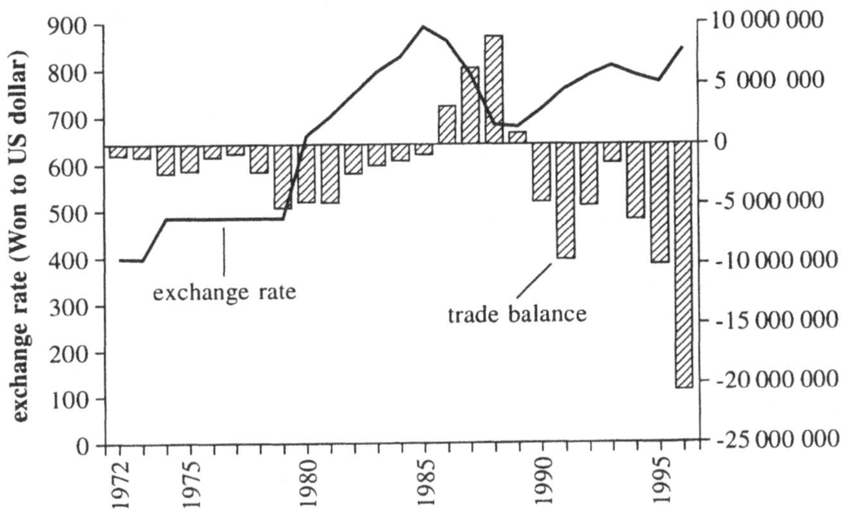

Source: The Bank of Korea, *Economic Statistics Yearbook;* Korea Foreign Trade Association, 1997, *The Trend of Foreign Trade*

Individual firms pursue different goals through their FDI. At present, FDI strategies among Korean chaebols represent a global solution to domestic profit loss so that the character of their FDI seems to be passive and defensive rather than active and offensive. So, how have Korean firms conducted this profit-defensive FDI?

Two factors since the late 1980s have made profit-defensive FDI possible. In reality, this period provided simultaneous conditions for both profit-squeezing and profit-creating for Korean firms by squeezing them from particular spatial economies and at the same time creating particular spatial 'fixes' for them. First, at a global level there have been more active exogenous economic strategies by host countries since the mid-1980s. In reality, forty-three countries have opened up FDI as part of their strategies for economic growth, and mergers and acquisitions (M&As) have been activated since then

(UNCTAD 1993, 1996b). These more liberal economic strategies of host countries can be regarded as pull factors at a global level and determine the geographical directions of Korean global production.

Second, as a background factor for Korean FDI at a national level, the state has played a critical role in its outward direct investment. This can be seen in the change of policies with regard to outward direct investment. The Korean state has changed or amended its FDI policies since the late 1980s, moving from regulation to deregulation through the relaxation of regulatory frameworks and through capital liberalisation (The Bank of Korea 1994, 1997).

Therefore, the globalisation of Korean FDI cannot be explained as a linear sequence on a particular spatial scale, nor can it be measured by a single factor. Korean FDI in the EU, in particular, provides a good example of the profit-squeezing and profit-creating pressures in force. One of the main push factors – trade regulations imposed by the EU – has squeezed Korean firms' profits regionally by protecting the EU against the import of goods from Korea; at the same time this mechanism of profit-squeezing led Korean firms to invest in the EU. Paradoxically, profit-squeezing on Korean firms conducted regionally by the EU also provides a solution to other economic pressures on both Korean firms and the old industrial regions of Europe.

BACKGROUND TO KOREAN FOREIGN DIRECT INVESTMENT IN THE EUROPEAN UNION

Since 1995, Korean FDI in Europe has overtaken its FDI in North America (figure 6.4) and tends to be concentrated in the European Union rather than the rest of Europe. For example, about 67 per cent of the total investment in Europe was focused upon the EU in 1996 (table 6.1). Regarding the motivation for Korean FDI in the EU, there are two main push and pull factors and one background force (figure 6.5). At the level of the EU, the main push factors are the trade regulations, such as anti-dumping tariffs, non-tariff barriers and quotas. The EU's anti-dumping actions against Korean consumer electronics goods have played a critical role in attracting Korean consumer electronics-based FDI to the EU and in encouraging large Korean electronics firms to concentrate on the EU. Individual member states played a significant role in the EU anti-dumping policy (Holmes and Kempton 1996) by squeezing Korean consumer electronics firms' profits at a regional level, and such a policy ultimately resulted in Korean FDI in the EU. Furthermore, extensions to anti-dumping regulations to cover screwdriver plants coupled with local content rules played a critical part in the attraction of chaebol subsidiaries. The market structure as a push factor relates to Korean small and medium-sized firms as well as to large firms. Apart from the Korean subcontractors to the large firms in the EU, these are independent and aim at extension or penetration into the EU market.

FIGURE 6.4: OUTFLOWS OF KOREAN FOREIGN DIRECT INVESTMENT IN MAIN REGIONS

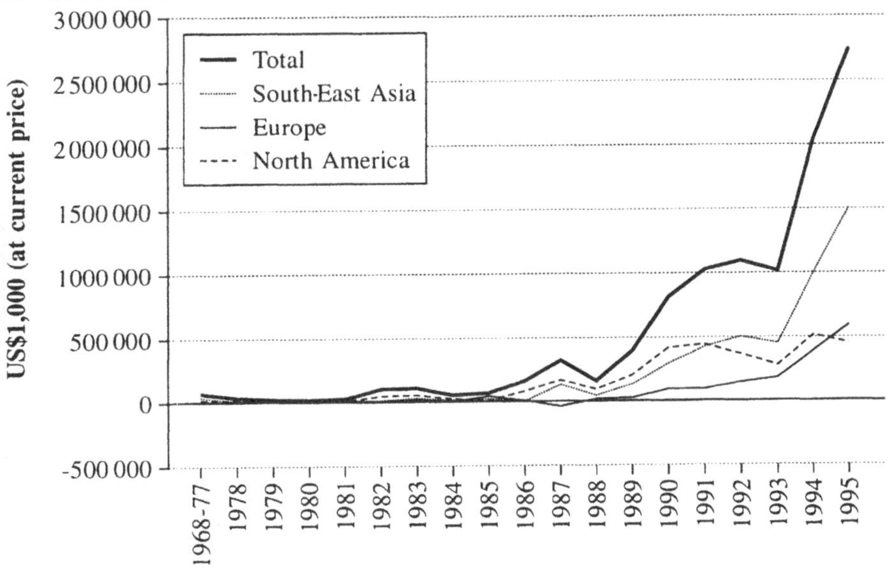

Source: The Bank of Korea, May 1996, *Yearbook of Overseas Direct Investment Statistics*

In terms of pull factors, exogenous regional economic strategies by the member states have provided opportunities for profit-creating with Korean firms in the EU. According to Dunford (1994), in these strategies 'competition for investment and subsidy wars occur and consequently unequal development is created as not all regions can emerge as winners though there are regional development programmes which do help redistribute gains from winners to losers'. In particular, the restructuring of the older industrial regions in the UK and France has played an important role in attracting Korean FDI. Along with Korean FDI those regions have themselves accumulated a new layer of investment. Opportunities for entering via mergers and acquisitions are a primary pull factor, too. Examples of this include the sales of former East German firms through privatisation by the German government, as a result of the German reunification.

With respect to the background force at a national (Korean) level, the deregulatory policy of the state has focused upon Korean FDI in the consumer electronics industry, where it has relaxed its profit-squeezing of firms as a reaction to the trade regulations of the EU. The most important fact in this domain is that the labour situation in Korea is not directly regarded as a significant push factor although it plays a critical role in Korean FDI in South-east Asia. In reality, EU trade regulations are more important to Korean firms in the EU as a push factor than the labour situation in Korea.

FIGURE 6.5: MOTIVATIONS FOR KOREAN FOREIGN DIRECT INVESTMENT IN THE EUROPEAN UNION ON A REGIONAL SCALE SINCE THE LATE 1980S

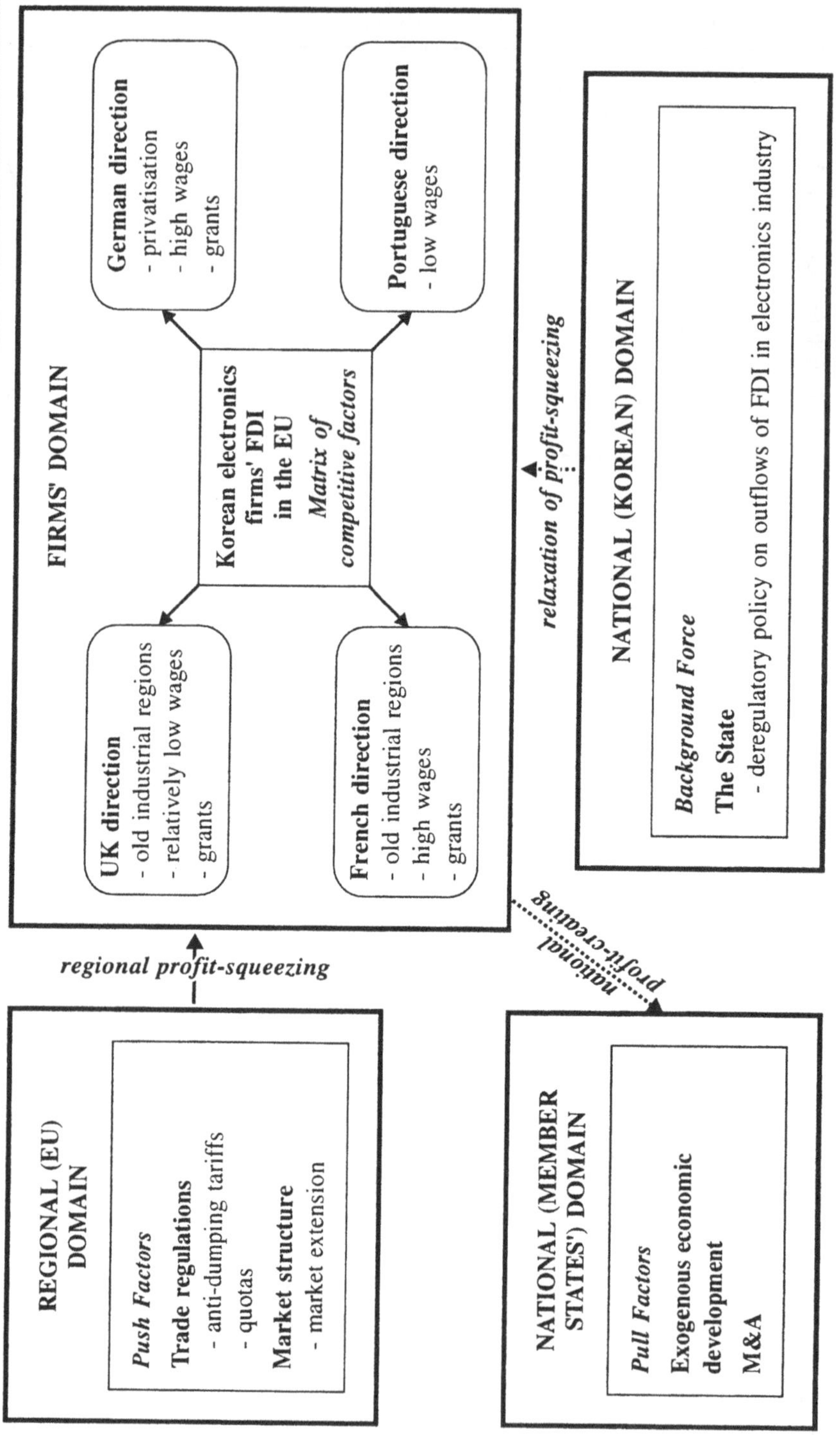

Along with these push and pull factors, Korean firms constitute part of a competitive matrix within the EU. The matrix determines the directions of its FDI in the EU. In this respect, motivations for Korean FDI focus on the locational determinants for its FDI at national and local levels. In general, there have been four main directions: the UK, Germany, France and Portugal (see table 6.1). The particular directions taken by firms critically influence the future formation of their production networks in the EU as well as in the rest of Europe. First of all, with regard to the direction of Korean FDI in the UK, large Korean electronics firms have invested considerably since the late 1980s. During interviews the main locational determinants for Korean firms' investment in the UK were revealed as lower wages than in Germany and France,[5] flexible employment legislation and grants from central and local government (Jung 1997b).

TABLE 6.1: KOREAN FDI IN THE EUROPEAN UNION BY INDUSTRIAL SECTOR, 1995

Unit: number, US$1,000

Industrial sector	**Manufacturing**		**Construction**		**Transport amd storage**		**Wholesale and retail**		**Others**		**Total**	
Region	*No.*	*amount*	*No.*	*amount*	*No.*	*amount*	*No.*	*amount*	*No.*	*amount*	*No.*	*amount*
Europe	110	843 450	3	5 052	3	1 537	156	497 465	31	179 811	313	1,544 383
EU	59	408 482	2	5 002	3	1 537	112	476 063	12	154 653	188	1,045 737
Germany	11	60 273			2	1 239	48	222 275	5	3 462	66	287 249
UK	23	104 274	2	5 002			24	130 457	1	354	50	240 087
Netherlands	3	20 211			1	298	12	6 685	1	146 903	17	174 097
France	9	97 290					11	69 806	2	2 297	22	169 393
Portugal	3	52 346									3	52 346
Spain	3	21 063					4	24 797			7	45 860
Italy	2	14 520					10	16 549	2	276	14	31 345
Ireland	3	23 526							1	1 361	4	24 887
Belgium	2	14 979					3	5 494			5	20 473

Source: The Bank of Korea, May 1996, *Yearbook of Overseas Direct Investment Statistics*

TABLE 6.2: GRANTS TO KOREAN CHAEBOLS BY MEMBER STATES IN THE EUROPEAN UNION

Chaebols	**Location**		**Grants**
	Country	**Region**	**(% as total investment)**
Samsung	UK	North-east of England	20[1]
LG	UK	North-east of England	14.5[1]
Daewoo	UK	Northern Ireland	71[2]
Daewoo	France	Lorraine	37[2]
Daewoo	France	Lorraine	37[2]
Daewoo	France	Lorraine	37[2]
Samsung	Germany	Berlin	44[2]

Notes: 1. The grants are based upon the total package including value of land.
2. These are based upon the percentage of the grants for the value of land and production equipment of the total investment.

Source: Companies' in-house data, Phelps, N, author's survey, 1997

Some other UK regions' experiences of Korean FDI are quite similar to those of Korean FDI in France. Those regions in the UK and France are nationally or EU-funded regions and this funding has been granted to Korean firms. Although the level of grant varies according to the regions, the grant is one of the main pull factors in attracting Korean FDI to those regions (table 6.2). The German attraction of Korean FDI was largely influenced by the government privatisation scheme which resulted from German reunification. In the case of Korean FDI in Portugal, low wages and grants were major determinants for Korean firms.

MAIN TRENDS OF KOREAN FDI IN THE EU

Korean FDI in manufacturing, as already illustrated, has increased dramatically since the late 1980s and is also true of its investment in wholesale retailing. Korean FDI in the EU has concentrated primarily on five EU member states: the UK, Germany, Netherlands, France and Portugal, with FDI in manufacturing tending to concentrate on the UK, while FDI in wholesale and retailing is focused upon Germany.

The ranking of Korean FDI has varied considerably among the member states. First of all, there is competition between the UK and Germany which have vied as the primary recipients of Korean FDI. None the less the UK was the main host country for Korean FDI between 1988 and 1996, with the exceptions of 1994 and 1995. The main reason for this preference is that the UK has had an influx of Korean chaebol manufacturing investments (such as Daewoo, Samsung, Lucky Goldstar (LG) and Hyundai) since the late 1980s, while Germany has been a sales platform for Korean wholesale and retail companies with the expectation of access to Eastern European markets. The 'cultural proximity' of the UK in terms of the English language has also contributed to the decision to invest there (Thomsen and Woolcock 1993; Christodoulou 1996; Jung, 1997a).

Competition for Korean FDI between the Netherlands, France, Portugal and Spain tends to be less intense. The rank of the Netherlands has risen sharply from ninth in 1991 to third in 1995 because of Samsung's investment in telecommunication services in the Netherlands, but the precise scale of this investment is unclear. In an interview with Samsung, staff stated they did not actually invest as much as the US$146m recorded for the Netherlands (see table 6.1). Bearing in mind these figures for the Netherlands, France is probably the third host country for Korean FDI as Daewoo has invested heavily in Lorraine. The position of Portugal is quite interesting as it has not received Korean FDI in wholesale, retail and manufacturing except for Samsung's investment. Leaving aside the Netherlands, Portugal is the fourth host country although it only has investment from Samsung. Alongside these trends and tendencies, there are five main characteristics of Korean FDI in the EU: trade-related, consumer electronics-based and chaebol-led FDI, attraction of Korean capital into the European old industrial regions, and the vertical integration of Korean production networks in the EU.

Trade-related, Consumer Electronics-based and Chaebol-led FDI

Korean FDI is mainly a trade-related phenomenon at the level of the EU. The EU's anti-dumping regime has played a critical role in attracting Korean FDI and, furthermore, processes of adaptation to this trade regulation by Korean firms have resulted in active locational shifts across the member states and even outside the EU. EU anti-dumping actions have largely taken place since the late 1980s. This period is mainly consistent with the sharp increase of Korean FDI at a global level as well as within the EU. The anti-dumping actions played an important role in determining the character of Korean FDI in the EU which can essentially be characterised as consumer electronics industry-based and chaebol-led FDI. For instance, to mid-1995, 59 per cent of the total value of Korean manufacturing FDI in the EU was in the radio, television and communications equipment and apparatus sector, while three chaebols (Samsung, LG and Daewoo) accounted for 68 per cent of the total value of Korean manufacturing FDI in the EU (Jung 1996).

The anti-dumping actions also gave rise to the activation of locational shifts of Korean firms in the EU. For example, when an EU anti-dumping investigation involving Korean microwave ovens (MWOs) was opened in 1986, Samsung invested in the UK the next year and Daewoo invested in France in 1988. As soon as the EU decided to withdraw anti-dumping regulations on Korean MWOs due to dumping margins of less than 5 per cent, Samsung withdrew the MWO production line from the UK. However, in 1995 when definitive duties on MWOs were imposed, Samsung immediately reinvested and LG also invested in the UK. A further example can be seen in the locational shift of Korean video cassette recorder (VCR) production. When an investigation into Korean VCRs was opened in 1987, LG invested in Germany. After that, when provisional duties were imposed by the EU, Samsung and Daewoo invested in the UK (in 1988). However, in 1997 LG shifted its production from Germany to one of the South-east Asian countries because the EU cancelled the anti-dumping duties on VCRs. The reason for this is that there are no European producers of VCRs within the EU because the main European producers have moved to South-east Asian countries. Additionally, in the case of LG, the increase of wages in Germany was one of the reasons for moving its production line. This reflects in part the fact that Korean FDI in the EU is based upon cost-competitiveness and profit-defensive FDI. As Young et al.(1991) pointed out earlier, 'the Pacific Rim investments being induced into the EC are chiefly import-substituting or market-share holding'. Therefore the impact of protectionism on Korean FDI in the EU still matters in terms of Korean firms' locational and relocational activities within and without the EU.

These trade-related investment and locational shifts of large Korean firms imply that Korean FDI in the EU is closely related to the improvement of cost-competitiveness through relocation or the switch between products within and outside the EU. In terms of locational and product shifts of large Korean firms, there are two different types concerned with sunk costs (Stafford 1991; Phelps 1997; Clark and Wrigley 1997). The first is concerned with locational shifts characterised by complete withdrawal from the EU. This can be shown in the cases of LG's withdrawal of refrigerator and freezer production from Italy in the early 1990s and of colour television (CTV) and VCR production from Germany in 1997. As a result, LG has abandoned sunk costs through its locational shifts across the EU as well as outside the EU. The second type is related to product shift *in situ*. This shift also accompanies locational shifts of a particular product with 'out of product line'. The example of Samsung's product shift in the UK as presented above is typical. These examples reflect the fact that, in order to secure a market-share holding within the EU, Korean firms search for market adaptability of a particular range of products through a continuous switch of products, and make strategic relocations based upon trade regulations and the search for applicable cost-competitive resources of host countries gearing into institutional, market and productivity contingency within the member states of the EU.

Attraction of Korean Capital into the EU's Older Industrial Regions

It has been shown that Korean manufacturing FDI in the EU has tended to be concentrated in particular member states. It has also been shown to be focused upon the grant-aided older industrial regions of the member states. This trend implies that Korean FDI in the EU is closely linked to programmes of job creation in local and regional economies within those member states (Alden 1997a). In this respect, Korean FDI has particular local concerns which stand apart from those connected with the globalisation and regionalisation of its investment. Therefore, while Korean FDI in manufacturing is structured by trade regulations, a Korean firm's location in a particular member state is determined by factors such as the level of wages, regional aid funding at state and EU levels, and regional and local economic policies. In other words, whereas investment decision-making of Korean FDI in the EU is concerned with the overall EU trade regime, Korean firms' locational decision-making within a member state is closely related to the characteristics of particular localities – producing a global–local interplay of Korean FDI below an interplay of FDI at the global–regional scale. As a result, along with the profit-squeezing of the Korean firms by trade regulations at EU level, the opening up of old industrial regions to large Korean firms, resulting from massive industrial and regional restructuring within some member states of the EU, has played a critical role in attracting Korean firms into particular regions of the member states. At the same time, this has led large Korean consumer electronics firms to form investment poles within particular member states such as the UK, France, Germany, Portugal and Spain (Jung 1997b). Alongside this trend, the continuous political and economic processes leading towards intensified and enlarged European integration will in turn influence Korean investment and reinvestment, the location and relocation of the firms, and product shifts within and outside the EU.

FIGURE 6.6: COLOUR TELEVISION PRODUCTION NETWORKS OF LG AND SAMSUNG IN THE EUROPEAN UNION

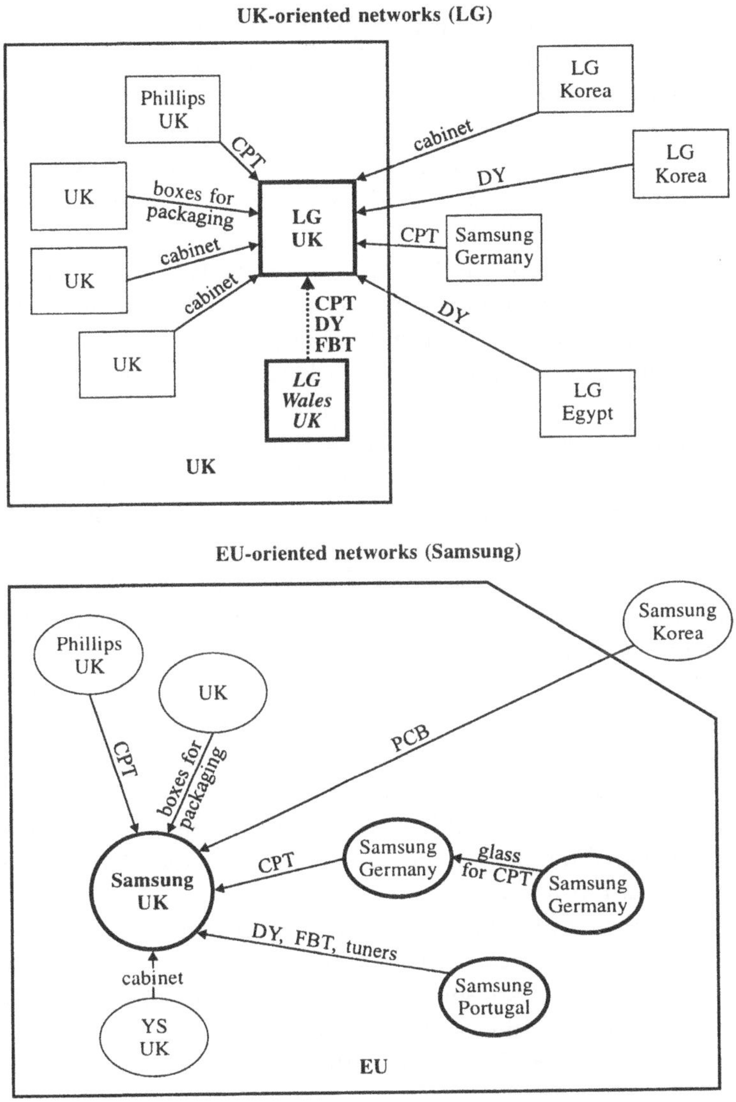

Trends and Tendencies of Vertical Integration of Korean Production Networks in the EU

Korean firms have integrated their production networks vertically within the EU. There are three main trends at the level of the EU and its member states. First, at EU level, Korean electronic chaebols have brought their subsidiaries to EU regions. For instance, Samsung Electronics Ltd producing CTVs in the north-east of England is supplied with components by its subsidiaries within the EU (figure 6.6). Of four main manufacturing-based subsidiaries of Samsung in the EU, three subsidiaries – Samsung Display Devices Ltd and Samsung Corning Ltd in Germany, and Samsung Electro-Mechanics Ltd in Portugal – have been producing colour picture tubes (CPTs), glass for CTV picture tubes and electronic tuners, deflection yokes (DYs) and flyback transformers (FBTs). In the case of the VCR plant of Daewoo Electronics Ltd in Northern Ireland, it has tuners supplied by Daewoo Electro-components Ltd in Northern Ireland. In Lorraine, France, Daewoo Electronics Ltd brought the CPT plant near to its CTV plant. Unlike these two examples, however, the CTV plant of LG Electronics Ltd in the north-east of England, was not provided with components by its subsidiaries in the EU. However, LG has now built its own CPT plant in Wales.

There are several reasons why large Korean firms have attempted vertical integration of their production networks in the EU. First, although they came to the EU to overcome the EU anti-dumping actions, extensions to anti-dumping regulations have meant that they have had to meet local content rules under which a certain amount of components have to be provided within the EU. Second, it was quite difficult for Korean firms to find specialised suppliers for their production in the EU. In other words, the improvement of cost-competitiveness on the European market can be achieved by the combination of proper costs for purchasing components. Third, the search for industrial sites in the EU by Korean chaebols is closely related to favourable policies of inward investment by the member states. For example, CPTs are very important to CTV production with regard to production cost and product quality. In the case of Samsung Display Devices Ltd in Germany, it took over an existing plant in the former German Democratic Republic which the German government sold at an extremely cheap rate through privatisation after German reunification, and for which it provided grants to Samsung. Samsung then established Samsung Corning Ltd in Tschernitz, Germany, where there is plenty of raw material for glass, in order to provide glass for CPTs to Samsung Display Devices Ltd in Berlin.

The result is that favourable policies towards inward investment of the member states has contributed partly to vertical integration of the main production networks of the Korean chaebols' subsidiaries in the EU. These processes of locational decision-making by Samsung in Germany are similar to those made by LG in Wales (Jung 1997b). A senior manager at LG

Electronics North of England Ltd said that:

> grants presented by the Welsh government were so high that the current industrial site was nearly free. Along with this, we decided to invest in the production of CPTs as well as semi-conductors and so on. For LG's CTV plant in the north-east of England, the CPT plant is as important as other plants. The production of CPTs requires many suppliers of glass, and in Wales there are many glass suppliers because Wales is a rich region of the raw material for glass. In addition to this, there are many electronics companies, especially Japanese electronics ones, so we could expect the availability of skilled labour. (Author's interviews)

At a national level some Korean subcontractors tend to be located adjacent to their parent firms. In the case of Korean firms in the UK, Samsung in the north-east of England, Daewoo in Northern Ireland and LG in Wales have all brought or will bring their Korean subcontractors over to the UK regions; a trend which is similar to that of Japanese FDI in the UK (Munday 1995). Currently, Samsung has six Korean small and medium-sized subcontractors around its plant which have worked for more than ten years in Korea on the basis of labour-intensive production rather than in monopolistic or oligopolistic transactions. Samsung brought them to the UK to meet the local content rules and to keep the cost of purchasing those components relatively low in order to attain cost-competitiveness. Equally, Korean subcontractors have invested in the UK so they can secure a relatively stable market, maintain the monopolistic role with Samsung and gain access to other producers in the UK and the EU under a special arrangement with Samsung.

Finally, the geographical scope of production networks in the EU can be divided into two types: regional (the EU) versus national (the UK) networks and companies like to combine the two. This tendency can be seen in Samsung's and LG's CTV production networks (figure 6.6). In the case of Samsung in the UK, its production networks are situated in various regions of the EU: for example, plants for tuners, FDT and DY in Portugal; a CPT plant and glass plant in Germany; another CPT plant and a plant for cabinets in the UK; and therefore Samsung in the UK needs to regulate supplier networks at the level of the EU. On the other hand, LG has kept its production network within the UK. LG has a plant in the north of England, and has also invested considerably in Wales, aiming to produce CTV components such as CPTs, CDTs, FBTs and DYs as well as semi-conductors. The ways in which these companies' geographical scope of production networks will influence success or failure cannot be predicted at present. Nevertheless, because the motives for bringing their subsidiaries to the EU are similar, whether these two firms succeed or fail will depend solely upon the national competitiveness of the individual member states for the production of CTV or relevant components.

CONCLUSION

The notion of 'global–regional interplay' contributes to create a new geographical concept in industrial and corporate geographies. In addition to this, it is premised by the global–local interplay through the global activities of Korean FDI. In terms of Korean FDI in the EU as well as in other countries, the global, national and local situations influence firms' activities and have a cyclical cause and effect relationship to its outward direct investment, reinvestment and disinvestment. Korean FDI as profit-defensive FDI based upon cost-competitiveness seems to be a product of profit-squeezing and profit-creating represented on different spatial scales but on a similar time scale. Therefore, Korean FDI in the EU can be characterised by a process of a cost-competitive combination towards various sources of competitiveness across different geographical scales. Along with these characteristics of its FDI in the EU as well as the rest of the world, what is more important is how Korean firms overseas will survive under the conditions of the recent turmoil in the Korean economy. It is also important to see how this domestic economic turbulence may be regarded as interdependent at a global level and therefore impact on Korean FDI in the new era of the IMF bail-out to the Korean economy. With these trends and tendencies, Korean FDI in the EU can be said to have 'globally taken off, made a locally incomplete landing' *en route* to a successful global–local destination.

NOTES

1. I would like to acknowledge the assistance given to me by Mick Dunford, Nicholas Phelps and Jeremy Alden and to thank them for their very helpful comments.

2. In this chapter 'Korea' refers to the Republic of Korea (South Korea).

3. Under 'global–regional,' the term 'region' indicates economic blocs such as the EU and the North America Free Trade Association (NAFTA).

4. This trend is indicative of recent developing country FDI. Since the mid-1980s, the growth rate of outflows of FDI from developing countries has increased sharply from 24 per cent between 1983 and 1987 to 52 per cent in 1993.

5. The 1995 wages at the UK plant of one Korean chaebol were rather lower than in France and actually similar to those in Korea on the basis of net wages (Jung 1997b).

YUKO AOYAMA[1]

7 Localisation Advantages for Multinational Firms: Views from the Japanese Electronics Industry in Europe

INTRODUCTION

Much of the existing theory of multinational firm location has been centred on the concept of 'offshoring' which typically involves the relocation of operations to low-wage areas that allow firms to be price competitive. The purpose of this chapter is to explore aspects of multinational firm location in 'high-cost' locations. While there are undoubtedly numerous factors that affect a firm's decision to relocate parts of its operations to areas which are generally considered 'high-cost', the focus of this chapter is on the competitive advantages that multinationals gain by having some kind of local market presence. Specifically, the chapter addresses both the perceived and actual business advantages gained from local market presence by the Japanese electronics industry in Europe.

I begin with a brief review of the literature on various aspects of 'localisation advantages' – the benefits firms perceive as well as actually gain through local market presence. In two further sections, I then examine the case of the Japanese electronics industry in Europe starting with a brief history of the locational dynamics of Japanese-owned establishments in Europe, drawing on a database which includes 3,200 overseas Japanese-owned establishments in three major world regions.[2] This is followed with empirical evidence on how Japanese firms perceive the importance of overseas market presence in the case of the European market. This empirical material is derived from survey findings and interview results. Interviews with employees of Japanese companies were conducted between 1994 and 1996 in offices in Japan, the United Kingdom, the Netherlands and Germany. The interview and survey material relates to eight major Japanese firms in the consumer and industrial electronics industry. Interviews were conducted in Japanese, and then later translated by the author.

MARKET PRESENCE AND THE GLOBAL LOCALISATION OF MULTINATIONALS IN THE 1990s

From Mass Markets to Mass Customisation and from Globalisation to Global-localisation

It has been suggested by Chandler (1977, pp. 285–376) that America's business success up to the 1970s was predicated on mass production and mass distribution for mass markets. Such assumptions about the nature of markets were implicit in important theories of overseas investment developed at the time, notably product cycle theory (Vernon 1966) and notions of a 'new international division of labour' (Fröbel *et al.* 1980). Both these theories are commonly credited with predicting a progressive shifting of foreign direct investment (FDI) toward lower cost locations. While this may be a reasonable caricature of the latter, with its emphasis on the labour process (see Schoenberger 1988 for a critique), it is a less valid caricature of the former.

In his reappraisal of the original product cycle model, Vernon suggested that a firm that has access to innovation and market information globally, in his term a 'global scanner', would have an absolute advantage over firms without such capacity. Vernon argued that 'ignorance or uncertainty is no longer a function of distance', as the cost of communication decreased over time (Vernon 1979, p. 261). Thus, global scanners can take advantage of their vast net of information in order to efficiently innovate and better serve overseas markets with their intimate knowledge of local market trends.

Vernon distinguishes between multinational firms that cater for homogeneous world demand versus those who cater to distinctive needs of individual markets. The latter group engages in what Vernon termed 'global optimisation', in which firms use their global networks to optimise information they acquire from various markets and use it effectively, differently, but also globally. The primary motivation for FDI associated with the idea of the global scanner is local market penetration, not cost reduction. Once a trade barrier is crossed, the firm has a tendency to locate in the areas where high-tech industries agglomerate to take advantage of existing infrastructures and labour pools for both skilled and semi-skilled workers, and favourable business climates for multinational firms. The global scanner with a segmented market demand not only has the capacity to scan technological and market information globally, but also to learn from different market trends, which contribute to innovative behaviour.

The suggestion of an evolution in the competitive logic of multinational location strategies has been taken up in subsequent accounts of multinational enterprise. Bartlett and Ghoshal (1989) argue that multinational firms are using their global strategies to remain competitive through continuous innovation. They argue that the size of the firm and international access to resources no longer provide sufficient conditions for multinational firms to compete successfully, since their competitors have gained the equivalent. Instead, what has become critical is a firm's ability to exploit new ideas and respond to creativity no matter where their origin. In sum, current multinational firms require the capability to manage globally, while retaining market sensitivity, innovative capacity and flexibility (Bartlett and Ghoshal 1989).

Since then it has been argued in business literature, that mass customisation has replaced mass production as the primary strategy for competition in the 1990s. This argument is based in part on the perceived need of companies to expand their product ranges and improve 'customer responsiveness' (Pine *et al.* 1993). Customer responsiveness has become the central objective for businesses seeking to capture and maintain their market share (Slocum *et al.* 1994). In order to remain competitive, firms have employed strategies to maintain customer intimacy (Seideman 1994; Partridge 1994).

Traditionally, the role of marketing has been considered nothing more than the icing on the cake for a firm's success. The apparent neglect of marketing and market research in the business and management literature's assessment of market demand stems from a perception developed from the traditional functional division of labour within firms. Porter's model of the value chain of firms, for instance, positions marketing along with sales at the end of the value chain before service (Porter 1985). This model suggests that the general functions of marketing, which include market research, advertising, promotion, and the development of sales aids and technical literature, have been considered distinct and entirely separate from other functions such as product design and the actual fabrication of products. Porter goes on to argue that firms whose organisational structure corresponds better to the value chain will improve their ability to create and sustain their competitive advantage. Yet the possibility of feedback from market demand to product development – so vital to achieving this correspondence – is not incorporated into his model. In more recent work, Porter emphasises what he calls 'buyers' needs' (Porter 1990). He argues that the firms that respond better to buyers' needs succeed, especially when those buyers are extremely sophisticated and demanding in their requirements. Here he stresses the importance of the capture of feedback from the market to product development within the function of marketing and market research.[3] In sum, market responsiveness has been addressed in business and management literature, although little discussion concerns the organisational and locational effects of market-sensitive firms.

Market Presence, Innovation and Product Development

The role of marketing has radically shifted during the last few decades. Until the mid-1970s, the role of marketing was restricted to simple reporting of facts by functional specialists in sales, advertising, promotion, distribution, market research and customer services. Since the mid-1970s, however, an increasing emphasis has been placed on the development of long-term objectives and customer relationships. Also, marketing has begun initiating the formation of networks through strategic alliances, seeking to improve or dramatically change a firm's competitive position (Miles and Snow 1986; Devlin and Bleakley 1988; Fujitake 1990; Webster 1992). With the increasing segmentation of markets due to rising income among advanced industrialised countries as well as increasingly differentiating tastes, firms competing in these developed markets are increasingly aware of the importance of consumer tastes in developing their scope. Market knowledge has become so important that some even argue that consumers have become partners in production (Fuchs 1968; Anderson and Narus 1991). Therefore, marketing has become integrated into product development, supplying market information from customers to production units. Marketing today should be considered as the channel that links production and consumption.

Lundvall (1985) has argued that user–producer interactions are an important aspect of innovation. The locational effects of innovative behaviour are agglomerative, since (1) long-distance interactions are prohibitively expensive in some phases of the technology life-cycle due to the 'cultural distance' involved, and (2) the 'learning-by-interaction' process reinforces historically developed user–producer linkages. The increasing importance of market demand responsiveness for multinational firms increases the importance of space as a provider of local market knowledge. As factors of technological advancement accumulate over time in various production factors (for example in capital investment and labour), locations that capture such advancement have competitive advantage over other locations. With institutional factors playing an increasing role in economic growth, the determinants of growth are increasingly identified as regionally and spatially embedded (Granovetter 1985). While various institutional factors have been identified (Freeman 1990; Scott 1988; Saxenian 1994), little is known about access to market knowledge as the determinant of location for multinational firms. Does the notion of regional embeddedness, social relations and labour extend to local market knowledge? Is there a type of local market knowledge that can only be sustained by firms' presence in a region, or can local market knowledge be easily exported? In a period of rapid technological change and shorter product life, has it become more important to maintain close contact with changing market demand?

The relationship between industrial location and customer intimacy has been studied to a limited extent (Cornish 1997; Gertler 1995; Schoenberger 1990). Schoenberger (1990) examined the relationship by using the American multinationals in Europe as an example. Since Europe was already a high-cost location at the time, Schoenberger sought to understand the motives behind the American firms moving to European locations. She found that access to local markets was their primary motivation.

Schoenberger also found that three-quarters of the foreign direct investment flowing into the USA in manufacturing in the late 1970s stemmed from acquisition of existing businesses rather than establishment of new businesses (Schoenberger 1984), noting the advantages of this mode of entry to firms unfamiliar with operating in the United States market.

Market Presence, Corporate Restructuring and the Networked Multinational

In order to better access local market trends and more efficiently reflect the knowledge in innovation and product adaptation, firms have opted to reorganise their corporate hierarchy. Here certain corporate structures are believed to be more receptive to innovatory processes. Recently, theorists have suggested that global forms of industrial organisation are evolving toward network forms which are more likely to facilitate continuous innovation and thus lead to successful business performance. The conceptualisation of corporate organisation in terms of networks instead of hierarchies has become a focal point for debate in the 1990s. For instance, Powell (1990) considers networks as being capable of more organic, reciprocal, flexible, indefinite and complex transactions than hierarchical organisations.

Several attempts at understanding globalisation have illuminated the importance of cross-border networks of local affiliates in shaping global networks (Bartlett and Goshal 1989; Imai 1992). Imai (1992) based his theory on an empirical study of the behaviour of Japanese multinational firms, and expanded the existing theory by attributing innovative business performance to network-oriented corporate organisations. Imai argues that Japanese multinationals are successful due to their unique organisational structure, which can be described as neither a vertically nor horizontally integrated hierarchy. Instead, many Japanese firms have assumed network forms of organisation. By adopting a network form of organisation, firms can benefit from information arising from various local and regional offices and can successfully convert it into innovative processes and products.

According to Imai, previous theories on multinational firms have focused on the redistribution of existing resources (management skills, products, etc.) across the globe. Because of this, the primary focus of these theories was on the control of these resources, as in the case of Hymer's theory for example (Hymer 1960). However, according to Imai, firms are globalising their functions based on a different logic since the mid-1980s. Japanese firms in particular are globalising their operations in order to take advantage of new opportunities arising from interacting with firms in other markets. Rather than redistributing existing resources, firms are seeking to create new opportunities and resources which did not exist previously through the process of globalisation.

However, critics of the network-organisation theory suggest that the role of corporate structure is over-emphasised in terms of its effects on innovation. Nonaka (1993), for example, argues that the critical factor for continuous innovation within a firm is not its structure, but its nature. Organisations that have been considered information processing in nature (Simon 1947) are now changing into knowledge-creating organisations in which innovation is encouraged and promoted. Others also warn against the widespread application of network-organisation theory. Dicken (1994) warns against the gap between theory and reality, concerning the pervasiveness of such network organisations, strategic alliances and learning corporations.

Having established in theoretical terms that there are good reasons for the localisation of activities in relatively high-cost locations due to advantages of market presence, I now wish to concentrate on Japanese electronics. Competition in the electronics industry, particularly the consumer electronics industry in which the Japanese firms are strongest is not simply based on technology; there is a strong component of market responsiveness in product design. Consumer electronics products can be the vehicles for the distribution and regeneration of information at the mass scale. This trend among multinational firms of gaining competitive advantages through extensive localisation I tentatively call 'localisation advantages'. In this respect Japanese electronics firms arguably have undergone the transition from domestic producers to 'global scanners' in the process of globalisation. Before going on to provide concrete examples of the localisation advantages derived by Japanese electronics firms operating in Europe, I provide some background to Japanese FDI, and specifically electronics FDI, in Europe.

GLOBALISATION AND THE MOVE TOWARD HIGH-COST LOCATIONS: JAPANESE ELECTRONICS IN EUROPE

Part of the increase in Japanese firms' investments offshore in relatively high-cost locations such as Western Europe and North America during the past decade is driven by the appreciation of the yen which made even some high-cost locations relatively affordable *vis-à-vis* domestic production in Japan. Yet, these locations still remain high-cost in comparison to many Asian locations.

Japanese investments toward high-cost locations have been characterised as a response to an increasing concern over import restrictions imposed by European and North American markets by means of tariffs, quotas (voluntary export restraints) and anti-dumping actions and associated local-content regulations starting from the late 1970s. Foreign direct investment by Japanese automobile manufacturers in Europe provides one example of the opening of production facilities in major overseas markets in order to evade tariff and quota barriers. While there is some debate on protectionism as a determinant of Japanese investment overseas, there seems little doubt that Japanese firms have been moving operations to overseas markets in spite of their cost with the object of evading the actual as well as the potential threat of protectionism.

However, for cost-based reasoning to prevail along with tariff-jumping as the major factor of globalisation, it is expected that a firm would prefer to locate in low-cost locations once inside target markets. Yet the evidence from the electronics industry shows that Japanese establishments in North America and Europe are not necessarily concentrated in low-cost areas within these regions. This appears to be the case irrespective of whether one considers the move into Europe in terms of the initial sales operations, regional office functions or manufacturing operations of Japanese firms which have been established over time.

In Europe, initial investments in the electronics industry began, not directly from Japan but through Japanese subsidiaries in the USA. One of the first investors to set up an office in Europe in this sector was Elco USA, an American subsidiary of Kyocera. Elco USA established Elco Europe in Copenhagen, Denmark in 1960. During the same year, Sony set up a finance office in Switzerland. Within a few years Elco USA then went on to build two manufacturing plants in Europe, one in Suffolk, England, and one near Düsseldorf in Germany. Sony, on the other hand, did not begin production in Europe for almost another decade. It was not until 1969 that Sony began manufacturing in Europe, at a plant in Surrey, England.

Thus, investment in Europe began with establishing sales offices. By 1965, Japanese electronics firms had offices in four countries: Germany, the UK, Switzerland and Denmark. From four countries in 1965, sales offices spread into

FIGURE 7.1: EUROPEAN SALES OFFICES OF JAPANESE ELECTRONICS MNEs, 1995

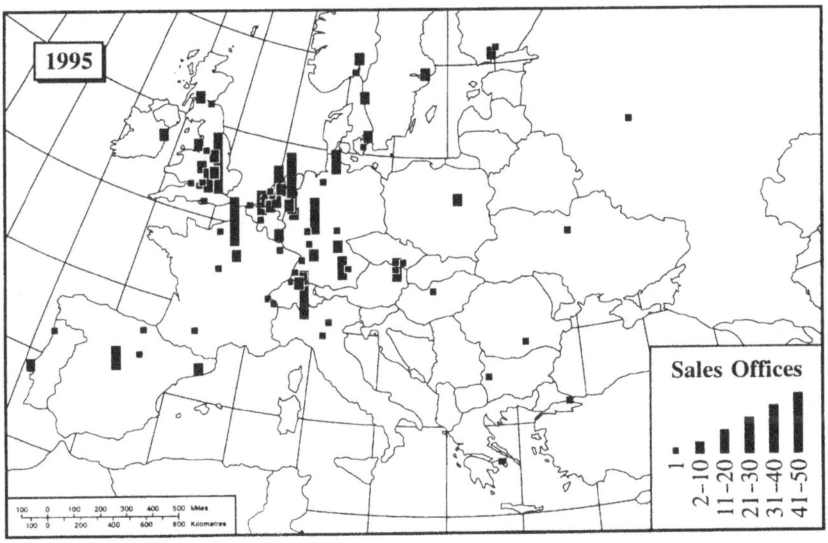

Source: Compiled from data provided by company reports, EIAJ and Tokyo Keizai Shuppan. Copyright: Yuko Aoyama 1996.

fourteen countries by 1975. The major concentrations of sales offices were to be found in London and its vicinity, Paris, the Düsseldorf–Cologne area, the Frankfurt area, Hamburg, Vienna and Zurich. These concentrations grew dramatically into major agglomerations for sales functions by 1985. In addition to the areas mentioned above, sales offices began agglomerating in and around Amsterdam and Brussels. As figure 7.1 shows, by 1995, four regions stood out as the biggest concentrations of sales offices for the Japanese electronics industry in Europe: London, Düsseldorf–Cologne, Hamburg and Milan. Also, with the opening of the markets in the former communist countries of Eastern Europe, sales offices have been established in Moscow, Kiev, Warsaw, Sofia and other areas. In Eastern Europe, Japanese firms are establishing their sales offices first, while manufacturing plants follow only much later on.

The regional headquarters of Japanese firms in Europe were first established in Hamburg, Germany, and Germany continues to be the major location for regional headquarters for the Japanese electronics industry. The map of regional headquarters in 1995 (see figure 7.2) indicates that they are largely restricted to cities in Germany, England, the Netherlands and Belgium. Regional headquarters in Europe have existed since the 1960s, but the number increased significantly only after the mid-1980s. This suggests that a major reorganisation has taken place since the 1980s, most likely as part of the effort to decentralise decision-making capabilities away from Japan. This was also done in response to the development of the European common market and the consolidation of corporate decision-making capacity of many European firms.

As for manufacturing plants, the surge of Japanese investment in Europe began in 1968. By 1975, they were in five major countries: Germany, the UK, France, Belgium and Spain. By 1985, investment spread to Italy, the Netherlands and Ireland, but most new establishments were in the original five countries. Finally, in 1995, figure 7.3 shows more agglomerations in those five countries, particularly in the UK and Germany, and to a lesser extent in France and Belgium. Manufacturing plants were also established in Denmark, the Netherlands, Austria and Poland, though to a much limited extent. Thus, while there are some recent investments into Central and Eastern Europe, the overwhelming majority of Japanese-owned manufacturing establishments are still located within Western Europe.

This evidence suggests that Japanese electronics firms in Europe as a whole are not necessarily channelling their investments toward low-cost areas within the trading bloc. The number of establishments remains comparatively small in areas such as Ireland and Spain. On the other hand, a large portion of the establishments have been directed toward the UK and Germany. There are clear advantages in locating in relatively high-cost countries, such as Germany and the UK, in spite of the cost disadvantages. These areas tend to provide a large pool of highly skilled engineers, experienced industrial workers and reliable industrial infrastructure along with familiarity with foreign-owned firms which in turn provides a relatively favourable political climate for firms to operate. In the following section I will examine how these factors, largely concerned with production, are also complemented by other more subtle advantages of keeping a close watch on local consumer preferences and market trends.

FIGURE 7.2: EUROPEAN REGIONAL HEADQUARTERS OF JAPANESE ELECTRONICS MNEs, 1995

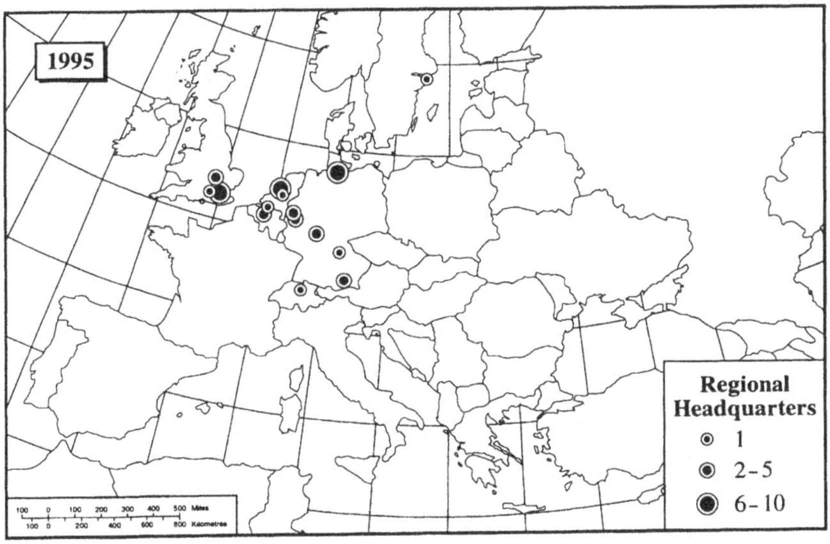

Source: Complied from data provided by company reports, EIAJ and Tokyo Keizai Shuppan. Copyright: Yuko Aoyama 1996.

FIGURE 7.3: EUROPEAN MANUFACTURING OPERATIONS OF JAPANESE ELECTRONICS MNEs, 1995

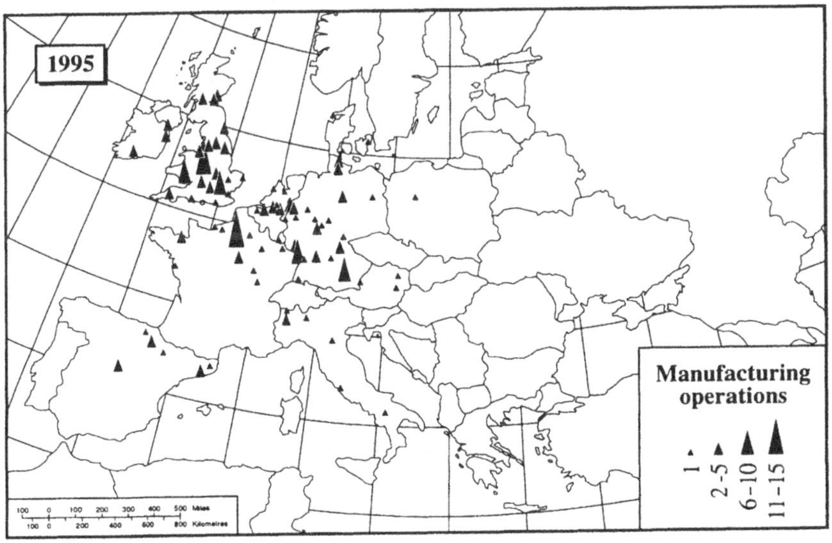

Source: Complied from data provided by company reports, EIAJ and Tokyo Keizai Shuppan. Copyright: Yuko Aoyama 1996.

LOCALISATION ADVANTAGES FOR JAPANESE ELECTRONICS INDUSTRY IN EUROPE

Some argue that Japanese firms possess unique abilities for acquiring new knowledge and disseminating it widely throughout their organisations (Nonaka 1991; Voisey 1993; Egan and McKiernan 1994). By exploiting the tacit and often highly subjective insights and intuitions of individual employees, Japanese firms have succeeded in transforming knowledge into a testable product. Perhaps the best known example of this is the entry of Japanese firms into the US automobile market with compact, fuel-efficient models in the aftermath of the oil crises of the 1970s. Most of the production was done within Japan and products were exported to overseas markets during the 1970s.

In contrast to the market situation in the 1970s, Japanese firms in the electronics industry in the 1990s face a much tougher market in Europe. This is partly because European markets, particularly when it comes to consumer electronics, have largely matured. Mature products, such as colour televisions, generally require more local sensitivity to ensure sustained sales, when compared with newly introduced products (Makino 1992). Generally, it is assumed that mature markets with mature products lead to competition among standardised products based on price. However, in reality, product differentiation frequently becomes the key to sustain demand for mature products.

Market Knowledge and Product Differentiation as a Competitive Strategy for the Consumer Electronics Industry

As a Toshiba executive in charge of consumer electronics commented, 'when it comes to mature products such as televisions, the business is all about volume'. In other words, as competition drives down prices, producers strive to earn profits by selling a massive number of units. Therefore, in dealing with mature markets, acquiring market share becomes critical for successful business performance. In order to gain market share for a mature product in a mature market such as Germany, it is critical that firms establish brand recognition and product differentiation. An Hitachi executive in Tokyo described how current competition intensifies the importance of market knowledge as follows:

> until the 1970s, almost anything and everything we produced got sold. This was because the economy was still growing globally, we had the price advantage and products simply had to have good quality standards. Now with this situation of intensified competition, recession and increasing cost of production due to the escalating value of the Yen, this is no longer the case. Also, these days with technological advancement, everybody can produce good quality products. So you have to differentiate your product from others in some other ways. Also, a shorter product cycle gives us more opportunities to differentiate. Knowing what customers want becomes really important. (Author's interview)

In other words, when growth in demand is limited and competition is fierce, the competitive advantage of firms lies not just in price but in product differentiation. In order to gain competitive edge in production differentiation, the combination of technology and knowledge of existing as well as hidden demand is a critical component for product development.

For instance, industry insiders stated that each market is entirely different in terms of how best to sell. They agree that the German consumer market poses a particular challenge for Japanese manufacturers. According to them, German consumers, unlike American or British consumers, are not as price sensitive. Instead, brand recognition is very important. A Sharp executive commented:

> Germany is a tough market because they still have very strong domestic companies like Grundig[4] and Telefunken, who command a lot of brand loyalty among older Germans. For them, Japanese, Koreans and Taiwanese producers are still all bunched up together and considered low-end producers. We have been recognised to some extent as a company that specialises in liquid crystal display, which is really lucky because otherwise the consumers still don't know us from Adam. (Author's interview)

A Toshiba executive responsible for television marketing in Europe, echoed this sentiment.

> Cracking the German market is tough, tough, tough! German consumers are a bit like Japanese consumers. They are somewhat prejudiced against foreign products. And brand recognition is extremely important. The only Japanese company selling TVs in the German market that has a powerful brand recognition is Sony. The rest of us are still struggling'. (Author's interview)

A variety of strategies have been employed to gain brand recognition. Another Toshiba executive even argued that the presence of an industrial electronics business can help sales in consumer electronics. 'It may be surprising, but being known among industrial clients as parts suppliers helps our consumer electronics businesses too. It's important that the name Toshiba is known among industrial clients. It definitely contributes to building brand recognition among German consumers' (author's interview).

While there may be a certain degree of standardisation, markets are still considerably different globally. Consumer markets in particular remain segmented locally as tastes and preferences are still distinctive. Research by McKinsey Global Institute (1993) on the electronics markets comparing Japan, the United States and Germany revealed some differences in product demand. Televisions, for example, are produced with different resolution levels because US and German consumers tend to watch television in darker rooms. Japanese consumers prefer multifunctional televisions with broadcasting satellite tuners or 'picture in picture' functions (a small screen showing another channel). A Sony executive has also been quoted as saying that in consumer electronics the Japanese market is different from the US market in that selling products with new technologies to the Japanese is easier. Compared with the Japanese, American consumers are more conservative about their choices of products.

With increasing technological sophistication, both consumer and industrial markets have become more sophisticated and demand is more customised than ever before. Therefore, assuming the existence of standardised markets does not allow multinational firms to prosper. The fact that markets are drastically different for various consumer markets was also echoed by another Toshiba executive based in the UK.

> It's true that some industrial applications, such as memory chips, already have a universal market. But you'll be surprised how different demand is for consumer electronics. For instance, take a VCR. You may think those VCRs look more or less the same everywhere you go, but if you look carefully, there are differences. In Japan, a VCR won't sell unless it has a stereo function. But try selling the same product here! The models that sell most in Britain are the simplest and cheapest ones, and it seems as if for the British, sound quality and stuff like that are low priority. We also have to deal with country specifications they have on electronic currents, plugs, MHz and things like that. Market knowledge is really important, because otherwise you go out of business by producing a bunch of stuff that won't sell. (Author's interview)

Statements such as these illustrate how assumptions about an increasingly standardised market at the global level may be premature. Yet assumptions that the globalisation of markets, through advancement in telecommunication technologies, has standardised various markets into a set of similar tastes and preferences are not without some foundation.

Another Sony executive in product planning pointed to the desire among firms to standardise production where possible.

> Sometimes I think we do too much for the consumers. If we keep customising everything, we end up spending way too much. As it is, we have something like twenty different models of television just for the German market, and if you start talking about things like headsets there are more than 300 models floating around in Europe. Interestingly enough, when the product is used closer to the body, there are more adjustments required. We'd love to standardise everything and sell one thing. For instance, marketers in Italy told us to eliminate the mute button on the remote control, because Italians don't use them. So we eliminated the mute button for the Italian market. Now this is what I mean by over-customisation. (Author's interview)

In sum, firms are faced with two conflicting interests: product customisation and cost reduction. In order to address both interests simultaneously, Japanese firms are experimenting with the development of a sophisticated global network of production and product development.

These statements by industry insiders reveal that markets for consumer electronics remain segmented, and that market strategies need to vary dramatically depending on the type and the characteristics of the market. Because competition has become fierce in this industry, Japanese firms echo the importance of intimate knowledge of these markets; this leads them to product differentiation and subsequent market capture.

Market Presence for Innovation and Product Adaptation

How important is it for a firm to have a presence in a market in order to succeed in capturing the market through locally based innovation and product adaptation? While views on product differentiation and competitive strategies vary among firms, almost all agreed that market presence is critical to the process of converting locally based knowledge into successful products. Executives claim 'global-localisation', as advocated by Honda's founder and adopted by other firms including Sony, is more than just rhetoric to please locals and to suppress criticism or anti-Japanese sentiments. Being present in the market is actually advantageous for firms to improve performance. Not only does it represent commitment of a firm toward a market, it also strengthens feedback of local market information to the manufacturer. A Sony executive in the UK offered the following comment on the importance of market presence.

> There are definitely things you can only understand when you are right there in the market. You have to experience the life in the UK, how people live and so forth to really know what they need. It's something you feel with your body. If you globalise marketing functions and hire locals, there are more chances of new ideas springing up, that is not originating in Tokyo. Product conception can now happen anywhere, and can be transmitted anywhere else, as long as they are useful. [To] Give you an example. The idea for My First Sony, consumer electronics for children, was conceived in our San Francisco office, then produced and marketed globally. It's true a lot of technological information, particularly for things like VCRs where Japanese producers have been strong, still originate in Tokyo. But product development is not just technological. (Author's interview)

Questions such as whether a firm needs to be present within the market to gain competitive advantage, and which function of the operation needs to be localised, are still under debate. Some Japanese firms seem to believe a total localisation, from conceiving product ideas to final distribution will be necessary, while others claim basic product development can be done in Tokyo. Sony is at the forefront of global-localisation, and Canon is also enthusiastically supporting the concept.

However, there are some disagreements as to how strategic Japanese firms are when it comes to global-localisation. Some firms are forced to look overseas because Japan's domestic market is considered saturated. A Canon executive, for example, downplayed the strategic component of the concept in suggesting: 'Globalisation sounds great now, doesn't it? But we aggressively globalised not because we were brilliant and foresighted. We were forced to globalise because we were a relatively new company compared with others and the domestic market was already dominated. We had to find a market elsewhere' (author's interview).

Similarly, a Sony executive downplayed the company strategy toward globalisation. 'I don't know what we are doing can be called a strategy. Sometimes we just do things as we go along, and then later call it a strategy, with some cute justification attached to it' (Author's interview). While this statement might more accurately describe the reality of the business world, Sony is continuously struggling to balance consumer needs with its production capability. At least for some firms then, the process of globalisation for the Japanese electronics industry began with a push out of domestic production due to high costs, trade barriers and domestic competition. However, Japanese firms are beginning to take advantage of their globalised positions with the new competitive advantage of the 1990s which involves competition based on innovation through the technological as well as market knowledge that is available locally.

For example, Europe has been an important location for the telecommunications industry. As the electronics industry becomes increasingly integrated with computers, communication and entertainment, Japanese companies interested in improving their technological capacity in telecommunications locate in Europe to benefit from technological alliances, joint ventures and other relationships with Europe's telecommunications firms.

Hitachi helped develop a pan-European cellular telephone with Nokia which became a hit in Europe. An Hitachi executive interviewed expressed the following view:

> Right now, Europe is like a small laboratory for globalisation. On the one hand, the regulatory environment is becoming increasingly standardised. On the other hand, there are still some enormous differences in consumer demand, requirements and use of products. We feel if we can do well right now in Europe, we can do well when the real globalisation hits the rest of the world. (Author's interview)

The same executive also insisted that such joint development could not have been possible during the 1980s.

> We developed custom ICs [Integrated Circuits] as part of this new product that became a hit product here. It's a pan-European digital cellular telephone (Nokia produces the 'unit' – the final product). But this wouldn't have been possible if we had not established this almost autonomous marketing and market research unit here in Europe in 1991. Even if we had come up with the same idea, Tokyo

> would have voted it down. It's really important that we listen to people in the field. (Author's interview)

Industry insiders stress that market presence does help ensure subsequent business success. One Sony executive said the following: 'You don't have to have market presence if your goal is to simply sell something. But if you want to lead a market, or if you want to be in the forefront of technology in a market, presence is critical.'

It is therefore clear why the Japanese electronics industry concentrates on highly sophisticated, highly competitive European markets in spite of cost. Industry insiders agree that substantial market presence is critical where fierce competition exists. These market competitive factors then provide the significant strategic motivations behind the locational dynamics of multinational operations. In the case of the Japanese electronics industry, rapidly changing and yet-to-be-standardised demand dictates firms' orientation toward market-based corporate structures.

Corporate Restructuring and Market Knowledge

The reality in the Japanese electronics industry reflects a variety of initiatives that allow firms to filter better and to use innovation more efficiently. Corporate reorganisations are also apparent in the case of overseas operations. Many are done to improve access to distribution channels and learn about local market demand. NEC, historically an industrially oriented company, began its consumer electronics operation because they predicted a shift in market demand from industrial to household clients. They thought that by learning from consumer electronics operations (including the establishment of distribution channels, marketing, etc.), they would be better equipped when the market shifted from industries to households. However, they had to scrap their European operations in the late 1980s since NEC's consumer electronics was always unprofitable. Simultaneously, the distribution side of the business is changing for the electronics industry around the world. In Europe, large discount distributors are making headway in retail businesses and, increasingly, Japanese firms in Europe are having to do business with them.

Furthermore, the establishment of the European Union encourages Japanese firms to consolidate their operations in Europe. Sharp, for instance, began locally based marketing for the European market in Germany in October 1995. The purpose of this reorganisation was to reflect the needs of customers better, particularly Europe's consumer markets. They have established *seikatsu sofuto centa* – a software research centre where various lifestyles and the use of consumer electronics are considered.

Finally, there is a consensus that electronics markets are shifting from industrial to consumer markets. Demand is increasing for products that formerly had only industrial applications but have now found consumer use (fax machines, cellular telephones, copiers, etc.). Most firms are eager to establish and/or strengthen distribution channels for consumer products and diversify into more sophisticated consumer products. The merging of consumer and industrial electronics poses a new challenge for some Japanese companies that are primarily industrially oriented. Many firms with origins in industrial electronics ignored general consumer demands since they catered to specific industrial clientele.[5] A shift to consumer markets would increase the importance of understanding market trends, thus increasing market research activities.

In an environment where boundaries between consumer and industrial electronics are increasingly blurred, firms are having to put some previously industrially oriented products on consumer distribution channels. For Japan's domestic corporate hierarchy, and as part of a major reorganisation in 1993, Toshiba moved its laptop operation from its computer division to its consumer electronics division, so that their laptops would be sold more efficiently as a consumer product. Toshiba has also opted for global localisation, by 'locating sales and marketing, production and product development in the regions the group serves' (Toshiba 1994).

Whether these initiatives are effective in promoting innovation remains to be seen. With the current economic downturn in much of Europe and Asia, it is difficult to isolate the effect of corporate reorganisation from economic cycles.

CONCLUSION

As Dicken (1994) has argued, multinational firms today need to be 'globally efficient, multinationally flexible and capable of capturing the benefits of worldwide learning all at the same time'. Interviews conducted with Japanese executives revealed that locating within a market is a subtle but critical tool for Japanese firms to function as 'global scanners' and enable them to compete more effectively in overseas markets. As the nature of competition shifts from cost-based competition to technology/knowledge-based competition, it has become increasingly clear that a successful technological venture is a nonlinear process that combines knowledge of both the supply side – technological advances – and the demand side – consumer needs and preferences – (see for instance Castells 1989 and Hepworth 1989). For multinational firms to achieve a worldwide dominance today, 'localisation advantages' – presence in lead markets where technologies are abundant and clients are sophisticated – constitutes a critical element for knowledge creation and sustained business success.

Industry insiders agree that worldwide learning through localisation is the advantage that Japanese firms are striving for when globalising their operations. The importance of capturing worldwide learning has increased, as firms face sluggish growth and intensified international competition in much of the industrialised world. To be an effective global scanner, it is critical that firms have a significant operational presence in markets where an abundance of technology and market information reside. Thus in spite of cost disadvantages, firms continue to hold on to operations in high-cost metropolitan areas of Western Europe in order to receive the advantages of localisation. However unquantifiable, subtle and vague these localisation advantages may be, industry insiders continue to stress presence as one of the most important requirements for success in overseas markets.

NOTES

1. My thanks to Nicholas Phelps for his invaluable comments on this chapter.

2. This database was constructed from information supplied from the Electronics Industry Association of Japan (EIAJ) and Tokyo Keizai shuppan. It includes establishments in Japanese ownership (defined as those with at least 10 per cent Japanese equity).

3. This aspect has been elaborated by Kline and Rosenberg (1986), who characterise the process of innovation as a series of multidirectional feedback links (a chain-linked model) rather than a linear, sequential model.

4. Recently, however, Philips acquired a 50 per cent stake in Grundig.

5. The exception to this general trend is Sony, which has been primarily oriented toward consumer electronics. Sony entered the PC market aggressively in the US (Fisher 1996; *Wall Street Journal*, 1996).

KEITH CHAPMAN[1]

8 Merger/Acquisition Activity and Regional Cohesion in the EU

INTRODUCTION

High levels of merger and acquisition activity[2] since the late 1980s have been characterised as the fourth 'wave' affecting developed economies following earlier 'waves', first at the turn of the century, then in the 1920s and early 1930s and later in the 1960s (see Sachwald 1994). These earlier 'waves' were, however, largely associated with the USA and the UK. Indeed, mergers and acquisitions have been described as a distinctively 'Anglo-Saxon phenomenon' (Bishop and Kay 1993, p. 3) and they have played a less significant role in shaping the commercial structure of other national economies. Nevertheless, this situation is changing and the impacts of the fourth 'wave' have certainly been felt in other European countries and in Japan (Walter 1994). Another important difference evident in recent events is the greater importance of cross-border deals relative to transactions conceived and implemented at the national scale (see Cooke 1988; UNCTC 1989; Waverman 1991; Hamill 1994; Economist Intelligence Unit 1996). The rise in cross-border transactions is linked to various dimensions of change associated with 'globalisation', including regional economic integration. This chapter describes recent trends in merger/acquisition activity in the EU, with particular reference to cross-border deals. The factors encouraging this activity are reviewed before examining the implications for various strands of public policy, notably relating to regional development and the cohesion agenda.

TRENDS IN MERGERS/ACQUISITIONS

Sachwald (1994, p. 17) notes, with reference to Europe, that 'a detailed examination of mergers, acquisitions and co-operative agreements is made difficult by the lack of adequate data'. Several data-bases have been deployed to draw together information from the multiple press reports, trade and financial publications which are the primary sources. These data-bases include Amdata, which is produced by the publishers of *Acquisitions Monthly*, DOME, started in 1971 by the Commission Directorate General for Competition (DG IV); and a KPMG data-base focusing upon cross-border statistics at a global scale. A recent assessment of these data-bases noted that 'there are many disparities between bases' and that 'particular care is required when using them' (CEC 1994, p. 14). The most accessible overall summaries are provided by the Annual Reports on Competition Policy to 1993 and an annual supplement to *European Economy* from 1994. Figure 8.1 expresses trends in different categories of mergers/acquisitions from 1986 to 1995 based on Amdata information. The trends reflect the number of transactions rather than their value.[3] Amdata makes no claim to provide a comprehensive record of transactions, but figure 8.1 may be regarded as a reliable indicator of change in the overall level of merger/acquisition activity.

FIGURE 8.1: MERGERS/MAJORITY ACQUISITIONS INVOLVING EU COMPANIES 1986–95

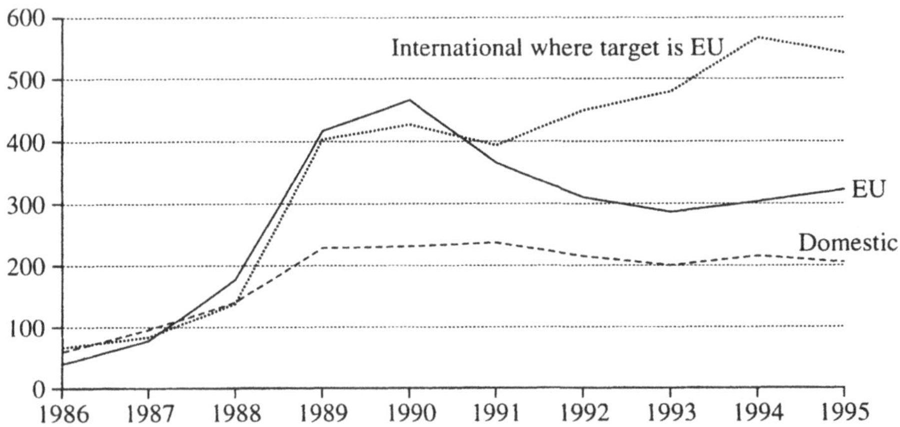

Index: average 1986–88 = 100

Figure 8.1 distinguishes between 'domestic', involving companies from the same industry, 'EU', involving companies from at least two member states, and 'international' deals in which EU firms are acquired by non-EU firms. The increase in the level of merger/acquisition activity, especially cross-border transactions (that is 'EU' and 'international') is clear and there is no doubt that this activity has been at historically high levels over the last ten years and certainly exceeds an earlier boost associated with the formation of the EEC (Yannopolous 1990). Although figure 8.1 shows a decline in the level of activity at the beginning of the 1990s, a recovery has been sustained since 1994 and '1997 looks likely to be a record year for mergers and acquisitions' [in Europe] (*Financial Times* 1997). It is also worth noting that Europe replaced the United States as the principal focus of inward acquisition investment in the global economy in the late 1980s, and the continuing attractiveness of EU companies as targets to non-EU acquirers is evident in the sustained upward trend of 'international' transactions in figure 8.1. The graph provides no indication of the absolute number of transactions. 'Domestic' transactions have increased less rapidly than cross-border deals, but they account for more than 70 per cent of the events included in the Amdata record upon which figure 8.1 is based (CEC 1996a, p. 117). This numerical dominance overstates their economic significance, however, in the sense that cross-border transactions tend to be larger (in value terms). Involvement in such transactions also varies among countries. Not surprisingly, cross-border transactions account for a higher proportion of total transactions involving companies based in the smaller, necessarily 'open' EU economies such as Austria and Ireland. There are also national differences in the ratio of acquiring to target firms in cross-border transactions. Companies based in the UK, France, Netherlands and Sweden tend to be more actively involved as acquirers while German, Spanish and Italian firms are disproportionately represented in the population of targets. Some implications of these differences in the balance of trade in corporate control within the EU, as expressed by the national identities of acquirers and targets, are considered later in this chapter.

There is a sectoral, as well as a geographical, dimension to merger/acquisition activity. Walter (1994) demonstrated very strong similarities in the sectoral distribution of merger/acquisition activity in the United States and Europe between 1985 and 1991. He ranked seventy sectors (classified by two-digit SIC codes) in terms of both the value and number of transactions. Spearman Rank correlation coefficients confirmed highly significant associations between the US and European data. 'Chemicals', 'oil and gas extraction' and 'food products' were, for example, all included in the top ten in both data sets (by number and value). Although these sectors, especially chemicals and food products, continue to figure prominently in European merger/acquisition activity, there has been a significant shift in the relative importance of the manufacturing and service sectors, with the former accounting for more than half of the transactions between 1986 and 1992 and the latter taking the lead from 1993.

It is clear that mergers/acquisitions are an important aspect of contemporary economic change, especially in the EU. They are implicated in 'a tidal wave of massive organisational and geographical restructuring [in Europe]' (Dicken and Öberg 1996, p. 15). Before considering some of the consequences of this restructuring with reference to the impacts of corporate strategies upon countries and communities, it is desirable to review some of the factors responsible for the proliferation of merger/acquisition activity in general and for European cross-border deals in particular.

MERGERS/ACQUISITIONS AND ECONOMIC INTEGRATION

Numerous motivating factors have been identified in studies of the merger/acquisition route to corporate growth. Explanations may be divided into four, overlapping strands. First, deriving from behavioural theories of the firm, mergers and acquisitions have been viewed as effective methods of fulfilling the presumed over-riding managerial objective of maximising sales growth (Cyert and March 1963). Second, attention is focused upon the interests of shareholders rather than managers in explanations which employ the logic of accountancy to explain the take-over process in terms of the ratio of the stock-market value of assets to their reported book value. Third, acquisitions are regarded as a consequence of the perceived economic benefits to the acquiring firm deriving from the reduced costs and/or enhanced revenues of an enlarged enterprise. Finally, longer-term strategic objectives, especially related to market control, may motivate the acquirer. In practice, specific merger/acquisition events can rarely be explained in terms of a single factor and the different 'strands' are, in any case, not mutually exclusive. It is often difficult, for example, to disentangle economic and strategic considerations. As a generalisation, these seem more relevant to an understanding of cross-border mergers and acquisitions than explanations based on behavioural

FIGURE 8.2: CORPORATE MOTIVATIONS IN MERGERS/ ACQUISITIONS

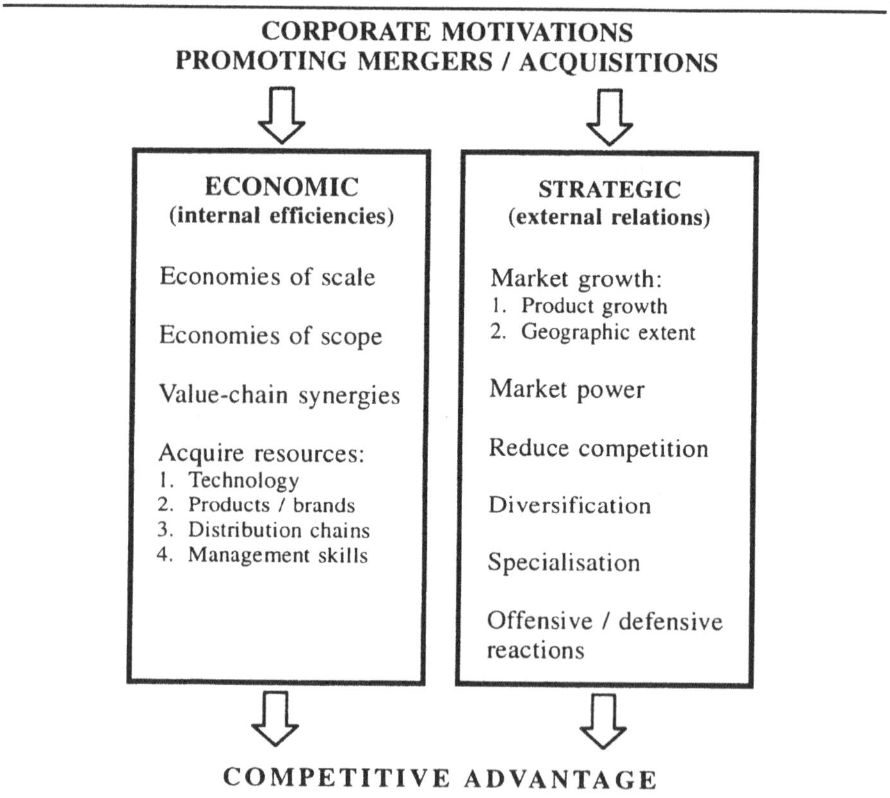

concepts or on share values. More specifically, there are good reasons to suggest that the kind of economic and strategic factors relevant to an understanding of merger/acquisition activity (figure 8.2) have been affected by the creation of the Single European Market (SEM).

Conventional theories or models of international production regard trade as a substitute for foreign direct investment. The rapid growth of intra-European trade during the first phase of European integration in the 1960s and 1970s was consistent with this view as the elimination of barriers made it easier for individual companies to serve the enlarged market by exports from their domestic plants (see Acocella 1992). However, the sharp rise in cross-border direct investment within Europe since the early 1980s (see Eurostat 1995) occurred at a time when ever closer economic integration may have been expected to reinforce the earlier corporate preference for trade over direct investment. Published statistics rarely distinguish between the different forms of foreign direct investment, but the growth in mergers/acquisitions indicated in figure 8.1 is directly related to the extension of cross-border operations. In the USA, for example, the proportion (by value) of acquisitions to total inward investment grew from 67 per cent in the first half of the 1980s to almost 80 per cent in the second half and similar trends occurred in the EU (OECD 1992, p. 21).

Several factors have contributed to the growth of merger/acquisition activity and it is difficult to isolate 'European' from 'global' influences. The realisation of economic efficiency gains was, on a strategic level, the fundamental objective underlying the creation of the SEM. The various studies of 'the cost of non-Europe', culminating in the Cechinni report (1988), were directed towards demonstrating the magnitude of these gains. One aspect of this agenda was the competitive position of European companies in global markets. It was recognised that the legacy of fragmented national markets was reflected in the smaller size of many European companies relative to their US and Japanese counterparts, a situation which weakened their ability to compete at the global scale. This issue was addressed in a study which sought to identify 'industries in which merger activity is *prima facie* beneficial' (Jacquemin *et al.* 1989). The study was, essentially, concerned with balancing the anticipated economic efficiency gains of larger companies against the possible risks of resulting reductions in competition within Europe. The sectors in which 'substantial efficiency gains' from mergers were predicted to more than offset the dangers of monopolisation shared certain common characteristics including: large economies of scale; high growth; openness to international trade; rapid rates of technical change. The global dimension is clearly important in sectors with these characteristics, not least because of the strategic need to establish a major European corporate presence in fast-growing, technology-intensive sectors.

It is clear that increased merger and acquisition activity may be consistent with the wider political and economic objectives of the European project in such sectors, but different considerations may promote similar activity in mature or declining industries. Although undesirable from the political perspective of competition policy, acquisitions in mature and declining industries are often commercially attractive and there are good reasons why they have become even more attractive within the SEM. Closely related to the premise that the SEM will promote economic efficiency is the implicit assumption of overcapacity in many sectors deriving from the inheritance of fragmented national markets. Such overcapacity is more likely to exist in mature sectors. By creating an enlarged corporate structure extending across national boundaries, mergers and acquisitions may be expected to facilitate the rationalisation of capacity. Thus by enhancing awareness of overcapacity at the European scale and by raising the prospect of increased competition in previously protected national markets, the SEM may indirectly encourage mergers and acquisitions motivated by industrial restructuring.

The SEM may be expected to stimulate mergers and acquisitions not only for economic reasons operating at the industry or sector level, but also for strategic reasons relevant to the behaviour of companies. The elimination of internal tariff and non-tariff barriers provides encouragement to firms to look beyond their traditional domestic markets to the wider European market. Such steps may be taken to derive first-mover advantages in anticipation of corresponding external threats to the domestic market. It has already been noted that trade and investment are not substitutes and that success in new geographic markets often depends upon a direct commercial presence, reflecting the importance of such factors as market intelligence and customer relations. Direct investment in production capacity in a new market brings geographic proximity but not necessarily 'presence' in the widest sense. Acquisition of an existing company is often a more attractive method of market entry because it brings not only production capacity but also less tangible commercial benefits such as established brand names, distribution networks and customer loyalty. These factors are all the more important when, as in Europe, language and other cultural barriers are more durable than economic ones. The strategic benefits of cross-border acquisitions in securing market access within the EU apply with even greater force to non-EU companies. Perceptions of 'Fortress Europe' may be expected to stimulate inward investment, including foreign acquisitions of EU companies.

The immediate factors encouraging one company to acquire the assets of another may be quite specific, but it is clear that there are certain general influences, related to the imperatives of economic integration, stimulating merger/acquisition activity in Europe. The Annual Reports on Competition Policy provide some circumstantial evidence of the impact of these influences. The DOME data-base (see above) was used to compile the statistical summaries in the annual reports to 1992. Reference to these summaries indicates that the share of 'community' (that is involving companies from different member states) mergers/acquisitions increased from 18.7 per cent of the total recorded transactions in 1983–4 to a peak of 41.3 per cent in 1990–1. The proportion of 'community' transactions in the Amdata record, which replaced DOME as the Commission's main source of annual merger/acquisition statistics in 1993, is much lower. This reflects fundamental differences in the scope of the two data-bases. DOME is restricted 'to operations involving the 1000 largest European industrial enterprises, the 500 largest worldwide firms, and the most important in the service sector' (CEC 1994, p. 14). The very large firms which are the focus of the DOME data-base are more likely to be involved in cross-border transactions than the wider population of firms, extending across a broader size-spectrum, that are included in Amdata. Nevertheless, Amdata also shows an increase in 'community' transactions from 15.5 per cent of the total record for the period 1986–9 to 18.7 per cent for 1990–5 (CEC 1996a, p. 117).

TABLE 8.1: DECLARED MOTIVES IN EC MERGERS/MAJORITY ACQUISITIONS (%)

	1985–6	1986–7	1987–8	1988–9	1989–90	1990–1	1991–2
Expansion	17.1	22.1	19.6	31.3	26.9	27.7	32.4
Diversification	17.6	5.8	8.3	7.1	3.0	2.8	2.1
Strengthening market position	10.6	11.5	25.4	42.2	45.3	48.2	44.4
Rationalisation and synergies	46.5	42.0	34.4	14.4	17.7	13.3	16.2
R&D	2.4	5.3	0.7	0.0	0.6	0.0	0.0
Other	5.9	13.3	11.6	4.9	6.4	8.0	5.0
	100.0	100.0	100.0	100.0	100.0	100.0	100.0

Source: CEC 1994

The general increase in the proportion of cross-border mergers/acquisitions within the EU immediately before and after 1992 is suggestive of corporate preparations for and adjustments to the SEM. More direct evidence of the influence of market factors is provided by table 8.1. This is a summary of the declared motivations of acquiring companies included in the DOME record to 1991–2.[4] The increasing importance of 'strengthening market position' and 'expansion' relative to other motivations is clear. Table 8.2 includes 'national' as well as cross-border (that is intra-EU and 'foreign' acquisitions of EU firms) transactions. Most analysts agree that market access is even more important in cross-border deals where it has been the dominating strategic influence upon acquiring firms – an influence shaped by the wider context of economic integration (see Davis 1990; Mayes 1991; Thomsen and Woolcock 1993; Dunning 1997a).

MERGERS/ACQUISITIONS AND CORPORATE CONTROL

Merger/acquisition activity has contributed to a significant increase in concentration in the EU. The market share of the top hundred firms in the manufacturing and energy industries of the EU rose from 14.8 per cent in 1982 to 20.0 per cent in 1988 (Amin and Tomaney 1995, p. 176), and 'For the average industry at EU level, the share of total sales by the leading four firms has increased from 20.5 to 22.8 per cent between 1987 and 1993' (CEC 1996a, p. 119). These average figures conceal wide variations between individual sectors with some of the biggest increases in industries associated with public procurement and substantial R&D expenditure (including aerospace and telecommunications). Although increased market power is not automatically associated with improved competitiveness, these trends are superficially consistent with the Commission's industrial policy objective of creating 'Eurochampions' capable of challenging US and Japanese firms in global markets. These trends are also a timely reminder, in the context of current preoccupations with small firms and 'flexibility', of the reality of increasing corporate power. This power finds expression in the role of the transnational corporation (TNC) as 'the single most important shaper – directly and indirectly – of the space economy at all geographical scales' (Nilsson and Schamp 1996, p. 123). Tangible evidence of this role is provided by changing corporate geographies resulting from mergers/acquisitions and by the collective impacts of such changes upon the European urban and regional system (see Fielding 1994; Nilsson and Schamp 1996). These impacts may be considered on two levels: first, with reference to the transfer of ownership itself; second, with reference to the nature of any subsequent adjustments in the enlarged corporate system affecting, for example, the size and distribution of production capacity and the disposition of various functions between centres of activity.

Mergers/acquisitions, by definition, involve changes in ownership and, therefore, in corporate control. These changes have a geographical dimension whether mergers/acquisitions are cross-border or take place within a single country. The potentially undesirable consequences of external control for countries and communities have attracted considerable attention in the economic development literature. This debate has been conducted with reference to external control at both regional and international scales. At the regional level, interest has focused on evaluating the economic impact of greenfield branch plants, although a subsidiary theme has been concerned with the consequences of the external acquisition of indigenous companies. In reviewing the evidence on this latter theme, Love (1989) concluded that it presented a discouraging picture incorporating the loss of key functions (with implications for innovative potential), weaker local linkages and diminished multiplier effects. These concerns are paralleled at the international scale where foreign penetration of national economies has always been a sensitive political issue. In the 1960s, inward investment by US companies was perceived by some as a threat to European economic sovereignty (Servan-Schreiber 1968). By the 1980s, the role was reversed with European and Japanese firms held responsible for the foreign take-over of corporate America (Hamill and Castledine 1992). Mergers/acquisitions have replaced greenfield investment as the principal mechanism of foreign direct investment, but the ownership and, by extension, control issues remain the same.

They reflect the premise that the presumed commercial benefits of a merger/acquisition will accrue disproportionately in favour of the country in which ultimate ownership lies. This premise has potentially profound implications for economic and social cohesion within the EU. These implications derive from the connections between two aspects of recent merger/acquisition activity: first, the role of economic integration is promoting such activity; second, the geographical dimension of cross-border activity as revealed by the nationality of acquiring and target companies. The evidence suggesting a causal link between economic integration and increasing merger/acquisition activity, especially cross-border, was reviewed in the previous section. Attention now turns to the evidence on the changing geography of corporate control.

Not surprisingly, companies based in the larger EU economies have been involved in a substantial proportion of EU mergers/acquisitions, although the level of activity is not directly related to the size of the economy. Reference to the Amdata record for 1990 to 1995 suggests that firms based in the UK, Netherlands and Ireland, for example, were involved in a significantly higher proportion than might have been expected on the basis of the size of their respective national economies relative to the rest of the EU. Conversely, firms from Italy and Spain were under-represented. Focusing attention on cross-border transactions, between-country differences in the *level* of activity are of less interest than differences in the *pattern* of activity as reflected in the respective roles of national companies as acquirers and targets. The data required to examine such patterns are not readily available, but detailed information has been assembled for the chemical industry, which has been characterised by higher levels of merger/acquisition activity than any other manufacturing sector. The Chemical Business Newsbase (CBNB), which is an abstracting service provided by the Royal Society of Chemistry, was used to derive a record of mergers/acquisitions occurring within the EU[5] from 1986 to 1994 inclusive. Expressing this record in quantitative terms (either as the number of value of transactions) raised significant methodological problems, not least the complexities of ownership relations. Mergers/acquisitions are better characterised as processes than events in the sense that the point at which one company secures a controlling interest in another may be the outcome of an evolving collaborative relationship which has proceeded from a loose alliance through successive incremental extensions of its financial stake. For the purposes of the study, an acquisition was defined as occurring when control passed from the target to the acquirer or its parent companies. Following this operational definition, a total of 2,860 merger/acquisition events was identified. Careful

TABLE 8.2: MERGERS/ACQUISITIONS IN EC CHEMICAL INDUSTRY 1986–1994 BY NATIONALITY OF ACQUIRING AND TARGET COMPANIES (NUMBER OF EVENTS)

Country of origin – acquirer	**Country of origin – target**													
	Belg	*Den*	*Ire*	*France*	*Germ*	*Greece*	*Italy*	*Lux*	*Neth*	*Port*	*Spain*	*UK*	*Mix EC*	*Total*
Belgium	1			4	10		7		1	1	5	8	3	40
Denmark	1	10		2	6		1					4	1	25
Ireland			3				1		2			10	1	17
France	8	2	2	168	38	2	43	1	5	6	26	25	11	337
Germany	7	5		44	213	3	28		20	5	16	27	5	373
Greece														0
Italy	1	1		14	4		70		2		4	3	1	100
Luxembourg				1										1
Netherlands	5	6	1	10	10		7		27		4	14	2	86
Portugal										2				2
Spain				5			2			3	18	4		32
UK	9	1	5	49	43		25		12		25	341	16	526
Mix EC	2	1	2	9	10		8		5	2	5	19	1	64
Total	34	26	13	306	334	5	192	1	74	19	103	455	41	1 603

Source: K Chapman and H Edmond, University of Aberdeen, 1997

cross-checking suggests that this record is more accurate and comprehensive than is available from any other source and for any other sector.

Table 8.2 is based on a subset of 1,603 mergers/acquisitions in which the ultimate ownership of both the acquirer and the target lies within the EU (that is excluding acquisitions by non-EU firms). It summarises the geographical pattern of corporate growth and control in the EU chemical industry. The rows represent acquisitions by companies based in each country and the columns indicate the national 'home' of targets. The diagonal indicates mergers/acquisitions involving companies from the same country; all other cells refer to cross-border transactions. The overwhelming dominance of UK, French and German companies in merger/acquisition activity is clear. This dominance acquires a particular significance when attention is focused on the ratio, for each country, of acquiring to target companies in cross-border transactions. A ratio exceeding 1.0 suggests an extension of corporate control by a country's national companies; a ratio of less than 1.0 suggests a loss of corporate control at the domestic levels.[6] Table 8.3 adds an extra step in calculating this ratio by expressing the acquisitions and targets in each country as a percentage of the respective totals. The ratio is then derived by expressing each country's percentage share of all acquisitions relative to its corresponding share of all targets. This approach is adopted to allow a comparison to be made between the data for the chemical industry derived from CBNB (included in table 8.2) and published information contained in a recent Commission report (CEC, 1996a, p. 118). This latter information shows the percentage breakdown of acquisitions and targets by country for cross-border mergers/acquisitions in all sectors between 1990 and 1995.[7]

There are considerable similarities in the ratios for individual countries derived from the chemical industry data and those derived from the data relating to all sectors, despite the fact that they cover different, partially overlapping periods. Only two countries – Belgium and Germany – have acquirer/target ratios for chemicals and all sectors lying on opposite sides of the 1.0 threshold value. Both have been net gainers of corporate control in chemicals, but net losers across the broader spectrum of economic activities. The position of German firms as targets for acquirers from other countries is surprising in view of their traditional competitive strength. More research is required to solve this problem, although it may be speculated that the size of the national economy makes the acquisition of German firms an attractive route to market entry. The questions raised by the case of Germany should not, however, divert attention from the overall consistency of the acquirer/-target ratios in table 8.3. These ratios suggest a systematic transfer of ownership from the countries of southern Europe to companies based in northern Europe. Expressed in terms of the number of transactions, the most significant net gainers are the UK and France; the most significant net losers are Italy and Spain.

TABLE 8.3: ACQUIRING AND TARGET COMPANIES BY COUNTRY:
a. chemical industry 1986–94
b. all sectors 1990–5

	(a) Chemical industry[1]			(b) All sectors[2]		
Country	***Acquirer (per cent)***	***Target (per cent)***	***Acquirer/ Target***	***Acquirer (per cent)***	***Target (per cent)***	***Acquirer/ Target***
Austria	nd	nd		1.7	1.3	1.31
Belgium	5.2	4.3	1.21	2.9	5.0	0.58
Denmark	2.0	2.0	1.00	4.8	3.9	1.23
Finland	nd	nd	—	4.0	3.1	1.29
France	22.5	18.3	1.23	18.5	13.8	1.34
Germany	21.3	16.1	1.32	14.4	25.5	0.56
Greece	0.0	0.7	α	0.1	0.4	0.25
Ireland	1.9	1.3	1.46	2.9	0.9	3.22
Italy	4.1	16.2	0.25	4.3	6.9	0.62
Luxembourg	0.0	0.0	—	1.0	0.6	1.67
Netherlands	7.7	6.5	1.18	9.1	7.5	1.21
Portugal	0.0	2.3	α	0.1	1.2	0.08
Spain	1.9	11.3	0.17	1.5	8.1	0.18
Sweden	nd	nd	—	8.2	4.5	1.82
United Kingdom	24.3	15.4	1.58	26.5	17.5	1.51
Mix EU*	9.1	5.6	1.62	na	na	na
EUR 12/15**	100.0	100.0		100.0	100.0	

Sources: 1 Adapted from personal database
2 Adopted from data in CEC 1996a

Notes:
* Relates to transactions where parent companies of acquirer and/or target are based in different EU countries
** EUR 12 for chemical industry; EUR15 for all sectors na not available nd no data oc cannot be calculated
na not available nd no data α cannot be calculated

MERGERS/ACQUISITIONS AND INDUSTRY RESTRUCTURING

This pattern is consistent with wider concerns regarding the implications of economic integration for 'north–south' relationships within Europe, but there is a lack of empirical research into the impact of mergers/acquisitions upon corporate systems. It is also difficult to resolve the counter-factual problem of establishing what would have happened in the absence of a change in ownership. It is easy to attribute factory closures and job losses following take-over of a national by a foreign firm to the loss of control, but it is important to remember that these undesirable trends may have occurred anyway or may even have been more pronounced where the acquisition was a failing company. This possibility emphasises the need to challenge the implicit assumption that the transfer of ownership beyond the boundaries of regions or countries necessarily has negative impacts upon their economic prospects. Indeed, changes in ownership are not always a precursor of changes in the disposition of facilities and functions. When market-entry is the principal motivation for an acquisition, it may be important to retain the 'local' presence of the acquired company's facilities. Increased market power based on an acquisition may also inhibit change. For example, Holmes (1989, p. 526) suggests that the wave of mergers/acquisitions in Europe in the 1960s and 1970s did not produce 'the expected rationalisation of production' because 'an oligopolistic live and let live atmosphere reduced the necessity to close old inefficient plants'. Despite these cases, there is no doubt that cross-border mergers/acquisitions are generally followed by visible change in corporate geographies.

It is difficult to generalise regarding the nature of such corporate restructuring and, therefore, its impact upon places. The specific motives of acquiring companies and the industry context influence the outcomes of post-merger/acquisition adjustments. Simplifying considerably, it is possible to detect two emerging trends in the geography of the European production system: first, the concentration of production within industries and companies at fewer sites; second, the development, in the largest companies, of corporate locational hierarchies extending across Europe. Mergers/acquisitions, especially cross-border transactions, have accelerated these trends by providing opportunities for acquiring companies to review the organisation of their enlarged corporate systems.

The elimination of frontier controls and improvements in transport infrastructure have effectively reduced the 'friction of distance' in Europe. This has altered the balance between production and distribution costs in some industries where the benefits of economies of scale and scope associated with the geographical concentration of production have more than offset any rise in distribution costs deriving from the extension of market areas (Brown 1993). The significance of this shift is a matter of debate. Phelps (1997, p. 49) notes that several factors, including public procurement policies and technical changes in methods of production, have inhibited any trend towards the concentration of capacity in fewer, larger plants.

Nevertheless, several mature or declining industries have displayed this characteristic. The European synthetic fertilizer industry, for example, has experienced major reductions in capacity and employment (from 140,000 in 1980 to 28,000 in 1995 (CEC 1996b, p. 2)). Mergers/acquisitions have led to increased concentration ratios with the top five producers accounting for 70.4 and 74.2 per cent of European capacity in the key products of ammonium nitrate and urea respectively in 1996 compared with corresponding percentages of 26.9 and 46.1 in 1981. They have also facilitated plant closures, and the number of production sites was reduced from sixty-one to forty-one for ammonium nitrate and from thirty-five to seventeen for urea over the same period. Smaller plants in peripheral agricultural areas, especially in France and Spain, have been most vulnerable to closure, and the net result of this rationalisation has been a significant shift in the distribution of fertilizer capacity across the EU with Belgium and the Netherlands accounting for more than 30 per cent by 1996 compared with approximately 20 per cent in 1981.

Mergers/acquisitions are not only associated with changes in production facilities but also with adjustments in the distribution of key corporate functions. Spatial divisions of labour have attracted much attention at national (see Massey 1984) and global (see Fröbel *et al.* 1980) scales. They have been less evident at the intermediate, continental scale. However, the growing importance of regional trading blocs is encouraging large companies to refine and develop locational hierarchies within these relatively new elements of economic organisation (see Cantwell 1992; Dicken and Quevit 1994). Only a few studies have made an explicit link between such hierarchies and regional development in Europe (see Amin *et al.* 1992; Howells 1992), but they clearly have the potential to widen the gap between 'core' and 'periphery' as control and R&D functions are clustered in the major metropolitan city regions (see Rozenblat and Pumain 1993; Curbelo and Albuqurque 1994; Amin and Tomaney 1995).

CONCLUSIONS

Mergers and acquisitions have played a major role in the recent restructuring of the European production system. There is a massive literature examining mergers/acquisitions from the perspective of industrial and competition policies. However, this activity also has implications for regional development and the cohesion agenda as a result of the connections between evolving corporate geographies and the places affected by decisions to close or expand factories, to transfer functions, to change suppliers and so on. Such decisions are obviously not restricted to the aftermath of mergers/acquisitions, but these circumstances necessarily invite a reappraisal of corporate strategies. Love (1994) argues that the collective impact of such reappraisals will exacerbate regional economic imbalances within the EU because of the increase in external control. On the other hand, the increasing complexity of corporate organisational structures means that external control is not always synonymous with limited autonomy and innovative capacity (see Dicken *et al.* 1994). These contradictions can only be resolved by detailed empirical study of the implications of mergers/acquisitions for companies, industries and places.

NOTES

1. Helen Edmond (Department of Geography, University of Aberdeen) was largely responsible for compiling the data-base of mergers/acquisitions in the EU chemical industry.

2. For the purposes of this chapter 'mergers' and 'acquisitions' are treated as synonymous. In fact, the number of acquisitions involving the transfer of ultimate control (that is more than a 50 per cent stake) from one company to another is far greater than the numbers of mergers.

3. It is difficult to obtain reliable information on the value of transactions. A general picture may be obtained by simple counts of the number of mergers/acquisitions, but this approach does not necessarily accurately represent their economic significance. Relatively few mega-deals typically account for a high proportion of the total value of mergers and acquisitions in any single year. Such deals have more profound potential implications for economic activity and employment at a European (or global) scale than any number of small-value transactions.

4. More recent information is not available because motivations are not identified in Amdata which replaced DOME in 1993 as the data source for Annual Reports on Competition Policy.

5. Excluding Austria, Finland and Sweden.

6. The qualifications expressed in note 3 obviously apply to the interpretation of this ratio.

7. The number of transactions represented by the percentages is not specified in the published source.

PART III:

NATIONAL EXPERIENCES OF FDI

9 Attracting Foreign Direct Investment to East European Economies: Can Lessons Be Learned from the UK Experience?

INTRODUCTION

The aim of this chapter is to examine the extent to which East European Economies (EEEs) have succeeded in attracting foreign direct investment (FDI) during the 1990s and to consider whether there are any lessons which can be learned from the well-developed inward investment policy of the UK and its regions.[1] A discussion of the theories of FDI and the multinational enterprise (MNE) is eschewed (for recent reviews, see Dunning 1993a and Caves 1996) and the chapter begins with a brief consideration of the locational requirements of MNEs, host country factors associated with the attraction of FDI and some specific factors pertaining to the EEEs. This is followed by an analysis, based on secondary data, of stocks of FDI in the EEEs and flows into them. The chapter concludes with a discussion of policy issues.

MNEs' LOCATIONAL REQUIREMENTS

There is considerable evidence on the locational requirements of inward investors (see Christodoulou 1996, for a review and annotated bibliography). The major locational requirements relate to labour, infrastructure, economic and political factors, and quality of life. With respect to labour the requirements are: availability of labour generally and university graduates in particular; low costs and high productivity; flexible employment legislation; good industrial relations; language skills and an effective Vocational Education and Training (VET) system. Infrastructure requirements include a good transport infrastructure; low cost and good provision of utilities; suitable sites and premises; and clearly specified environmental regulations and procedures.

While the availability of suitable serviced sites with development consent and expansion possibilities is still very important, a good information technology (IT) and telecommunications infrastructure is of increasing importance. Economic and political requirements include suitable economic and fiscal policies; the availability of financial incentives; political stability and a welcoming attitude. Quality of life requirements include cultural affinity; good education; low crime rates; good housing and leisure facilities; and a relatively low cost of living. In addition, there are sector specific requirements with respect to markets, a track record in the sector, the presence of related and supporting industries, and close ties with the nation or locality.

There is no single factor that will successfully attract an inward investor although the absence of one key factor can lose a project. 'It is a mix of requirements structured in a competitive package matched to the specific business needs of an inward investor that is crucial' (Christodoulou 1996, p. 21). However, two overall trends in locational requirements are noteworthy: the increasing importance of quality factors, such as quality of labour, as a result of the production process becoming more knowledge based; and the decrease in the relative importance of location factors that operate at a national level as opposed to regional trading bloc factors such as the completion of the Single European Market (Netherlands Economic Institute and Ernst and Young 1993).

Christodoulou's review (1996) suggests that for a nation or region to reach the shortlist for any inward investment project it must meet a minimum set of criteria. These are: an adequate supply of quality labour especially those with intermediate skills; access to markets and suppliers; a track record of success with endorsement by existing inward investors; a good image; and a welcoming attitude and professional approach towards inward investors. Once these criteria are met a number of other factors may come into play such as financial incentives and tax treatment, sites and premises and the cost of labour. Any one could be crucial depending on the stage of decision-making and where other requirements are equal between regions or sites. For example, the role of financial incentives is important at the point of determining the regional choice and is also particularly important for high-tech capital-intensive projects.

FDI AND HOST COUNTRY FACTORS

Dunning (1997c) provides evidence, based on executives' perceptions, that MNEs derive an important proportion of their competitive advantages from their presence in foreign countries. Two aspects of the evidence are particularly relevant here. First, there are some differences in the perceptions of firms depending upon their country of origin. With respect to access to resources and assets, firms from high-wage economies such as the USA rank the sourcing of unskilled labour in foreign countries relatively highly while Japanese investors do so for foreign natural resources. MNEs with a European or US origin value access in foreign locations to created assets, such as organisational capacity and management, more than do Japanese investors. With respect to demand conditions, inter-firm competition and related and supporting activities, European-owned firms seem to rely more on foreign sources of competitiveness than do firms of US or Japanese origin. A second aspect of the evidence relates to the different types of competitive advantage available to MNEs which are associated with particular foreign countries. Developing countries are perceived to provide access to natural resources, the USA to provide more than the average share of managerial assets and consumer demand conditions, and Germany and Japan are regarded as providing more than the average share of technological assets. Relative to other countries, Germany, Japan and the USA are perceived as good locations for establishing inter-firm linkages and these are perceived to offer a more competitive stimulus.

The review by Caves (1996) contains a discussion of the theoretical propositions and the results of empirical tests on the characteristics of host countries which may attract or deter FDI. His review suggests that a number of factors are of importance. Contrary to the theoretical proposition that there will be large capital inflows to capital-poor countries and large capital outflows from capital-rich countries, the evidence suggests that host country FDI increases with national income per capita. FDI is also induced by tariff walls with investors setting up production facilities within the tariff boundary. Other host country factors which attract FDI are a liberal policy towards foreign investment, a sound legal framework of industrial property rights and a good economic and physical infrastructure. Factors which deter investment include a difficult language and different culture, political instability and a high-risk environment. Mixed evidence exists with respect to labour costs, but evidence on two-way FDI shows that flows are affected by differences in skilled labour endowments. With respect to flows between countries, one connection is through colonisation, with exports to the colony replaced by direct investment after independence. Other factors affecting flows between countries include neighbour effects, a common language and similar cultures.

EEEs AND FDI: SOME SPECIFIC FACTORS

Estrin *et al.* (1997, p. 13) have argued that the main deterrents to FDI in the EEEs have been 'risk and uncertainty, the poor legal framework and weak infrastructure, and a lack of reliable information about the region'. Other inhibiting factors have been difficulties in finding suitable local suppliers and a lack of managerial expertise. Richet (1996, p. 59) has argued that while the 'lack of attractiveness of EEEs can largely be explained by the existence of many factors remaining from the old system', the changes which have taken place have opened up new opportunities for FDI. Institutional changes and modifications of the economic environment have taken place in all EEEs. These have included privatisation programmes, the clarifying of property rights, the adoption and enforcement of bankruptcy laws, the adoption of favourable legislation towards FDI, price liberalisation, the creation of financial markets and the quasi-convertibility of currencies. This has provided a more appropriate context for foreign investors to be attracted by the new markets available in Eastern Europe. However, Sadler *et al.* (1993) have pointed out, with respect to motor car ownership specifically, that a large potential market may take a number of years to materialise. Estrin *et al.* (1997) have argued that, while expected market growth can attract FDI to the region, other factors include the trade policy regime and costs of inputs. For example, they argue that MNEs from outside the EU may invest in the expectation that a country may obtain full EU membership so that the MNE can operate inside the tariff barrier. With respect to input costs the main attraction is that labour costs, at least by Western standards, are low and are of relevance especially for firms from neighbouring countries such as Germany.

The potential benefits of FDI to the EEEs have been recognised. At the microeconomic level, FDI is seen as providing business expertise and Western technology and contributing to modernisation. As Hunya puts it: 'Foreigners transfer not only capital, but also knowledge of modern business behaviour and techniques' (Hunya 1992, p. 501). At the macro level, the flow of foreign capital is seen as a means to generate exports, substitute imports with domestic production and thereby help reduce the trade deficit (Gibb and Michalak 1994). However, one factor in deterring FDI by acquisition is the reluctance to sell 'crown jewels' to foreigners. Moreover, the average size of investment projects has been constrained by regulations concerning privatisations which limit the stake of foreign investors and by the process of privatisation through vouchers. It is also the case that some investments have been of the classic branch-plant type with limited local linkages, although some FDI has taken the form of 'relatively locally-embedded production facilities within a European production system' (Sadler *et al.* 1993, p. 348). It has been argued by Marton (1993), with particular respect to Hungary, that it is through the development of linkages that the positive contributions of MNEs can be enhanced.

THE EEEs: STOCKS AND FLOWS OF FDI

Global Context

Globally the level of FDI that flows into Central and Eastern Europe (EECs) is still relatively small despite significant growth in investment since 1990. At the start of the decade the stock of FDI in the EEEs was virtually non-existent, accounting for just 0.1 per cent of global foreign direct investment (table 9.1). By 1995 the stock had increased twelvefold to account for 1.25 per cent of global FDI. At this time just over $33 billion had been invested by foreign-owned companies in the EEEs. However, the region, in terms of accumulated investment, still lagged behind other developing regions such as Africa, which accounted for 2.2 per cent of the stock, and Latin America/Caribbean (8.5 per cent). However, the twelvefold increase in the stock of FDI in the EEEs between 1990 and 1995 represents a significant performance particularly when considering that the stock in Asian/Pacific countries, the next best performer, increased by only a factor of 1.3. Particularly noteworthy is the fact that the global share of annual FDI inflows accounted for by Western Europe and North America had declined from 78 per cent in 1990 to 59 per cent in 1995. At the same time the developing regions of Latin America, Asia/Pacific, Central and Eastern Europe and Africa have increased their global share of annual FDI inflows from 17 per cent to 35 per cent (table 9.2).

TABLE 9.1: STOCK OF INWARD FDI, BY HOST REGION (£ MILLION)

	1990	**(%)**	**1995**	**(%)**	**% increase**
Western Europe	758 682	44.2	1 087 594	40.9	43.4
North America	507 965	29.6	681 425	25.6	34.1
Asia and Pacific	178 050	10.4	406 457	15.3	128.3
Latin America/Caribbean	121 330	7.1	225 805	8.5	86.1
Other developed countries	106 681	6.2	163 723	6.2	53.5
Central and Eastern Europe	2 568	0.1	33 291	1.2	1 196.4
Africa	41 573	2.4	59 565	2.2	43.3
Total	**1 716 849**		**2 657 860**		**54.8**

Source: UNCTAD 1996

TABLE 9.2: FDI INFLOWS BY HOST REGION, 1990 AND 1995

	FDI inflows			
	1990		**1995**	
Host Region	**£ million**	**%**	**£ million**	**%**
Western Europe	103 393	50.7	115 630	36.7
North America	55 773	27.3	71 418	22.7
Asia and Pacific	22 419	11.0	68 158	21.6
Latin America/Caribbean	10 612	5.2	26 560	8.4
Other developed countries	8 900	4.4	16 120	5.1
Central and Eastern Europe	2 303	1.1	12 391	3.9
Africa	413	0.2	4 657	1.5
Total	**203 813**	**100**	**314 934**	**100**

Source: UNCTAD 1996

FIGURE 9.1: FDI INFLOWS TO EEEs 1990–1995

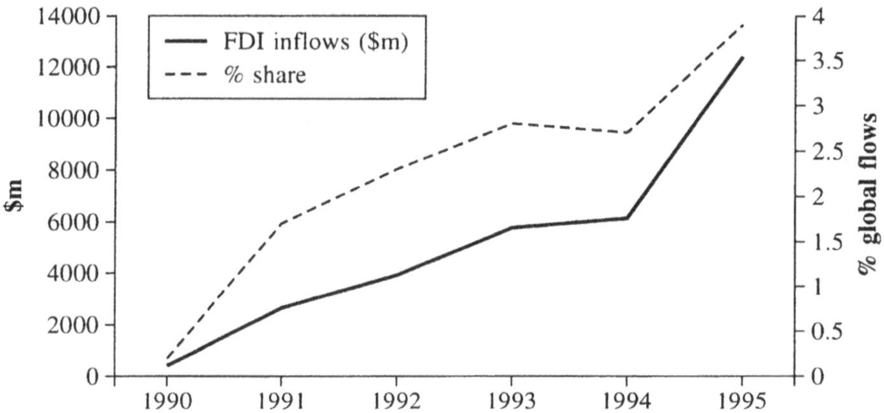

Source: UNCTAD 1996

The increase in the stock of FDI in the EEEs is accounted for by significantly improved annual inflows of investment during the transition (figure 9.1). In 1990 just $413 million was invested in EEEs by foreign-owned companies, representing 0.2 per cent of global inflows in that year. However, in 1991 FDI inflows into the EEEs amounted to $2.6 billion, representing 1.7 per cent of global flows. Both the annual value of investment to the EEEs and the annual global share increased markedly between 1991 and 1993. There was a slight decrease in the annual global share in 1994 followed by a significant increase in 1995 when the annual flow of investment doubled from the previous year. In 1995 FDI inflows into the EEEs represented almost 4 per cent of the global total.

The Host Countries

Generally there is now a much more conducive environment in the EEEs facing potential foreign direct investors. Markets are being opened up, regulations are being relaxed and privatisation programmes are continuing apace (Richet 1996). However, the speed of change has not been uniform across all the East European economies. Particular differences are observed both between countries and between the three regions: Eastern Europe, European CIS and the Baltic States.

Between 1989 and 1993 FDI inflows to the EEEs were heavily concentrated in three countries: the Czech Republic, Poland and especially Hungary, which itself accounted for over 50 per cent of flows (table 9.3). The Czech Republic accounted for 19 per cent and Poland almost 9 per cent. Total flows into these three countries during this period amounted to almost $9 billion. Elsewhere in Eastern Europe, Slovakia and Slovenia were the next largest

TABLE 9.3: FDI FLOWS INTO EAST EUROPEAN ECONOMIES, 1989–96
($ millions and %)

Country	1989–93	%	1994	%	1995	%	1996 (est.)	%	1994–96	%	Cumulative flows 1989–96	%
Albania	77	0.1	53	1.1	70	0.6	95	1.0	218	0.8	295	0.8
Bulgaria	97	0.9	105	2.1	98	0.8	150	1.6	353	1.4	450	1.2
Croatia	105	0.9	98	2.0	81	0.7	300	3.2	479	1.8	584	1.6
Czech Republic	2 131	18.8	750	15.3	525	21.5	1 200	13.0	4 475	17.3	6 606	17.8
Hungary	5 767	50.9	1 146	23.3	4 453	37.9	1 900	20.6	7 499	28.9	13 266	35.6
Poland	981	8.7	542	11.0	1 134	9.7	2 300	24.9	3 976	15.3	4 957	13.3
Romania	171	1.5	341	6.9	367	3.1	555	6.0	1 263	4.9	1 434	3.8
Slovakia	256	2.3	181	3.7	180	1.5	150	1.6	511	2.0	767	2.1
Slovenia	267	2.4	128	2.6	176	1.5	160	1.7	464	1.8	731	2.0
TFYR Macedonia	0	0	24	0.5	14	0.1	–	–	38	0.1	38	0.1
Eastern Europe	**9 852**	**86.9**	**3 368**	**68.5**	**9 098**	**77.3**	**6 810**	**73.7**	**19 276**	**74.4**	**29 128**	**78.2**
Belarus	75	0.7	10	0.2	7	0.1	18	0.2	35	0.1	110	0.3
Moldova	14	0.1	18	0.4	72	0.6	46	0.5	136	0.5	150	0.4
Russian Federation	600	5.3	1 000	20.3	1 900	16.1	1 600	17.3	4 500	17.4	5 100	13.7
Ukraine	370	3.3	91	1.9	266	2.3	440	4.8	797	3.1	1 167	3.1
European CIS	1 059	9.3	1 119	22.8	2 245	19.1	**2 104**	**22.8**	**5 468**	**21.1**	**6 527**	**17.5**
Estonia	219	1.9	214	4.3	204	1.8	70	0.8	488	1.9	707	1.9
Latvia	94	0.8	155	3.1	165	1.4	171	1.8	491	1.9	585	1.6
Lithuania	113	1.0	60	1.2	55	0.5	80	0.9	195	0.8	308	0.1
Baltic States	**426**	**3.8**	**429**	**8.7**	**424**	**3.6**	**321**	**3.5**	**1 174**	**4.5**	**1 600**	**4.3**
Total	**11 337**	**100**	**4,916**	**100**	**11 767**	**100**	**9 235**	**100**	**25 918**	**100**	**37 255**	**100**

Source: Financial Times Survey 11 April 1997

recipients of FDI, each with just over 2 per cent of total flows. Taken together the Eastern Europe countries accounted for 87 per cent of flows to the EEEs with the remainder going to the European CIS and the Baltic States. Of the European CIS states the Russian Federation and the Ukraine were the major players accounting for over 90 per cent of flows into the European CIS and almost 9 per cent of total flows into the EEEs. The Baltic states (Estonia, Latvia and Lithuania) accounted for just 4 per cent of the total investment with Estonia being the largest recipient at almost 2 per cent.

The balance of attractiveness, with respect to FDI inflows, between Eastern Europe and the European CIS changed markedly between 1994 and 1996 primarily due to significant flows into the Russian Federation. During this period FDI flows into the Russian Federation accounted for 17 per cent of the total, bringing the European CIS share up to 21 per cent. Hungary remained the principal recipient of FDI inflows albeit with a significantly reduced proportionate share. Elsewhere in Eastern Europe flows into Poland increased markedly between 1994 and 1996 with the result that its proportionate share of the total flows increased to 15 per cent. The Czech Republic maintained its strong position while there were also noticeable improvements in flows to Romania, Croatia, Bulgaria and Latvia. In the other European CIS states of Belarus and Moldova, as well as the other Baltic States, little change can be noted.

As flows into the region before 1989 were virtually non-existent, an indication of the distribution of the current stock of FDI in the EEEs can be gained from looking at the cumulative flows between 1989 and 1996. Estimates suggest that the EEEs had attracted $37 billion worth of investment by the end of 1996 (UNCTAD 1996b). The majority of this investment (78 per cent) is in East European countries and especially Hungary, the Czech Republic and Poland. Together these three account for two-thirds of the total investment in the EEEs. Together with the Russian Federation (14 per cent) it can be noted that 80 per cent of FDI stock in EEEs is accounted for by just four countries.

Another measure of the performance of individual EEEs in attracting FDI inflows is to consider per capita investment (table 9.4). Between 1989 and 1996, per capita investment for the EEEs as a whole was $113. However, significant differences can be observed between Eastern Europe, European CIS and the Baltic States, and between individual countries. Eastern Europe, with per capita investment at $270 can be seen to be attracting more than its 'fair-share' of FDI inflows, particularly at the expense of the European CIS where per capita investment stood at only $30. Despite significant investment in the Russian Federation since 1993 it is still not achieving anything like its 'fair-share' of investment flows based on the size of the country. Despite relatively low levels of investment the Baltic States, and especially Estonia and Latvia, have performed well in terms of per capita investment with figures of $459 and $234 respectively. Within Eastern Europe, Hungary, the Czech Republic,

Poland and Slovenia, are performing well in terms of per capita investment. The case of Hungary is particularly noteworthy where per capita investment between 1989 and 1996 amounted to $1,288. Considering per capita investment for 1996 a similar pattern emerges: Eastern Europe states such as Hungary, the Czech Republic, Poland, Slovenia and the Baltic states of Latvia and Estonia again lead the way. At the same time countries such as Albania, Bulgaria, Romania, Slovakia, Lithuania and the whole of European CIS lag behind.

Origins of FDI into the EEEs

Most FDI flows into the EEEs originate from the European Union. EU countries account for some 75 per cent of the FDI stock in Hungary and Bulgaria, and as much as two-thirds in the Czech Republic, Poland, Slovakia and Slovenia. In the Baltic States the EU accounts for over 50 per cent of the FDI stock. In the European CIS the EU accounts for 68 per cent of FDI in Moldova, 43 per cent in the Ukraine and 38 per cent in Belarus (UNCTAD 1996b). The notable exception is the Russian Federation where investment from the USA and Switzerland accounts for over 50 per cent of the stock. Overall the USA accounts for 15 per cent of the total inward FDI stock in the EEEs. Investment from Japan accounts for just 1 per cent (UNCTAD 1996b).

TABLE 9.4: CUMULATIVE FDI FLOWS INTO EAST EUROPEAN ECONOMIES, 1989–96

Country	1989–96 ($m)	1989–96 %	1989–96 (per capita, $)	1996 (per capita, $)
Albania	295	0.8	92	30
Bulgaria	450	1.2	54	18
Croatia	584	1.6	118	63
Czech Republic	6 606	17.8	642	117
Hungary	13 266	35.6	1 288	184
Poland	4 957	13.3	234	68
Romania	1 434	3.8	63	24
Slovakia	767	2.1	144	28
Slovenia	731	2.0	366	80
TFYR Macedonia	38	0.1	18	n.a.
Eastern Europe	**29 128**	**78.2**	**269.6**	**63.0**
Belarus	110	0.3	11	2
Moldova	150	0.4	35	11
Russian Federation	5 100	13.7	34	11
Ukraine	1 167	3.1	23	9
European CIS	**6 527**	**17.5**	**30.3**	**9.8**
Estonia	707	1.9	459	45
Latvia	585	1.6	234	68
Lithuania	308	0.1	83	21
Baltic States	**1 600**	**4.3**	**206.4**	**41.4**
Total	**37 255**	**100**	**112.6**	**27.9**

Source: Financial Times Survey 11 April 1997; EBRD 1996

The evidence of Lansbury *et al.* (1996) suggests that strong existing trade links have been an influencial factor in determining flows of FDI into Hungary, Poland, the Czech Republic and Slovakia from OECD source countries. For example, the relatively high amount of FDI from Germany and Austria was partly a reflection of long-standing business linkages associated with geographical proximity. The EEEs' trade has been increasingly reoriented towards EU economies, and the desire for even closer links is likely to be reflected in efforts to retain and attract FDI from EU sources.

Given that relative labour costs are important in the attraction of FDI to the EEEs (Lansbury *et al.* 1996), as is typical in developing countries, it might be argued that the EEEs represent the less-developed, low-cost periphery of the relatively high cost EU. However, for the EEEs to become more fully integrated would require the EU to resolve the conflict between the deepening of political and economic integration represented by the Maastricht Treaty and enlargement incorporating the EEEs (Gibb and Michalac 1994).

TABLE 9.5: FDI PROJECTS IN SELECTED EEES BY MODE OF INVESTMENT, OCTOBER 1991–MARCH 1993

	Acquisitions		**Joint ventures**		**Greenfield investments**		**total investments**	
Country	***No.***	***%***	***No.***	***%***	***No.***	***%***	***No.***	***%***
Czech Republic	62	34	60	33	59	33	181	100
Hungary	121	36	121	36	92	28	334	100
Poland	48	30	46	28	68	42	162	100
Russian Federation	113	3	285	71	106	26	402	100
Total	**242**	**21**	**519**	**48**	**325**	**30**	**1 079**	**100**

Source: Richet 1996

Types of FDI in the EEEs

The mode of FDI into EEEs is influenced by the operating environment within individual countries. Joint ventures are likely to be favoured in countries where economic uncertainty, and hence risk, remains high. Where property rights are clearly defined, where there have been mass privatisations and risk factors are low a mix of greenfield investments, acquisitions and joint ventures is likely. This is reflected in the data shown in table 9.5 where the three modes of FDI have almost equal importance in countries such as the Czech Republic, Hungary, Slovenia, Slovakia and Poland, while joint ventures have a large majority in Russia (Richet 1996). In the case of Hungary it has been suggested that increased confidence in political and economic stability has, over time, been one of the factors leading to a greater willingness by inward investors to move from minority to majority ownership in joint ventures and to make fully-owned foreign investment (Lane 1994). It may also reflect a development process which sees joint ventures as an initial stage in the inward investment process which later results in greenfield investment.

Case Studies: the Czech Republic, Poland and Hungary

It has been demonstrated that the Czech Republic, Poland and Hungary are the major recipients of FDI flows into the EEEs. These three accounted for some two-thirds of foreign direct investment into the region between 1989 and 1996. It is therefore important to consider these in isolation to discuss the origins of FDI, the type, the preferred sectors, the FDI environment and other factors which make these three countries particularly attractive.

Origins of FDI

As previously established the majority of foreign direct investment in EEEs originates from neighbouring European Union countries. This is certainly the case with respect to Hungary, the Czech Republic and Poland. Data for 1996 suggests that over 60 per cent of the FDI stock in the Czech Republic and Poland originated from the EU, while in 1995, 75 per cent of Hungary's FDI stock was EU in origin. More detailed country of origin data is available. In Hungary between 1992 and 1996 the five largest investors were Germany, Austria, Netherlands, France and the USA. No data is available on their relative shares. In the case of the Czech Republic and Poland, German, Dutch and US investors again emerge as important (figure 9.2). German investors accounted for 29 per cent of the total FDI stock in the Czech Republic, in September 1996, and 13 per cent of the total stock in Poland (December 1996). Investors from the USA have a greater presence in Poland with 25 per cent of the total investment compared with 15 per cent in the Czech Republic. Significantly in the Czech Republic six countries account for 86 per cent of the total stock, while in the case of Poland the largest five investors account for 63 per cent (MITT 1997a; Czech Invest 1997a; *Warsaw Voice* 1997).

Sectional Analysis

Some evidence exists on the preferred sectors of foreign direct investors. In Poland the majority of investment (63 per cent) has gone into manufacturing and in particular into the food, drinks and tobacco industry (21 per cent), the transport equipment industry (12 per cent) and pulp and paper products (6 per cent). The financial intermediation sector (real estate, banking and finance) is also important accounting for 19 per cent of the stock. In the Czech Republic almost one-quarter of investment has gone into the transportation and communications sector. The automotive industry accounts for 16 per cent and consumer goods and tobacco (13 per cent). The construction industry (8 per cent), the chemical industry (8 per cent) and the financial sector (7 per cent) are also important sectors in the Czech Republic. In Hungary

FIGURE 9.2: ORIGIN OF FDI

Czech Republic (Sept 1996)

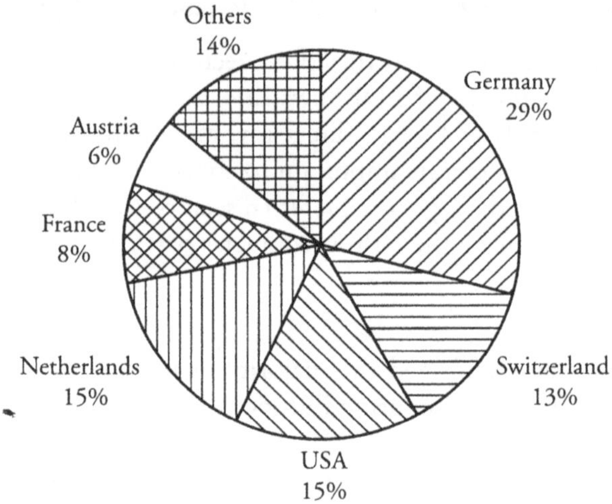

Poland (Dec 1996)

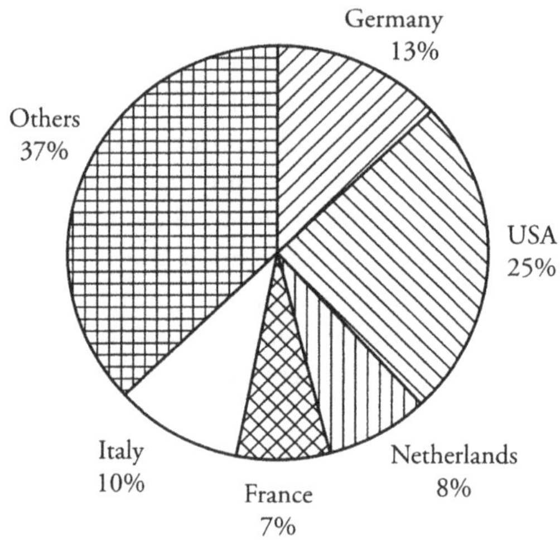

Sources: Czech Invest, *Business Briefing Publishing,* 1996; Polish Agency for Foreign Investment, *Warsaw Voice,* 1996

annual flow data for 1996 shows that only 20 per cent of foreign investment was in manufacturing, the preferred sectors being real estate, leasing and business/financial activities (MITT 1997a; Czech Invest 1997a; *Warsaw Voice* 1997; Reuters Ltd 1997a).

Some explanations

Why is it that FDI has been particularly attracted to these three countries? Evidence suggests that foreign investors sought first to invest in those EEEs where economic performance had improved and where political stability was likely to be maintained (UNCTAD 1996b). Poland, the first EEE country to receive significant flows of FDI, was the first to achieve economic growth following the initial transition period, but political instability became a deterrent to FDI (Hany 1995) and Poland was surpassed as a host country by the Czech Republic and especially Hungary. Significant flows in these countries have largely been linked to privatisation (UNCTAD 1996b) with the timing and form of privatisation influencing the geographical pattern of FDI (Lansbury *et al.* 1996; Hunya 1992). This in particular helps explain the relatively high level of FDI flows to Hungary in the early 1990s. However, it is anticipated that FDI inflows into Hungary and the Czech Republic will settle at a level below that in Poland where non-privatisation-related FDI flows have been much more important. In Hungary in particular signs of recession and increased risk are deterring new investment (*Warsaw Voice* 1996). Economic decline in the Baltic state of Latvia during the initial transition period prompted investors to be cautious. Privatisation in the telecommunications sector has since helped Latvia become the largest FDI recipient among the Baltic states. The low level of investment in Lithuania is attributed to the small size of its domestic market. It has also been suggested that foreign companies sought to invest in Russia in order to establish first-mover advantages (UNCTAD 1996b). However, the flows are, of course, sensitive to changes in political and economic stability.

Attractiveness Factors

The Czech Republic, Poland and Hungary have not only proved the most attractive locations in terms of economic stability but they also have the most conducive regulation environments. Those countries with increased purchasing power, that have large domestic markets and have made considerable market changes are most attractive to foreign investors (*Warsaw Voice* 1996).

Evidence from the Policy Agency for Foreign Investment suggests that Poland is currently perceived as a more attractive location for FDI for a number of reasons: skilled labour force; competitively priced labour; large market for goods and services; geographical position and improving infrastructure. Events have also been organised for foreign businessmen and journalists to negate fears regarding the Polish workforce and business environment (Reuters Ltd 1997a). The Foreign Investment Act of 1991 was designed to open up the economy to foreign investors, enabling foreign and domestic investors to trade under the same conditions. However, greenfield investments in Poland have been limited by strict regulations on the purchase of land by foreigners. It is also thought that high corporate taxes in comparison with countries such as Hungary have discouraged greater levels of investment (Styczek 1996).

Czech Invest cites '10 good reasons to invest in the Czech Republic'(Czech Invest 1995). These are economic and political stability, low risk, high level of international business confidence, accessibility to both Eastern Europe and the large EU market, availability and cost of labour, favourable levels of productivity, an expanding domestic market, an established infrastructure and supply base, a good portfolio of sites and the existence of Czech Invest to assist potential investors. Czech law also enables foreign investors to trade under the same conditions as their indigenous counterparts. Since April 1991 no formal approval is required for foreign investment except that involving banking, finance or defence or where it occurs through a large privatisation programme (Czech Invest 1997b).

The performance of foreign companies in the Czech Republic has also been good. They have out-performed indigenous companies on several measures. In 1995, they produced 11.2 per cent of the economy's total output from 8.5 per cent of the workforce, and although they only represent less than 3 per cent of the total stock of firms they 'invest more, produce more, export more and pay better than indigenous companies' (Zemplinerova 1997).

In Hungary incentives for potential foreign investors are available through preferences in the taxation system as well as direct forms of subsidisation (MITT 1997b). Being open longer to market forces and to Western influence, as well as having the most sophisticated banking, regulatory and management infrastructure of all EEEs, Hungary has reaped benefits in terms of the attraction of FDI. This enabled Hungary to steal a march on its rivals. However, austerity measures introduced in the mid-1990s stifled economic growth and served to push investors towards the Czech Republic and Poland (Randolph 1997).

Other countries, aware of the benefits accruing to Hungary, Poland and the Czech Republic are also introducing measures to try and stimulate greater levels of foreign direct investment. For example, in June 1997 the Slovak Finance Ministry announced plans to give tax breaks to foreign investors, aware that the country is lagging behind its neighbours in attracting FDI flows (Reuters Ltd 1997b).

Policy Issues

Policies to encourage and support the attraction and development of inward investment are well developed in the UK both at national level through the activities of central government departments and at the regional level through Regional Development Organisations (RDOs) and Agencies (RDAs). In Scotland and Wales the RDAs have a wide range of economic development powers providing potential inward investors with a clear organisational structure within which to operate. The development of policy towards the attraction of inward investment to the UK regions therefore has a long and successful track record. This track record has developed in response to changing global patterns of inward investment which has seen the dominance of North American inward investment in the 1950s and 1960s, followed by increasing flows of investment from other European Union countries after 1970. In recent years high profile investment from Pacific Rim countries has attracted particular attention from policy-makers. The approach adopted by UK policy-makers to the attraction of inward investment, from a wide range of source countries, provide important lessons for EEEs. Of particular value is identifying those factors which are known to be important to FDI and recognising how policies have been formulated to respond to the changing global and corporate frameworks within which investment decisions are made by multinational enterprises.

It is evident from the analysis in earlier sections of this chapter that potential inward investors into the EEEs are likely to attract increasing attention from those agencies and organisations seeking to promote and secure the economic development of EEEs. Agencies and organsiations designed to encourage new inward investment are growing in prominence in the EEEs. In the Czech Republic, Czech Invest was established in the early 1990s as an agency of the Ministry of Industry and Trade with a mission to foster greenfield and strategic joint venture investment. The primary role of Czech Invest is to provide quality information with an emphasis upon selected industries, such as electronics and those in high-tech activities. The Hungarian Investment and Trade Development Agency (ITD) was established in 1993 to promote both exports and foreign investment in Hungary. ITD provides information on investment opportunities, including joint venture partners, and assists investors with contacts in the public and private sectors. In Poland, the Polish Agency for Foreign Investment (PAIZ) was established in 1992. It again operates nationally, linked to government ministries, and helps to provide a network of contacts, information on investment opportunities and independent consultancy advice. It is evident that in all three of the above examples of support for overseas investment the emphasis is upon national agencies, linked to central government departments and supported through EU initiatives such as Pologne-Hongrie: Actions pour la reconversion économique (PHARE).

While the circumstances and factors which can lead to inward investment into EEEs may differ from those which face the UK economy it is, in our view, a valuable exercise for the reasons set out above, to draw upon UK experience. In doing so it is recognised that while at the national level there are arrangements for promoting and encouraging flows of inward investment, it is generally at the subnational level of government that policies towards the attraction of inward investment are most developed in the UK.

A review of the policy implications of the changing profile of inward investment into the West Midlands Region of the UK (Roberts and Noon 1987) provides a useful starting point for evaluating the implications for policy of the growing levels of inward investment flowing into EEEs. While there has been a rising level of inward investment into EEEs in general during the 1990s, flows to many of these countries; have been modest and therefore, as advocated for UK policy (ibid.), it is important to ensure that activities to attract inward investment, for example promotion and marketing, are appropriate in scale having regard to the likely contribution such investment will make to economic restructuring. Of equal, or perhaps even greater importance, is ensuring that local competitiveness is enhanced through investment in local infrastructure and skills training. It is important to note that many of the factors which attract inward investing companies such as: good communications, a skilled workforce and availability of land and premises are also major factors in the successful development of indigenous businesses. The wider local economic development context is therefore of paramount importance.

Drawing lessons from recent Polish experience, Hany (1995) observes that the factors influencing the potential for inward investment include the state of telecommunications infrastructure, the development of human capital and the attitude of the host country's population. He also emphasises the significance of national factors such as economic and political stability, market-orientated changes, including privatisation, and effective legal, fiscal and banking frameworks. These conclusions reinforce the notion of a global shopping list of locational attractions pursued by multinational enterprises. In the case of EEEs the potential of these economies was constrained until the early 1990s by restrictive legal and regulatory frameworks which resulted in FDI seeking alternative destinations. Now that these barriers have been removed, there is evidence of strong attractiveness factors which need to be highlighted and effectively promoted.

There has been an extensive and continuing policy debate in the UK on the contribution made by inward investment to local and regional economic development. Dicken and Tickell (1992, p. 99) observed that 'attitudes remain strongly polarised towards the rightful place of inward investment in a regional or local economic development strategy'. Policy-makers need to be explicit about the anticipated benefits of inward investment: for example, is the primary objective one of creating new jobs or to attract technologically advanced capital intensive investment? The priorities attached to economic development objectives will determine the approach taken towards inward investment, such as targeting particular sectors as potential sources of new investment. Additionally, Collis and Noon (1994, p. 846) have observed that 'the approach taken to inward investment will be informed by an appraisal of a locality's potential to attracting inward investment'. Indeed it is paramount that the role of inward investment in a wider economic development strategy for EEEs is effectively informed by the evaluation of a locality's strengths and weaknesses.

The significant level of joint ventures and acquisitions, in the first wave of inward investment into the EEEs, has already been highlighted by Lane (1994). There has been a rapid growth of joint ventures in Hungary and it is evident that this was often a preferred initial mode of inward investment, taking advantage of the many privatisation opportunities. This suggests that the spread of joint ventures and other forms of strategic alliances is now being reflected in the flows of inward investment to the EEEs. This again raises public policy issues in terms of the actions and activities of economic development agencies. For example, there is a brokerage role, supported by well-developed data-bases, to be played in matching and bringing together potential partners. It is important to recognise that very often a joint venture is regarded by multinational enterprises as a cost effective way of gaining access to a new market with minimum risk and as a possible precursor to greenfield investment. The development of good working relationships by economic development agencies with joint venture partners is therefore important in enhancing the prospects for long-term investment. This is a particularly important element in the context of EEEs where the joint venture arrangement, linked to privatisation, often represents the start of major capital investment and company restructuring.

Studies of the relocation process have demonstrated the importance of promotional agencies being involved at an early stage in the decision-making process so that they can both influence and respond to the needs of MNEs (Roberts and Noon 1987). This is most effectively achieved through direct contact with corporate decision-makers as strategy is being formulated. One means of doing this is to target those companies and sectors which have already demonstrated some interest in investing overseas as well as working with companies who have already made an overseas investment but may then be looking to expand their operations. To support the growth and development of previous inward investment, there is a growing awareness in the UK and other countries of the importance of effective 'aftercare' programmes. The benefits of developing comprehensive aftercare is well documented by Peck and Burdis (1996), and their work points to the need for aftercare programmes to take account of wider regional development issues. In the case of EEEs it is particularly important to develop a means of effective communication between government organisations and inward investors to overcome operational problems and remove barriers to further investment. However, the key to the success is the continued flow of investment to support restructuring; and therefore policies to support this, through aftercare arrangements, are likely to gain in significance in EEEs. It is also important that effective aftercare activities are in place to maximise the opportunities for greenfield developments which may flow from an initial joint venture.

CONCLUSIONS

There is evidence from the information presented in the earlier sections of this chapter that a degree of concentration exists in both the origin and destination of inward investment into the EEEs. Germany and Austria are the major source countries for inward investment into EEEs while Hungary, Poland and the Czech Republic are preferred destinations. There is also a sectoral focus with significant flows of investment into those sectors associated with physical reconstruction (for example transport, construction), with growing disposable incomes (for example consumer goods) and with a burgeoning financial services sector. These sectors are likely to continue to be among the most significant sources of inward investment for the EEEs and therefore provide policy-makers with an opportunity to focus and target their marketing activities. It also provides the opportunity to assess the anticipated benefits to which different types of investment are likely to give rise.

The evidence available on the factors which have attracted inward investment into the EEEs, particularly Hungary, Poland and the Czech Republic, suggest that relatively low wage costs for skilled labour, geographical and cultural proximity combined with access to Western markets, the potential for local markets to develop further and a growing sense of economic and political stability have had the most influence. It is important for the EEEs to maintain and extend their attractiveness through well-developed education and training facilities, improved infrastructure (including telecommunications) and continued support for related and supporting indigenous enterprises. The development of Regional Supply Offices in the UK is an example of how support for indigenous businesses in the UK can be linked to inward investment in a way which is designed to bring mutual benefits.

To date it would appear that the emphasis of policy incentives in EEEs has been the use of fiscal policies, such as lower tax rates and capital investment allowances, to encourage FDI. However, Estrin *et al.* (1997) observe that given low profit levels in the early years of new investments these incentives may not be particularly important. Instead positive action by Government, to provide information to investors, is more important and it is noted that this may bias investment into those sectors which have traditionally been active in the region, for example capital equipment and engineering. Estrin *et al.* conclude their analysis by commenting: 'The main role of inward investment agencies in these countries, therefore, may be in providing and effectively disseminating information about their respective economies and the opportunities and advantages that the transitional environment can provide' (Estrin *et al.* 1997, p. 244). Such a role depends on up to date and comprehensive local information and Estrin observes that what may be required is a more active regional/industrial policy such as high-quality local supply networks to reduce the barriers to development and to facilitate the flow of information between local firms, regional government and multinationals. Clearly the approach of local authorities and development agencies in the UK provide important insights into how these services might be delivered.

NOTE

1. The definition of EEEs covers the countries of Eastern Europe, the European CIS and the Baltic States (see table 9.3).

MAX MUNDAY AND MICHAEL PEEL

10 Assessing Changes in the Economic Performance of the Japanese Transplant Sector in the UK

INTRODUCTION

Japanese transplant manufacturers have been credited with the creation of significant new employment opportunities in the UK. However, concentrations of highly productive Japanese manufacturing capital may have other significant impacts on the UK economy. The presence of Japanese manufacturing capital could represent one means of improving the competitiveness of domestic UK manufacturing – for example, through technological transfer or through increased competitive pressure. Much has been made of the potential for the 'Japanisation' of UK industry whereby UK firms adopt 'new' production techniques and 'hybrid' forms of personnel management successfully transplanted to the UK industrial environment. However, the developmental potential of Japanese capital has been questioned by a number of commentators who suggest that Japanese subsidiaries in the UK are, in fact, characterised by comparatively poor performance, and that this poor performance is underlined by reference to the marginal nature of Japanese manufacturing operations in the UK periphery. These conclusions have been supported by recent evidence which reveals the relatively low profitability of Japanese subsidiaries in the UK. (see for example Munday and Peel 1997).

However, little previous research has used cross-sectional corporate data to examine changes in the performance of foreign-owned companies located in the UK. Building on our earlier cross-sectional study (Munday and Peel 1997), which examined the relative performance of matched samples of Japanese and domestic manufacturing companies using data for 1994, the purpose of this chapter is to examine changes in the performance of the

Japanese transplant manufacturing sector in the UK using reported financial data, supplemented by information from other published sources. The chapter focuses on an empirical analysis of the comparative performance of Japanese subsidiaries in the UK over the period 1991–4. The analysis demonstrates how Japanese manufacturers measured up to a matched sample of domestic manufacturing firms on a variety of performance variables relating to employment, productivity, profitability and liquidity. In particular, changes in these performance measures are assessed for the 1991–4 period, thus highlighting the responses of domestic and Japanese firms to recessionary pressures, and providing new evidence on the comparative stability of the foreign-owned sector in the UK.

The remainder of the chapter is structured as follows. The second section contains background information on the development of the Japanese manufacturing sector in the UK. The third section reviews previous research on the contribution of the Japanese transplant sector to the UK national and regional economy and focuses on studies which have examined the performance of Japanese transplants. The fourth section provides details of the study method, and the fifth section contains the analysis and results. The final section concludes with a summary of the key findings and associated policy implications.

THE JAPANESE MANUFACTURING SECTOR IN THE UK

The first significant Japanese manufacturing inward investments into the UK occurred during the late 1960s and early 1970s. Initial entrants included YKK (Runcorn), Sony (Bridgend), Matsushita (Cardiff), Mitsubishi (Haddington, Scotland) and Hitachi (Hirwaun). Pathfinder Japanese investments were comparatively small, with the vast majority involving the manufacture of consumer electronics products, largely colour televisions. By 1981, the Census of Production showed that there were seventeen Japanese enterprises in the UK employing approximately three thousand people. The bulk of this employment was in the periphery, with Wales and Scotland being particularly successful in attracting Japanese transplants. Japanese firms locating in the UK periphery sought to balance access to more favourable regional production conditions with the need to gain access to UK and European markets.

Steady growth of Japanese investment continued until 1984–5. Thereafter, in the period to 1990, investment by Japanese companies in the UK soared. In 1985, total Japanese net investment in the UK (manufacturing and non-manufacturing) was £154m, amounting to just 3.5 per cent of total net inward investment into the UK during that year. By 1990 net inward investment by Japanese firms had reached £2.1bn, representing 12.2 per cent of total UK net inward investment (Business Monitor 1997).

New manufacturing investment partly resulted from growing pressure on Japanese imports into the EU, with the period 1984–7 seeing anti-dumping duties placed on an increasing range of Japanese consumer electronics goods and key components. Growth of the Japanese transplant sector in the period 1985–90 was also characterised by several new features. First, investment outside of the consumer electronics sector – most notably in the motor and motor components sector – increased substantially. Second, the period 1985–90 was characterised by a significant increase in 'second wave' investment from Japanese suppliers to the UK electronics sector. This was largely to support existing Japanese original equipment manufacturers (OEMs) and to develop market share in the UK. Third, 1985–90 was a period which witnessed a spatial shift in Japanese manufacturing investment, with a higher proportion of new firms selecting sites in the East and West Midlands, and the northern region, as opposed to Wales and Scotland, which had received the bulk of investment prior to 1984. Fourth, Japanese firms increasingly turned to acquisitions and joint ventures as a means of UK entry.

More recently, the collapse of the Japanese 'bubble economy' in 1989–90 curtailed the 'boom' in Japanese inward investment. However, by 1992, 117 Japanese manufacturing enterprises employed 58,000 people in the UK. These Japanese enterprises accounted for £6.1bn of sales and just over £2.5bn of net output in 1992 (Business Monitor 1995). Following the slowdown of the Japanese economy in the early 1990s, Japanese inward investment into the UK has continued to grow in recent years. This has occurred despite persistent problems in the Japanese economy, and despite stronger competition from other EU states to attract such investment. Data derived from information from the annual Japanese External Trade Organisation (JETRO) survey of Japanese manufacturing affiliates in Europe, and from data from the Invest in Britain Bureau of the Department of Trade and Industry indicates that Japanese manufacturers in 1995 employed around 73,000 people in the UK (comprising 2 per cent of UK manufacturing employment). The precise distribution of Japanese investment across industrial sectors is difficult to ascertain since several large component producers supply both the electronics and motor industry sectors and because classification is dependent on which of the two sources is used. This noted, the consumer electronics and electronics sectors represented 44 per cent of this employment, while motor vehicles and components manufacturers accounted for 31 per cent.

The electronics industry represents the largest proportion of investment. In 1995, the total net book value of Japanese manufacturing investment in the UK was £1.4bn, of which electrical engineering and electronics accounted for 42 per cent, mechanical engineering 21 per cent, transport 20 per cent and other manufacturing sectors 17 per cent (Business Monitor 1997).

As noted above, it is the regions in the periphery that have been most successful in attracting Japanese manufacturing investment. In 1995 Japanese firms in Wales, northern England and Scotland employed nearly 34,000 people (46 per cent of Japanese manufacturing employment in the UK). Growth of Japanese manufacturing employment in the West Midlands increased significantly in the late 1980s which partly reflects a concentration of Japanese companies in Telford (including NEC, Maxell and Ricoh), and, more importantly, the fact that areas in the West Midlands received Assisted Area status in the mid-1980s.

In summary, Japanese investment in the UK grew rapidly after 1985 and continues to develop in terms of industrial diversity and spatial spread. For several UK regions, Japan now ranks second behind the USA as the largest source of new foreign manufacturing inward investment.

THE PERFORMANCE OF THE JAPANESE MANUFACTURING SECTOR

It has been hypothesised that UK domestic manufacturing might benefit or learn from the presence of Japanese (or other foreign) multinational transplants (Eltis and Fraser 1992). By implication, this suggests that foreign-owned subsidiaries located in the UK should outperform their domestic counterparts in the same industrial sector. There is theoretical support for this proposition. The international activities of multinational enterprises (MNEs) focus on their having specific ownership advantages (Dunning 1993a). These might be in terms of the possession of proprietary knowledge, management or process skills and special technology. These tangible and intangible assets have advantageous income-generating potential. Moreover, access to, and the use of, these assets may more than compensate MNEs for the additional costs borne when operating far from the home economy. In addition, Dunning (1986) argues that the ownership advantage of Japanese MNEs is partly tied to their organisation of manufacturing processes (for example systems emphasising just-in-time production and total quality management). The existence of ownership advantages (from whatever source) suggests that foreign-owned subsidiaries should be more efficient, productive and profitable than their domestic counterparts (see for example Dunning 1993a; Pitelis and Sugden 1991).

Foreign-owned competitors may also benefit from other advantages over their domestic counterparts. For example, the competitive advantages of MNEs may not only derive from the possession of specific assets but may also result from the way MNEs internalise transactions in specific assets and intermediate products (including know-how) between productive units (Buckley and Casson 1976). Where uncertainty increases the transaction costs of a market exchange (for example via licensing production/technology to domestic firms), then markets are internalised within firms, decreasing risk and protecting proprietary knowledge and skills. The protection accorded to proprietary knowledge by this internalisation process also suggests that MNEs may be able to maintain an advantage over domestic firms (Buckley and Casson 1976).

General empirical evidence supports the contention that these advantages lead to foreign-owned subsidiaries outperforming their domestic counterparts on productivity measures (see for example Davies and Lyons 1991). Higher productivity, coupled with the extended global reach of MNEs, leads to the contention that foreign firms should also outperform their domestic counterparts on a range of financial and performance variables. For example, Shapiro (1983) examined the determinants of the profitability of 750 of Canada's largest manufacturing firms over the period 1968–72. Profit rates were related to a series of control variables including corporate size, gearing, capital intensity and industrial concentration. After controlling for these factors, foreign-owned firms were still found to be significantly more profitable than indigenous firms. It was suggested that this was consistent with the fact that MNEs in Canada had advantages over domestic firms in terms of patents, trade marks, pools of management talent and technology (together with the benefits of reduced transactions costs resulting from the internalisation of markets).

Improved performance may also be reflected in the comparative operational stability of MNE operations in terms of growth of output and employment, with the greater size and 'reach' of MNEs, together with their more diversified operations, protecting them from economic shocks and national recessions (see for example Dunning 1993a; Killick 1982; McAleese and Counahan 1979). Following this rationale, it might also be expected that, in relation to their domestic counterparts, foreign-owned subsidiaries would be less prone to close/fail. For example, Li and Guisinger (1991), in an analysis of failure rates among foreign- and domestically owned firms in the USA, reported that foreign firms tended to be much less failure prone than their domestic counterparts. In the UK, a large number of studies have examined the economic impact and performance of Japanese manufacturing FDI – including: the spatial distribution of investment (Taylor 1993), overall investment growth (Morris *et al.* 1993), the impact on domestic competitors (Dunning 1986; Brech and Sharp 1984; Strange 1993), and the contribution to regional and national development (Dillow 1989; Munday *et al.* 1995; Morris 1988; Strange 1993; Trevor 1985). However, studies of Japanese manufacturing performance at the firm level are rare (see Munday and Peel 1997), although some studies have examined the comparative productivity of Japanese plants in the UK and Japan (Dunning 1986; Strange 1993). In addition, several studies have focused on the declared objectives of Japanese enterprises in the UK, compared to UK and other foreign-owned enterprises, and have emphasised the propensity for Japanese subsidiaries to seek longer-term strategic objectives in terms of, for example, increasing market share as opposed to profit maximisation (see Doyle *et al.* 1992; Bromwich and Inoue 1994).

The UK Census of Production provides some evidence relating to the comparative performance of Japanese enterprises at the aggregate level. Based on 1995 Census of Production data, table 10.1 shows that Japanese subsidiaries (compared to UK-owned manufacturing enterprises) perform relatively well on most of the standard productivity measures. For example, on average, gross value added per employee in Japanese manufacturing subsidiaries was 51 per cent higher than in UK-owned manufacturing firms in 1995, with sales per employee being over 89 per cent higher in the Japanese manufacturing sector. Moreover, the wages to sales ratio in Japanese-owned enterprises was 42 per cent below that in UK-owned manufacturing enterprises in 1995. The gross value added to sales ratio of Japanese firms was, however, lower than in the UK manufacturing sector, probably in consequence of Japanese enterprises importing a high proportion of materials and semi-finished products (Munday *et al.* 1995). It should be noted, however, that Census of Production data may not be the best basis for comparison, since observed differences may result from structural variations (for example industry, size, and capital intensity) in the populations of foreign and domestic firms (see for example Davies and Lyons 1991).

TABLE 10.1: INDEX OF THE RELATIVE PERFORMANCE OF JAPANESE FIRMS, 1995

Measure	**Index for Japanese firms (UK firms = 100)**
Gross value added per employee	150.7
Gross value added to sales	79.5
Stock turnover	117.4
Sales per employee	189.3
Net output per employee	141.9
Earnings (administration and technical)	113.7
Earnings (operators)	107.0
Wages to sales ratio	58.2

Source: Derived from 1995 Census of Production.

In this context, the encouraging Japanese performance indicators from the Census of Production have not been replicated in studies which have examined the reported financial performance of Japanese enterprises at the firm or plant level. Research here has focused on the poor reported profits of Japanese subsidiaries in the UK (see for example Oyelere and Emmanuel 1996; Williams *et al.* 1992; Munday and Peel 1997), and the influence of transfer pricing policies on the reported profits of Japanese subsidiaries (see Buckley and Hughes 1997).

Conclusions on the comparative performance of Japanese manufacturing investment have important implications, with much claimed for this sector in terms of process efficiency and human resource management, and with large subsidies used to attract Japanese subsidiaries to locate in the UK. The success of the UK's policy of subsidising Japanese transplant investment as one means of promoting national development centres on the ability of these firms to create additional employment. Clearly, Japanese firms have been successful in job creation, although the quality of employment, in terms of earnings and occupation, and the quality of manufacturing operations undertaken, has been questioned (see Strange 1993; Morris *et al.* 1993; Haslam *et al.* 1995; and Williams *et al.* 1992). Whether Japanese manufacturers have acted as a catalyst to improve domestic manufacturing competitiveness is doubtful if such investors are shown to be underperforming when exposed to the UK manufacturing environment.

The remainder of this chapter seeks to provide some new empirical evidence on the relative performance of matched samples of Japanese and domestic manufacturing firms over the period 1991–94. Building on a previous study by the authors (Munday and Peel 1997), which examined the performance differentials of the two samples in 1994, the current study extends the analysis to focus on changes in performance over a three-year period.[1] In the following section, changes in the performance of matched samples of Japanese and domestic subsidiaries are evaluated with reference to variables relating to employment, remuneration, profitability, labour and asset productivity, stock efficiency, liquidity and gearing.

RESEARCH DESIGN AND METHOD

The FAME CD-ROM data-base (compiled by Jordan's) provides annual financial and non-financial information (mainly drawn from company annual reports) on companies registered in Britain (see Munday and Peel 1997 for a discussion of the database). In September 1995, the data-base contained 193 Japanese subsidiaries classified as having primary activities in manufacturing (defined as SIC 1980 2,3,4). Excluding subsidiaries which had inadequate sales data (a matching criterion), and/or companies which were subsidiaries of other firms in the sample, and/or companies which had failed/ceased trading, reduced the available sample of Japanese subsidiaries to 108.

The 1993/4 turnover and three-digit SIC code for each Japanese subsidiary were used as a basis for matching each Japanese subsidiary to a domestically owned subsidiary, the expectation being that a matched sample design would avoid any bias relating to corporate size, subsidiary status and industrial sector (see Davies and Lyons 1991). The majority of selected Japanese subsidiaries had financial data available for the year ending in 1994, but in twenty-one cases data was only available for 1993. Hence, each Japanese subsidiary was matched to a domestic subsidiary on the basis of sales (plus or minus 5 per cent), primary SIC code and year (1993 or 1994) of data. On this basis it was possible to match ninety seven Japanese subsidiaries to domestic subsidiaries drawn from the following sectors: metals and other metal goods (six), chemicals (six), mechanical engineering (eleven), office machinery (seven), electronics (thirty-one), motors (three), instrument engineering (six), food and drink (three), textiles and clothing (eight), paper and print (three), rubber and plastics (eight), other sectors (five).

Data relating to nineteen performance variables was collected from each corporate record for 1991 and 1993/4 (hereafter referred to as 1994), focusing on both labour and asset productivity, profitability, stock efficiency, liquidity and gearing. In some cases, firms in one sample had missing values (for either 1991 or 1994) for the variables described below. Where this occurred, each firm's matched counterpart was assigned a missing value to ensure that, for all variables, the analysis was based on equal-sized matched (in 1994) samples.

Detailed definitions of the variables are reported in the Appendix. The first five variables cover size and remuneration characteristics. These are turnover (TUR), total assets (TAS), fixed assets (FAS), number of employees (EMP) and average annual employee pay (REM). Three variables capture profitability characteristics: net profit margin (NPM); a dummy variable (LOS), coded 1 for a loss-making subsidiary (on the basis of net profit before tax) and zero otherwise; and return on capital employed (REC). Six variables focus upon the efficiency and productivity characteristics of the sample firms. These are remuneration as a proportion (percentage) of sales (ERS); sales per employee (SEM); net profit per employee (PEM); turnover divided by fixed assets (TFA) and turnover divided by total assets (TTA) which are standard ratios which assess the efficiency (productivity) of firms to generate revenue from assets; and average days stock held (DST).

The last five variables in the appendix cover liquidity and gearing characteristics. The first two (DAD, DAC) are ratios which focus on relative cash flows in terms of outstanding (days) debtors (cash owed from customers) and creditors (cash owed to suppliers), with DAC representing the average number of days' credit given by suppliers. Liquidity was analysed using the current ratio (LIQ = current assets to current liabilities). Financial risk was evaluated using the gearing ratio (GEAR), which is the ratio of total liabilities to total assets, and interest cover (ICOV), defined as the ratio of net profit before interest and tax to interest paid.

THE COMPARATIVE PERFORMANCE OF THE JAPANESE SECTOR

In the descriptive analysis and tables which follow, the Japanese and domestic subsamples are compared on a matched basis, with variables suffixed with 94 and 91 to indicate the year the variable relates to and with changes in variables (1994 minus 1991 values) prefixed by the letter 'C'. For each variable, the mean, standard deviation and median are reported. Students' t-tests were used to test for differences between mean values, with non-parametric Mann–Whitney U tests employed to test whether variable distributions (medians) in the two samples differed significantly.

Corporate Size, Remuneration and Growth Characteristics

Table 10.2 reports the results on size and remuneration characteristics. As expected, and confirming the accuracy of the matching procedure, the mean and median sales values (TUR94) of the Japanese and domestic subsamples (in 1994) do not differ significantly. This conclusion also holds for 1991 turnover values (TUR91). However, turnover in the domestic sample grew slightly faster (CTURN) than that in the Japanese sample (with a mean growth of 17.7 per cent against 14.9 per cent for Japanese subsidiaries), but the difference is not statistically significant. The mean values of fixed and total assets (TAS, FAS) for Japanese and domestic firms also do not differ significantly, although the median values of fixed assets in 1994 and 1991 are significantly higher in the Japanese sample.

Contrary to prior expectations, the table reveals that the total assets of domestic firms grew significantly faster than in the Japanese subsample (CTTA). This result is, however, not a complete surprise. In the early 1990s the Japanese economy experienced slow domestic growth and a fall in stock prices, accompanied by Yen appreciation, and pressure on Japanese corporations in Japan to restructure and reduce production costs (Norimoto 1996). As a consequence of these pressures several large Japanese corporations reduced their investment in Europe.

Japanese subsidiaries, on average, employed significantly fewer people (415) in 1994 (EMP94) than their domestic counterparts (607). To the extent that the higher fixed asset levels in Japanese subsidiaries proxy for capital intensity, lower employment is perhaps to be expected. Employment changes over the period 1991–4 do not differ significantly between the two samples. However, the mean increase in employment (CEMP) in the domestic sample between 1991 and 1994 amounted to 7.2 per cent, while it decreased by 3.5 per cent in the Japanese sample. Negative growth in employment in the Japanese sample is consistent with the comparatively slow asset growth (CTAS) in Japanese subsidiaries over the period.

Perhaps the most interesting finding reported in table 10.3 relates to pay levels. Japanese firms paid their employees significantly more than their matched domestic counterparts in both 1994 and 1991. Furthermore, average remuneration in Japanese subsidiaries (CREM) increased at a significantly faster rate (27 per cent) than it did for domestic firms (22 per cent). The results here support those in table 10.1 drawn from the Census of Production. These findings should be interpreted with some caution, since the samples were not matched in terms of location, with manufacturing pay rates in the UK differing significantly by region, and with Japanese subsidiaries tending not to concentrate in high manufacturing wage areas of the UK. These findings are important in the light of concerns about low pay levels in Japanese subsidiaries (Williams *et al.* 1992), argued to be a reflection of the low value added nature of manufacturing operations and poor diversity of functions.

TABLE 10.2: EMPLOYMENT SIZE AND REMUNERATION CHARACTERISTICS

	JAPANESE		DOMESTIC	
Variables	Mean[1] (st.dev.)	Median (n=)	Mean[1] (st.dev.)	Median (n=)
TUR94	44 539.1 (66 959.9)	16 174.5 (n=94)	43 667.7 (64 233.2)	16 150.5 (n=94)
TUR91	38 768.7 (57 439.0)	16 453.0 (n=94)	37 091.1 (58 496.3)	13 143.0 (n=94)
CTUR	5 770.5 (30457.9)	1 168.5 (n=94)	6 576.6 (26301.8)	1 821.5 (n=94)
TAS94	32 082.7 (43 595.8)	13 628.5 (n=96)	32 640.6 (55 507.9)	10 195.5 (n=96)
TAS91	30 244.3 (43 658.3)	13 762.0† (n=96)	25 008.1 (39 868.6)	8 443.0† (n=96)
CTAS	1 838.4* (23 910.5)	371.5 (n=96)	7 632.4* (27 041.6)	600.0 (n=96)
FAS94	12 218.2 (19 641.4)	3 895.5† (n=96)	11 084.2 (23 599.2)	2 762.5† (n=96)
FAS91	11 717.3 (18 835.4)	4 118.5†† (n=96)	8 784.9 (15 554.9)	2 289.0†† (n=96)
CFAS	500.9 (10 423.9)	–94.0 (n=96)	2 299.3 (12 716.5)	22.0 (n=96)
EMP94	399.8** (598.7)	193.0† (n=85)	650.8** (927.4)	223.0† (n=85)
EMP91	414.5 (667.4)	183.0 (n=85)	607.2 (898.9)	221.0 (n=85)
CEMP	–14.7 (199.8)	–7.0 (n=85)	43.7 (375.2)	0.0 (n=85)
REM94	18 680.4*** (7 796.1)	17 546.3† (n=84)	16 304.1*** (4 354.8)	15 475.1† (n=84)
REM91	14 668.2* (5 817.9)	13 509.6 (n=84)	13 315.5* (3 960.5)	13 031.0 (n=84)
CREM	4 012.2* (4 989.9)	3 527.3 (n=84)	2 988.6* (2 521.2)	2 931.2 (n=84)

Notes:

[1]Means are unbracketed with standard deviations shown in parenthesis

***,**,* indicates sample means are significantly different at the 1%, 5% and 10% levels, respectively (two-tailed t-tests)

††,† indicates medians are significantly different at the 5% and 10% levels, respectively (two-tailed Mann–Whitney rank sum tests)

Comparative Profitability

Table 10.3 reports the profitability variables for the two samples. For each of the three profitability indicators (net profit margin, percentage of loss-making firms and return on capital employed), Japanese subsidiaries significantly underperformed their matched domestic counterparts. In 1991, the mean net profit margin (NPM91) of the Japanese subsidiaries was –18.9 per cent, improving to –2.16 per cent by 1994 (NPM94). Similarly, the mean return on capital employed (REC) in the Japanese sample was negative in both years. In the case of the domestic sample, the profitability ratios (NPM, REC) were positive in both years and were significantly higher (by reference to both means and medians) than for their matched Japanese counterparts. The table also shows that the domestic and Japanese subsidiaries improved profitability (CNPM, CREC) between 1991 and 1994 – this being a reflection of improving conditions in the Japanese and UK economies – albeit with some Japanese firms still being adversely affected by recession in key export markets.

TABLE 10.3: PROFITABILITY CHARACTERISTICS

	JAPANESE		DOMESTIC	
Variables	Mean[1] (st.dev.)	Median (n=)	Mean[1] (st.dev.)	Median (n=)
NPM94	–2.16*** (20.30)	0.242††† (n=94)	7.03*** (8.63)	6.46††† (n=94)
NPM91	–18.89* (132.48)	0.663††† (n=94)	5.19* (10.38)	5.57††† (n=94)
CNPM	16.73 (126.72)	1.20 (n=94)	1.84 (10.55)	0.695 (n=94)
LOS94	46.88+ (N/A)	N/A (n=96)	19.79+ (N/A)	N/A (n=96)
LOS91	42.71+ (N/A)	N/A (n=96)	18.75+ (N/A)	N/A (n=96)
CLOS	4.17 (N/A)	N/A (n=96)	1.04 (N/A)	N/A (n=96)
REC94	–0.264*** (21.49)	0.330††† (n=96)	10.77*** (13.27)	10.59††† (n=96)
REC91	–3.18*** (26.90)	1.09††† (n=96)	7.70*** (16.56)	8.15††† (n=96)
CREC	2.92 (29.43)	0.979 (n=96)	3.06 (16.30)	0.683 (n=96)

Notes:
[1]Means are unbracketed with standard deviations shown in parenthesis
***,* indicates sample means are significantly different at the 1% and 10% levels, respectively (two-tailed t-tests)
††† indicates medians are significantly different at the 1% level (two-tailed Mann–Whitney rank sum tests)
+ indicates sample proportions are significantly different at the 1% level (Chi-square tests)

Table 10.3 also shows that over twice as many Japanese subsidiaries experienced losses (LOS) than did domestic firms in both 1991 and 1994. Overall, the summary statistics for each of the three profit variables demonstrate the poor comparative profitability of Japanese firms in both 1991 and 1994. These findings were confirmed when an analysis of the population of manufacturing companies (with primary manufacturing SIC codes) on the FAME data-base was conducted. Using the FAME software, it was possible to

TABLE 10.4: LOSS-MAKING MANUFACTURING FIRMS, 1994–5 AND 1995–6

	Percentage Loss-Making[1]	
Samples*	1994/5[2]	1995/6[3]
Japanese subsidiaries	40.3% (n=159)	34.7% (n=98)
Other Foreign-owned subsidiaries	25.8% (n=3 293)	23.1% (n=2 164)
British-owned subsidiaries	18.9% (n=4 473)	17.0% (n=3 278)
Independent British firms	22.2% (n=12 976)	19.1% (n=9 967)
All companies	22.2% (n=20 901)	19.1% (n=15 507)

Note:
*All failed firms analysed in table 10.5 are excluded
[1]Percentages refer to the proportion of firms (shown in parenthesis) which were loss-making (negative net profit before tax)
[2]Analysis is based on all live firms on the FAME data-base with a primary manufacturing SIC code, with account year ends falling in the period 1.4.94 to 31.3.95, and which disclosed their net profit before tax figure
[3]Analysis is based on all live firms on the FAME data-base with a primary manufacturing SIC code, with account year ends falling in the period 1.4.95 to 31.3.96, and which disclosed their net profit before tax figure
The data for 1994/5 is also reported in Munday and Peel (1997)

TABLE 10.5: MANUFACTURING FIRM FAILURES AND CLOSURES 1994–5 AND 1995–6

	Percentage failing/closing[1]	
Samples*	1994/5[2]	1995/6[3]
Japanese subsidiaries	0.598% (n=167)	0.0% (n=105)
Other Foreign-owned subsidiaries	0.862% (n=3 827)	0.351% (n=2 564)
British-owned subsidiaries	0.643% (n=4 980)	0.501% (n=3 791)
Independent British firms	0.978% (n=19 528)	0.617% (n=16 856)
All companies	0.902% (n=28 502)	0.566% (n=23 316)

Note:
[1]Failure/closures are all corporate deaths resulting from liquidation/insolvency/ceased trading/receivership and administration
[2]The analysis is based on all firms on the FAME data-base with a primary manufacturing SIC code and with annual account year ends falling in the period 1.4.94 to 31.3.95 (1994/5) and in the period 1.4.95 to 31.3.96 (1995/6), respectively
*Percentages refer to the proportion of all firms (shown in parenthesis) which failed/ceased trading
The data for 1994/5 is also reported in Munday and Peel (1997)

examine the characteristics of all the Japanese, other foreign-owned and British manufacturing companies (whether independent or held as subsidiaries) contained in the data-base, and to derive frequency statistics on the proportion of firms in each sample that were loss-making (negative net profits before tax), together with the proportion failing or closing. The analyses in tables 10.4 and 10.5 are presented for the financial years 1994/5 and 1995/6.

Table 10.4 reports the proportion of firms (excluding failed ones, see table 10.5) which were loss-making in the two periods. For both years, a higher proportion of Japanese subsidiaries with primary manufacturing SIC codes were loss-making than were other foreign-owned subsidiaries, British subsidiaries or independent British firms. For example, in 1994/5, 40.3 per cent of Japanese subsidiaries (n=159) declared losses against 18.9 per cent of British-owned subsidiaries (n=34,473), 25.8 per cent of other foreign-owned subsidiaries (n=3,293), and 22.2 per cent for all companies on the database (n=20,901). A similar picture is evident for 1995/6, although with fewer companies in all samples declaring losses. Hence for both periods these results confirm that Japanese-owned manufacturing firms were much more likely to experience losses.

Given these findings, it might be expected that Japanese manufacturing subsidiaries in the UK will suffer from relatively high failure rates. Table 10.5 demonstrates that the opposite holds. Failure rates in the Japanese sample in 1994/5 (0.60 per cent), and 1995/6 (0.0 per cent) are much lower than for the other samples analysed. As we noted earlier (Munday and Peel 1997), one explanation for this finding is that Japanese subsidiaries are prima facie more failure prone but receive more support from their parent company. Another explanation is that transfer pricing strategies are reducing the 'objective' profitability of Japanese-owned subsidiaries, resulting in poor disclosed profitability, which hides true firm health.

Using the same database (for 1994) as that used in this chapter Munday and Peel (1997) investigated the factors underpinning the poor profitability of Japanese subsidiaries in the UK in 1994, together with the role of transfer pricing, and came to the following conclusions: (a) that it was comparatively high input prices (that is raw materials, components and semi-finished goods, etc.) that were largely responsible for the relatively low profitability of Japanese subsidiaries and which appeared to be consistent with transfer pricing to avoid taxation or to minimise exchange rate risks; (b) that poor comparative profitability was not confined to Japanese subsidiaries in the UK since Japanese firms in other EU states also disclosed poor profits, and with poor profitability being reported in Japanese subsidiaries over a long period; (c) that poor comparative profitability was only partly due to the specific economic problems damaging Japanese economic prospects in the early 1990s; and (d) that pure tax avoidance was unlikely to be the motivation for Japanese transfer pricing practices – with differences in the corporation tax rates in Japan and the UK favouring profit declaration in the latter – rather that Japanese transfer pricing strategies may be conducted to concentrate cash centrally and to reduce inflation and exchange rate risks. In this latter context, Buckley and Hughes (1997) noted that the Japanese business culture favours subsidiaries generating profit for the home-based parent, and that this policy effectively

TABLE 10.6: EFFICIENCY AND PRODUCTIVITY CHARACTERISTICS

	JAPANESE		DOMESTIC	
Variables	Mean[1] (st.dev.)	Median (n=)	Mean[1] (st.dev.)	Median (n=)
ERS94	22.04*** (12.36)	20.36††† (n=87)	27.33*** (9.25)	27.34 (n=87)
ERS91	26.72 (36.77)	20.76††† (n=87)	26.82 (9.90)	26.48††† (n=87)
CERS	–4.68 (34.96)	1.26 (n=87)	0.508 (5.56)	1.12 (n=87)
SEM94	127 924.8*** (134 173.4)	86 921.6††† (n=82)	69 485.1*** (39 131.8)	57 179.7††† (n=82)
SEM91	114 082.1 (121 499.1)	65 142.4††† (n=82)	60 563.1 (51 881.0)	49 278.7††† (n=82)
CSEM	13 842.7 (83 491.2)	12 177.6 (n=82)	8 921.9 (33 204.6)	8 020.2 (n=82)
PEM94	1 471.7 (20 455.8)	488.6††† (n=84)	4 879.3 (7 965.5)	3 472.5††† (n=84)
PEM91	–952.2 (29 030.7)	412.1††† (n=84)	3 759.2 (7 721.7)	2 825.6††† (n=84)
CPEM	2 423.9 (29 278.1)	854.0 (n=84)	1 120.2 (7 651.3)	825.0 (n=84)
TTA94	1.44* (0.824)	1.33††† (n=94)	1.63* (0.585)	1.52††† (n=94)
TTA91	1.39** (0.869)	1.21††† (n=94)	1.65** (0.783)	1.49††† (n=94)
CTTA	0.048 (0.595)	0.051 (n=94)	–0.018 (0.558)	0.042 (n=94)
TFA94	7.18** (9.25)	4.51††† (n=94)	9.96** (10.31)	6.57††† (n=94)
TFA91	7.11 (10.44)	4.40††† (n=94)	11.44 (24.7)	5.39††† (n=94)
CTFA	0.07 (8.46)	0.25 (n=94)	–1.48 (17.92)	0.62 (n=94)
DST94	78.09*** (71.29)	58.38††† (n=92)	50.93*** (33.82)	45.76††† (n=92)
DST91	90.53*** (106.01)	63.88††† (n=92)	54.92*** (37.25)	43.90††† (n=92)
CDST	–12.44 (86.72)	–3.03 (n=92)	–4.00 (21.68)	–0.740 (n=92)

Notes:

[1]Means are unbracketed with standard deviations shown in parenthesis

***,**,* indicates sample means are significantly different at the 1%, 5% and 10% levels, respectively (two-tailed t-tests)

††† indicates sample medians significantly different at the 1% level (two-tailed Mann Whitney tests)

drives the Japanese intra-firm pricing structure (that is in this scenario the Japanese firm is seen as a collective body, so that an overseas subsidiary acting as a profit centre would be viewed as highly dysfunctional).

In summary, it is doubtful how far the reported profitability of Japanese subsidiaries in the UK presents a true and fair view of their financial health. This problem is not restricted to the reported financial information for Japanese subsidiaries, since successive UK governments have been taking ever more strident steps to discourage unfair pricing of international intra-firm transfers (see Munday and Peel 1997).

Productivity and Efficiency Characteristics

Table 10.6 reports details of the productivity and efficiency characteristics of the Japanese and domestic samples in 1991 and 1994, together with changes between these years. It shows that employee remuneration as a proportion of sales (ERS) was, on average, significantly lower for the Japanese subsidiaries in 1994 (22.04 per cent) than for matched domestic subsidiaries (27.33 per cent). However, for 1991, there are no significant differences between the sample means (although, for both periods), median earnings as a proportion of sales are significantly higher in the domestic sample. Hence, for Japanese subsidiaries, there is some evidence that the ratio (CERS) improved over this period.

Table 10.6 also shows that Japanese subsidiaries generated significantly higher sales per employee in both periods, with mean 1994 sales per employee in the Japanese sample amounting to £128,000, compared to just £70,000 in the domestic sample. Similar results are evident for 1991, though the level of sales per employee in both samples was lower in 1991 than in 1994. Hence both Japanese and domestic firms experienced improving ERS ratios between 1991 and 1994, though the change in the ratio (CERS) did not differ significantly between the two samples. Although a superior measure of labour productivity is gross value added per employee (which is not available on the FAME database), the evidence presented here (combined with findings from the Census of Production) does suggest that Japanese companies are characterised by comparatively high labour productivity.

However, with reference to the net profit generated per employee (PEM), the table reveals that domestic firms outperformed their Japanese counterparts in both years, and significantly so in respect of the median value of the ratio. These results are perhaps unsurprising, given the poor profitability characteristics of the Japanese sample described above. They do demonstrate, however, that conclusions made in respect of employee productivity are sensitive to the measures adopted (sales versus profit). Also noteworthy, is the fact that, as with the ratio of sales to employees, the net profit to employee ratio improved in both samples between 1991 and 1994, as companies traded out of the recession. However, the change in the ratio of net profit to employees (CPEM) between 1991 and 1994 does not differ significantly between the samples with reference to both mean and median values.

Contrary to prior expectations, in terms of the generation of sales from total assets (TTA), table 10.6 shows that, with reference to both mean and median values of TTA, domestic subsidiaries had significantly higher asset turnover ratios than their Japanese counterparts in both 1991 and 1994. A similar pattern is also evident in respect of the ratio of sales to fixed assets, although the mean value of this ratio (TFA) does not differ significantly between the samples in 1991, nor do changes in the asset turnover ratios (CTTA, CTFA).

There is a strong expectation that the adoption of 'Japanese' production systems, with their emphasis on stock reduction and accelerated materials flows, would have resulted in Japanese subsidiaries holding relatively low levels of stock. Support for this is found in the summary statistics from the Census of Production (table 10.1), which show that the Japanese manufacturing sector in the UK was characterised by a favourable stock turnover performance. However, table 10.6 reveals that, when differences in industry and size are taken into account, domestic subsidiaries significantly outperformed (with reference to mean and median values of DST) their Japanese counterparts in both 1991 and 1994. The findings on stock holdings also show that both domestic and Japanese subsidiaries succeeded in reducing stock holdings (CDST) between 1991 and 1994 as the economy recovered. However, in both periods domestic firms were, on average, holding around a third less days' stock than their Japanese counterparts. These findings support the earlier research of Bromwich and Inoue (1994) who reported that Japanese subsidiaries in the UK in 1991 held relatively high levels of inventory. In part, this finding may reflect the need of Japanese subsidiaries to schedule high value parts from the Far East many months in advance of use (Munday *et al.* 1995).

Liquidity and Gearing Characteristics

Table 10.7 reports summary statistics relating to the liquidity and gearing characteristics of the two samples. Japanese multinational firms have been credited with efficient managerial practices, and in consequence there is an expectation that this will be reflected in their relative efficiency in the management of cash flows. Days debtors (DAD) measures the number of days sales represented by outstanding debtors, while days creditors (DAC) is the number of days sales represented by credit from suppliers. The table shows that both Japanese and domestic firms reduced their outstanding days debtors between 1991 and 1994 since debtors paid more promptly as the economy moved out of the recession. However, there are no significant differences between the two samples in respect of the debtor collection periods for either 1991 or 1994, or between changes in debtor collection periods (CDAD) between these years.

Table 10.7 also reveals that, with reference to both the mean and median, the level of days creditors in 1994 (DAC94) was significantly higher for domestic subsidiaries than for their matched Japanese counterparts. This may be due to the fact that Japanese companies received poor credit ratings in this period (Munday and Peel 1997), largely in consequence of their poor financial performance. In consequence, Japanese subsidiaries were less able to 'stretch' creditors than domestic firms.

TABLE 10.7: LIQUIDITY, SOLVENCY AND GEARING CHARACTERISTICS

	JAPANESE		DOMESTIC	
Variables	Mean[1] (st.dev.)	Median (n=)	Mean[1] (st.dev.)	Median (n=)
DAD94	51.13 (38.17)	47.09 (n=87)	55.03 (30.98)	54.27 (n=87)
DAD91	69.46 (71.84)	61.94 (n=87)	65.25 (26.83)	70.19 (n=87)
CDAD	−18.33 (66.16)	−8.03 (n=87)	−10.22 (27.09)	−7.04 (n=87)
DAC94	28.07*** (23.72)	20.82††† (n=90)	36.83*** (22.22)	36.70††† (n=90)
DAC91	74.62 (156.64)	39.76†† (n=90)	54.29 (37.66)	50.70†† (n=90)
CDAC	−46.55* (150.45)	−15.07† (n=90)	−17.45* (38.98)	−8.84† (n=90)
LIQ94	1.50 (1.18)	1.13† (n=96)	1.57 (0.971)	1.31† (n=96)
LIQ91	1.41 (0.838)	1.22 (n=96)	1.55 (0.854)	1.31 (n=96)
CLIQ	0.093 (0.919)	−0.078 (n=96)	0.019 (0.675)	0.003 (n=96)
GEAR94	0.787 (0.536)	0.741 (n=96)	0.694 (0.337)	0.686 (n=96)
GEAR91	0.693 (0.256)	0.702 (n=96)	0.714 (0.361)	0.679 (n=96)
CGEAR	0.094** (0.400)	0.016† (n=96)	−0.020** (0.273)	−0.001† (n=96)
ICOV94	10.39* (47.76)	1.13††† (n=52)	216.48* (822.56)	4.71††† (n=52)
ICOV91	3.65** (15.21)	1.30††† (n=52)	51.66** (161.25)	2.67††† (n=52)
CICOV	6.74 (50.25)	0.480††† (n=52)	164.82 (732.29)	2.93††† (n=52)

Notes:
[1]Means are unbracketed with standard deviations shown in parenthesis
***,**,* indicates sample means are significantly different at the 1%, 5% and 10% levels, respectively (two-tailed t-tests)
†††,††,† indicates sample medians are significantly different at the 1%, 5% and 10% levels, respectively (two-tailed Mann–Whitney rank sum tests)

However, the table shows that Japanese subsidiaries had higher mean creditors in 1991 (DAC91), but that the median value of days creditors was significantly lower in the Japanese sample in 1991. This is reflected in the finding that days creditors decreased (CDAC) by a significantly greater amount (by reference to both the mean and median) in the Japanese sample between 1991 and 1994. In summary, domestic subsidiaries, on average, 'stretched' creditors to a greater extent in 1994, with Japanese subsidiaries suffering greater reduction in days credit between 1991 and 1994.

With reference to corporate liquidity (that is the ability to meet short-term liabilities from short-term assets) the table shows little difference between the current ratios (LIQ) of the two samples for either period. However, the median liquidity for Japanese firms was generally lower, although only the median figure for 1994 (LIQ94), differs significantly between the two samples. There is also an indication that the average liquidity of firms in both samples improved (CLIQ) between 1991 and 1994. Table 10.7 also reveals that Japanese subsidiaries exhibited higher mean and median gearing ratios (GEAR) than their matched domestic counterparts in 1994 (although not significantly so), but slightly lower gearing levels in 1991. Hence, the average gearing level of the Japanese subsidiaries increased significantly more than that of domestic subsidiaries between 1991 and 1994 (CGEAR); domestic firms succeeded in reducing leverage during the economic upturn.

Finally Table 10.7 reports the mean and median values for interest cover (ICOV), a measure of income gearing. This shows how far interest payments are covered by net profits, with higher values of this ratio indicating lower financial risk. In line with the previous discussion on comparative profitability, domestic firms performed much better than their matched Japanese counterparts on this risk measure. For both Japanese and domestic subsidiaries, the mean interest cover ratio improved between 1991 and 1994 as profitability improved (CICOV). However, due to the large variance of this ratio, the median value of ICOV is perhaps more appropriate as a measure of central tendency. Table 10.7 shows that in both periods the median level of interest cover was significantly higher in the domestic sample, with the median Japanese company only just making sufficient net profits to cover fixed interest payments in 1991 and 1994. In addition, the median change (increase) in interest cover (CICOV) was significantly higher in the domestic sample.

CONCLUSIONS

Although evidence from a number of sources has examined the relative performances of the foreign-owned (and Japanese) manufacturing transplants in the UK, few previous studies have utilised cross-sectional data derived from company annual reports, and even fewer studies have examined changes in company performance using such data. Building on our earlier study by (Munday and Peel 1997), the purpose of this chapter has been to provide some new evidence on changes in the relative performance of Japanese subsidiaries between 1991 and 1994, with reference to a wide range of variables derived from company annual reports.

The empirical analysis suggested the following. Domestic subsidiaries actually grew faster (in terms of both sales and assets) than their Japanese counterparts over the period 1991 and 1994, partially reflecting adverse economic conditions in Japan. This was confirmed with respect to employment levels. Japanese subsidiaries, on average, employed fewer people than domestic subsidiaries in both 1991 and 1994. Moreover, employment levels in Japanese subsidiaries fell marginally between the two periods. At the same time, earnings in the Japanese firms increased faster than those in matched domestic subsidiaries.

Japanese subsidiaries scored comparatively badly on several indicators of profitability over both years. The evidence cited here suggests that poor Japanese subsidiary profit performance is not restricted either to the UK, or to particular periods. In spite of an improvement in economic conditions both in Japan and the UK, the results of this study indicated that more than twice as many Japanese (as compared to domestic) subsidiaries were making losses in both 1991 and 1994. This, it was suggested, is prima facie evidence of transfer pricing practices, although the objective of transfer pricing manipulation may reflect the inner dynamics of Japanese enterprises rather than representing a systematic attempt to minimise UK tax liability.

On productivity and efficiency variables, Japanese firms performed comparatively well compared to their matched domestic counterparts. Earnings as a proportion of sales were lower for the Japanese subsidiaries in 1994, and earnings as a proportion of sales actually fell in the Japanese sample between 1991 and 1994, in spite of average pay increasing at a faster rate in the Japanese sample over this period. Labour productivity, in terms of sales generated per employee, was also significantly higher in the Japanese sample over both periods. However, domestic firms generally produced a higher level of sales from a given asset base. This is important, as conclusions on productivity vary between assets and employment denominators, and between sales and profit numerators.

Contrary to prior expectations, Japanese subsidiaries also carried comparatively high levels of stock over both periods, although they and domestic firms did manage to reduce stocks between 1991 and 1994 as trading conditions in the UK improved.

The results of this empirical analysis do question the claimed efficiency of the Japanese transplant sector in the UK. Although the Japanese sector performs well on selected labour productivity measures, on other key performance variables (relating to profits, asset efficiency and stock holdings), the results are disappointing. Clearly such results do call into question the extent to which Japanese transplants are able to deliver the hypothesised benefits claimed in the literature, particularly given the generous subsidies extended to attract overseas investment. The results also raise questions pertaining to the contribution of Japanese firms to longer-term national development. If Japanese firms are found to be performing at a similar (or lower) level to their domestic counterparts (both in terms of employment and investment growth and financial performance), then the possibility of the domestic sector benefiting from Japanese investment may be reduced (that is, there may be little to learn from subsidiaries that are performing at the same level under similar manufacturing conditions). This is particularly germane since technology and knowledge transfer is one objective underpinning UK government aid to foreign companies.

NOTE

1. It should be noted that the values of the 1994 variables reported in Munday and Peel (1997) differ from those reported in this chapter, because of missing data for 1991. Thus in this chapter, data for 1994 is only used where equivalent data for 1991 is also available.

APPENDIX TO CHAPTER 10: VARIABLE DEFINITIONS

Note: In the text, variables are suffixed with 94 and 91 to indicate the year to which the variable refers (1991 and 1993/4). Changes in variables (1993/4 minus 1991 values) are prefixed by the letter C.

TUR:	Turnover (£000).
TAS:	Total assets [total capital employed] (£000).
FAS:	Fixed assets (£000).
EMP	Number of employees.
REM:	Average employee remuneration [total wage bill/employment] (£).
NPM:	Net profit margin: net profit before tax/TUR(per cent).
LOS:	1 = negative net profit before tax; zero otherwise (per cent).
REC:	Return on capital employed: net profit before tax/TAS (per cent).
ERS:	Total wage bill/TUR (per cent).
SEM:	Sales (TUR) per employee (£).
PEM:	Net profit before tax/EMP (£).
TTA:	TUR/TAS.
TFA:	TUR/FAS.
DST:	Days stock held: (stock/sales) x 365.
DAD:	Debtor collection period in days: (debtor/sales) x 365.
DAC:	Credit period (as a proportion sales) in days: (debtors/sales) x 365.
LIQ:	Current assets/current liabilities.
GEAR:	Total liabilities/TASS.
ICOV:	Net profit before interest and tax/interest paid.

11 The Impact of FDI on Domestic Employment: The Phenomenon of Industrial Hollowing-out in Japan

INTRODUCTION

The increasing globalisation of economic activities with new trends and patterns of investment, trade and inter-firm collaboration is rapidly changing the world map of industrial activity. International direct investment, in particular, grew rapidly during the 1980s and after a slow-down in the early 1990s showed renewed growth starting in 1993. Growth in flows of foreign direct investment (FDI) outstripped the growth in international trade that had been the primary engine of international economic growth until the end of the 1970s. Meanwhile, the annual sales of goods and services by foreign affiliates have reached one and a half times the value of world exports (OECD 1996, p. 15–21).

At the firm level, this relocation of manufacturing activities within industrialised countries and from industrialised to developing countries has generally strengthened the competitiveness of the multinational companies concerned. In contrast, at the country level, the consequent capital outflow has raised the fear of industrialisation. Apart from the issue of safeguarding international competitiveness, the main concern is with a decline in industrial employment. While in the USA and Western Europe the debate about FDI being a substitute for or complementary to trade, and, by extension, to domestic production and employment, dates back as far as the 1970s (Frank and Freeman 1978; Owens 1980; Kravis and Lipsey 1988; Glickman and Woodward 1989; Beyfuss and Kitterer 1990; Kokko 1993), this discussion did not become a major topic in Japan, however, until the beginning of the 1990s.[1]

For the first time then, the Japanese manufacturing sector has shown both a rapid increase in outward FDI and a substantial decline in domestic production and employment at the same time. More than the absolute increase in FDI, its strong regional concentration on Asian countries has become the focus of interest. In many cases, FDI in Asia did not just add to production in Japan, as in the past, but substituted for domestic production. This trend can be observed in many fields but is best illustrated by the shift of video cassette recorder (VCR) production by Japanese companies from Japan to abroad, mainly to Asian countries.

This has led to the widespread acceptance of a thesis that argues for a causal relation between a rise in FDI to Asia and a decline in domestic employment. This thesis is based on the assumption that the recent trend of shifting manufacturing activities abroad results in fewer exports from and more imports to Japan and thus to a delocalisation of domestic production and employment, foreshadowing an industrial hollowing out of the Japanese economy over the long term (in Japanese: *sangyô kûdôka*).

However, this view neglects important positive effects of FDI in both the short and the long run that range from a direct stimulation of exports to the role of FDI in the dynamic process of structural adjustment. By analysing these effects as well, the chapter seeks to achieve a more balanced view of the impact of Japanese FDI on the Japanese economy. Within this analysis, the chapter focuses on Asia, defined as East and South-east Asia, as the main recipient region of recent Japanese FDI in manufacturing. Concentrating on distinctions between the effects of FDI in Asia and that in Europe and North America, the chapter will elaborate on the special role of Asia as a whole rather than differentiate between single Asian countries.

Section two describes recent changes in Japanese manufacturing and FDI, and presents the factors that led to a widespread acceptance of the hollowing out thesis in Japan. Section three shows the direct effects of Japanese FDI on trade, production and employment from 1991 to 1995 by using detailed data provided by the Ministry of International Trade and Industry (MITI). In addition, it identifies the indirect effects of FDI during the same period. The final section touches on future prospects, emphasising the positive role of FDI in the process of a restructuring of companies, industries and the Japanese economy as a whole.

FACTORS SUPPORTING THE HOLLOWING-OUT THESIS

So far, 1991 has been the year of the highest industrial activity in Japan, as measured by shipments, value added and the number of employees in the manufacturing sector.[2] After a sharp decline over the following two years, a moderate increase began in 1994. However, the numbers are still below the record figures of 1991, and the employment figures even continued to decrease in 1995 and 1996 (Sômuchô Tôkeikyoku 1998). Table 11.1 presents the main changes by industries between 1991 and 1995.

TABLE 11.1: CHANGES IN THE JAPANESE MANUFACTURING SECTOR BY INDUSTRY, 1991–5 (establishments with four or more employees)

	Number of establishments		**Shipments (trillion yen)**		**Employees (Thousands)**		
	absolute in 1995	***% of 1991***	***absolute in 1995***	***% of 1991***	***absolute in 1995***	***change from 1991***	***% of 1991***
Lumber/wood	16 373	84.3	4.2	91.3	212	–33	86.5
Pulp/paper	10 558	94.4	8.5	94.4	269	–14	95.1
Chemicals	5 230	97.0	23.4	96.3	392	–14	96.6
Petroleum/coal	1 109	101.5	7.6	85.4	34	0	100.0
Ceramic/stone/clay	19 419	93.9	10.2	91.9	429	–30	93.5
Iron and steel	5 808	90.7	14.1	75.8	297	–43	87.4
Non–ferrous metals	3 793	91.0	6.5	84.4	161	–13	92.5
Plastics/rubber	24 312	93.2	13.8	89.6	601	–28	95.5
Food/beverages	47 577	96.1	34.7	100.3	1,259	+25	102.0
Textiles	16 045	53.9	4.2	53.2	265	–254	51.1
Leather	4 792	81.3	1.0	76.9	62	–17	78.5
Furniture	15 213	89.8	3.6	85.7	204	–26	88.7
Fabricated metals	47 668	93.4	17.6	87.1	817	–49	94.3
General machinery	42 138	91.1	30.3	83.5	1,094	–140	88.7
Electrical machinery	31 342	84.8	54.8	93.5	1,750	–233	88.3
Transport equipment	14 506	93.7	44.2	90.2	914	–70	92.9
Precision instruments	5 923	83.3	4.1	74.5	198	–56	78.0
Others	63 988	98.6	13.7	94.5	1026	–37	96.5
Total	**387 726**	**90.1**	**306.0**	**89.8**	**10,321**	**–1,030**	**90.9**

Source: TSDKCT 1993, 1997

With the exception of a small increase in the food and beverage industry, there is a clear negative trend across all industries that reflects the relative stagnation of the Japanese economy at the time. Nevertheless, a closer look at the employment changes reveals that four industries suffered especially hard from both a relative and an absolute decline in employment: namely, textiles, general machinery, electrical machinery and precision instruments. Although the decrease was less than average, another 70,000 jobs lost in the fourth machinery industry, transportation equipment, also contributed strongly to the total absolute decline. Textiles and the four machinery industries together account for more than 70 per cent of the overall employment loss of one million jobs between 1991 and 1995.

Although this development has to be largely attributed to a number of domestic factors and the worldwide economic stagnation in the early 1990s, Japanese FDI in Asia has often been cited as a main reason for the prolonged decline in manufacturing employment (Okajima 1996; Chôgin Sôgô Kenkyûsho 1996; Keizai Kikakuchô Chôsakyoku 1996). At first sight, this view seems to be supported by a number of factors that relate to the overseas activities of Japanese manufacturers at the same time, regarding the rapid increase of FDI as well as its sectoral and regional distribution.

TABLE 11.2: JAPANESE FDI IN MANUFACTURING BY REGION AND SELECTED INDUSTRIES, 1951–95 ($ MILLION, %)

	1951–85	*1986–90*	*1991*	*1992*	*1993*	*1994*	*1995*	*1991–5*
Total	**24 413**	**57 203**	**12 311**	**10 057**	**11 132**	**13 784**	**18 623**	**65 907**
Textiles	11.5%	3.1%	5.0%	4.3%	4.5%	4.7%	5.6%	4.9%
Gen. machinery	9.0%	10.4%	10.4%	11.0%	10.5%	11.8%	10.0%	10.7%
Electr. machinery	16.8%	22.0%	18.6%	18.1%	24.8%	19.1%	28.4%	22.5%
Transp. equipment	14.8%	13.1%	16.2%	11.8%	8.5%	14.7%	10.7%	12.3%
Other industries	47.9%	51.4%	49.8%	54.8%	51.7%	49.7%	45.3%	49.6%
Asia	7 600	11 141	2 928	3 104	3 659	5 181	8 058	22 930
Textiles	15.6%	10.0%	7.4%	7.3%	8.2%	9.6%	9.3%	8.7%
Gen. machinery	7.6%	8.8%	8.7%	6.9%	11.9%	7.7%	9.8%	9.1%
Electr. machinery	11.0%	22.4%	29.7%	17.4%	24.2%	26.6%	30.4%	26.7%
Transp. equipment	9.1%	8.8%	8.7%	6.9%	11.9%	7.7%	9.8%	8.2%
Other industries	56.7%	50.0%	45.5%	61.5%	43.8%	48.4%	40.7%	47.3%
North America	**7 824**	**32 617**	**5 868**	**4 177**	**4 146**	**4 763**	**7 326**	**26 280**
Europe	**2 115**	**10 452**	**2 690**	**2 101**	**2 040**	**1 855**	**1 995**	**10 681**
Other regions	**6 874**	**2 993**	**825**	**675**	**1 287**	**1 985**	**1 244**	**6 016**

Source: Tsûshô Sangyôshô 1996, p. 421–4

Notes: Japanese investment statistics do not always offer special data on precision instruments

Investment figures for Japan are usually given on a notification basis that does not include reinvested profits. Estimates on reinvested profits for the 1980s and available data for the years 1992 through 1995, totalling $54 bn, half of this in Asia, suggest that the total investment volume for the first half of the 1990s exceeded all cumulative investment in manufacturing until then (Tsûshô Sangyôshô 1997a: 31)

Three points arise from the statistics shown in table 11.2. First, total Japanese FDI in manufacturing from 1951 to 1995 clearly exceeded that of the first investment wave between 1986 and 1990; this rise becomes even more obvious when reinvested profits are included. Second, textiles and the three main machinery industries accounted for more than 50 per cent of the investment, with the textile industry accounting for the smallest share. The aggregated share of these four industries even rose slightly compared to the second half of the 1980s. Third, Asia's share as an investment destination increased remarkably (43.3 per cent of all FDI in 1995, 46.2 per cent including reinvested profits) while that of developed countries in North America and Europe dropped correspondingly.

Beside its volume, the recent concentration on Asia is of special consequence because Japanese investment motives in Asia clearly differ from those in Europe and North America. While market expansion has long been, by far, the most important motive for FDI in the Western developed countries, this factor has only recently gained importance in Asia. In contrast, the use of cheap labour and other input factors is still a main investment motive for Japanese manufacturers in Asia even in the Asian Newly Industrialising Economies (NIEs).

This is shown not only by numerous surveys on the investment motives of Japanese manufactures abroad (Takagi and Tsuchiya 1995, pp. 25–7; Kikai Shinkô Kyôkai 1996, p. 7–11; Tsûshô Sangyôshô 1997a, p. 3), but also by the high share of goods that are exported from Japanese affiliates in Asia to Europe, North America and Japan (table 11.3). The continuous rise of exports from Japanese affiliates abroad to Japan – often misleadingly labelled as reimports – is of special relevance here, for they appear directly to substitute for production and employment in Japan. This important point will be examined in detail in the next section.

TABLE 11.3: REGIONAL SALES DESTINATIONS BY JAPANESE MANUFACTURING OVERSEAS AFFILIATES IN DIFFERENT REGIONS, 1988–94 (%)

	1988	1991	1994
North America			
Intra-regional sale	93.8	89.4	86.3
Export out of region	6.2	10.6	13.7
to Japan	4.0	4.1	4.7
to others	2.2	6.5	9.0
Europe			
Intra-regional sale	95.6	93.9	81.7
Export out of region	4.4	6.1	18.3
to Japan	1.7	1.9	8.5
to others	2.7	4.2	9.8
Asia			
Intra-regional sale	71.2	70.1	73.4
Export out of region	28.8	29.9	26.6
to Japan	13.7	15.5	16.6
to North America	8.7	8.5	6.5
to Europe	4.5	4.3	2.8
to others	1.9	1.6	0.7

Source: Tsûshô Sangyôshô 1993, p. 22; Tsûshô Sangyôshô 1996, p. 170–9

While figures on FDI can serve as indicators for an absolute increase in foreign production, the relative extent of foreign production, as compared to domestic, is of even higher relevance for our topic here. This ratio is described by the foreign production quota, which measures sales of manufacturing affiliates abroad as a percent of sales of manufacturing firms at home and offers the best indicator for the degree of production internationalisation.

There has been a substantial rise of the foreign production quota over all industries for Japanese companies since 1991 (table 11.4) with electrical machinery and transportation equipment reaching the highest degree of foreign production. This corresponds to the large amount of FDI for these industries. In contrast, the ratio for the textile industry has stayed far below the industrial average. One reason for this is the relatively low average value of Japanese textile production abroad which is mainly located in Asia and is of the labour-intensive character.[3]

The uneven development of investment in plant and equipment in Japan and in overseas affiliates is another factor adding to the fear of industrial hollowing out. Neglecting the absolute decline after 1991, which was a direct result of the Japanese recession, there has been a trend towards a larger share of plant and equipment investment conducted abroad (figure 11.1). This shift indicates a build-up in production capacity abroad possibly affecting production levels in Japan. A sectoral differentiation reveals that electrical machinery and transportation equipment have been the leading sectors throughout the 1990s. A regional breakdown shows a strong shift from North America to Asia. In 1994 and 1995, Japanese production facilities in Asia captured more than half of all Japanese plant and equipment investment abroad, indicating a strong capacity shift to this region. While in Europe and North America half of the investment accounted for rationalisation, R&D, maintenance and repair, in Asia more than 70 per cent of this investment was directed at new production equipment and an expansion of capacity (Tsûshô Sangyôshô 1996, 1997a).

TABLE 11.4: FOREIGN PRODUCTION QUOTA OF SELECTED JAPANESE INDUSTRIES, 1991–5 (%)

	1991	*1992*	*1993*	*1994*	*1995*
Lumber/wood/pulp/paper	1.6	1.4	1.9	2.1	2.2
Iron and steel	4.9	5.0	6.3	5.4	6.8
Food/beverages	1.2	1.3	2.4	3.2	2.6
Textiles	2.6	2.3	3.2	4.0	3.5
Non-ferrous metals	5.2	7.8	6.5	8.8	6.7
General machinery	7.6	4.1	5.8	8.1	8.1
Electrical machinery	11.0	10.8	12.6	15.0	15.5
Transportation equipment	13.7	17.5	17.3	20.3	20.6
Total average	**6.0**	**6.2**	**7.4**	**8.6**	**9.0**

Source: Tsûshô Sangyôshô 1997a, p. 18

Note: foreign production quota = value of overseas production sales / value of domestic production sales

FIGURE 11.1: PLANT AND EQUIPMENT INVESTMENT OF JAPANESE MANUFACTURERS IN JAPAN AND IN OVERSEAS AFFILIATES, 1989–95

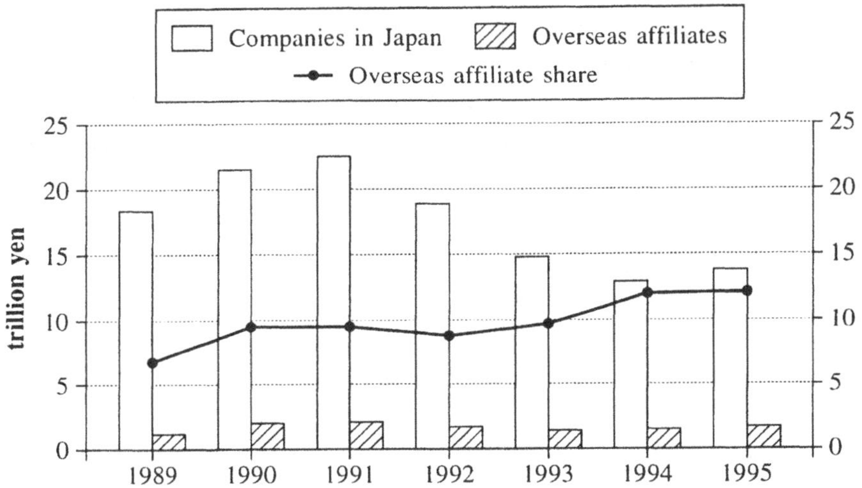

Overseas affiliate share=Plant and equipment investment in overseas affiliates/plant and equipment investment in Japan

Source: Tsûshô Sangyôshô 1997a, p. 27

Finally, our discussion of data that seem to support the hollowing-out thesis will return directly to the topic of employment. The view that employment loss in Japan is at least partly due to increased production activity by Japanese manufacturers in Asia seems to be most strongly supported by looking at the new jobs that have been created in Japanese overseas affiliates. This holds true for the number, as well as for the industrial and regional distribution, of these new jobs abroad since 1991.

Table 11.5 shows that most of these jobs abroad have been created in textiles, electrical machinery and transportation equipment, three of the five industries with the highest employment loss in Japan. Especially in electrical machinery, there is a striking parallel between jobs lost in Japan and new ones created overseas. Eighty per cent of the new jobs overseas have been created in Asia. While in transportation equipment the Asian share is only 40 per cent, in textiles, non-ferrous metals, general and electrical machinery, and other industries, Asia accounts for nearly all new jobs created abroad by Japanese FDI.

Summarising the findings of this section, it seems plausible to suggest that Japanese FDI in the first half of the 1990s, especially that in Asia, spurred imports from overseas affiliates and reduced exports, and thus led to a net loss of production and jobs in Japan. However, our discussion did not touch upon either the direct positive effects on exports or upon indirect effects of FDI that might have worked in the opposite direction. The next section will address both direct and indirect effects of Japanese FDI up to 1995.

TABLE 11.5: CHANGES IN DOMESTIC AND FOREIGN EMPLOYMENT OF JAPANESE MANUFACTURING COMPANIES, 1991–5%

	Employees in Japan (Thousands)			*Employees in overseas affiliates all regions/Asia (Thousands)*		
	1991	*1995*	*change*	*1991*	*1995*	*change*
Lumber/wood/pulp/paper	528	481	-47	19/3	13/4	-6/-1
Chemicals	406	392	-14	72/28	112/48	+40/+20
Petroleum/coal	34	34	0	5/1	2/1	-3/0
Iron and steel	340	297	-43	33/11	27/15	-6/+4
Non-ferrous metals	174	161	-13	34/20	58/40	+24/+20
Food/beverages	1 234	1 259	+25	33/15	63/35	+30/+20
Textiles	519	265	-254	91/69	154/129	+63/+60
General machinery	1 234	1 094	-140	88/18	111/40	+23/+22
Electrical machinery	1 983	1 750	-233	419/249	604/435	+185/+186
Transportation equipment	984	914	-70	230/91	354/143	+124/+52
Precision instruments	254	198	-56	31/23	39/27	+8/+4
Others	3 664	3 477	-187	188/66	226/113	+38/+47
Total	**11 354**	**10 322**	**-1 032**	**1 243/594**	**1 763/1 030**	**+520/+436**

Source: TSDKCT 1993, 1997; Tsûshô Sangyôshô 1992, 1996

IMPACT OF JAPANESE FDI ON TRADE, PRODUCTION AND EMPLOYMENT IN JAPAN BETWEEN 1991 AND 1995

Methodological Remarks

Numerous theoretical and empirical studies have been undertaken in Western countries throughout the last twenty-five years to examine the trade, production and employment effects of outward FDI in manufacturing industries. No consensus has emerged either on the signs of the effects or on their magnitudes. This has to be seen primarily as a reflection of poor data availability combined with the complexities of the analysis and methodological problems. Beside lacking data, measurement problems arise from the existence of direct and indirect effects as well as important differences between static and dynamic, microeconomic and macroeconomic approaches (for a good overview of methodological problems and empirical findings see OECD 1995, pp. 140–5).

In analysing the effects of Japanese FDI between 1991 and 1995 on domestic production and employment, both a direct and an indirect impact can be identified. In the main, the presentation and analysis of the direct impact is based on figures provided by MITI that calculate changes in trade flows to and from Japan which are directly due to the overseas activities of Japanese manufacturers.[4] By using industrial input–output tables, these changes in Japanese exports and imports are converted to changes in domestic production and employment. Although this method is open to a number of possible errors concerning the resulting absolute figures, it offers a reasonable basis for measuring the extent and the changes in the direct influence of FDI on domestic employment. In addition, an analysis of the indirect impact will address effects that go beyond mere changes in trade flows and will try to examine how much an absence of investment abroad would have affected production and employment in Japan through 1995.

Direct Impact

There are three main effects that determine the direct relationship between FDI and trade, and between FDI and domestic production and employment, namely the export stimulation effect, the import effect and the export displacement effect (see Tsûshô Sangyôshô 1995, p.33). According to MITI's calculation method, the single trade effects can be described as follows:[5]

The *export stimulation effect* measures the increase in exports of capital and intermediate goods from Japan by calculating exports to Japanese overseas affiliates. Accordingly, the effect must be divided into two sub-effects describing the export increase of capital goods for fixed capital formation overseas and that of components serving as input factors for the production in overseas affiliates.

$$\text{export stimulation effect} = \left\{\begin{array}{l}\text{volume of fixed capital formation}\\ \text{in overseas affiliates}\end{array} \times \begin{array}{l}\text{ratio of capital goods}\\ \text{from Japan}\end{array}\right\} + \left\{\begin{array}{l}\text{component purchase volume of}\\ \text{overseas affiliates}\end{array} \times \begin{array}{l}\text{ratio of components}\\ \text{from Japan}\end{array}\right\}$$

The *import effect* measures the increase of imports to Japan by calculating imports from Japanese affiliates abroad. These goods are supposed to replace production that has formerly taken place in Japan for the domestic market.

$$\text{import effect} = \text{volume of sales of overseas affiliates} \times \text{ratio of sales to Japan}$$

The *export displacement effect* measures the decrease of exports originating in Japan due to an increase in overseas production of Japanese affiliates abroad. These overseas produced goods are supposed to replace exports from Japan that formerly have been either directed at the country of the overseas affiliate or that have been exported to other countries.

$$\text{export displacement effect} = \text{volume of sales of overseas affiliates} \times (1 - \text{ratio of sales to Japan}) \times \text{Japanese share of world imports}$$

$$\text{Japanese share of world imports} = \text{world import volume of industry } i \text{ from Japan} \div \text{total world import volume of industry } i$$

Before we refer to the calculated figures, it is important to mention two methodological problems associated with the three formulas presented above. First, the formula for the import effect suggests that imports to Japan from Japanese overseas affiliates replace only production in Japan although these imports might also crowd out imports from foreign companies. Thus, this calculation of the import effect tends to overestimate the negative impact on production in Japan. However, the low import penetration rate of Japan suggests that this takes place only to a very limited extent and therefore does not significantly affect the calculated result for the import effect.

A more critical issue is the calculation of the export displacement effect. The formula implies that production in overseas affiliates replaces exports from Japan according to the Japanese share of world imports of respective industries. This assumption is highly speculative but, but given the lack of a better indicator, is probably the most realistic. However, most observers (including representatives of the MITI) agree that this calculation tends to overestimate the displacement effect.[6]

Based on the calculation method explained above, figure 11.2 shows the direct effects of Japanese FDI on exports from and imports to Japan between 1991 and 1995. These data yield two main findings. First, the

FIGURE 11.2: DIRECT TRADE EFFECTS OF JAPANESE FDI, 1991–5

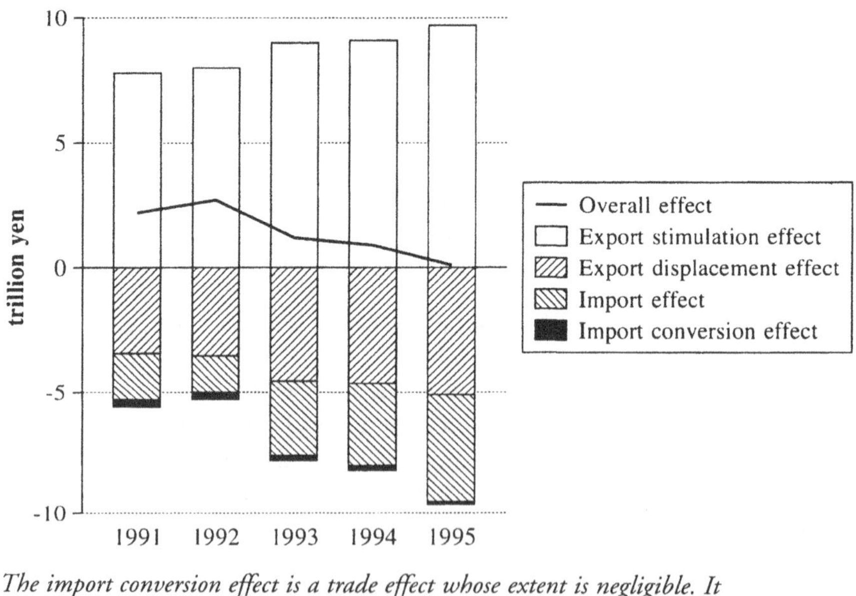

The import conversion effect is a trade effect whose extent is negligible. It measures increases and decreases in material imports for production in Japan that arise for FDI induced changes of the production level in Japan.

Source: Tsûshô Sangyôshô 1997a, p. 36

numbers clearly show that a growing share of Japanese foreign trade is related to FDI and conducted between Japan and affiliates of Japanese companies abroad. In 1995, nearly one-quarter of all Japanese exports went to overseas affiliates that had been the destination for less than 19 per cent of all exports in 1991. With respect to capital goods only, the share of overseas affiliates rose to more than 35 per cent of all Japanese exports compared to 30 per cent in 1991 (Tsûshô Sangyôshô 1996, p. 70). Similarly, FDI led to a strong absolute and relative rise of imports from Japanese overseas affiliates to 15 per cent of all imports in 1995; the number rises to more than 18 per cent if only consumer goods are counted (Tsûshô Sangyôshô 1996, p. 70).

Second, the overall influence of Japanese FDI on Japan's trade balance has been positive so far. Or, in other words, the influence of FDI on Japanese trade has been of a complementary, rather than of a substitutive, character. This result is of utmost importance, for it stands in sharp contrast to the hollowing out argument and general expectations based on the discussion in the previous section. Although FDI replaced exports and led to an increase in imports, at the same time it also stimulated exports of capital and intermediate goods to an extent that outweighed the negative impact of FDI on the Japanese trade balance. Accounting for a probable overestimation of the import and export displacement effects, the real positive net effect on trade might be even larger. However, this positive net effect shows a clear tendency to level off, suggesting that it might turn negative in the future.

These findings are directly reflected in the sectoral changes in the Japanese trade balance (table 11.6) which is increasingly influenced by trade between Japan and Japanese overseas affiliates as shown before. A striking feature of recent changes in the Japanese trade structure is the absolute and relative decline of consumer goods on the export side in contrast to an enormous rise in imported consumer goods, especially of electric household appliances and motor cars. The quantity of capital goods imported to Japan also rose strongly between 1991 and 1995. But, in contrast, this rise in imports to Japan is clearly outweighed in absolute terms by the increase in capital and intermediate goods exported from Japan within the same time.

A regional break-down of the trade flows reveals that Asia has become by far the most important trade region for Japan, with exports to Asia rising much more strongly than imports from that region (table 11.7). This development stands in obvious contrast to the shrinking trade surplus, or rising deficit, with all other regions. Although these figures are only indirectly related to Japanese FDI, they suggest that the changes in FDI-induced trade flows to and from Asia did not have a negative, but rather a positive, influence on the Japanese trade balance.

TABLE 11.6: SECTORAL CHANGES IN THE JAPANESE TRADE BALANCE, 1991–5 ($100 MILLION, %)

a) Exports	**1991**	**1992**	**1993**	**1994**	**1995**	**change 1991–5**	
Total exports	**3 145**	**3 396**	**3 609**	**3 956**	**4 429**	**+1 284**	**+40.8%**
Food, direct consumer goods	17	18	18	18	18	+1	+5.9%
Industrial materials and supplies	549	583	615	682	846	+297	+54.1%
Capital goods	1 716	1 881	2 080	2 377	2 730	+1 014	+59.1%
general machinery	696	764	829	931	1,070	+374	+53.7%
electrical machinery	555	598	681	807	980	+425	+76.6%
transportation equipment	313	360	400	448	456	+143	+45.7%
Consumer goods	806	853	828	795	764	-42	-5.2%
non-durable consumer goods	26	30	31	32	35	+9	+34.6%
textile products	8	9	9	8	8	0	0.0%
durable consumer goods	780	823	797	763	729	-51	-6.5%
electric household appliances	62	62	58	53	48	-14	-22.6%
motor cars	447	486	468	448	416	-31	-6.9%

b) Imports	**1991**	**1992**	**1993**	**1994**	**1995**	**change 1991–5**	
Total imports	**2 367**	**2 330**	**2 407**	**2 747**	**3 361**	**+994**	**+42.0%**
Food, direct consumer goods	322	373	395	464	507	+185	+57.5%
Industrial materials and supplies	1 280	1 187	1 177	1 239	1 462	+182	+14.2%
Capital goods	329	356	389	488	689	+360	+109.4%
general machinery	141	146	151	181	277	+136	+96.5%
electrical machinery	130	128	155	206	305	+175	+134.6%
transportation equipment	55	55	53	63	55	0	0.0%
Consumer goods	326	346	379	476	609	+283	+86.8%
non-durable consumer goods	155	178	199	242	296	+141	+91.0%
textile products	100	118	133	161	196	+96	+96.0%
durable consumer goods	171	168	180	234	313	+142	+83.0%
electric household appliances	15	17	19	28	41	+26	+173.3%
motor cars	52	50	51	70	100	+48	+92.3%

Source: JETRO 1996b, pp. 12, 20

TABLE 11.7: REGIONAL CHANGES IN THE JAPANESE TRADE BALANCE, 1991–5 ($100 MILLION, %)

	1991	**1992**	**1993**	**1994**	**1995**	**change 1991–5**	
Total exports	**3 145**	**3 396**	**3 609**	**3 956**	**4 429**	**+1 284**	**+40.8%**
to USA	915	958	1 054	1 176	1 209	+294	+32.1%
to EU	592	625	564	575	703	+111	+18.8%
to Asia	1 008	1 121	1 305	1 528	1 865	+857	+85.0%
to other regions	630	692	686	677	652	+22	+3.5%
Total imports	**2 367**	**2 330**	**2 407**	**2 747**	**3 361**	**+994**	**+42.0%**
to USA	533	522	552	627	754	+221	+41.5%
to EU	318	313	301	355	488	+170	+53.5%
to Asia	683	703	766	907	1 155	+472	+69.1%
to other regions	833	792	788	858	964	+131	+15.7%
Trade balance	**778**	**1 066**	**1 202**	**1 209**	**1 068**	**+290**	**+37.3%**
with USA	382	436	502	549	455	+73	+19.1%
with EU	274	312	263	220	215	-59	-21.5%
with Asia	325	418	539	621	710	+385	+118.5%
with other regions	-203	-100	-102	-181	-312	-109	-53.7%

Source: JETRO 1996b, pp. 15, 22
Note: Data for EU until 1994 for EU 12, in 1995 for EU 15

To measure the effects of FDI-induced changes in trade flows, we return to the data provided by MITI that has applied the trade effects shown in figure 11.3 directly to changes in production and employment in Japan. To do this, industrial input–output tables that differentiate between a hundred kinds of

FIGURE 11.3: DIRECT PRODUCTION EFFECTS OF JAPANESE FDI, 1991–5

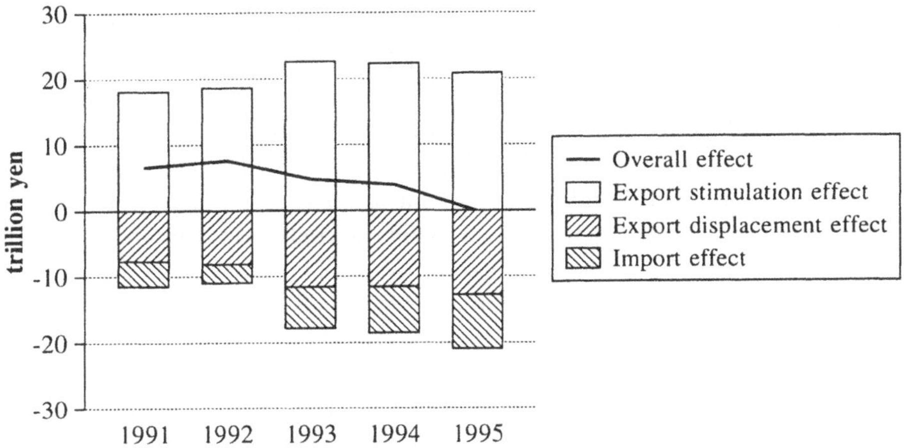

Source: Tsûshô Sangyôshô 1997a, p. 38

FIGURE 11.4: DIRECT NET EMPLOYMENT EFFECT OF JAPANESE FDI, 1991–5

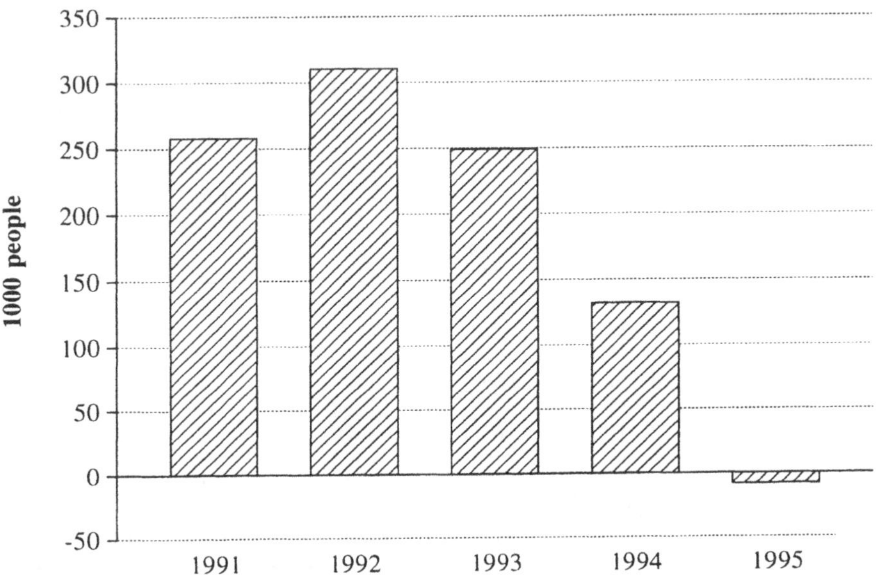

Source: Tsûshô Sangyôshô 1997a, p. 39

goods have been used to calculate the effects, first on domestic production, and then on domestic employment in a second step.[7] Although this method also raises some methodological problems, such as how to deal with changes in the yen rate, it can be regarded as a reasonable approach here. As could be expected by the changes in trade flows described above, the net direct impact of trade changes on production and employment in Japan induced by Japanese FDI has, until recently, been positive (figures 11.3 and 11.4).

It is important to note that the effects shown here have been calculated for the whole Japanese economy and not only for the manufacturing sector. The fact that the slight positive trade effect in 1995 resulted in a slight negative effect on employment reflects the shift to more capital- and technology-intensive production in Japan, substituting for more labour-intensive processes that have been shifted abroad (see table 11.8). Overall, the picture, as given in figures 11.3 and 11.4, shows a positive net influence of FDI on production and employment in Japan, which started to decrease in 1993 and then levelled off in 1995. Presuming some overestimation of the negative trade effects, it can be concluded that, even in 1995, the direct net effect of Japanese FDI on domestic employment has been positive.

TABLE 11.8: DIRECT PRODUCTION AND EMPLOYMENT EFFECTS OF JAPANESE FDI BY INDUSTRY, 1994

	Export stim. effect *billion yen*	**Export displ. effect** *billion yen*	**Import effect** *billion yen*	**Production net effect** *billion yen*	**Employment net effect** *persons*
Agriculture/forestry/fishery	27	–13	–147	–133	–4,261
Mining	33	–10	–10	13	452
Construction	130	–55	–82	–7	–372
Manufacturing	**17 984**	**–9 309**	**–5 305**	**3 370**	**93 900**
food/beverages	43	–14	–426	–397	–17 204
textiles	201	–61	–298	–158	–12 509
lumber/wood/pulp/paper	313	–89	–229	–5	–251
chemicals	1 511	–496	–401	614	12 094
petroleum/coal	465	–97	–513	–145	–491
iron and steel	2 019	–588	–215	1 216	16 821
non-ferrous metals	857	–208	–127	522	13 275
general machinery	1 194	–465	–269	460	16 517
electrical machinery	4 149	–2 774	–1 585	–210	–7 710
transportation equipment	4 400	–3 659	–609	132	2 918
precision instruments	125	–7	–8	110	6 444
others	2 707	–851	–626	1 230	63 996
Commerce	848	–464	–302	82	10 441
Service	1 569	–927	–493	149	13 090
Others	1 684	–776	–524	384	19 200
Total	**22 275**	**–11 554**	**–6 864**	**3 857**	**132 450**

Source: Tsûshô Sangyôshô 1996, p. 355

Finally, we will address differences in the effects of FDI by industry and region. Although there are no data available that show the development of trade, production and employment effects of Japanese FDI by industry over a number of years, figures for 1994 display the existence of differences between individual industries (table 11.8). These figures also show that only 70 per cent of the employment effects of FDI in 1994 related to the manufacturing sector directly, with commerce and other services accounting for the remaining 30 per cent.

Within the manufacturing sector, only food/beverages, textiles and electrical machinery showed strong net negative effects. Most manufacturing industries, including the other three machinery industries, offset negative import and export displacement effects by an even stronger stimulation of exports of capital and intermediate goods to overseas affiliates. This result includes some inter-industrial balancing: for example, a negative import effect of increased overseas production of electrical goods compensated by an increase in general machinery exports. Preliminary figures for 1995 indicate that this structure remained nearly the same in the following year with one exception. Production and employment effects for the transport equipment industry also turned negative for the first time due to a strong export displacement by overseas production (Tsûshô Sangyôshô 1997a, p. 75).

This allows for a distinction between two types of industries with negative net effects, separate from those displaying positive or neutral ones. In food/beverages and textiles, the decrease in production and employment in Japan has been mainly due to a strong import effect of FDI, while for electrical machinery and transportation equipment the export displacement effect has been of greater relevance. These findings are also reflected in the sectoral changes of the Japanese trade balance as described in table 11.6.

Although there are no data available that differentiate the effects of FDI by region, data on trade flows of overseas affiliates clearly show that FDI in Asia gained strongly in importance for both negative and positive effects on production and employment in Japan. Obviously, the import effect is mainly related to FDI in Asia. Figure 11.5 shows that Asia accounted for nearly 70 per cent of all imports from Japanese overseas affiliates since 1991. Considering the strong growth of these imports in absolute terms, this relative figure becomes even more significant. As described above, the negative influence of the import effect has had the fastest growing influence on production and employment in Japan.

Looking at export stimulation effects, the significance of FDI in Asia rose in both absolute and relative terms. Purchases of intermediate goods from Japan by manufacturing affiliates in Asia nearly tripled from 1991 to 1995, expanding the Asian share from 31 per cent to 40 per cent of all purchases of this kind worldwide. Similarly, Asia accounted for the largest positive impact on exports from Japan for plant and equipment investment in

FIGURE 11.5: VALUE OF IMPORTS OF OVERSEAS AFFILIATES TO JAPAN BY REGION, 1991–5

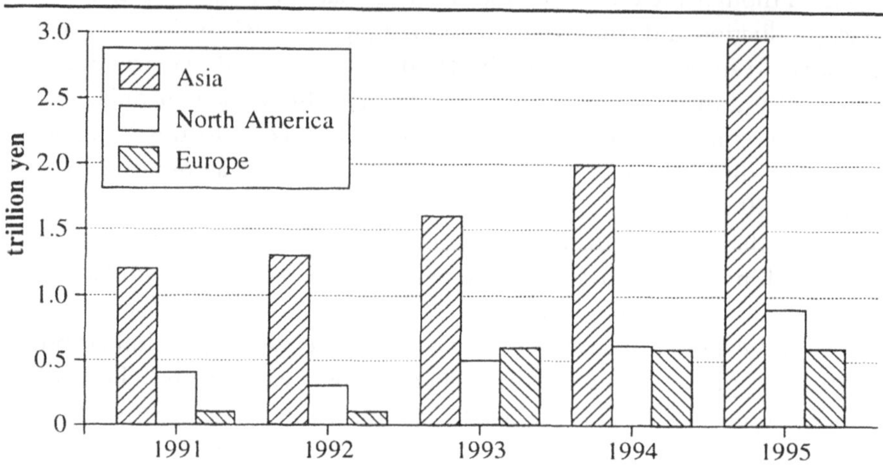

Figures for 1995 are preliminary ones and differ slightly from those in figure 11.3

Source: Tsûshô Sangyôshô 1997a, p. 39

overseas affiliates. Asian affiliates did not only invest the most in plant and equipment in 1994 and 1995, but also imported relatively more from Japan than from affiliates in other regions – 37 per cent in Asia versus 26 per cent in North America and 23 per cent in Europe in 1995 (Tsûshô Sangyôshô 1997a, pp. 27, 52).

Summarising the analysis of the *direct* impact of FDI up to 1995, three results have to be stressed. First, the overall net influence of FDI on the Japanese economy has been positive rather than negative. Although FDI resulted in some direct delocalisation of production activities, this loss was more than offset by an extra export to overseas affiliates. This finding stands in sharp contrast to the hollowing out thesis that partly attributes the overall decline in manufacturing employment observed in Japan since 1991 to FDI. However, these effects vary remarkably between industries.

Second, the rise of FDI in Asia is of special importance, for it has contributed the largest share to both negative and positive effects on production and employment in Japan. Regarding the strong growth of exports of intermediate and capital goods to Asia, it can be suggested that the net effect of FDI in this region has been positive so far. This conclusion is also supported by the strong rise of the Japanese trade surplus with Asian countries up to 1995.

Third, the positive overall effect started to decrease in 1993 and levelled off in 1995. Even accounting for an overestimation of negative trade effects, this trend shows that the direct effect of FDI on employment in Japan might turn negative in the future, especially regarding the shift of labour intensive production to other countries.

Indirect Impact

The calculation method above measured the direct impact of actual Japanese FDI, but did not address important indirect effects and alternative scenarios with less or no FDI. We will touch on this indirect impact briefly here and examine it in detail in the last section.

Even in the 1990s, a large share of Japanese FDI has been directed to markets where Japanese exports are still threatened by trade restrictions. This holds true for large parts of the automobile and electronic sectors in North America and Europe but also for a number of different sectors in Asia, especially in China. It is justifiable to assume that Japanese manufacturers would have had big problems penetrating these markets to the same extent using only exports (Dicken 1988; Negandhi and Serapio 1995; Fukushima and Kwan 1995). This means that Japanese FDI in such sectors partly resulted in additional production abroad and, thus, did not displace exports which would not have taken place otherwise. Rather, FDI allowed for an extra export of capital and intermediate goods to overseas affiliates that would not have occurred without FDI.

Even in the absence of trade barriers, overseas investment can lead to a strengthening of the global competitiveness of companies investing abroad. This strengthening is achieved by better access to a wide range of input factors (for example, technology, skilled labour, cheap labour, infrastructure, investment incentives) as well as proximity to local customers and competitors, enabling fast and flexible responses to market changes (Dunning 1988). Accordingly, it can be taken for granted that overseas activity has also helped Japanese manufacturers to secure and further explore foreign markets to an extent unreachable without FDI and, thus, indirectly affected production and employment in Japan.

Taking a dynamic perspective, the most important point is the change in comparative advantage. It goes without saying that a large part of FDI-relocated production could not have been kept in Japan over the long term for the simple reason of high domestic production costs.[8] In addition, the rapid appreciation of the yen since 1990 raised the pressure on both export-intensive industries and those principally open to imports. Accepting such production loss in certain areas as inevitable, FDI proves to be a useful countermeasure, for it permits the export of intermediate and capital goods. It also secures cheaper imports that can strengthen the competitiveness of the investing, and other domestic, companies and might even prevent complete firm closure (Madeuf 1995). Although only reflecting the basic theory of comparative advantage, this argument is highly relevant to our discussion since a large share of Japanese FDI to Asia falls into this category (Kwan 1997).

This brief presentation of only the most important indirect effects shows the limitations of any approach that solely calculates the direct effects of FDI. It also indicates that the overall effect of Japanese FDI on domestic production and employment until 1995 has clearly been more positive than described in the previous chapter.

THE ROLE OF JAPANESE FDI WITHIN INDUSTRIAL AND ECONOMIC RESTRUCTURING

As shown before, domestic production and employment have clearly benefited from the overall impact of Japanese FDI in the first half of the nineties. As related to the direct effects of FDI, however, this positive outcome has been due to a special historic set of factors that seems to have run its course.

So far, negative effects have been limited by the fact that overseas production, especially in Asia, only very recently reached an extent that results in significant exports to Japan. Regarding the ongoing shift of Japanese production activities abroad, the amount of all imports from Japanese overseas affiliates is expected to increase strongly in the future. According to one estimate of the MITI, these imports will rise from 4.4 trillion yen in 1995 to 10 trillion yen in the year 2000 (SSKK 1996, pp. 14–15).

On the other hand, the strong increase in capital good exports that was due to the rapid expansion of production in Asia must not be expected to continue at the same pace in the future. A rising local and regional procurement of capital goods by Japanese affiliates abroad will directly reduce imports from Japan. The overall share of these purchases had already declined continuously from 44.8 per cent in 1990 to 36.5 per cent in 1995 (Tsûshô Sangyôshô 1992–1997a). This trend will continue, especially for exports of intermediate goods to Asia where the industrial infrastructure is constantly improving and thus facilitating local/regional procurement.

In addition, the substitution of labour-intensive processes in Japan with capital- and technology-intensive ones will continue and lead to a relative shift of jobs to Asia. Regarding this outlook, positive indirect effects of overseas investment even gain in importance for Japan and for our hollowing out discussion and the evaluation of an overall effect of FDI. Changes in comparative advantages and the need for restructuring of the domestic industry have to be taken into account in particular.

In this respect, the situation in Japan seems to resemble that of western industrial countries where the discussion of the effects of outward investment has been focusing on domestic location conditions for a long time. While such a point of view is correct in general, it neglects a fact that requires an important distinction when evaluating the role of FDI for Japan and for her Western counterparts. Although Japan has meanwhile caught up to the leading industrial nations with regard to technology and has also become one of the most expensive places for industrial production worldwide, the internationalisation of the Japanese economy and the change of its industrial structure did not keep up with these changes.

Despite the strong rise in overseas investment during the last ten years, the extent of Japanese production abroad remains low by international standards. Even in the electrical machinery and transportation equipment industries, Japanese companies are much less internationalised than their counterparts in Germany or the USA (table 11.9). Although individual companies like Sony or Toyota have without doubt reached the status of global player, the average Japanese industry still shows a surprising low degree of internationalisation.

The following factors explain this low degree of internationalisation and the insufficient structural adjustments of Japanese industry at home. As an industrial latecomer, Japan still regulated foreign trade and capital exchange strictly until the 1960s. After the abolition of most of these regulations, the peripheral location of Japan towards the economic centres of Europe and North America continued to limit the international exchange of goods and capital to a certain extent. Even after 1980 and the economic rise of Asian countries, rising cost levels in Japan and an appreciation of the yen started to impel production internationalisation and structural adjustment at home. However, strong domestic demand during the 'bubble economy' until 1991 once again prevented this restructuring process from becoming thorough-going. In addition, the low penetration of Japan by imports and FDI from abroad have delayed internationalisation and economic restructuring until the present because their low levels not only reduce competitive pressure in Japan but also limit the import of new knowledge and technologies (Legewie 1998, pp. 294–310).

TABLE 11.9: INTERNATIONAL COMPARISON OF FOREIGN PRODUCTION QUOTAS IN SELECTED INDUSTRIES (%)

	Japan 1995	USA 1994	Germany 1994
Food/beverages	2.6	23.9	4.9
Textiles	3.5	—	11.1
Chemicals	8.3	42.3	66.0
Iron and steel	6.8	—	12.5
General machinery	8.1	38.4	19.9
Electrical machinery	15.5	26.9	34.5
Transportation equipment	23.9	46.6	46.0
Total average	**9.1**	**26.0**	**23.0**

Source: Tsûshô Sangyôshô 1997a, p. 18
Note: Foreign production quota = value of overseas production sales / value of domestic production sales

The slow internationalisation of production came about with an obvious declining competitiveness of the domestic industry by international standards. A comparison of the Japanese export portfolio with that of other industrialised countries based on a product classification of SITC (Standard International Trade Classification) goods at the lowest level of aggregation suggests that in 1992 Japanese exports were concentrated in sectors with low-growth propensity and also in goods that faced strong competition from low-wage countries, indicating limited growth potential and a high level of international pressure on domestic manufacturing.

This pressure has to be seen as the real driving force behind the recent rise in Japanese FDI in manufacturing which was only accelerated by the rapid appreciation of the yen until April 1995. Such a view is supported by the continued rise in FDI outflows after that time, reaching a new record high with more than $20 billion in 1996 (Ministry of Finance 1997).[9] Although the internationalisation of production has meanwhile gained strong momentum in Japan, Japanese industry remains under special strains to spur restructuring and to move to new sectors that are able to secure domestic production and employment over the long term. Within this process, FDI plays a crucial role. It allows for extra export of capital goods and better access to foreign markets and, most importantly, simultaneously accelerates the necessary allocation of resources in Japan. In addition, overseas affiliates can strongly support the shift in the domestic industrial structure by generating profits and thus providing necessary capital for new investment in Japan.

Even the MITI acknowledges the inevitable loss in further areas of production in Japan. In its White Paper on International Trade 1997, it stresses strongly not only the positive role of outward investment, but also of inward investment for the necessary reallocation process of labour and capital in Japan, resulting in policies to promote both (Tsûshô Sangyôshô 1997b). Although this process represents a perpetual task for all industrial countries, it forms a special need in Japan. Regarding the still low degree of production internationalisation, the positive role of further FDI appears to be even more important in Japan than elsewhere.

CONCLUSION

Summarising the findings, we see that the rapid change of comparative advantage and the relative worsening of the Japanese domestic industry in terms of international competitiveness at the beginning of this decade have accelerated the need for far-reaching structural adjustment in Japan. Within this process, the relocation of industries that have lost their competitive edge to developing countries serves as an important tool to enable a shift to new, high value-added sectors that can keep production, employment and wages high in Japan. Thus, the recent rise in FDI has to be seen as one important pillar in companies' efforts at restructuring. It has already contributed to the impressive recovery of Japanese manufacturers, with some export-intensive companies even posting record earnings in 1996 and overall exports rising strongly, far surpassing the increase of imports since the beginning of 1997 (Sômuchô Tôkeikyoku 1998).

However, the trend towards more capital- and technology-intensive industries and the higher productivity growth in manufacturing compared to the service sector make it unlikely that the employment of the manufacturing sector will remain at its current level or even rise again over the long term. Rather, a relative shift of jobs to the service sector has to be expected. Accordingly, industrial restructuring must comprise the whole economic sector in Japan, emphasising employment opportunities in new fields of the service sector, like software development or financial services, that might be closely related to the globalisation of manufacturing activities.

Within this restructuring process, FDI can play an important role, but it cannot solve structural problems that hinder the growth of new industries and impede a prolonged revitalisation of the Japanese economy. Overly high domestic prices for services in excessively regulated sectors like energy, transportation or finance and overly strong rigidities in Japan's budget system, as well as in the Japanese education and employment systems, have turned out to be important domestic factors that prevent an optimal allocation of resources within Japan (Economic Planning Agency 1996; Kwan 1997, p. 73; several contributions in Deutsches Institut für Japanstudien 1998). If FDI rises as a result of these factors, it might pose an actual threat to production and employment in Japan. However, this kind of delocalisation would occur only as a symptom, not as the root of an industrial hollowing out.

NOTES

1. Reflecting the first wave of Japanese FDI after 1985, deindustrialisation in Japan started to be discussed in the second half of the 1980s. However, the continuing rise of employment in the manufacturing sector until 1991 restricted the discussion mainly to the academic field (Karatsu 1986; Rôdôsha Kyôiku Kyôkai 1988; Tomizawa 1989).

2. Yearly figures refer to the Japanese fiscal year that runs from April of the given year to March of the following year.

3. The low foreign production quota for the textile industry also suggests that only a small part of the production that was abandoned in Japan went overseas in the form of FDI, reflecting its relatively small share compared to the machinery industries as seen in table 11.2.

4. In 1970, MITI conducted the first annual survey on overseas activities of all Japanese companies only excluding those in banking, finance, insurance and real estate. The contents of this survey have been constantly extended and provide detailed information on production activities and trade flows of Japanese overseas affiliates. Among other big industrial countries, similar data are available only for the United States. Since 1993 the number of respondent overseas affiliates has always exceeded 10,000, representing a high coverage rate of more than 60 per cent (Tsûshô Sangyôshô 1996: 22).

5. For a detailed discussion of the different effects mentioned above, see Tsûshô Sangyôshô (1995: 33).

6. Due to its large leverage effect, this estimate of substitutability presents the biggest problem for all approaches that try to calculate the impact of FDI on domestic production and employment, (see also Frank and Freeman 1978; Glickman and Woodward 1989 and Madeuf 1995).

7. For a detailed description of this method of calculation and related problems, refer to Tsûshô Sangyôshô (1995, pp. 33–41).

8. Of course, this holds true only if higher costs cannot be offset by higher productivity.

9. This also implies that Japanese FDI in manufacturing will stay relatively high over the long term despite the current economic downturn in Southeast Asia and the economic stagnation at home.

PART IV:
FDI AND SUBNATIONAL DEVELOPMENT

JEREMY ALDEN[1]

12 The Impact of Foreign Direct Investment on Job Creation: the Experience of Wales

THE ROLE OF THE FIRM AND THE INSTITUTIONAL FRAMEWORK IN FDI AND JOB CREATION

Foreign Direct Investment has become a major issue for economic development policies at all spatial levels, from global to local. In the UK, FDI has been seen as a key component of regional policy in helping to reduce regional economic disparities. Development agencies and local authorities have been targeting FDI in an attempt to create jobs and strengthen their local and regional economies. Nowhere has this been more the case than in Wales, where the Welsh Development Agency has been working closely with local authorities and others to attract FDI. One of the main reasons cited by the government in support of the Welsh Assembly, created in 1999, has been the strategic advantages it provides for Wales in attracting FDI.

A good example of the result of such activity has been the attraction of the South Korean firm LG (Electronics and Semiconductors) to South Wales. LG announced its decision in 1996 to invest £1.7 billion to construct (a) an integrated plant for the manufacture of television monitors and other electrical equipment (LG Electronics), and (b) a wafer fabrication and assembly plant (LG Semicon). The two plants represent the largest FDI project ever to come to the UK or Europe. They will occupy a 250-acre site in Imperial Park at Newport with room for further expansion. The WDA offered LG their most prestigious industrial site, and government grants and land to the value of £247 million was agreed by the European Commission. This amount of aid worked out at some £40,000 per direct job created. In 1996 when the LG investment was announced, it was expected to create 6,100 direct jobs and another 10,000 indirect jobs by 2002. By 1998 the job creation expectations had been increased to some 20,000 overall, including increases for both direct and indirect job creation. It would be the largest manufacturing firm in Wales. The LG investment was expected to create a large number of jobs overall because of the extent of local suppliers involved and their concentration in electronics along the M4 corridor. It is expected that many of the jobs will be high quality and high skilled, and taken by people living within a twenty-five-mile radius of Imperial Park, Newport. The overall impact of the LG project on the locality of Newport and its wider subregion is expected to be significant for a range of planning issues in addition to job creation. The number of jobs created by the LG project has in fact been much lower than that predicted because of the delay in progressing the semi-conductor plant. The number of direct jobs associated with the two plants on the site is currently less than 2,000.

Is Wales getting value for money from this FDI? How much can localities and the region expect to gain in terms of job creation? This chapter examines the impact of FDI on job creation in Wales in recent years. It analyses data on job creation recently made available by the Economics Advice and Statistical Directorate at the Welsh Office (Cardiff), and by the Invest in Britain Bureau (London) in relation to FDI. The chapter also examines the extent to which local planning authorities have sought to achieve 'planning gain' from FDI projects through 'planning obligations' and Section 106 Agreements. The issue of planning gain has become one of the most controversial and central aspects of land-use planning in Britain. The practice of planning gain has become increasingly widespread and sophisticated in recent years.

Recent theories of innovation and local/regional economic development have acknowledged the extent to which the firm is the key institution in economic development (Cooke and Morgan 1998). Morgan (1997), in his article 'The Learning Region' has stressed the important interdependence between the firm, local institutions and other actors in developing regional innovation strategies to promote economic development. These strategies include aftercare services, retention strategies, marriage brokering, greater support for investors and sectorial initiatives (Christoloulou 1996). A wide array of public and private institutions, including local authorities, regional development agencies, universities and other higher educational establishments, training agencies, etc. are involved in fostering local and regional economic development. The main institutional characteristics of the so-called innovative, intelligent or successful region have been examined by numerous researchers (for example Amin and Thrift 1994).

However, the firm remains the key institution in local and regional economic development. It produces an output, creates jobs which employ people and provides incomes which are injected into the local economy. Dunning (1996) has examined in some depth the reasons why firms wish to engage in foreign production. Profit maximisation is clearly the driving force of the modern business enterprise, with the principal stakeholders being employees, managers and shareholders, rather than that of the wider community of which they are part. Any discussion of FDI must not underestimate the power of the market mechanism and the driving force of the firm in local economic development. The 1980s and 1990s in Britain have seen a market-led approach to planning, where the focus has been on private sector-led growth. Planning has moved away from the control of development and more towards enabling development to take place. Planners have become enablers and promoters of development as have the development agencies. This changing relationship between the state and market in the development process has raised interesting questions regarding the reality of job creation and planning gains from FDI.

REGIONAL DISPARITIES IN THE UK: THE PROSPERITY GAP FACING WALES

The importance of FDI for Wales is closely related to a period of rapid and extensive industrial restructuring. Wales faces a 'prosperity gap' compared to the UK as a whole. As Dunford (1993) has illustrated in his article on regional disparities in the EU, regional GDP per capita is the most common indicator of regional inequality. Table 12.1 shows that in 1995 Wales's GDP per capita was only 83.3 per cent of the UK average: that is a gap between Wales and the UK of almost 17 per cent. Wales's relative position has worsened over the past twenty-five years as shown in table 12.1. It now ranks lowest in the UK alongside Northern Ireland. However, Northern Ireland's position has improved markedly in contrast to Wales. Also, as shown in table 12.2, since 1991 Wales has had the slowest growth of GDP per head of any region in the UK, that is, 16.8 per cent compared with 20.1 per cent for the UK (and 22.7 per cent for the West Midlands). This suggests that the Welsh economy has performed poorly in recent years. This persistent prosperity gap facing Wales is supported by Mackay (1997), in his review of Welsh economic performance over the past twenty years. It appears that Wales seems unable to break back through the elusive 90 per cent of UK average GDP per capita or income/earnings figures which it enjoyed in the mid 1970s.

TABLE 12.1: WALES GDP PER CAPITA POSITION COMPARED TO UK REGIONS, 1971–95 (UK = 100)

Region	**1971**	**1972**	**1977**	**1985**	**1990**	**1993**	**1995**
North	87.1	94.5	94.2	92.9	87.9	88.9	88.1
Yorkshire and Humberside	92.8	94.5	95.1	94.2	91.2	90.0	90.4
East Midlands	95.7	96.5	95.5	99.0	97.1	96.9	97.9
East Anglia	94.6	92.5	92.4	101.3	101.6	100.9	100.9
South-east	114.1	113.3	113.0	114.8	117.4	117.1	116.2
South-west	93.9	90.8	91.5	94.1	94.5	95.2	95.3
West Midlands	102.9	100.1	99.9	92.1	93.5	92.9	95.2
North-west	96.4	96.0	97.0	94.6	90.6	90.2	90.6
Wales	88.0	90.0	87.8	83.6	85.9	82.8	83.3
Scotland	92.4	95.5	96.4	96.1	95.9	98.7	97.4
N Ireland	75.4	75.7	75.5	78.3	78.2	82.3	83.0

Sources: Compiled by the author from *Regional Statistics* No. 15 1980 and *Economic Trends* No. 519 January/February 1997 HMSO

TABLE 12.2: GROWTH IN GDP PER CAPITA FOR UK REGIONS, 1991–5 (FACTOR COST: £ PER HEAD)

Region	1991	1995	Percentage Growth Rate 1991–5
North	7 534	8 932	18.6
Yorkshire and Humberside	7 765	9 166	18.0
East Midlands	8 294	9 926	19.7
East Anglia	8 553	10 226	19.6
Greater London	10 519	12 503	18.9
Rest of south-east	9 516	11 310	18.9
South-west	8 058	9 663	19.9
West Midlands	7 865	9 649	22.7
North-west	7 614	9 181	20.6
Wales	7 228	8 440	16.8
Scotland	8 242	9 872	19.8
Northern Ireland	6 955	8 410	20.9
UK	8 481	10 137	19.5

Source: Compiled by the author from *Economic Trends* No. 521. table 12.2, p. 19, April 1997. *Regional Economic Indicators* HMSO

However, the evidence on unemployment and employment growth provides a different picture. Wales has faced high rates of unemployment for many decades, but in the early 1990s unemployment rates fell as new jobs were created. In 1992 Wales had an unemployment rate below that of the UK (9.7 per cent and 9.8 per cent respectively) for the first time since regional records were kept in the 1920s. By 1993 the Welsh unemployment rate had fallen even below that of south-east England, the most prosperous region in the UK. This relatively good performance of the Welsh economy in recent years on unemployment has continued, as shown in table 12.3, with Wales keeping within a percentage point of the UK overall rate.

TABLE 12.3: UNEMPLOYMENT RATES IN WALES COMPARED TO UK, 1973–97*

Annual Average	Wales Male	Wales Female	Wales Total	UK Male	UK Female	UK Total
1993	14.4	5.1	10.4	14.0	5.6	10.3
1994	12.7	4.9	9.4	12.7	5.1	9.4
1995	12.2	4.5	8.8	11.2	4.5	8.3
1996	11.4	4.3	8.2	10.3	4.1	7.6
October 1997	8.0	2.9	5.7	7.0	2.8	5.1

Source: Labour Market Trends HMSO
Note: * Percentage of workforce

FDI in Wales has focused on the manufacturing sector. The European Commission's document *Europe 2000+* (CEC 1994c), in its section on FDI, noted the importance of FDI for the industrial development and restructuring of the Welsh economy. Along with other observers (for example Dicken 1992), it drew attention to the trend towards the growing proportion of FDI in the service sector. This could aggravate spatial imbalances by reinforcing the growth of the strongest economic areas in each country and of large cities in particular. With the loss of its coal and steel jobs, FDI has brought new jobs to Wales. Table 12.4 shows that manufacturing employment has performed better in Wales than Great Britain as a whole. The 1991–3 period was a recessionary one nationally as with FDI globally. Both the UK and FDI economies have expanded since 1993. There is no doubt that FDI has brought new manufacturing jobs to Wales. The exact extent of these gains is examined below.

The Welsh Development Agency is largely responsible for the attraction of FDI to Wales. In its 1995 Corporate Plan it identified its main objective as being to promote the growth of quality jobs. The focus of FDI in Wales must be to attract high-value-added activities and raise income levels. As Phelps (1997) has emphasised, Wales continues to attract cost-minimising manufacturing investments. He cites the example of Ronson International's decision to shift production of lighters from its Korean to its Welsh factory. The need in Wales is to raise the quality of its multinational investments. UNCTAD in its World Investment Reports has stressed that multinationals are increasingly looking for an educated, skilled and committed workforce, combined with a social and physical infrastructure capable of generating high productivity. As Alden (1996) has noted in relation to the Welsh economy, the UK regions most successful in attracting FDI have been those in which productivity growth has interacted with relatively low earnings to push unit labour costs well below the UK average.

It should also be noted that the relatively low GDP, earnings and income levels in Wales are partly due to (a) a relatively small working age population, (b) a relatively high proportion of retired persons, (c) low labour force participation rates compared to other regions of the UK and (d) lower earnings levels due to job mix rather than low rates of pay *per se*. Earnings in manufacturing are

TABLE 12.4: CHANGES IN MANUFACTURING EMPLOYMENT IN WALES AND GREAT BRITAIN, 1991–5 (employees in employment)

	Wales	**Great Britain**
1991	207 500	4 162 160
1995	208 400	3 944 700
% change 1991–5	+0.4%	–5.2%

Source: Nomis Data; Government Employment Service

comparable with those of the UK as a whole. There is also a higher incidence of sickness/long-term illness in Wales than elsewhere in the UK. Measured in terms of GDP per person employed rather than per head of population, Wales's relative position in the UK would be significantly improved.

These points have been emphasised by the Welsh Office (1997) in its *Economic Strategy for Wales.* The foreword by the Welsh Industry Minister (P Hain, MP) recognises the label attached to Wales in the past as a low-cost nation/region. Lower pay bills and lower property costs were seen as attractive features for inward investors looking to use Wales and Britain as a platform into Europe. However, the 1997 *Economic Strategy for Wales* emphasises that any strategy relying on low costs is doomed to failure. The only serious option for Wales is seen as a high-quality one: that is, an economy producing high-value-added products, at the leading edge of innovation, with new technology which establishes a competitive edge through quality.

There has been an on-going controversy in Wales regarding just how well the economy has been performing (Lovering 1996; Morgan 1996). The evidence shows that Wales has been successful in reducing its unemployment rate differentials with other regions, in expanding its manufacturing employment and attracting new jobs via FDI. The evidence on GDP and incomes/earnings shows a less successful picture and the need to raise the quality of jobs and income levels. The Secretary of State for Wales has emphasised the need for Wales to improve its GDP per capita ratings, and to continue to be successful in attracting FDI. The Labour government's proposals for an enlarged Welsh Development Agency (WDA) and a Welsh Assembly are very much oriented to developing Wales's strategic capability to compete globally for FDI. The 1997 *Economic Strategy for Wales* has stressed the importance of corporate and institutional dynamics in FDI. It is envisaged that the Welsh Assembly will be better placed to tailor policies to Welsh needs, and mobilise the support needed to implement them. It will direct the new Welsh Development Agency created by amalgamating the WDA, the Development Board for Rural Wales (DBRW) and the Land Authority for Wales. Within the simpler framework of a single organisation, the agency will be able to offer comprehensive coverage across Wales, and a single point of contact for inward investors.

THE REGIONAL DISTRIBUTION OF FOREIGN DIRECT INVESTMENT IN THE UK: WHO GAINS?

In terms of the relative regional performance on FDI projects and new jobs created in Britain, Wales has been the most successful. Hill and Munday (1994) have shown that although Wales is small in respect of its share of UK employment, it has consistently attracted a higher share of new foreign projects and jobs. Table 12.5 provides Hill and Munday's regional league table of inward investment success in terms of new projects and new jobs attracted for the ten-year period, 1982–92.

TABLE 12.5: REGIONAL PERFORMANCE INDEX ON FDI IN BRITAIN, 1982–92

Region	Average 1982–92 Project index*	Average 1982–92 New jobs index
Wales	3.82	3.71
North	2.03	2.68
Scotland	1.77	2.33
West Midlands	1.65	1.48
North-west	1.10	0.72
Yorkshire and Humberside	0.71	0.69
East Midlands	0.71	0.69
South-west	0.42	0.56
South-east	0.41	0.30

Source: Hill and Munday (1994: Table 3.8, p. 43

Note: * Both regional shares of new projects and associated jobs are divided by regional shares of employment to provide a relative regional performance index. A value higher than one indicates the attraction of a share of projects greater than its equivalent employment share

Wales has continued to be the most successful region in attracting FDI. The author has analysed FDI data recently made available by Invest in Britain Bureau (IBB) by region for the financial years 1987–96, showing the number of projects, new jobs created and jobs safeguarded. The IBB data cover projects and jobs in both the manufacturing and service sectors. The author's analysis covers the UK whereas that by Hill and Munday covered Great Britain, excludes Northern Ireland. Table 12.6 provides the regional performance index on new projects, and table 12.7 shows new jobs created. A summary table is provided in table 12.8 to compare with the Hill and Munday table. The tables show that while Wales has continued to perform well on the number of projects, it has done relatively less well in terms of the number of new jobs created in the 1990s compared to the early 1980s, but it still leads the UK regions. Indeed, for the ten-year period 1987–96, the number of new jobs created from FDI for Wales was 156,824 for the five years 1992–96 compared to 140,647 for the five years 1987–91. However, despite this absolute improvement for Wales, other regions have been improving their position. Northern Ireland has performed particularly well on FDI, coming a close second to Wales in terms of new jobs created, although further behind in the number of projects. It should be noted that the Wales 1996 figure is for the financial year up to end-March 1996 and excludes the very large South Korean LG project, which will be recorded in the 1997 figures. The new jobs created index also shows a continued strong performance by Scotland and the North-East, confirming the continued strong performance by the 'peripheral' regions.

TABLE 12.6: REGIONAL PERFORMANCE INDEX ON NUMBER OF FDI PROJECTS IN UK, 1987–96

Region	(a) Number of projects	(b) Regional share of UK FDI	(c) Percentage regional share of UK national employment[1]	(d) Average project index[2]
East Midlands	158	4.49	7.00	0.64
North-east	353	10.03	4.95	2.02
Northern Ireland	169	4.80	2.60	1.84
North-west	429	12.20	10.47	1.16
Scotland	513	14.59	8.87	1.64
South-east	305	8.67	32.47	0.26
South-west	93	2.64	8.05	0.32
Wales	539	15.32	4.44	3.45
West Midlands	616	17.51	8.98	1.94
Yorkshire and Humberside	268	7.62	8.32	0.91
East Anglia	73	2.07	3.77	0.54
Total UK	**3 516**	**100.00**	**100.00**	

Source: Compiled by author from data supplied by IBB

Notes: 1 1995 employees in employment
2 Index is column (b) divided by column (c)

TABLE 12.7: REGIONAL PERFORMANCE INDEX ON NUMBERS OF FDI NEW JOBS CREATED IN UK, 1987–96

Region	(a) Number of new jobs	(b) Regional share of UK FDI new jobs	(c) Percentage regional share of UK national employment[1]	(d) Average new jobs index[2]
East Midlands	15 085	5.42	7.00	0.77
North-east	32 608	11.73	4.95	2.36
Northern Ireland	19 865	7.14	2.60	2.74
North-west	19 907	7.16	10.47	0.68
Scotland	56 678	20.38	8.87	2.29
South-east	28 713	10.32	32.47	0.31
South-west	10 023	3.60	8.05	0.44
Wales	36 236	13.03	4.44	2.93
West Midlands	37 952	13.65	8.98	1.52
Yorkshire and Humberside	17 463	6.28	8.34	0.75
East Anglia	3 441	1.23	3.77	0.32
Total UK	**277 971**	**100.00**	**100.00**	

Source: Compiled by author from data supplied by IBB

Notes: 1 1995 employees in employment
2 Index is column (b) divided by column (c)

TABLE 12.8: SUMMARY REGIONAL PERFORMANCE INDEX ON FDI IN UK, 1987–96

Region	Average 1987–96 project index	Average 1987–96 new jobs index
Wales	3.45	2.93
North-east	2.02	2.36
Northern Ireland	1.84	2.74
West Midlands	1.94	1.52
Scotland	1.64	2.29
North-west	1.16	0.68
Yorkshire and Humberside	0.91	0.75
East Midlands	0.64	0.77
East Anglia	0.54	0.32
South-west	0.32	0.44
South-east	0.26	0.31

Source: Compiled by author (1997) from tables 12.6 and 12.7

THE IMPACT OF FOREIGN DIRECT INVESTMENT IN WALES ON JOB CREATION: WHO GAINS?

Wales has been the most successful of the UK regions on FDI over the past ten to fifteen years. Some areas within Wales have become quite dependent on FDI investment and jobs. Taylor (1993) has noted, for example, that some 40 per cent of manufacturing employment in Mid Glamorgan has been based on Japanese investment, where assisted area status has played an important part in attracting FDI. The location of FDI plants within Wales has been determined by a number of factors. As Phelps (1997) has noted, despite an emphasis on institutional support, it is still the traditional attractions such as labour costs and availability, financial incentives, availability of suitable sites, and transport and communications which have made Wales a favoured location for FDI compared to other regions of the UK or European Union (EU). Hill and Roberts (1993) reached a similar conclusion in their article on inward investment in Wales in a special issue of the *Welsh Economic Review* on this topic. Within Wales, the areas of north-east and south-east Wales have been the main beneficiaries in terms of attracting FDI in recent years, with the north-west and south-west of Wales finding it more difficult to attract inward investment and revitalise their economies. While the latest detailed published data on FDI employment in Wales is that for 1994 contained in *Welsh Economic Trends 1995*, the Welsh Office has made available data for the period 1985–96, providing an analysis of change for both the stock of FDI plants and for employment. The data has been provided by the Welsh Office's Economics Advice and Statistical Directorate, which operates the Welsh Register of Manufacturing Employment (WRME).

Table 12.9 provides the components of change analysis of employment at overseas-owned manufacturing plants in Wales for the period 1985–96. It shows that over this period, Wales gained 28,900 manufacturing jobs net from FDI. In 1996 there were 75,400 people employed in overseas-owned manufacturing plants. This figure represents 36 per cent of total manufacturing employment in Wales (some 208,000) . It compares to a corresponding figure of only 22 per cent in 1985 (with 46,500 employed in overseas-owned manufacturing plants). With the recent and continued attraction of overseas-owned plants to Wales, particularly from Japan, South Korea and Taiwan, it is quite possible that by the year 2000 there will be 100,000 people employed in Wales in such plants, representing 50 per cent of total Welsh manufacturing employment.

Table 12.9 shows that the net change of 28,900 jobs is the result of much larger gross flows of increases (+50,800 from new openings, expansions and acquisitions) and decreases (-21,900 from divestments, closures and contractions). The data in table 12.9 show that acquisitions have accounted for more jobs (22,200) than new plant openings (17,600). The table also shows the highest percentage change (47 per cent) for jobs via acquisitions over the period, followed by 37 per cent for jobs via new plant openings. The data also show that these acquisitions have involved mainly American and European companies rather than the Japanese. While they may not represent new jobs to Wales they are jobs retained that are now in the hands of overseas-owned manufacturing plants. Lovering (1997) has made the point that FDI has had a larger effect on the ownership of Welsh manufacturing than the jobs it provides.

Another important trend change is that Japanese plants now record the largest net employment additions, a position formerly held by plants in the ownership of EU countries. Table 12.9 shows that over the period 1985–96, Japan was responsible for more FDI jobs in Wales than any other region of the world. Japanese firms were also notable for their high proportion of jobs coming from new plant openings rather than acquisitions. It is also noticeable that employment in Japanese-owned firms increased nearly five-fold over the period 1985–96, from 3,500 to 16,900. It is also a feature of FDI employment that jobs lost as a result of plant closures account for a relatively small element in the components of employment change analysis. FDI plants, with substantial long-term investments at stake, have not shared the branch plant syndrome of cutting back jobs in recessionary periods.

FDI employment in Wales had hitherto been dominated by American and European plants, accounting for over 70 per cent of all FDI jobs in Wales as at 1996. However Japan has increased its share of all FDI employment in Wales from 7.5 per cent in 1984 to 22.4 per cent in 1996. The recent additions from South Korea and Taiwan will increase further the South-East Asian presence in Wales.

Another feature of FDI plants is their relatively large size in terms of jobs provision. The attraction of large employers is at a premium in local and regional economic development. Table 12.10 illustrates that of the 75,400

TABLE 12.9: ANALYSIS OF EMPLOYMENT CHANGE AT OVERSEAS-OWNED MANUFACTURING PLANTS IN WALES (INCLUDING ADJUSTMENTS FOR ACQUISITIONS AND DIVESTMENTS OF EXISTING OVERSEAS-OWNED PLANTS), 1985–96

	Employment in 1985	**Employment change 1985–96 Increases**			**Employment change 1985–96 Decreases**				**Employment in 1996**
Region	***Employees***	*New Plant* ***Openings***	***Expansions***	***Acquisitions***	***Divestments***	***Closures***	***Contractions***	*Net* ***Change***	***Employees***
North America	31 600	6 200	3 500	8 800	7 500	3 400	5 300	+2 300	33 900
Europe	10 200	5 000	2 800	8 700	2 500	1 200	900	+12 000	22 200
EU	8 400	4 500	2 400	8 600	1 900	1 000	800	+11 800	20 200
Non-EU	1 800	500	400	100	500	200	100	+100	1 900
Japan	3 500	5 700	4 500	3 600	—	100	300	+13 400	16 900
Other	1 300	700	100	1 100	200	500	—	+1 200	2 500
Totals	**46 500**	**17 600**	**11 000**	**22 200**	**10 100**	**5 200**	**6 600**	**+28 900**	**75 400**
Percentage change over 1985		37.8	23.7	47.7	21.7	11.2	14.2		

Source: Welsh Office 1997

FDI jobs in Wales in 1996, 75.5 per cent were in plants employing two hundred or more people. This compares to a corresponding figure of 53.2 per cent for all plants in Wales.

TABLE 12.10: EMPLOYMENT IN FOREIGN-OWNED MANUFACURING PLANTS BY SIZE OF PLANT, 1996

Employment size group	Number of plants	Employment (thousands)
1–10	25	0.2
11–19	15	0.2
20–49	65	2.2
50–99	91	6.4
100–199	69	9.6
200-499	83	26.6
500–999	24	15.9
1000 and over	9	14.4
Total	**381**	**75.4**

Source: Welsh Register of Manufacuring Employment: Welsh Office

Data has recently become available from the Welsh Office on employment in overseas-owned manufacturing plants as at 1996 for the twenty-two new unitary authorities in Wales. The analysis presented in table 12.11 provides a profile of FDI success at local level in Wales. Table 12.11 shows that FDI has brought job creation gains to all the unitary authorities in Wales. However, the gains have been unevenly distributed as illustrated by the range of location quotients, with localities in north-east Wales and south-east Wales being the main beneficiaries.

The United Nations 1996 *World Investment Report* has illustrated the extent to which the global FDI recession of the early 1990s ended in 1993. World investment flows increased by 9 per cent in 1994 and 40 per cent in 1995, to reach a record $315 billion for inflows.

An upsurge in FDI to the UK regions, including Wales also appeared in 1993. The latest increase in world FDI reflects the fact that an increasing number of firms, including those from developing countries, are becoming more active globally in response to competitive pressures, liberalisation and the opening up of new areas for investment. These firms are using mergers and acquisitions as a central corporate strategy for establishing production facilities abroad to protect, consolidate and advance their international competitiveness.

Another important feature has been the growth of FDI outflows from South Korea, Singapore, Hong Kong and Taiwan. In 1980 their outflows amounted to only $0.1 billion. However, by 1990 they had increased to $2.3 billion. Their

TABLE 12.11: EMPLOYMENT IN FOREIGN-OWNED MANUFACTURING PLANTS BY NEW UNITARY AUTHORITIES IN WALES, 1996

Unitary Authority	(a) Number of plants	(b) Employment (thousands)	(c) Employment as a percentage of total in overseas-owned plants in Wales	(d) Total employment in areas as a percentage of rural employment in Wales	(e) Location quotients: i.e. column (c) divided by column (d)
Anglesey	5	0.7	0.9	1.6	0.6
Gwynedd	*	0.7	0.9	4.2	0.2
Aberconwy and Colwyn	*	0.5	0.7	2.9	0.2
Denbighshire	*	1.8	2.4	2.9	0.8
Flintshire	48	6.3	8.4	5.4	1.6
Wrexham	40	6.9	9.2	4.8	1.6
Powys	9	3	4.0	4.0	1.0
Ceredigion	6	3	4.0	1.8	2.2
Pembrokeshire	5	1.2	1.6	2.7	0.6
Carmarthenshire	13	2.8	3.7	5.2	0.7
Swansea	14	3.3	4.4	8.3	0.5
Neath Port Talbot	15	4.1	5.4	4.1	1.3
Bridgend	19	7.6	10.1	3.3	3.1
Vale of Glamorgan	11	4.5	6.0	4.8	1.3
Rhondda	41	6.9	9.2	6.9	1.3
Cynon Taff					
Merthyr Tydfil	9	1.6	2.1	1.8	1.2
Caerphilly	48	6.6	8.8	4.5	1.9
Blaenau Gwent	24	3.2	4.2	1.9	2.2
Torfaen	21	3.6	4.8	3.6	1.3
Monmouthshire	5	1.1	1.5	2.8	0.5
Newport	19	3.9	5.2	16.6	0.9
Cardiff	20	4.9	6.5	16.6	0.4
Wales	381	75.4	100.0	100.0	1.0

Sources: (a) Welsh Register of Manufacturing Employment (WRME); (b) Annual Employment Survey 1995; (c) compiled by the author

Note: Location quotient of 1.0 equals a locality's 'fair' share of PDI in Wales, above 1.0 equals a greater than average share and below 1.0 a smaller than average share

outflows in the early 1980s were concentrated in labour-intensive industries in the low-cost countries of Asia. Through the 1990s they began to invest in the OECD countries to avoid trade protection. By the end of the 1980s about 80 per cent of their stock of FDI was located in North America. However, in the 1990s they began to invest in Western and Eastern Europe. FDI from these so called 'Tiger economies' has been a major new source for Europe. Following the attraction of the South Korean firm Samsung to the north-east of England in 1994, other Korean firms have moved to the UK. These include the largest inward investment ever to come to Europe, namely LG (Electronics and Semicon), which in 1996 announced a $2.5 billion investment in South Wales. This single investment is equivalent to the entire outward FDI investment by Korea, Singapore, Hong Kong and Taiwan combined as at 1990. The Korean investment by LG in Wales is considered further later in this paper.

The European Commission's Fifth Periodic Report, *Competitiveness and Cohesion: Trends in the Regions* (CEC 1994b) emphasised that the 1990s have been a difficult period for reducing regional disparities because of the deep recession between 1989 and 1993. However, the volume of world FDI has increased markedly since 1993. The Fifth Periodic Report emphasised the extent to which the creation of a Single Market has favoured EU regions as a whole for new investment. This has led to a large gross inflow of FDI into the EU from third countries, estimated at nearly ECU 120 billion between 1986 and 1991. When combined with the flows between member states, some ECU 150 billion between 1986 and 1991, FDI represents a significant source of potential investment for the EU's weaker regions and, except in the case of Greece, has outstripped the transfers from the Structural Funds. In July 1997 the European Commission announced its negotiations with six potential new EU members: Hungary, Poland, the Czech Republic, Estonia, Slovenia and Cyprus.

While nearly 50 per cent of the EU budget is spent on the Common Agricultural Policy, some 40 per cent is spent on the Structural Funds and regional aid. In July 1997 the president of the European Commission presented 'Agenda 2000' which introduced the map of a new twenty-one member EU (fifteen existing members and the six new ones identified above), and radical spending reforms which will affect both the Common Agricultural Policy and Structural Funds. This review is likely to lead to less funding being available to the weaker regions of relatively strong economies like the United Kingdom with more going to the weaker regions of less-developed economies, as illustrated by the new member countries from Southern Europe and Eastern Europe. The Objective 2 regions, like South Wales, are particularly under threat of reduced support from the Structural Funds. In the future, therefore, FDI will play an even greater role in regional economic development for regions like Wales, seeking increased investment, quality employment and income generation.

FOREIGN DIRECT INVESTMENT AND PLANNING GAIN IN WALES: INTERFACE BETWEEN LAND-USE PLANNING AND DEVELOPMENT

There is considerable interest in Britain on the issue of 'planning gain'. Local planning authorities have increasingly looked towards major new development projects as a source of planning gain: that is, to gain benefits for their locality from the granting of planning permission to a developer. With the high profile attached to FDI projects in the UK generally, and in Wales in particular, the extent to which FDI projects are subject to planning gain is a topic of considerable interest. FDI projects do produce gains in terms of job creation. Is this also the case with planning gain? The power to grant or refuse planning permission for development is at the heart of the British system of land-use planning. As a Department of Environment report on *The Use of Planning Agreements* (1992) has noted, authorities also have powers to attach planning conditions to the granting of planning permission and, in addition, to enter into legal agreements with anyone who has an interest in land. The use of these powers can exert considerable control over development that is permitted.

Powers to enter planning agreements with owners of land were first created by the Housing, Town Planning Act of 1909, and developed through the 1932 and 1947 Town and Country Planning Acts. The Town and Country Planning Act 1971 introduced, in Section 52, new legislative authority for planning agreements. These powers are now contained within Section 106 of the Town and Country Planning Act 1990 and replaced by Section 12 of the Planning and Compensation Act 1991. In terms of terminology, common reference is made to Section 106 agreements and planning conditions as ways of addressing planning gain and appropriate development. The government's policy position on the use of planning obligations is contained in Circular 1/97 'Planning Obligations' (January 1997). As confirmed in Planning Policy Guidance (PPG)1 (revised February 1997), the planning system should operate in the public interest, and should aim to foster sustainable development, providing homes, investment and jobs in a way that adds to rather than detracts from the quality of the environment. These objectives are achieved through the preparation of development plans and the exercise of development control functions.

It has become normal practice for local planning authorities to seek planning gain from large development projects. The South Korean LG example is an interesting one. All large projects in the UK require an Environmental Statement. For certain projects they are compulsory, for example a nuclear power station. LG were required to submit an Environmental Statement alongside their planning application. The LG planning application was received in July 1996 and went to Newport Borough Council Planning Committee in September 1996. The Welsh Office, the seat of Government in Wales agreed not to call in the application. The statutory twenty-one day consultation process began on 4 September and planning permission was granted on 24 September. During this period all objections were dealt with, consultations made and agreement reached. This process was completed in record time. Planning permission was granted subject to twenty-nine conditions. There was no Section 106 Agreement. With international competition for FDI projects being so intense, the planning process is seen as a hurdle to overcome for developers. Insistence on a Section 106 Agreement could frighten off an FDI proposal. There would, of course, be a planning gain to the locality of Newport and its subregion in terms of job creation and all its associated benefits.

The overriding concern for both the region and the locality was to secure the LG investment in the face of fierce international competition. Given the local and regional context of the needs for jobs, and especially quality jobs, planning gain and job creation were seen as one and the same thing. This also appears to be the case with other FDI projects in Wales. The author has reviewed the cases of ten recent prestigious FDI projects distributed throughout Wales. These are shown in table 12.12. The local authorities responsible for the granting of planning permission all confirmed that none had sought to enter into Section 106 Agreements with the firms concerned for the reasons cited above. They all considered the job creation associated with the projects equivalent to planning gain.

FOREIGN DIRECT INVESTMENT: THE WELSH EXPERIENCE: SOME CONCLUSIONS

The main conclusions of this chapter on job creation and planning gain in relation to FDI are twofold. First, Wales has been very successful in recent years in attracting FDI projects which have created new jobs. However, the extent of the job creation needs to be treated with some caution as a significant number of jobs have involved acquisitions rather than new openings. FDI has, therefore, had a large effect on the ownership of Welsh manufacturing as well as the provision of jobs. Second, evidence to date suggests that while local planning authorities have been active in seeking planning gain from large residential, retail or mixed-use developments, they have been reluctant to negotiate planning gain agreements with large, high-profile FDI projects. With international competition for FDI projects being so intense, the planning process is seen as a hurdle to be overcome for developers. Insistence on a Section 106 Agreement could frighten off an FDI proposal. The general view of the development agencies and local authorities in Wales is that the job creation associated with FDI projects equates to planning gain achieved. This manifests itself in various ways including the number of jobs created, the quality of the jobs, access to the jobs by local people and those within a wider catchment area, incomes generated and injected into the local economy, and other spin-offs including the attraction of further inward investment. For large FDI projects, the authorities are driven by the commercial and business requirements of the investor, and the job creation needs of localities and regions.

TABLE 12.12: FDI PROJECTS RECENTLY ESTABLISHED IN WALES AND PRESENCE OR ABSENCE OF SECTION 106 AGREEMENT

Firm	Year established	Business	No. employed	Section106 Agreement: yes or no	Nationality of plant ownership	Location within Wales
LG	1996	Electronics and semiconductors	6 100	No	South Korean	Newport, South Wales
Halla	1996	Excavators and fork lift trucks	300	No	South Korean	Merthyr, South Wales
Bosch	1991	Alternators for automobiles	1 100	No	German	Miskin, South Wales
Sony	1992	TV monitors, tubes and components	2 500	No	Japanese	Pencoed, South Wales
Showa	1996	Suspension and steering parts for automotive industry	200	No	Japanese	Aberdare, South Wales
Nippon Electric Glass	1994	Glass for cathode ray tubes	750	No	Japanese/German	Cardiff, South Wales
MVO	1996	Precision instruments	45	No	Italian	Welshpool, Mid Wales
Toyota	1991	Automobile engines	130	No	Japanese	Deeside, North Wales
G C Hahn	1985	Food stabilisers	50	No	German	Mold, North Wales
Amcor	1992	Fibre/cardboard packaging	75	No	Australian	Mold, North Wales

Source: Compiled by the author with assistance of local authorities

While Wales has been successful in the past in attracting FDI, the future is less certain. Within the UK we are likely to see much greater competition between areas for FDI with some regions able to identify only a small number of strategic FDI sites. While the UK has been an attractive location in the past for FDI, other regions of the world may emerge as more attractive. Global competition for FDI in the future can be expected to be as great as in the past. Wales is seeking to close the prosperity gap between itself and the rest of the UK. This is proving to be a difficult task. It will be made all the harder with the likely cutbacks coming from a revised EU Structural Funds programme. This will make FDI even more of a priority as an instrument of local and regional economic development. While the institutional framework for promoting and maintaining local economic development and prosperity will also continue to be an important component of FDI, the role and behaviour of individual firms will also continue to dominate the process of local and regional economic development.

As Young *et al.* (1994) have observed, there is no easy route to generating a dynamic comparative advantage. In a world of increasing global mobile capital, there is no option for Wales and individual areas but to view FDI very seriously. The OECD (1993) and the European Commission (1994) have stressed that increasing competition between areas means there will be winners and losers in terms of economic development. This enhances the role of institutional capacities for local and regional economic development and the role of inward investment and job creation.

NOTE

1. The author wishes to thank both the Invest in Britain Bureau in London and the Economic Advice and Statistical Directorate in the Welsh Office in Cardiff for information and advice received for purposes of producing this chapter.

13 *In Situ* Restructuring in Branch Plants and their Local Economic Development Implications[1]

INTRODUCTION

The 'branch plant economy' has encapsulated many of the recurrent problems associated with precarious forms of industrialisation that have continued to undermine the development of economically peripheral regions. The history of dependent development within such localities has had a marked effect in perpetuating uneven and unequal geographies of local and regional economic prosperity. While the 'branch plant economy' has a long tradition in the regional economic development literature (Dicken 1976; Firn 1975; Massey 1995; Townroe 1975; Watts 1981), recent claims have been made concerning the emergence of a new type of branch plant with more progressive and developmental implications for local economies. These accounts of new 'performance' and 'networked' production plants have emphasised their qualitatively different character from their branch plant predecessors and their changed potential for local economic development (Amin *et al.* 1994; Cooke 1995; Morgan 1995; Morgan and Sayer 1988; Phelps 1993; Young *et al.* 1994). This work has tended to focus on greenfield developments associated with inward investment and their local and regional economic spin-offs.

This chapter makes a critical examination of the alleged change in the 'branch plant economy' and contributes to the literature on in-situ restructuring through a consideration of reorganisation in existing brownfield plants of US-owned 'Motor Co.' and 'Car Co.' in the automobile industry in the old industrial region of 'Riverside' (Morgan and Sayer 1988; Norcliffe 1995; F Peck 1996; Rutherford 1994). The identities of the plants and the region have been disguised to maintain confidentiality. These plants were chosen since both were established as archetypal 'branch plants' in the early 1960s and both have survived while undergoing significant changes. The study employed an intensive research methodology and thirty interviews were conducted with management, trades unions and workforces within the two plants between 1991 and 1993. Automobile production has historically been associated with the creation of 'branch plant economies' (O'Dowd 1985) and recent developments have been aligned with the emergence of 'performance plants' with heightened local economic development potential (Mair 1993). Empirical evidence is examined across several dimensions, comprising: role and autonomy; labour process; labour–management relations; labour market strategies; supplier linkages; and local economic development implications.

The argument is that the alleged changes in the type of production plant and their implications for local economies can be understood by addressing the inter-relations between structure, agency and contingency. The historical tradition of the branch plant economy tended to overemphasise the 'top-down' determinism of structures of ownership and control external to host local economies. More recent 'revisionist' literature has highlighted the 'bottom-up' potential for both individual and collective institutional agency at the conjunction of the plant and locality. These latter accounts have incorporated contingency – from localities, firm strategies, plant histories, labour relations and so on – into their explanations. The chapter employs political economy notions of the inter-relations between structure, agency and contingency to go beyond the description of unique cases and move toward explanation of their general significance (Hudson and Sadler 1986; Lovering 1989; Martin 1994; Phelps 1995; Sayer 1995). In-situ restructuring at 'Motor Co.' and 'Car Co.' in 'Riverside' suggests a narrow increase in plant responsibility, the limited upgrading of functions and the introduction of new techniques. The changes in the type of plant are partial, revealing the overlap of old and new practices, and the implications for local economic development appear limited and contingent upon the ability of local institutions to exploit the more positive developments.

A SHIFT FROM THE 'BRANCH PLANT ECONOMY' TRADITION?

The branch plant economy has had a long tradition in the regional economic development literature. Branch plants were seen as specialised in a narrow range of lower-level execution functions and hierarchical links were maintained between the command and conception activities – centralised at headquarters – and R&D facilities and the branch plants to exert control and monitor performance. The branch plants were often duplicate facilities, allowing production to be switched between sites, and links between them were kept weak to prevent collective action (Fujita and Child Hill 1995). Corporate internalisation limited local linkage formation, which did little to stimulate activity among local economic development institutions, and regional policy often guided their investment to assisted areas. The literature emphasised how branch plants have acted as points of insertion for local economies, often linking them to increasingly internationalised webs of external ownership and control (Fröebel *et al.* 1980). In this way, the place of the host region in the broader spatial division of labour was shaped by the functional specialisation of certain local economies in particular stages of the production process. New rounds of investment were seen to reinforce these roles, cementing the uneven development between regions through capital's search for low labour costs, pliant industrial relations and the potential for workforce 'feminisation' (Breathnach 1993).

The branch plant economy tradition has endured due to its conceptual clarity and the substantial weight of supporting evidence. Critiques have focused on: the uncritical, overgeneralised and stereotypical use of the concept (Lovering 1989; Sayer 1985); the emphasis on the causal power of the firm's organisation ahead of historically developed forces including technology, labour relations and competitive conditions (Clarke and Beaney 1993; Walker 1989; see also Dicken and Thrift 1992 in response); and the relative failure to be sufficiently open to change and evolution (Storper and Walker 1989). In addition, the branch plant economy tradition has overplayed the more obvious 'top-down' structural constraints of external ownership and control in explanations and has paid relatively too little attention to the 'bottom-up' influence of agency and contingency at the conjunction of the plant and local institutions in mediating particular sets of outcomes.

The branch plant economy tradition has been stirred by these critiques. Recent 'revisionist' work has suggested the emergence of a new and qualitatively different type of plant with more progressive implications for local economic development (Young *et al.* 1994). The new work emphasises the reorganisation of modes of corporate economic coordination and the potential for a changed role for branch plant economies in the spatial division of labour. The latter development prospects are seen as contingent on the combination of plant changes and the capacity of the locality to exploit them. Change in the type of plant has been captured by the loose distinction between the 'performance' and 'cost/price-based' branch plant (Amin *et al.* 1994). Phelps's (1993) discussion of the networked branch plant spans the above distinction and acknowledges more continuities with the branch plant economy tradition. Economic coordination within and without the multiplant and multilocational firm has increased. Intra- and inter-firm integration and 'networking' have fostered organisational decentralisation, 'flattened hierarchies' and the potential devolution of strategies and operating autonomy to individual plants. Transnational and plant specialisation strategies have increased interdependency, and geographical market and/or product mandates and parent–subsidiary relations have shaped new roles for plants (Howells and Wood 1993). 'Performance' plants are said to be at the forefront of such changes and to have implemented the most advanced practices (Amin *et al.* 1994). Formerly sequential and departmentalised structures have been reintegrated, including R&D at production plants to reduce development lead times and improve 'manufacturability'. Positive interpretations of the new type of plant illustrate the advantages of branch plant industrialisation as a vehicle for local economic development due to the catalytic effect of its sophisticated demands and upgrading efforts upon the local economy (Morgan 1995; Potter 1995). Cost/price-based plants, in contrast, illustrate continuities with their branch plant predecessors. While more integrated within corporate networks, these plants continue to occupy peripheral roles and embed their host economies into structures of external control (Phelps 1993). Their heightened interdependency has meant that upgrading can occur at one plant at the expense of corporate rationalisation elsewhere and that such reorganisation may conclude with little change in the overall structural position of the plant and its workforce (Breathnach 1993). In addition, the splintering and reintegration of R&D networks is seen to strengthen 'global' corporate competencies rather than 'local' technical capability at individual plants.

The extent of such dimensions of 'embeddedness' of these new types of plants and their developmental consequences for local economies has been questioned (Oinas 1997). Such enhanced developmental prospects are often only on offer to a few favoured locations and should not disguise the wide variety of TNC-local relations existing between the stereotypical conception of 'placeless globalisation' and 'localised embeddedness' (Dicken *et al.* 1994).

The recent revisionist accounts encompass both change and continuity relative to the branch plant economy tradition. The more positive work emphasises the extent of change and stresses how external ownership and control act as the link to advanced developments and investment capable of upgrading the local economy. The more sceptical, or at least qualified, accounts recognise continuities despite the evidence of some changes. Both strands of work agree on the enhanced degree of autonomy and that the plants seem to be more porous and integrated with networks, often localised, other than those solely associated with external ownership and control and with a potential leverage in relation to activities in the plant stimulating local development. Table 13.1 is used as a summary device rather than a dualistic 'before and after' writing strategy (Sayer 1989). It details several dimensions of change and their local economic development implications from the preceding discussion.

IN SITU RESTRUCTURING AT MOTOR CO. AND CAR CO.

The remainder of this chapter focuses on the extent and nature of changes in the type of plant and their local economic development implications resulting from in-situ restructuring. The framework of dimensions of change is utilised to examine empirical evidence from the automobile industry of in-situ restructuring in the branch plants of Motor Co. and Car Co. in Riverside. This approach is taken due to the overemphasis in the debate on greenfield developments, the constraints in-situ change place on capital and the alleged recent changes in automobile plants (Berggren 1995; Pike 1996; Schamp 1991; Shaiken 1994). In-situ restructuring has been evident since the bulk of

TABLE 13.1: SUMMARY TABLE OF DIMENSIONS OF TYPE OF PLANT AND LOCAL ECONOMIC DEVELOPMENT IMPLICATIONS

	Branch plant	Performance/networked branch plant
Role and autonomy	External ownership and control; structured position and constrained autonomy; truncated and narrow functional structure involved in part-process production and/or assembly; cloned capacity and vertically integrated with limited nodes capable of external local linkage (for example suppliers, technology); state-policy subsidised establishment via automatic grants to broadly designated areas.	External ownership and control but possible enhanced strategic and operating autonomy as well as responsibility for performance increased within a 'flattened' hierarchical structure; wider functional structure involved in full process production tilted toward manufacturing rather than solely assembly; sole capacity with product (range), division or market mandate at the expense of rationalisation elsewhere; increased nodes capable of linkage (for example R&D with technology support, human resources with training); state-policy support for establishment on selective and regulated basis (for example job creation, local content).
Labour process	Labour-intensive, semi- and unskilled work; 'routinised' and specific tasks within refined technical division of labour; high-volume production of low- to medium-technology products; standardised process technology; short-term, task-specific, 'on-the-job' training integrated with production.	Capital and technology intensive, semi- and skilled work with increased need for diagnostic and cognitive skills; recombined job tasks and individual/team responsibility for performance; low to high technology and low- to high-volume production flexibility; flexible and reprogrammable process technology; longer-term, coordinated with investment, 'on-' and 'off-the-job' training.
Labour–management relations	Organised and unionised labour; job classifications, task assignments and work/supervision rules linked to seniority-based pay scales; formalised and collective negotiation and bargaining tied to employment contract; personnel management with administrative focus.	Business unionism; reduction and streamlining of grading, job titles and meritocratic salary structure; shift to company-based non-(traditional) union arenas; individualised negotiation and bargaining tied to 'enabling' agreements; Human Resource Management techniques.
Labour market strategies	Employees considered interchangeable, replaceable and in need of constant supervision; limited screening and high labour turnover and absenteeism; reliance on external labour market.	Rigorous scrutiny and increased selectivity in recruitment; employees as human resources needing investment; teamworking to reduce labour turnover and identify employee with the goals of the company; development of core internal labour market and peripheral (part-time, temporary) segments.
Supplier linkages	Limited since integration with broader corporate structures of production and supply chains; intra-firm linkages substituted for local ties; limited local supply chain knowledge and greater awareness of potential suppliers in headquarters region.	Outsourcing increase with JIT and synchronous suppliers; increased potential for local procurement and supplier agglomeration; 1st and 2nd tier supply chain management; increased global sourcing and partnership relations; growth in dependence in the local supply network; geographically distributed production networks and JIT operated over international distances.
Local economic development implications	Externally owned and controlled plants with limited decision-making powers locally ('dependent development', 'branch plant economy') vulnerable to closure or relocation ('footloose', 'runaway industries', 'hyper-mobile capital'; limited growth rates in employment and output; low technology and skills ('screwdriver plants'); few local linkages ('enclave development'), 'dual economy', 'industrialisation without growth', 'cathedrals in the desert'); diversified industries not building upon or modernising existing regional industrial strengths; limited innovation potential and technology transfer from dedicated production processes and suppliers.	New concepts of externally owned and controlled plant with increased decision-making autonomy for strategic and operational issues, more rooted and anchored in the local economy ('embedded firm'), higher levels of technology and skills, higher innovative potential, more local linkages and increased technology transfer through research and technological development functions; supplier links upgrading process technology improvement and partnership development with suppliers; potential for the plant to be a 'propulsive local growth pole', 'vehicle/catalyst for local economic development' and capable of setting in train 'sustainable development'.

automobile manufacturing capacity and employment is concentrated in existing sites, and, due to its cost structure, the historical circumstance of the industry remains influential in its geography (Dicken 1992a).

This analysis emphasises the inter-relations between structure, agency and contingency in understanding contemporary processes of capitalist development (Hudson and Sadler 1986; Lovering 1989; Martin 1994; Phelps 1995). The approach taken is alive to the socio-economics literature which situates economic action within its social structure (Matzner and Streeck 1991) and the 'old' institutionalism that emphasises the role of institutions in shaping economic, social, political and cultural life (Sunley 1996), which have latterly revived regional political economy. Influential in this work is an interpretation of the outcomes of the economic imperatives incorporated in restructuring as historically contingent and spatially heterogeneous (Clark 1990; Tomaney *et al.* 1999).

In this chapter, the tendency for the 'branch plant economy' tradition to give preference to structural concerns is countered by giving recognition to the agency or scope that individual plants and local institutions, working individually and collectively, have for action in reshaping the position of plants within corporate organisational structures and the role of local and regional economies within spatial divisions of labour.

Motor Co. and Car Co. in Riverside

'Motor Co.' and 'Car Co.' were established in the Riverside Assisted Area in the early 1960s, following the refusal of Industrial Development Certificates (IDCs) for expansion at existing sites of both firms in the south-east region. Riverside was experiencing increased unemployment, due to the collapse of its port-based industries and a (then) rising population, which together provided a low-cost labour supply (Salt 1967). Inflated land prices, escalating wage demands and labour retention problems coupled with disputes, stoppages and absenteeism underlined the decision to decentralise production from the south-east. Each plant was set up to broaden existing model ranges, rather than simply expand capacity, and further component manufacturing investment consolidated their positions. From the outset, both greenfield sites pursued new production techniques and working practices with a carefully selected workforce recruited from the slack local labour market (Beynon, 1984). Each plant mirrored its parent company's productivity, quality and labour relations problems, and nearly fell victim to the wave of rationalisation in the 1980s which befell other plants established in Riverside during the 1960s (O'Dowd 1985). 'Car Co.' was only saved following integration with its parent's German subsidiary and its downgrading to assembly-only status. Motor Co. and Car Co. have survived into the 1990s, attracting considerable regional policy support, despite the 'brinksmanship' of periodic closure threats and exhortations to close the performance 'gap' with both their continental 'sister' plants and the Japanese transplants in the UK.[2]

The establishment of Motor Co. and Car Co. in Riverside as 'typical' branch plants in the 1960s and their survival into the 1990s provides empirical material concerning in-situ restructuring in brownfield plants and their local economic development implications. The evidence suggests that there has been some heightening of plant responsibility, the limited upgrading of plant functions and the introduction of an array of new techniques. The changes are partial, revealing the overlap of new and old practices, and the benefits for local economic development appear limited.

Shifting Roles and Autonomy

As part of moves to increase transnational integration, Motor Co. and Car Co.'s parent companies have introduced programmes of decentralisation with integration. For Motor Co. and Car Co. these have increased operating autonomy, especially in terms of responsibility for performance, and have devolved a degree of strategic autonomy, particularly in bidding for new investment projects. Car Co. claim they are more stand-alone while simultaneously more integrated (Author's interview, 1992). Intra-corporate competition between plants has intensified. The criteria is increasingly cost-driven and final decision-making power remains centralised at both plants' pan-European headquarters located in the south-east of the UK and Germany and Switzerland. The range of functions at Motor Co. has been constant while Car Co. has come full circle from a fully integrated manufacturing plant through assembly-only to vehicle assembly and engine manufacture. The capacity of both plants is duplicated elsewhere due to dual sourcing strategies to maintain security of supply, and because they produce models for the high-volume, medium-sized market segment.[3] The need for cost, quality and productivity performance comparison has underpinned the standardisation in 'technically identical' plants. Motor Co. and Car Co. produce numerous variants of single models, mainly for the UK and continental Europe markets, although there are sole source mandates for some model variants, pressings and powertrain systems, and low-volume production for some export markets. Both plants remain reliant on centralised corporate functions for production engineering and scheduling, purchasing, product and process R&D. Plant engineering liaison functions have been bolstered for 'de-bugging', incremental product and process change, and input into new model design to improve 'manufacturability'.

The strategy of each plant remains based on model specialisation and breaking into export markets in tandem with the in-situ improvement of productivity, capacity utilisation and cost reduction. Car Co. has benefited from a new plant-wide labour agreement introduced as a prerequisite for the recent engine investment. This was 'won' ahead of another Car Co. German plant due to surplus capacity and labour on-site, the UK supplier base and low labour costs. The model specialisation strategy has endured since it generates scale economies, reduces manufacturing complexity and raises the profile of the plant by becoming a sole (often export) source within the company. However, specialisation also entails dependence upon a narrow product range and closer integration with intra-corporate supply chains and other 'sister' plants. This specialisation within the intra-firm division of labour has created new inter-plant dependencies. 'Lead' sites with superior performance have emerged to begin new model production in parallel with product and process engineering functions. This allows time for 'de-bugging' models before they are released to full-scale production elsewhere in 'follower' plants. Lead sites have had historically higher relative levels of investment in 'state-of-the-art' process plant than other solely production-oriented capacity, and they gain from the productivity and quality head start. Motor Co. and Car Co.'s lead plants are in Germany. Despite being twice the size and producing fewer model variants, the UK plants' performance is compared on a 'like with like' basis with all the plants. Car Co. was even forced to become a 'swing plant' to absorb fluctuations in output, while the production volume at its lead plant was kept constant to maintain three-shift working. In this way, the lead plant's privileged position directly affected output and employment levels at the follow plant in Riverside. Capacity expansion at both plants has been seen as critical to upgrading and matching the scale of the lead plants.

Labour Process Reorganisation

A technical and social reorganisation of production is apparent at Motor Co. and Car Co. The emblem of 'lean production' has guided the choice of techniques which increase integration between more specialised stages of production and reduce manufacturing complexity (see Williams, Williams and Haslam 1992). The aim has been to increase capacity, rates of production, quality, cost efficiency and improve productivity through reducing labour hours per vehicle. Motor Co. are moving beyond the planning stage while Car Co.'s new labour agreement has underpinned significant changes. 'Soft', reprogrammable automation has been utilised to improve cost efficiency but progress has been uneven due to the desire to reduce fixed costs per model.[4] JIT and outsourcing have been used to reduce inventory, increase cost efficiency and improve quality. Internal plant functions have been scrutinised on a 'make or buy' basis but outsourcing has been contested by trade unions anxious to prevent the loss of work to often non-union, lower-wage suppliers. Motor Co. outsourced seat assembly to a nearby factory operated by a specialist supplier whose investment has been supported by a long-term supply contract. Local economic development institutions have interpreted this development as the beginning of a putative supplier park capable of creating local jobs. There appears to be no guarantee with this strategy since seat cover production was outsourced to Eastern Europe with the loss of 270, mainly female, jobs, leaving a net employment reduction in Riverside. Car Co. secured trade union concessions on working practices and staffing which reduced costs and kept seat assembly in-house although a quirk of the existing plant layout, which situated the assembly operations alongside where they would have had to be delivered, also helped.

Changes in working practices have focused on teamworking. The Car Co. workforce claim there are 'teams but not teamworking' (author's interview 1992). Job demarcation has been replaced by team demarcation (Roberts and Corcoran Nantes 1992), labour flexibility has been enhanced horizontally across grades rather than vertically between grades and work rates have intensified with indirect tasks (for example maintenance) being tacked onto direct workloads. *Kaizen* (continuous improvement) programmes have often not yielded the expected labour savings, and some areas are considered 'lean to the bone' with little room for further improvement without fundamental change in car design. Both brownfield plants have had problems with reluctance by an ageing workforce to move between jobs and their vulnerability to the rising intensity and dexterity required for modern work on the line. Training efforts have intensified at both plants, often in conflict with output requirements. Employees have been encouraged to take more educational courses in an attempt to implant a 'learning culture' on the shopfloor. Some skills have been rendered obsolete (for example, mechanical fitters) and others combined (for example, 'mechelec' technicians from electricians and mechanics). Overall, the workforces of both plants have experienced 'multi-tasking' through an increase in the number of jobs of roughly equivalent skill levels rather than through skills upgrading.

Realigning Labour–Management Relations

The employee–company relationship and trade union representation have been realigned at Motor Co. and Car Co. Both plants have experienced the 'new realism' in UK industrial relations (Beardwell 1992) due to intensified competition, their specific histories of near closure, previous disputes, ongoing pressure to reduce workforce numbers and entrenched unemployment in Riverside. Such 'realities' have fostered a more cooperative attitude between labour and management. Motor Co. and Car Co. have instigated shifts away from the adversarial industrial relations traditions, often assumed to be synonymous with Riverside, in the direction of business unionism. The realignment of trade union interests with that of the company has become the quid pro quo for the continued acceptance of trade unionism in the plants. 'Enabling' employment agreements, which aim to cover both current and future contingencies, have been used to codify the framework for change and to formalise the commitment to teamworking and engender the feeling between employee and company that 'we're all on the same side, there is no "us" and "them" anymore' (author's interview 1992). Such agreements have become longer term to reduce negotiation costs and dispute threats, and include pay incentives to promote and reward the acceptance of change. Management secures longer-term benefits for one-off payments. Car Co.'s recent agreement at Riverside originated from negotiations to save another

Car Co. plant from closure. The agreement was made a prerequisite for the engine plant bid on Riverside since it was thought that the workforce was more militant and not quite as willing to accept change (author's interview 1992). Since then the agreement has been considered a 'blueprint' for the company's European operations. Bargaining has been decentralised and more locally driven to disengage the plants from national collective structures and heighten plant management's flexibility and autonomy.[5] This has opened up the potential for the 'leveraging down' of terms and conditions between plants due to competitive pressures for investment securing concessions in terms and conditions. Although, paradoxically, trade unions within Motor Co. and Car Co. claim they are stronger in plant level negotiations since they have a better understanding of the detail of local issues and managerial intent.

Reorganising Labour Market Engagement

Motor Co. and Car Co.'s recruitment practices have become increasingly selective and sophisticated. Previous methods based on vetting applications for educational attainment and suitability in relation to basic criteria, supported by the high number of applicants from the slack local labour market, have been replaced by a system where applications are scrutinised rigorously. The aim has been to enhance the adaptability of the workforce, especially their manual and mental dexterity, by requiring higher levels of basic education. Pressures for 'kith and kin' recruitment from the existing workforce have been resisted through such measures. Graduate recruitment has been used to fill the gap created by the rationalisation of middle management. A dilemma for both brownfield plants has been their ageing workforces. In the context of strategies for reducing labour hours per vehicle and relatively low recruitment levels, each has had to balance the level of exits, through early voluntary retirement or redundancy, with the entry of new recruits.

Temporary employment tested the apparent *rapprochement* between labour and management at Motor Co. and Car Co. due to Riverside's unhappy history of casual dock-related work. While ostensibly to meet peak periods in demand as in continental European plants, temporary labour was central to the company's attempt to develop a labour market structure with core and peripheral segments.

Safeguards were won but the initial utilisation of temporary labour was typical of Car Co.'s follower role relative to its lead German plant. The lack of press shop capacity at the German plant led the European headquarters to insist that Car Co. bring in temporary labour to staff its own press shop to provide the extra capacity. Otherwise, its assembly line speed would be slowed to generate the extra labour, leaving the German plant to make up the output shortfall. The use of temporary employees has been rejected at Motor Co. (except as cover for absentees) after union campaigning for permanent status for all jobs within the plant.

Changing Relations with Suppliers

Motor Co. and Car Co.'s relatively increased autonomy has led to heightened discretion over material costs and supply linkages. Reorganisation of both internal, intra-corporate and external, inter-corporate links are evident. External sourcing in particular has increased in a bid to reduce costs and labour hours per vehicle, raise quality, productivity and efficiency as well as externalise uncertainty and gain flexibility. Each plant has had to confront the cost of generating surplus labour and potential redundancies due to outsourcing and has had to utilise 'insourcing' strategies of bringing or maintaining work in-house to maintain capacity utilisation. Arrangements with external suppliers have been marked by longer-term and closer relations with a reduced supplier base. Services were among the first to be contracted out, including energy supply, building maintenance, security and catering. The purchasing departments of Motor Co. and Car Co.'s parent companies have become increasingly centralised, however, in the search for purchasing economies, shared components between models and a 'global' perspective. This has created a tension between the benefits of global sourcing, promoted by centralised purchasing functions anxious to reap scale economies, and 'local' just-in-time (JIT) supply links, desired by individual plants aiming to reduce material costs and logistic management complexity. Indeed, the current practice of global sourcing often translates into a process at odds with the current partnership sourcing models whereby global low-cost sources are sought out and used to extract concessions from existing suppliers. Due to their lack of technological development functions, Motor Co. and Car Co. have had limited leverage over design and procurement decisions. The co-location of the centralised purchasing functions of the parent companies with their R&D and technical development centres in the south-east region of the UK, and Hessen, Germany, has created problems due to the close linkages fostered between design and procurement. Suppliers locally adjacent to these strategic decision-making centres tend to be incorporated early into the product specification, since most of the cost-critical decisions are made early in car design. Supply chain development initiatives pursued by local institutions have been further hampered by the historically low levels of local sourcing and reliance on imports at the plants, rationalisation amongst the existing supply base within Riverside and the need to compete for new supplier investment against even lower-cost Central and Eastern European regions. Localised JIT links with suppliers at both plants have been confined to bulkier, lower value-added components with which suppliers have greater scale economies and those components fitted to every vehicle. Motor Co. have utilised a haulage company to establish a transitional 'JIT warehouse' or 'sequencing centre' (three or four others within a thirty-mile radius are planned) on site, in which material is consolidated before crossing the physical and financial threshold into the plant. Both plants have made substantial one-off inventory and indirect labour savings through JIT, but their existing layout has often hampered the quick turnaround JIT delivery and presentation of materials to the 'lineside'.

Each plant is planning adjacent supplier 'park' or 'village' initiatives in conjunction with local institutions anxious to create job opportunities in the context of Riverside's relatively high unemployment levels. Motor Co.'s initial aim was to develop a 'wrap-around factory', as used by its lead plants in Germany and Spain, where dedicated suppliers are located on an adjacent 'supplier park' linked directly to the production lines by conveyors. Drawn by the promise of five hundred jobs, a local partnership, including the local authority and English Partnerships, worked closely with the plant to redevelop a site using national and EU funding. Indeed, Motor Co. included the new industrial park as a key element in their bid to win the investment for the new version of their current model. However, the viability of earlier plans by the local partnership was thrown into question when it was revealed that the new model investment would go to other Motor Co. plants in Germany and Spain, and any further investment in vehicle assembly in Riverside was dependent upon performance improvement, market development and discussions concerning grant aid with the Department of Trade and Industry. A deal was eventually secured for a new niche vehicle for another subsidiary of the parent company to be assembled at Motor Co. through a package worth £15m, comprising Regional Selective Assistance and training delivered through the TEC and local providers.

CONCLUSIONS

This chapter has argued that addressing the inter-relations between structure, agency and contingency can help in an understanding of the changes in the branch plants and their local economic prospects.

Both plants and their host local and regional economy have experienced limited changes in their positions within the wider structures of corporate and spatial divisions of labour. The role of the plants continued to be of low-volume, duplicate capacity, producing numerous variants of single products, and they remain reliant on external ownership, control and the support of centralised intra-corporate services. Agency at the plant and locality level had changed through the reshaping of each plant's scope for action. Heightened autonomy and responsibility for operational performance issues and preparing bids for intra-corporate investment competitions were evident. Decisions were also marked by the intervention of organisational politics . There was evidence also of the plants becoming simultaneously more 'stand alone' and 'integrated'. Discretion in the plants concerning bids for investment projects, new labour agreement negotiations, local supplier arrangements and input to product manufacturing and process engineering all had potential implications for local economic development. The extent to which this heightened scope led to more progressive developments in the local economy, as suggested in the more positive accounts of change, was limited, however. The structural role of Motor Co. and uncertainty over future investment questioned the viability of the local partnership's attempt to redevelop a supplier park to support the plant's bid for investment. Contingency also played a role in unravelling the meaning of changes. The port-related, 'casualised' employment history of Riverside impinged on the trade union responses to the utilisation of temporary labour. Labour relations were shaped by the specific local histories of perceived militancy, disputes and closure threats as well as the ability of the management to get 'delivery' on employment agreements. 'Outsourcing' was resisted in both plants, and workforces were unwilling to surrender safeguards won as a result of historic disputes. The particular history of the industrial structure of Riverside and historic problems of the traditional 'branch plant economy' (North West Partnership 1996) also played a role, since rationalisation of the existing supply base influenced the extent to which purchasing at the plants could be localised and required local economic development institutions to work in partnership with the plants to encourage inward investment in the supply sector and the regeneration of industrial sites.

Changes in both plants were characterised by experimentation with new strategies that sometimes echoed the hallmarks of previous developments. Motor Co. and Car Co.'s autonomy increased their operational responsibility for performance and strategic scope for change, especially as part of bidding for intra-corporate investment. Local economic development institutions have perhaps had more of an opportunity to be involved in responding to grant packages offered elsewhere and working closely with the companies on strategic issues, such as the local supplier park plan. Decentralisation was tempered with further integration within parent company structures, with increasingly pan-European and global perspectives and new dependencies emerging through 'lead' and 'follower' roles. The engineering liaison upgrade is a development, but it is clearly instrumental to central monitoring and 'de-bugging' capability for production elsewhere and manufacturing input to new product development. The intra-corporate focus of such change has limited the degree of local linkages with the local technology support infra-structure. R&D and purchasing co-location at lead sites has also reinforced their capacity to contract more actively with their local suppliers and technology-based institutions outside Riverside. In this context, the fact that each plant remains relatively low-volume duplicate capacity raises questions for their futures. Investments continue to be tied to winning intra-corporate battles, and current cost competitiveness may be insufficient in relation to the needs of organisational politics to spread investment between existing and/or new sites and the bidding competitions between local institutions regarding the level of public subsidy. Reorganisation for lean production was uneven and marked by a reluctance to change among an ageing workforce.

The technical and social reorganisation of production and accompanying investment means it is hard to sustain a depiction of the jobs as characteristic of 'screwdriver' plants, but multitasking appears a more appropriate description than multiskilling. The changes in labour–management relations suggest a willingness to accept, or inability to reject, working within a framework of business unionism on the part of employees and trade unions. Developments in Car Co. are even being 'exported' as the blueprint for other plants, implying the weakening of workplace solidarity in affected local economies by a 'ratcheting down' of employment safeguards to the current lowest common denominator standard. Resistance has been evident in Riverside, at least in part due to the specific labour history of the locality, for instance to temporary employees, outsourcing and 'off-the-job' discussion groups, suggesting that change does not always go uncontested. Experimentation with new supply chain strategies provoked tensions between trade unions, manufacturing and materials management within the plants and between the plant and centralised purchasing functions. Outsourcing is set to continue and presents a threat to jobs when plant specialisation and sole source strategies focus on cost-sensitive and labour-intensive production stages. Supplier linkages were dealt with in a pragmatic manner through transitionary measures, comprising 'JIT warehouses' and 'warehouses on wheels'. JIT was implemented over longer distances and proliferated rather modest local supply base development. These developments, coupled with uncertainty over future model plans, render the hopes of local economic development institutions for job creation through supplier park-types of initiative problematic. More possibilities exist through moving existing suppliers onto JIT but, again, this is not necessarily 'local' nor will it guarantee the establishment of new factories in the local economy. While both plants remain significant employers, growth prospects are modest due to ongoing efficiency drives, strategies for reducing labour hours per vehicle and redeployment. Both plants are able to produce more cars with a given workforce and absorb expansion. The 'quality' of the jobs at Motor Co. and Car Co. is more difficult to assess. More is expected of those remaining in work with intensification reinforced by continuous pressure for ongoing rationalisation, efficiency improvement and the incorporation of an expanding array of direct and indirect production tasks within teams. The nature and net level of employment were also questioned by developments.

The evidence of in-situ restructuring in the automobile industry in Riverside provides a cautionary tale for economic development policy-makers. The overlap of old and new practices may yield limited benefits for local economic development and become increasingly contingent upon the capability of local institutions to build on such developments. Indeed, despite their best intentions, the forces underlying these fashionable initiatives aimed at enhancing the ties of local economies with the fortunes of the emergent type of 'branch plant economy' may subsequently prove problematic.

NOTES

1. This research was supported by the ESRC. Thanks are due to: the management, trades unions and workforce at Motor Co. and Car Co. for participating in this research; Michelle Wood and Nick Phelps for their comments; and LATTS, Noisy-le-Grand, for hosting the European Commission-funded European Network on Innovation and Territory (EUNIT) fellowship. The usual disclaimers, as always, apply.

2. Minimum efficient scales for car assembly plants are 250–300,000 units annually.

3. The approximate proportion (per cent) of automation for Motor Co. and Car Co. in the four key areas respectively are: press shop (50:60), body shop (70:90), paint shop (30:45) and final assembly (5:20) (author's interviews 1992).

4. The more recent establishment of European Works Councils at Motor Co. and Car Co. occurred after this research was undertaken.

FRANK PECK AND JONATHAN DURNIN[1]

14 Institutional Marginalisation and Inward Investment Strategies in the North of England: the Case of Cumbria

INTRODUCTION

The role and influence of institutions in local economic development has been the subject of considerable debate in recent literature (Amin and Thrift 1994; Cooke and Morgan 1993; Dicken 1994; Morgan 1997). While, in general, there appears to be widespread acceptance of the idea that institutions play a significant role in regional development, the effectiveness of strategies designed to build up institutional capacity in weaker regions remains a point of debate (Bennet 1997). The role of institutions has been debated prominently in the context of strategies designed to attract new inward investment and embed existing inward investment within host regions. Many of the ideas related to the concept of 'institutional thickness' suggest that companies will tend to be drawn towards regions which can demonstrate an institutional capacity to support firms through periods of very rapid change (Dicken 1994). As far as weaker peripheral regions are concerned, these ideas can be extended in different ways. One policy response, for instance, might be to build up institutional capacity by creating new institutions and strengthening local networks between firms and public sector agencies and authorities. However, others have argued that the relative power and influence of local institutions may represent another form of uneven development which is highly persistent through time (Hudson 1997). The claims made by those who advocate an institutionally based strategy for local economic development may therefore be overstated. In the context of these debates, this chapter explores the effects of institutional marginalisation in the context of strategies to attract inward investment to the relatively isolated industrial areas of the county of Cumbria in the north of England.

INWARD INVESTMENT AND INSTITUTIONAL CAPACITY IN REGIONAL ECONOMIES

Local institutional support has always been critical in the process of attracting new inward investment. However, in this highly competitive field, inward investment agencies have needed to become increasingly sophisticated in their approach to winning new projects. Various inter-related changes in industrial organisation induced by powerful competitive processes have led to much greater selectivity in the locational choice of companies and closer attention to the kinds of support which a regional economy may be able to provide in the longer term. As a consequence, inward investment agencies have been under increasing pressure to demonstrate a region's capacity (and willingness) to provide a wider range of services and access to public resources over an extended period of time beyond the initial set-up period.

In recent literature, however, consideration of the role of inward investment agencies in influencing investment flows has been subsumed within wider discussions concerning the role of institutions in regional economies in general. These debates have moved attention away from the role of inward investment agencies *per se* towards the construction of explanatory frameworks within which networks of relationships between numerous local institutions can be analysed. There has, for example, been much discussion of the concept of 'institutional thickness' in local economic development. This suggests that the success of regions in the global economy may depend on the 'articulation between institutional thickness and "economic" variables which make it worthwhile for industry to remain in a locality' (Amin and Thrift 1994, p. 16). Local economies vary in institutional capacity in terms of their number, diversity, connectivity and access to resources. This framework of analysis implies that regions which have a dense network of institutions may create special advantages for investors in terms of the capacity of regions to support incoming firms and assist subsequent *in situ* corporate adjustments through collective action and pooling of resources.

While it is widely accepted that the concept of institutional thickness encapsulates something important about the way in which local economies develop, the precise meaning of the term raises difficulties. In a superficial sense, 'thickness' can be taken to mean something to do with the formal structures that exist: the number, the variety of institutions (institutional presence), the resources available to them or the way in which these institutions collaborate with one another (institutional networks). Amin and Thrift (1994), however, attempt to develop a much broader concept which includes aspects of institutional *performance and behaviour* which relate to other less formal structures, social conventions, habits and routines which may be unique to particular places. In these terms, institutional thickness is not simply about structures, but also represents an attempt to encapsulate the behaviour and motivations of individuals and institutions within particular local contexts. It also embodies the notion of institutionalisation – a process of change whereby institutions sustain themselves and work towards the development of trust and reciprocity.

The relationship between formal networks and informal social/institutional practices is also given prominence by Cooke and Morgan (1993) who elevate this approach to the status of a new paradigm in regional development. The focus of their approach is on the networks that exist in the industrial system. Large-firm networks consist of formal links such as joint ventures and strategic alliances but also involve more informal arrangements that exist between producers, some of which operate at a regional level. Large firms also network with small and medium-sized firms (SMEs) in supply chains, which can become the basis of mutual learning and problem solving. SMEs can also develop inter-firm networks that become a basis for mutual support and innovative behaviour. Cooke and Morgan argue that these networks lead to the creation of unique locally produced and locally embedded knowledge resources which can improve the competitiveness of established firms and act as a magnet for new investors who wish to acquire that specialist knowledge. These intra- and inter-firms networks are supported by the activities of other public and private institutions which act as animateurs in the process of economic development and these institutions become vital repositories of local knowledge (Lundvall 1992; Morgan 1997).

These arguments are now fairly familiar in the literature on regional development. In policy terms, they imply that some types of regions can create conditions in which production facilities are highly embedded through the existence of dense local networks of support. In such regions, production units are less likely to be selected for closure because they demonstrate a capacity to adapt to change, display high levels of innovation supported by other institutions and firms that share the risks involved. These networks also generate an archive of highly specific and specialised knowledge that is both formal but also tacit – knowledge which is only acquired by acting and interacting with others (Lundvall 1992; Morgan 1997). This tacit knowledge, in particular, is not easily replicated in new locations and becomes a specialised resource that forms a basis for regional competitive advantage which can be used to attract new investors and to embed existing ones. In relation to policy, these arguments tend to lead to the conclusion that strategies can be constructed around the objective of strengthening local institutional capacity as a means of embedding existing firms and attracting new inward investment.

INSTITUTIONS AND UNEVEN DEVELOPMENT

While there does appear to be some consensus about the importance of institutions in current processes of regional development, Hudson (1997) has argued that some of these ideas need to be treated with caution. Locations that have many well-resourced institutions and are able and willing to support private capital will undoubtedly attract mobile investment and retain existing firms. This arises because firms seek locations which not only have labour reserves, but which also possess 'social and cultural settings that shift the cost of reproducing labour power onto local societies and states' (Hudson 1997, p. 473). Quite clearly, strong regions with deep institutional capacity will be attractive to inward investors. However, it is quite another matter to suggest that weaker regions can improve their performance by developing deeper institutional structures. A new emphasis on institutions in regional development may simply create a new form of uneven development as resource-rich institutions in powerful regions are able to exercise control over policy design and implementation and the directions in which resources flow. Simply creating new institutions may not provide economic solutions for weaker regions which may remain marginalised due to the highly uneven distribution of institutional power and resources.

It is, of course, possible that regions that are characterised by 'thick' institutional structures can lose their supremacy. As Amin and Thrift (1994, p. 260) observe, institutions can become ossified even in successful regions which provides other regions with opportunities to replace them if they find the right 'institutional mix'. Similarly, Bennett (1997) suggests that anti-growth sentiments can strengthen over time in successful regions, particularly in response to concerns for the environment, conservation and quality of life. In other situations, a lack of common purpose can work to reinforce sectional or institutional interests rather than the creation of new investment. However, in the short term at least, the power associations built up between neighbouring territories and regions tend to persist through time. This implies that the creation of new institutional arrangements in marginalised local areas is unlikely to have a major impact on local development unless it is accompanied by the repositioning of territories within the power networks that control the development process.

These are significant points of departure for this chapter, which develops a critique of ideas concerning institutional capacity building. We argue that the power relationships which exist between institutions operating in different territories and at different levels of spatial aggregation play a vital role in determining not only the direction of flow of resources but also in determining prevailing attitudes, ideologies and policy responses. In other words, some local economies in the UK may be disadvantaged not only by their relatively poor access to external resources but also by their inability to influence policy agendas. Socio-political processes that operate at a wider European and national level with strong feedback links to the more powerful regional metropolitan cores primarily shape such agendas.

As a consequence, not only do some local economies find difficulty in securing external resources for development, but the models of development applied to those areas may not be the most appropriate response to local circumstance, and it is indeed possible that the two may be connected. Such responses may instead be driven by the necessity to appease demands created by dominant political opinion and public perceptions of what constitutes 'success' in local development. In the remainder of this chapter, we develop these arguments using a case study of policy responses towards inward investment promotion in the county of Cumbria.

Peripherality and Institutional Marginalisation in Cumbria

Cumbria provides a clear example of a subregion that has experienced the effects of various forms of institutional marginalisation. One of the more obvious illustrations of the effects of this is provided by the attempts by agencies in Cumbria to work through regional and national agencies to secure inward investment projects during the 1990s. In comparison with many other counties in northern England, Cumbria has not been a major destination for new greenfield investment. Some of the reasons for this, which have been analysed elsewhere, include the effects of labour market change in established firms (see Peck *et al.* 1997a, 1997b) the impact of perceptions of Cumbria and the difficulties associated with transport infrastructure (Hague and Wylie 1996; F Peck 1996). However, Cumbria has also experienced the effects of various forms of institutional marginalisation due, in part, to a lack of clarity regarding its formal regional place that was only recently resolved.

Cumbria is situated in the north-west extremity of England and its core areas contain the Lake District National Park, which is a major tourist destination in the UK. After North Yorkshire, Cumbria is the second largest county in England, covering an area of approximately 680,000 hectares. The majority of the population live in the more peripheral areas of the county, dictated by the central location of the Cumbrian fells, which creates relatively long distances between settlements and relative difficulty in providing transport networks. The largest centre of population is Carlisle (approx. 80,000) and although there are industrial towns to the west and south of the county at Whitehaven, Workington and Barrow, 48 per cent of the population live in settlements of less than 10,000 (Cumbria County Council 1995).

As a consequence of Cumbria's large area, the sparsity of its population and the eccentricity of its settlement pattern dictated by topography, there has been much debate as to the structure of local government in Cumbria over the last twenty years. The present county of Cumbria was established in the 1974 reorganisation of local government by drawing together the two former counties of Cumberland and Westmorland and adjacent parts of North Lancashire and the West Riding of Yorkshire. The two-tier structure in Cumbria consisted of a county council and six local authority Districts of Allerdale, Barrow-in-Furness, Carlisle, Copeland, Eden and South Lakeland. In spite of intense local debate, this county boundary and two-tier structure of local government survived the 1994 review of local government.

While there are in-built tensions in the structure of local government created by strong local identities and localised attachments to place, the position of Cumbria as a whole within the regional framework of northern England has also been problematic. The Standard Regions used by government for official statistical purposes have placed Cumbria in the 'Northern Region' with a focus on Newcastle upon Tyne. However, for the purpose of central government administration, Cumbria comes under the jurisdiction of Government Office North West (GONW) based in Manchester. A wide range of public and private sector institutions, some of which coordinate their activities in Cumbria from Newcastle while others link the county to Manchester, mirror this situation. The question of regional identity is complex and not independent of local attachments to place and divisions within the county. In general terms, communities in the south of the county have close affinity to the north- west, while areas to the north (and possibly in the west) express stronger attachment to the north-east of England.

INWARD INVESTMENT IN CUMBRIA: THE INSTITUTIONAL FRAMEWORK

The institutional framework within which inward investment projects are currently managed within the UK has evolved incrementally over the past two decades (Dicken and Tickell 1992; Roberts and Noon 1987). At a national level, the Invest in Britain Bureau (IBB) was set up in 1977 as a specialised unit within the Department of Trade and Industry (DTI). Its role and operations have been examined elsewhere (see, for example, Dicken 1990). The key point as far as Cumbria is concerned is that all enquiries generated by the IBB are routed through INWARD, which is the agency responsible for securing inward investment projects for the north-west region. According to officials at INWARD, approximately 45 per cent of all their enquiries in recent years have been routed from the IBB. However, INWARD also generates its own enquiries through its overseas offices in Chicago and in Tokyo. INWARD therefore generates 55 per cent of its inward investment enquiries independently from the IBB.

The situation in Cumbria is made more complex by the county's relationship to Northern Development Company (NDC), which parallels INWARD's activity based in Newcastle upon Tyne, serving primarily the north-east of England (Dicken and Tickell 1992). NDC was established in its present form in 1987 with the original intention of serving the whole of the Northern Region, which included Cumbria. The local authorities in Cumbria were given the option to access NDC services in addition to those provided by INWARD. An agreement was reached whereby the Cumbrian contribution to NDC would include 50 per cent from the county council and the rest divided equally among the six local authority districts. The county council has been a consistent supporter of NDC, but the response from the districts has varied. The communities in the south of the county within the districts of

Barrow-in-Furness and South Lakeland have stronger economic and cultural ties with the North-West and have not subscribed to NDC. However the West Cumbria Partnership (incorporating Allerdale and Copeland Districts) and the City of Carlisle have made regular contributions to NDC.

In terms of its regional setting therefore, Cumbria lies at the spatial margins of these two regional inward investment agencies and this fact has had an important effect upon the development of institutions within Cumbria. Many of the local structures have evolved to try to compensate for real (and perceived) disadvantage experienced by the county because of its spatial and institutional peripherality as a subregion within the Government Office North West and the Standard Northern Region. These local structures, however, have also evolved in response to a series of major job losses affecting large employers since the late 1980s (for a more detailed account of these changes, see Peck *et al.* 1997).

In the west of the county, economic development strategies in the boroughs of Allerdale and Copeland have evolved since 1988 under the umbrella of the West Cumbria Partnership, which was created as a local response to intensified employment decline created by redundancies from British Nuclear Fuels (BNFL). This decline was associated with the end of the construction phase of the Thermal Oxide Reprocessing Plant (THORP) at Sellafield (PIEDA 1991). These job losses added to those created by the long-term decline of coal mining, iron, steel and engineering industries which affected the town of Workington in particular in the early 1980s. The West Cumbria Development Agency was set up to spearhead regeneration. As part of this response, the economic strategy of the partnership highlighted inward investment as a means of securing alternative employment (West Cumbria Partnership 1994, 1996; Ernst and Young 1995). The promotion of inward investment was enhanced in 1993 by the creation of a specialist unit operating through an Inward Investment Office at Cockermouth (West Cumbria Development Agency 1994). The office has been working closely with both NDC and INWARD to process inward investment enquiries and organise site inspections and visits.

More recently, in the south of the county, Furness Enterprise was established in 1991 in response to similar problems created by redundancies at Vickers Shipbuilding and Engineering Ltd (VSEL) at Barrow-in-Furness (PIEDA 1992a). The agency's target was to generate 5,000 new jobs within ten years of operation through local expansions, new starts and greenfield inward investment (Furness Enterprise 1992, 1996, 1997). In relation to inward investment, the agency works primarily with INWARD at a regional level but has also developed local strategies to search for new inward investment projects. According to the agency, Furness Enterprise received 307 enquiries from potential inward investors in the financial year 1995–6 and of these, 72 per cent were generated by the agency itself. Both Furness and West Cumbria are eligible for European Regional Development Funding under Objective 2.

Policy-makers in Cumbria anticipated some difficulty in attracting inward investment due to a lack of awareness among potential investors of the industrial traditions of the county. In an attempt to counter this and compensate for institutional marginalisation the Cumbria Marketing Initiative (CMI) was set up in 1992 in an attempt to promote the whole of Cumbria as a destination for inward investment. The CMI was financed by a combination of local partners including Cumbria County Council, Cumbria TEC, West Cumbria Development Agency, DTI Cumbria Action Team (now GONW), BNFL and Furness Enterprise. Research conducted by CMI confirmed expectations that there was a basic lack of knowledge about Cumbria as a location for economic activity (see Hague and Wylie 1994, 1996). The Lake District as a holiday destination conditioned common perceptions of industrialists, but little was known about the industrial areas in the south and west of the county. The CMI operation therefore led to a sequence of imaginative ways of raising the public awareness of Cumbria across the UK using advertisements in the national press and opportunities presented by various projects, such as promotions associated with the warship *HMS Cumberland.* Subsequently, the 'Ambassadors for Cumbria' scheme involved contacting well-known personalities with links to Cumbria who were asked to raise the profile of County whenever it was appropriate to do so with potential investors (Lord Whitelaw, Chris Bonnington, Melvyn Bragg, Edward Stobart, Anna Ford).

CMI literature also drew attention to the existing key specialist areas of industry in Cumbria which might act as anchor points for other incoming firms in paper, board, film and packaging, pharmaceuticals, engineering, automotive components, food, textiles, clothing and footwear. Listing existing firms in these sectors to persuade potential investors that Cumbria could sustain and support leading firms in these sectors reinforced the message. As well as marketing, CMI was also intended as a first point for receiving inward investment enquiries generated by its own marketing activities.

STRATEGIES FOR INWARD INVESTMENT IN CUMBRIA, 1991–97

The manner in which these institutional frameworks have evolved in Cumbria has produced tensions in policy design and delivery. English inward investment agencies in the 1990s operate under considerable constraints, most of which arise from the highly competitive nature of the process of attracting inward investment. The objective of INWARD and NDC as regional agencies has been to create as many inward investment projects in their respective territories as a whole and their success has been measured in these terms. In preparing responses to enquiries, therefore, sites have been selected which maximise the attractiveness of their region as a whole. There is clearly a tension in this process between even-handedness across the region, and the pressure to focus on a small number of more accessible flagship sites close to the major conurbations to attract the attention of investors. Cumbrian practitioners, therefore, have had limited control over the way in which Cumbrian locations have been incorporated into responses to potential investors.

This point is evident in the attempt by INWARD in the early 1990s to develop a more systematic approach to site selection and definition. Key employment sites across the region with over eight hectares of development land were categorised into five types using criteria shown in table 14.1. The critical point in this context is the criteria to define 'flagship sites', which must be within one hour's driving time from an international airport. This requirement effectively eliminated the whole of Cumbria from this category. The application of these criteria to strategic sites in Cumbria is shown in table 14.2. Although there are no 'flagship sites', the major industrial site at Lillyhall near Workington, West Cumbria and others in the vicinity of Barrow are

TABLE 14.1: INWARD STRATEGIC EMPLOYMENT SITES IN THE NORTH-WEST REGION – CLASSIFICATION CRITERIA

Flagship sites
More than fifty hectares of undeveloped land
International airport within sixty minutes' driving time
Freight rail access within thirty minutes
Public transport facility access within ten minutes
Within five minutes from either motorway or dual carriageway
Special use – airport
Airport access within twenty minutes
Public transport facility access within ten minutes
Motorway or dual carriageway access within ten minutes
Special use – port
Port access within ten minutes
Special use – R&D
Higher education institute within thirty minutes
Airport access within sixty minutes
Public transport facility access within ten minutes
Motorway or dual carriageway access within ten minutes
Regional warehouse sites
More than fifty hectares of undeveloped land
Freight rail access within ten minutes
Motorway or dual carriageway access within ten minutes
Other unclassified sites
More than eight hectares of undeveloped land available

Source: Cumbria County Council

TABLE 14.2: INWARD DESIGNATED STRATEGIC EMPLOYMENT SITES FOR INWARD INVESTMENT IN CUMBRIA, 1996

Site		Type	Ha
	Allerdale		
1	Lillyhall Industrial Estate	Special use: port	47.5
2	Oldside, Workington	Special use: port	8.0
	Barrow		
3	Sowerby Woods Business Park	Special use: port	8.0
4	Furness Business Park	Special use: port	16.4
5	Sandscale Park (Courtaulds site)	Special use: port	20.0
6	Ramsden Dock	Special use: port	?
	Carlisle		
7	Kingmoor Park, West	Regional warehouse	25.0
8	Kingmoor Park, East (RAF 14MU)	Regional warehouse	30.0
9	Parkhouse Industrial Estate	Unclassified	9.9
10	Carlisle Airport, Crosby-on-Eden	Unclassified	22.0
	Copeland		
11	Westlakes Science and Tech. Park	Unclassified	50.4
12	Whitehaven Commercial Park	Unclassified	12.9
13	Keekle Opencast Site	Unclassified	?
14	Cleator Moor Industrial Estate	Unclassified	8.3
15	Millom Pier	Unclassified	8.1
	Eden		
16	Gilwilly Industrial Estate, Penrith	Unclassified	8.9
	South Lakeland		
17	Libby's Factory, Milnthorpe	Special use: R&D	8.5
18	Low Mill Tannery, Ulverston	Unclassified	9.0

Note: all available sites above eight hectares
Source: Cumbria County Council

included in a special category as they are within a ten-minutes drive of port facilities. In Carlisle, the former site of the RAF Maintenance Unit (14 MU), which is adjacent to the M6 motorway, is included as a location specified for regional warehouse activity. It is clear from this analysis that INWARD do not perceive nor do they present sites in Cumbria as 'flagship' locations which might attract a wide range of potential investors to the region. They are, as implied by the classification, sites which will only be suitable for 'special use' by particular companies which do not insist on sites close to an international airport.

Even so, according to information provided by INWARD for the twenty-one months between April 1995 and January 1997, 223 property bids were sent out by the agency and a Cumbrian location was included in about half of these cases. Table 14.3 shows the overall picture of INWARD's attempts to incorporate Cumbria sites into their bids in response to enquiries. Records collated by Cumbria County Council over the past five years show that sites in Cumbria have been incorporated into responses to enquiries on 310 occasions. The largest number includes bids to North American enquiries, reflecting the presence of INWARD offices in the USA. By comparison, bids to Japanese investors are relatively few, although the recent increase in the 'rest of world' category reflects increasing flows of potential investment from the Far East outside Japan. Bids to potential European investors have also increased marginally since 1992.

Similar tensions also apply to NDC's approach to Cumbria. One major difference is that NDC is not obliged to cover Cumbria for enquiries routed from IBB (referrals for Cumbria come via INWARD). NDC, however, has extended its services for inward investment to Cumbria on the basis of its own self-generated projects. The outcomes in terms of bids including sites in Cumbria is shown in table 14.4. Interestingly, the total of 310 bids is exactly the same as that of INWARD. The figures show some other parallels with INWARD, including a down-turn in 1993 during the recession. There are, however, some interesting differences in terms of country of origin. NDC

TABLE 14.3: INWARD INVESTMENT ENQUIRIES INCORPORATING POTENTIAL SITES IN CUMBRIA

Country	1992	1993	1994	1995	1996	Total
Japan	4	0	3	6	6	19
North America	35	23	40	29	18	145
UK	13	3	3	5	8	32
Europe	8	5	13	12	14	52
Rest of World	4	3	22	10	16	55
Total	**64**	**34**	**81**	**62**	**62**	**303**

Source: Cumbria County Council

Note: Table includes all enquiries which led to the inclusion of proposals for sites in Cumbria. These include all enquiries directed to INWARD from IBB as well as other INWARD self-generated projects.

TABLE 14.4: NORTHERN DEVELOPMENT COMPANY INWARD INVESTMENT ENQUIRIES INCORPORATING POTENTIAL SITES IN CUMBRIA

Country	1992	1993	1994	1995	1996	Total
Japan	10	2	6	6	12	36
North America	26	24	26	16	25	117
UK	15	4	12	19	12	62
Europe	9	8	3	2	3	25
Rest of World	18	16	16	12	8	70
Total	**78**	**54**	**63**	**55**	**60**	**310**

Source: Cumbria County Council

Note: Table includes all enquiries which led to the inclusion of proposals for sites in Cumbria. These are NDC-generated enquiries only (excludes all enquiries directed to NDC via IBB).

presented fewer bids to North American enquiries, but has suggested sites in Cumbria to a greater number of Japanese and European investors. The distribution of these enquiries across Cumbria reflects the location of principal employment sites (table 14.5). The largest number of bids has involved redeveloped industrial sites in Barrow, while the high number of bids in Allerdale is associated with the Lillyhall Industrial Estate, which lies close to the boundary with Copeland and acts as a strategic site for the whole of West Cumbria. The increase in the number of bids from the Carlisle area after 1994 reflects the expectation that the RAF 14 MU site would be available for development by an inward investor.

TABLE 14.5: NDC INWARD INVESTMENT ENQUIRIES FOR CUMBRIA

District	1993	1994	1995	1996 (to Sept.)	Total
Allerdale	31	37	23	15	106
Carlisle	1	8	10	4	23
Eden	0	0	0	0	0
Copeland	0	2	4	5	11
South Lakeland	0	1	5	0	6
Barrow	38	52	31	14	135
Total	**70**	**100**	**73**	**38**	**281**

Source: Northern Development Company

TABLE 14.6: NDC INWARD INVESTMENT VISITS TO CUMBRIA BY DISTRICT

District	1993	1994	1995	1996 (to Sept.)	Total
Allerdale	6	5	7	0	18
Carlisle	0	1	0	0	1
Eden	0	0	0	0	0
Copeland	0	0	0	0	0
South Lakeland	0	0	0	0	0
Barrow	1	5	1	0	7
Total	**7**	**11**	**8**	**0**	**26**

Source: Northern Development Company

Once potential inward investors have received details of bids from regional inward investment agencies, the most likely next step is a site visit. At this stage, the logistics of visits can have an important effect as visitors from overseas form first impressions. Parties of international visitors organised by INWARD or NDC usually enter the north of England via Manchester or Newcastle airports. Time is generally fairly short, and INWARD and NDC understandably need to be convinced that the potential benefits of visiting sites in Cumbria can justify a long journey. In other cases, the visitors themselves may have dismissed sites in Cumbria because the bids include equally appropriate sites with the same amenities which are closer to the metropolitan areas. For all these reasons, the number of site visits in Cumbria is much lower than the number of enquiries. This can be seen in table 14.6 which shows the pattern of NDC- organised visits to Cumbria which total twenty-six (equivalent to only 9 per cent of all enquiries incorporating a Cumbrian site).

Since 1990, there has been only one international investment in Cumbria derived from all the enquiries channelled through the regional agencies. This investment was secured as a consequence of an NDC mission which involved the Korean firm Sammi Sound who were looking for a UK location to produce loudspeakers for customers in the UK and Germany. It has been noted that Korean firms in the UK tend to be more dispersed across the regions of the UK compared to Japanese firms which display a more clustered location pattern (Burge 1996, 1997). The Sammi Sound decision suggests that part of the reason for this may be a desire by executives to move into areas that are not already dominated by larger Far Eastern companies. Initially, Sammi Sound assembled components delivered from Korea and had plans to expand to 90 employees over three years. Ownership changes in Korea, however, have altered the corporate approach to the UK investment and the planned expansion of production facilities has not taken place.

It is clear from this account that recent attempts to secure overseas investment for Cumbria through formal channels provided by IBB, NDC and INWARD have been frustrated by intensified competition for mobile international investment and the imperative for regionally based agencies to maximise investment flows in their core territories. Using a model of inward investment promotion which has proved highly successful in neighbouring territories in north-east England in particular, their attempts to work with local partners to secure investments in Cumbria have met with difficulty and frustration. Experience has demonstrated that Cumbria is unlikely to secure a large overseas assembly plant that requires a dense localised supply base of related firms and a large skilled-labour reserve. Indeed, it is questionable whether this is even desirable, given the possible negative effects of large inward investors on established firms' skill shortages (Peck and Stone 1991).

LOCAL INITIATIVES IN INWARD INVESTMENT PROMOTION

While the attraction of new greenfield investment from overseas has become increasingly difficult, Cumbria has secured a number of new investments through local initiatives. These cases illustrate two key points in analysing the experience of Cumbria in the 1990s. The chances of attracting investors is heightened considerably when the promotion of the local economy is conducted through informal networks of relationships which have an important bearing on building trust between agencies, existing local firms and potential inward investors. Such chances are also improved if agencies target their efforts on particular types of activity that relate to existing strengths in the local economy. These points can be illustrated by the recent experience of Furness Enterprise, the West Cumbria Development Agency and the Cumbria Marketing Initiative. These principles are also emerging as significant aspects of the approach being developed by the newly formed Cumbria Inward Investment Agency (see below).

A good illustration of the importance of these principles is provided by the American candle manufacturer Candle Corporation Worldwide (CCW). CCW announced plans in 1997 to invest £16 million in a new facility in Barrow, making this the largest new inward investment in Cumbria in recent years, employing an estimated 260 people. The firm is building a new factory on the former site of Courtauld's factory. The process was coordinated locally by Furness Enterprise in collaboration with Colony Gift Corporation, an established firm in Furness which had existing links with CCW. (Colony Gift is currently 50 per cent owned by CCW.) It was reported that the investment was secured against competition from sites in Ireland, Germany and Holland (*Newcastle Journal* 5 December 1996). The process involved persuading executives of CCW that Cumbria could be an effective base for its European operations. The demonstration effect provided by Colony Gift Corporation, which was already operating in the area, was a vital part of this process. This meant CCW could access information from a verifiable source about the capability of the local labour market and the quality of relationships between local private-and public-sector agencies.

In West Cumbria, an important network of relationships was also a significant element in attracting Newport Components, based in Milton Keynes, to set up branch establishments in Workington to manufacture in 1991. Since Newport Components is a supplier to several major original equipment manufacturers (OEMs) including IBM, Honeywell, Philips and Siemens, this investment demonstrates the capacity of Cumbrian agencies to service the suppliers to larger investors in the United Kingdom. More recently, the West Cumbria Development Agency has also been instrumental in securing a new occupant for the former Campbell's factory at Maryport. The new company, Cumbrian Seafoods, will initially employ eighty workers to process fish for large customers in the food supply industry. The presence of potential employees with previous experience of working in the food industry was undoubtedly a local resource that attracted the incoming firm.

Cumbria has also attracted a number of investments in the service sector, including back office and call centre activity. In Furness, BT set up a call centre to handle Directory Assistance services in 1992 and a recent expansion of this facility increased employment from 100 to 170. The most recent project of this type has involved 150 public-sector jobs located in Workington in a new cattle tracking centre operated by the Ministry of Agriculture, Forestry and Fisheries (MAFF) (*Cumberland News* 1 August 1997). Finally, there have been several significant inward investments associated with the tourism sector.

These cases provide the clearest illustration of the way in which the unique characteristics of Cumbria can be used to generate forms of inward investment. The development of the Oasis Holiday Village south of Penrith financed by the Rank Group is by far the largest of these projects and which received considerable publicity in the lead up to opening during 1997. It is estimated that this project could create as many as 1,000 jobs in peak season. Several of the important tourism projects in West Cumbria have also involved investments by UK organisations located outside Cumbria, including the hotel group Campbell's, who own the Lakeland Sheep and Wool Centre at Cockermouth which acts as a gateway leading into the west of the Lake District.

CONCLUSIONS AND POLICY IMPLICATIONS

The experience of Cumbria provides useful insights into the ways in which local economies can experience institutional marginalisation. While there is undoubtedly unevenness in the distribution of institutional resources between local economies and regions, this case shows how such marginalisation can also diminish the influence that can be exercised over policy agendas determined at a regional level. This can mean that the legitimate concerns of some localities and the kinds of strategies that might address them may not be given equal attention in policy debates at a regional level. Instead, the interests of powerful national interests mediated through the regional metropolitan cores can overshadow these local issues.

These points are exemplified by the kinds of difficulties that can affect marginalised local economies in their attempts to compete for new inward investment. Cumbria has needed to compete for inward investment through an institutional structure that has not been set up primarily to serve the particular needs of the county, which has many unique features. As a consequence, the models of development via inward investment that have worked elsewhere have not proved effective in Cumbria. Significantly, the new inward investment that has been created has been secured by other means working at a local level. As a consequence, the types of inward investment coming to Cumbria have been quite varied in character, including UK relocations, call centre developments and investment in tourist attractions. These cases demonstrate that the prospects for securing new projects depend critically on working through existing formal and informal networks of relationships at different spatial scales and the development of investment promotion based on realistic assessments of local resources.

This experience has implications for our understanding of the role of institutions in regional development. The arguments developed in this chapter suggest that 'deepening' institutional structures by the creation of new institutions *per se* will not necessarily solve the problems of marginalised local economies unless these new structures enable local policy-makers to exercise greater influence over the strategic priorities at a regional level. Local policy-makers must also build on existing networks of relationships between local authorities, public-sector agencies and private-sector organisations in the local economy. In this context, it is significant that Cumbria has recently set up a new inward investment agency (CiiA) as part of an attempt to improve coordination of inward investment strategy across the County. Also, the Labour Party's plans for setting up Regional Development Agencies in the English regions have created considerable institutional uncertainty in the North-West. One of the key tasks of the new RDA after April 1999 will be to design an economic strategy for the region. In this context, there may well be a unique opportunity for local authorities and development agencies in Cumbria to establish new working relationships and to influence the emerging strategies at the regional level within the north-west of England.

NOTE

1. The authors acknowledge assistance and helpful comments provided by representatives of the county council and district councils in Cumbria, Cumbria TEC, West Cumbria Development Agency, Furness Enterprise, Northern Development Company, INWARD, IBB, Cumbria Tourist Board, Cumbria Marketing Initiative and Government Office North-West. The interpretations in the chapter, however, are those of the authors only.

Earlier versions of this chapter were presented at the British and Irish Section of the Regional Science Association conference, Falmouth, Cornwall, 10–12 September 1997 and at the Regional Studies Association 'Regional Frontiers' European Urban and Regional Research Network Conference, Frankfurt-on-Oder, Germany, 20–23 September 1997.

JOHN DUNNING AND LORNA WALLACE

15 New Jersey in a Globalising Economy

INTRODUCTION

Contrary to the claims of some analysts about how 'the logic and dynamics of territorial development are increasingly placeless' (Castells and Henderson 1987, p. 7), or those who predict either the end of geography (O'Brien 1992) or of the nation state (Ohmae 1995), we tend to agree with Allen Scott (1986) when he suggests that the global economy is entering a phase of capitalist development in which the local or subnational concentration of production is becoming more rather than less pronounced as a mode of spatial economic organisation.

This chapter provides an overview of the impact of the ongoing globalisation on the economy of the state of New Jersey (NJ). In addition, it discusses key executive identified dimensions which influence locational decisions on the part of multinational enterprises (MNEs) conducting operations in the state.

Inward, inbound or foreign direct investment (FDI) in the United States (USA) has rarely been rigorously analysed at the subnational level, yet an understanding of FDI at this level, provides an opportunity for identifying areas or industries for strategic priority setting, and the formulation of policies by state governments for most effectively upgrading the resources and capabilities within their areas of jurisdiction. It also assists in identifying the particular role of an individual state, as opposed to that of the federal government, in attracting and retaining desirable mobile investment, and how it can best contribute to the economic welfare of the region. By reducing the size of the more commonly used spatial unit of analysis – the nation-state – to that of the subnational segment, scholars are presented with an approach which provides a more micro perspective from which to examine the continued relevancy of the interdisciplinary theories related to foreign direct investment and to increase understanding of global trade and investment flows (Graham and Krugman 1995).

RESEARCH METHODS

Two research methods are used to examine and relate inbound FDI in New Jersey to received theory and regional policy formulation. These are: first, a statistical analysis of secondary data; and second, field interviews with key executives of selected corporations engaging in FDI in the state of New Jersey. These approaches differ in two significant ways. First, the statistical analysis aims to discover patterns in the outcomes of locational decisions by multinational enterprises (MNEs), whereas the interviews inquire more directly about the underlying managerial motivations. Second, because of the coverage of available statistical data, the quantitative results provide a reasonably comprehensive but broad treatment of FDI in New Jersey, while the interview results offer useful additional data but from a relatively small sample of corporations. In addition, the two methods serve as checks and balances on each other – interviews as 'reality checks' and statistics as 'generality checks' (Gomes-Casseres 1985).

HISTORY, TRENDS, SIGNIFICANCE, CONCENTRATION AND THE ROLE OF FDI INTO THE STATE OF NEW JERSEY

History

Foreign investments into the United States have always been an integral part of its economic development. Indeed, the colonisation of the USA itself, has been described as 'a massive foreign investment' (Arpan 1977, p. 99).

Foreign investment into New Jersey has included many varieties and kinds of enterprises, some of which have flourished for a time and disappeared, while others have continued to expand with the growth of the economy (Lewis 1938). The early development of FDI into New Jersey was often associated with the increasing industrialisation of the USA behind tariff walls.

FDI had more impact on the pre-World War I American chemical industry than on any other US manufacturing sector. In the period 1887–1914, in no other industry were Europeans so far in advance of Americans; in no other single industry was the foreign technological contribution so dramatic (Wilkins 1989; Merck Archives 1992). In this era chemical production in New Jersey shifted competitive advantage from small apothecary shops to large manufacturing plants and finally to integrated research and development (R&D) MNE operations. The early decades of the twentieth century therefore witnessed the location of MNE facilities, first in manufacturing and later in R&D, to New Jersey. Concurrent with these changes was the added importance accorded to marketing and distribution facilities in the State (Feldman and Schreuder 1996).

New Jersey was also fortunate to have, in its inheritance, a number of well-known and significant entrepreneurs. These included Thomas A Edison, Alexander Graham Bell, John D Rockefeller and the Johnson Brothers. This early knowledge-intensity of New Jersey industry undoubtedly acted as a stimulus to innovatory activity. The path dependence or 'follow the leader' nature of FDI (Knickerbocker 1973) was fashioned by this technological inheritance as well as the state's traditional low rate of corporate taxes, its excellent harbours and its direct access to rail, interstate highways and international airports, combined with its proximity to Manhattan (New York). These locational advantages established NJ as a site for many manufacturing, marketing and distribution activities of foreign firms; and also of headquarters of US MNEs. In addition, over the years, the size, richness and concentration of the regional market (that is, the Tri states of New York, New Jersey and Connecticut) and a skilled labour pool have influenced numerous small knowledge- and technology-intensive-based firms to locate in the state.

Trends of FDI into New Jersey

Figure 15.1 shows the fluctuating trends of FDI in the state of persons employed by the US affiliates of foreign firms in New Jersey over the period 1977–1994. Employment is frequently used as a proxy to analyse FDI because, in its simplest form, it is perhaps the single most important variable that is both quantitatively captured by the US Department of Commerce in their statistical gathering efforts and watched by both politicians and the public alike.

Table 15.1 shows that in 1994 there were 1,615 US affiliates of foreign firms with property, plant and equipment from fifty-eight countries operating in NJ, employing more than 211,200 persons. Between 1977 and 1994 the number of such affiliates nearly tripled from 551 to 1,615 and their employment more than doubled, increasing at an average annual rate of 5.7 per cent.

FIGURE 15.1: FOREIGN DIRECT INVESTMENT INTO NEW JERSEY (EMPLOYMENT) 1977–94

Source: as Table 15.1

TABLE 15.1: FOREIGN DIRECT INVESTMENT INTO NEW JERSEY AND THE UNITED STATES, 1977–94

Year	Number of employers (thousands) NJ	Rate of change (%)	Number of employers (thousands) US	NJ % of US
1977	85.0	—	1 218.7	6.98
1978	98.0	15.3	1 429.9	6.85
1979	110.5	12.8	1 753.2	6.30
1980	120.5	9.1	2 033.9	5.93
1981	134.9	12.0	2 416.6	5.58
1982	132.1	(2.1)	2 448.1	5.40
1983	136.5	3.3	2 546.5	5.36
1984	140.8	3.2	2 714.3	5.19
1985	154.8	9.9	2 862.2	5.41
1986	161.7	4.5	2 937.9	5.50
1987	173.3	7.2	3 224.3	5.38
1988	203.9	17.7	3 844.2	5.30
1989	222.8	9.3	4 511.5	4.94
1990	227.0	1.9	4 734.5	4.80
1991	229.6	1.2	4 871.9	4.71
1992	216.3	(5.8)	4 715.4	4.59
1993	212.6	(1.5)	4 765.6	4.46
1994	211.2	(0.7)	4 866.6	4.34

Source: US Department of Commerce, Bureau of Economics and Statistics, Annual records, 1977 – Preliminary Estimates 1994 (Published July 1996)

From 1977 to 1981, the average annual rate of increase in affiliate employment was approximately 12.3 per cent, compared with 19.7 per cent for the USA as a whole. Following a brief decline during the 1982 recession, foreign employment in New Jersey continued to expand from 1982 through 1991, although at a decreased annual rate of 6.5 per cent, approximately half the 12.6 per cent annual growth rate of change for the USA. Therefore, although FDI into New Jersey increased from 1977 to 1991, it grew at a decreased rate. Since 1991, there has been an absolute decline in employment in foreign-owned businesses in the state. A useful way to analyse FDI into a subnational area is by comparison with like subnational areas in the economy.

Of the fifty US states, New Jersey ranked seventh in employment by foreign-owned affiliates in 1994. In that year it accounted for 4.34 per cent of all employment in foreign-owned affiliates in the USA. As shown by table 15.2, this ranking is lower than in previous years, thus indicating that NJ's share of the total FDI coming into the USA has declined relative to that of other states.

TABLE 15.2: TOP TEN STATES RANKED BY EMPLOYMENT IN US AFFILIATES OF FOREIGN-OWNED COMPANIES 1977–94 (THOUSANDS OF EMPLOYEES)

							FDI Employment in			
Rank	**1977**	**1980**	**1991**	**1992**	**1993**	**1994**	**1977**		**1994**	
1	California	CA	CA	CA	CA	CA	CA	124.2	CA	552.4
2	New York	NY	NY	NY	NY	NY	NY	121.6	NY	356.0
3	New Jersey	TX	TX	TX	TX	TX	NJ	85.0	TX	320.1
4	Illinois	NJ	IL	IL	PA	IL	IL	73.8	IL	233.1
5	Texas	PA	NJ	NJ	IL	PA	TX	66.6	PA	229.0
6	Pennsylvania	IL	PA	PA	NJ	NC	PA	64.5	NC	221.8
7	Ohio	OH	OH	OH	NC	NJ	OH	55.8	NJ	211.2
8	North Carolina	NC	FL	FL	OH	OH	NC	45.7	OH	209.4
9	South Carolina	GA	NC	NC	FL	FL	SC	35.1	FL	198.2
10	Georgia	FL	GA	GA	GA	GA	GA	30.7	GA	173.7

Source: US Department of Commerce, Bureau of Economics and Statistics, Annual records, 1977 – Preliminary Estimates 1993, and Preliminary Estimates, 1994 (published July 1996)
Note: Florida was ranked thirteenth in 1977 and had FDI employment of 28,300. South Carolina was ranked sixteenth in 1994 and had FDI employment of 105,100.

Economic Significance of FDI into the state of New Jersey

The growing economic significance of FDI to NJ is shown by the contribution of employment by foreign firms as compared to all private-sector employment. FDI into NJ accounted for 3.6 per cent of the total private-sector employment in the state in 1977; by 1992 this figure had risen to 5.2 per cent. Widespread empirical research has suggested that inward FDI is frequently more productive than investment by domestic firms; and that foreign affiliates record better rates of productivity growth than their indigenous counterparts (Dunning 1993a). In addition, foreign-owned MNE productivity gains generally result from adding capacity and from the use of more advanced technology (OECD 1994). By contrast, productivity increases at locally owned companies often result from downsizing and layoffs.

Concentration of FDI in the State of New Jersey

An identification of industries in which New Jersey is 'competitive' relies on the calculation of the state's revealed comparative advantage (RCA) across industries (Dunning 1988).[1] As table 15.3 shows, NJ had an RCA in six industrial categories in 1991. New Jersey had a comparative advantage in three broad industrial categories: chemicals; wholesale trade; finance as well as other industries.

TABLE 15.3: NEW JERSEY'S COMPARATIVE ADVANTAGE, BY INDUSTRY[A]

Industry	1980	1991	1993
Petroleum	0.33	0.32	0.33
Total manufacturing	1.10	1.04	1.04
Food and kindred products	0.73	0.89	na
Chemical and allied products	2.29	2.06	na
Primary and fabricated metals	0.90	0.73	na
Machinery	0.69	0.70	na
Other manufacturing	0.59	0.70	na
Wholesale trade	1.64	1.53	1.45
Retail trade	0.80	1.00	0.85
Finance (except banking)	0.19	1.43	1.37
Insurance	1.17	0.85	0.90
Real estate	na	0.61	0.46
Services	na	0.61	0.77
Other industries	0.65	1.09	1.10
Total number of RCA	4	6	

Note: A The table gives the computed 'revealed comparative advantage' (see text for definition) in different industries based on employment in the industry and therefore applies to the existing amount or stock of inward foreign direct investment and not to any flow measure.
na = not available.

The Geographical Source of FDI in New Jersey

An understanding of the source countries for FDI into the state of New Jersey is important to our understanding of the cultural thrust of this investment. Table 15.4 shows that the most dramatic changes in the sources of FDI in NJ are the declining share of European MNEs and the corresponding increase of that of Canadian and Asian investors. This is not surprising given the implementation of the Canada–US Free Trade Agreement during the late 1980s, and the shift of Japanese outward investment largely away from portfolio to direct investment (attributable, in part at least, to the surge in the strength of the yen against the dollar – particularly after the Plaza Accord in 1985).

THE CHALLENGE TO POLICY-MAKING

The number of dimensions which can and do influence locational decisions on the part of MNEs is substantial. The methodology undertaken for this portion of the research includes open-ended field interviews with key executives of selected, representative corporations engaging in FDI in New Jersey. Executives from the public (PSE&G Company; NJ Small Business Development Center), government (Prosperity NJ; NJ State Department of International Trade and Investment) and the private sector (KPMG Peat Marwick; Wadley-Donovan Group, Ltd) are included. Nine determinants or motivations for FDI into the state of New Jersey, as revealed by the practitioners interviewed, are summarised and listed below.

TABLE 15.4: FDI INTO NEW JERSEY BY SOURCE COUNTRY

	1980		1993	
	Percent of total	RCA	Percent of total	RCA
Canada	4.34	0.2	11.92	0.8
Total Europe	83.98	1.2	64.57	1.2
France	6.58	0.9	4.60	0.7
Germany	15.88	1.4	15.04	1.7
Netherlands	11.05	0.5	8.25	0.9
Switzerland	30.82	5.9	18.97	5.1
United Kingdom	12.97	0.7	12.14	0.7
Other Europe	6.68	1.4	6.50	1.1
Japan	3.02	0.7	13.71	0.7
Middle East	1.16	0.7	2.40	0.8
Latin America and Other W. Hemis.	2.78	0.9	2.31	0.8
Other Africa, Asia and Pacific	0.44	0.5	na	na
Other	4.28	3.8	na	na

Source: Foreign Direct Investment in the US, 1980; Foreign Direct Investment in the US, 1993 Preliminary Estimates, US Dept. of Commerce
Note: FDI measured by gross property and plant and equipment of affiliates

Market Access

The size and rate of growth of the American market is probably the most frequently cited reason for investing in the USA (Kieschnich 1981; Bartik 1989; Crone 1997). The strong regional consumer market based in New York (primarily New York City), New Jersey, Connecticut and Pennsylvania is a critical attribute of the region. According to the research of Dunning and Narula (1995), the size of local or adjacent markets leads resident firms to evolve a comparative advantage in technological innovation.

New Jersey is located in the heart of the world's richest consumer market. More than sixty billion consumers with a collective purchasing power of $800 billion are within a 250-mile radius (Connell 1996). New Jersey also has the second highest per capita income in the USA.

Labour

In the knowledge-based economy of the 1990s, low labour costs are no longer a major attraction in the site selection process, especially at the subnational level within the USA (Maturi 1995). Labour cost minimization emphasis has been replaced by the significance of labour availability and quality which Venable (1995) views as a reflection of the increasing knowledge intensity of many manufacturing and service activities.[2] The availability of skilled workers

– which includes the importance of a network of firms in the same industry in a site as well as an undertaking to upgrade labour to suit the needs of an incoming firm – is now being seen as a crucial determinant of subnational foreign MNE location strategy, especially for Schumpeterian firms (Kieschnich 1981; Hekman 1982; Stafford 1985; Calzonetti and Walker 1991).

There are more than fifty-five colleges and universities in the state of New Jersey and many more, such as Columbia University, New York University, the University of Pennsylvania and Yale within commuting distance, offer added educational and training facilities for New Jersey residents.

Infrastructure

'If you build it, they will come'. This was true when 'it' was railroads: jobs and the people to fill them soon followed. The adequacy of a region's infrastructure is tied to its future productivity and living standards (Carlino and Mills 1987; Bartik 1989; Mofidi and Stone 1990).

The research of Biehl (1991) argues that public investment in infrastructure improves both the levels of productivity of existing businesses and the attractiveness of regions for new investment. Quality, sophisticated and advanced infrastructure (such as fibre-optic lines and digital switching systems and access to the Internet) are all increasingly significant determinants in influencing the short-listing of possible locations, although rarely is such infrastructure viewed as the decisive factor in the final decision (Diamond and Spence 1984; Ball and Pratt 1994). This may be due to the public goods nature of infrastructure which, by definition, refers to those facilities which provide 'the collective and integrative basis of economic activity' (Spence 1992, p. 229). However, according to F W Peck (1996), potential inward investors focus in not only upon the *general* level and quality of such infrastructure in a geographic area; but they also try to meet their own *specific* requirements through customised space. This concept of a tailored infrastructure and of a set of resources and capabilities contained within a particular spatial area is now being increasingly explored by geographers, sociologists and economists (see for example the works of Amin *et al.* 1994 Young and Hood 1993; Storper 1995; Scott 1986; Wheeler and Mody 1992; and Dunning 1998). It also has exceedingly interesting implications for state policy-makers. In many respects, regions are like firms: they need to identify and continually upgrade their unique competitive advantages.

Regulatory Environment

The regulatory or commercial environment includes the 'hassle costs' of doing business as well as the degree of restriction on activities which the region of location imposes through government. Examples are:

- the existence of safety laws governing workers;

- the freedom of action of firms with respect to pricing products and engaging in cooperative strategic alliances;
- environmental protection legislation;
- regulation with respect to the employment of foreigners, or the participation of foreign firms in local research and development consortia; and
- the time required for permit approval processing.

While investment incentives, differences in labour availability and costs, etc. may affect *de novo* FDI, ever-increasing globalisation is likely to enhance the importance of other locational variables. These include the general business climate within the subregion for international investment and trade, the extent of regional integration, the efficiency of markets for intermediate products transferred across national boundaries, the international market structure in which MNEs compete and economies of scale. Finding the 'optimum' degree of regulation, and focusing on generating a cost-efficient means of regulating, in which compliance costs are identified as a cost of doing business, are also components of successful macro-organisational strategy.

Several academic studies (Contractor 1990; UNCTAD 1993 and 1994; World Economic Forum 1995) have shown that a negative correlation exists between inward FDI and imposed regulatory requirements. The rapid rise in FDI in many developing countries since the mid-1980s has followed a widespread reduction in government-imposed obstacles to FDI (UNCTAD 1997). The executive interviews conducted suggest that there has, in the past, been a sense that the state of New Jersey was anti-business. This perception persisted for a time, when businesses, seeking to expand facilities, found themselves caught in the labyrinth of the state's regulatory and approval process. The vice president of a major chemical MNE is reported to have said that he would not even try to modernise the company's large plant in New Jersey because the permissioning process would take longer than the technological life span of the new equipment the company wanted to install! (Houston 1995).

The regulation and regulatory difficulties experienced by firms in New Jersey are substantial. It routinely takes six months for a foreign firm to get a permit to start business in New Jersey as opposed to thirty to ninety days in, for example, North Carolina. This disadvantage turns into a revenue loss for MNEs. In today's global economy, speed-to-market and first-mover advantages are becoming increasingly significant and put a premium on rapid permit approval (Stalk and Hout 1990; Smith and Reinertsen 1991).[3] With respect to New Jersey's environmental regulations, it is not so much the concept of compliance that poses a problem for business as the administration of the regulations (Schmenner 1982; Hake *et al.* 1985; Stafford 1985; Bartik 1988; McConnell and Schwab 1990; Duffy-Deno 1992; Garofalo and Malhotra 1995; Houston 1995).

Incentives

Financial incentives affect the profitability of MNEs directly. They are designed either to increase the rate of return of a particular FDI initiative, or to reduce its costs or risks (UNCTAD 1996). They may include everything from subsidised job training programmes and reimbursement for moving expenses, foreign trade and enterprise zones, to tax credits and rebates, loan assistance and reduced rates for utility consumption.[4]

In addition to training and other cost reduction incentives, New Jersey offers a host of fiscal incentives including: property tax abatements and exemptions for commercial and industrial properties in areas in need of redevelopment; new jobs investment tax credits; manufacturing equipment and employment investment tax credits; reduced corporate tax rates for qualifying firms; and research and development tax credits for corporate businesses. Such incentives are important because they can be clearly defined; and their effect is easily calculated because they can be entered directly into net-present-value computations.[5] The corporate interviews and practitioner literature reviewed for this research reveal that incentives are increasing in significance as an FDI location determinant at the subnational level within the USA.

Other things being equal, incentives within the USA are designed to 'tilt the scales' in favour of a particular state as host for FDI. They were originally designed for, and primarily geared towards, manufacturers who could provide a community with large payrolls and politicians with easily visible facilities (Whittington 1995). Incentives may be granted either conditionally or unconditionally (UNCTAD 1996). As regional authorities become more experienced, incentive packages have evolved from virtual free-for-all give-aways in some states and municipalities to more carefully negotiated contracts with longer-term phase-in periods. The suggestion has been made that increased audit and accountability requirements should be built into these incentive packages (Whittington 1995; Guisinger 1985).

Efforts to influence the location decisions of MNEs have led many governments to offer fiscal and other inducements to attract investment into their borders and often away from other geographic areas. 'Investment contests result when two or more states vie to attract the location of a specific investment' (Atik 1992, p. 840); they may be likened to locational tournaments! (Mytelka 1996). As a result, there is a growing debate about the role of incentives as a policy tool to attract investment, and, more specifically, about whether their benefits to the recipient economy exceed their costs (UNCTAD 1996; Ipsen 1997).

The significance of incentives as a determinant influencing the location strategy of MNEs, at other than the subnational level is debatable.[6] However, from the UNCTAD (1996) research we know that incentives do appear to have an effect on investors' decisions within a country or a region. This suggests that incentives (as with marketing and promotion efforts) become more important for smaller spatial units, especially for projects that are cost-oriented and 'footloose'.

'Incentives are more readily accepted in practice than in theory' (UNCTAD 1996, p. 9). Academic analyses stress the point that financial incentives do a great deal to promote relocation and very little to promote new jobs or new tax revenues within the larger area, that is the country, macro-region or the global economy. It seems improbable that the process is a completely zero-sum game because the process does impose a transfer from the consumer to the corporate sector, but it would be very difficult to distinguish any increase in total investment and the process does, in some of its manifestations, involve skill upgrading programmes for labour (Agarwal 1980).[7]

Access

In order to gain or sustain a unique competitive advantage in today's global economy, the efficient movement of goods to market is of primary importance. This involves efficient intermodal systems linking together different transportation modes. The ability of the intermodal system to transfer cargo from one mode of transportation to another without additional packing and handling makes it efficient, cost-effective and fast. The efficiency of this kind of infrastructure is especially important for a region that has its large consumer market as a prime attribute.

To access major markets, the state of New Jersey offers more than 35,000 miles of highways, twelve airports, the port of Newark/Elizabeth and the most railway tracks per square mile in the United States. New Jersey has the physical location advantage of a time zone which is relatively compatible with that of Europe. Dennis Donovan, in an executive interview, explained that the simple fact that European supervisors are awake during the normal work hours gives this state an advantage for inbound European direct investment. But technological improvements are gradually replacing the traditional nine-to-five 'same place/same time' concept with the 'anytime/anyplace' office concept, a fact that must be considered in the FDI development, retention and attraction issue.

The issue of trade-offs between time and space is especially important in the case of foreign direct investment. Investments in transportation and communications infrastructure aim to reduce not only the monetary costs of movement over space but the reduction of time in circulation (Schoenberger 1997). Distance equals time because, as Marx noted, 'the important thing is not the market's distance in space but the speed with which it can be reached' (quoted in Schoenberger 1997, p. 22).

State information availability

Investment promotion represents efforts by the government of the state of New Jersey (and other interested parties such as the main public utility producers) to transfer information to foreign investors about the nature of the state's investment climate, and to persuade and assist these MNEs to invest, expand investments and continue to maintain their investment(s) in the state (Wells and Wint 1990; Wint 1992). The annual budgets other subnational areas allocate for business retention or expansion are considerably higher than New Jersey's: New York, $3.1 million; California, $2.9 million; North Carolina, $2.4 million; Alabama and Virginia, $1.3 million each. The city of Jacksonville spends $3 million a year. Charlotte and Kansas City each spend $20 million. The competition is increasing. At just over $0.5 million, the monies that the state of New Jersey allocates to attract and keep business annually are relatively modest. The research of Wint (1992) emphasizes the significance of marketing the state of New Jersey. He points out that investment promotion operates 'at the margin': that is, it is most successful in situations where the MNE has identified the particular region of the world in which to produce for example: NAFTA, the USA, or, at the subnational level, the New York City area.

Modelling techniques now play a part in location selection by generating a 'short list' of possibilities (that is, they are capable of eliminating obvious misfits). Some state and regional investment-promoting administrations have facilitated their inclusion in such models by ensuring that data on their states are easily available from electronic sources. In New Jersey, the leading electricity supplier PSE&G has produced a CD to address many of the questions that prospective site selectors may be interested in.

Every US state and hundreds of communities currently use 'the Web' to attract companies, open new markets for business and to promote tourism. A web location is a necessity for New Jersey both for the corporate site selector, and for the sake of the state at least appearing to be competitive. New Jersey, through PSE&G, shares a Website and is presently developing a location of its own as an economic development tool for the State. According to Bob Henningsen, Bureau Chief of Marketing and National Expansions for the Iowa Department of Economic Development in Des Moines, 'the states that succeed will be those that manage their information best and can present it to their best advantage' (Venable 1995).

Quality of Life

Quality-of-life considerations can be important attributes of a site, but the importance varies according to such factors as the size of the locating company, individual preferences of its top management and activity to be undertaken (Kolz 1995). The mix of transferred and newly hired personnel is also important. New Jersey seems to be most favoured for its accessibility to the cultural and sports entertainment of New York City and Philadelphia, but New Jersey has its own symphony, opera and ballet companies. There are more than 235 golf courses, the Meadowlands Sports Complex, and vast pinelands, hills and beaches along the 127-mile Jersey shore. Atlantic City is home to gambling casinos; there is also the Thomas H Kean New Jersey State Aquarium and Liberty Science Center offering additional activities for people of all ages (Kolz

1995). According to George Tobjy, a location consultant with KPMG Peat Marwick, the service base for international business is in the four northern New Jersey counties, and the beaches at the New Jersey shore are not the attraction.

Clusters of Firm Activities

'When analysing the local environment of globally-competitive firms, geographic clustering of production appears as a striking feature' (OECD 1994, p. 4). Business scholars focusing of the MNE (for example Prahalad and Doz 1987; Bartlett and Ghoshal 1990; Hedlund and Rolander 1990; Ridderstrale 1997) have conveyed doubts about the local environment having an important role to play with regard to how global firms formulate their location strategies and build competitiveness (Malmberg *et al.* 1996). This view is now being increasingly questioned by scholars.

Agglomeration economies, as first identified by Alfred Marshall (1920) and built upon and extended to explain regional production systems (Scott 1988b; Storper 1995), industrial districts (Piore and Sabel 1984; Markusen 1994), learning regions (Saxenian 1994), innovative milieux (Aydalot 1986; Maillat 1995) and industry clusters (Porter 1990 and 1994 and 1996) are shown not only as a significant determinant in subnational FDI location decision-making but as an important dynamic competitive advantage to the participating firms. The state of New Jersey is the home of a cluster of worldwide high value-adding MNE activities in a number of knowledge-intensive industries, especially pharmaceuticals and telecommunications. In both sectors it is attracting mobile investment, geared to accessing the human and physical resources and learning capabilities which New Jersey has to offer. At the same time New Jersey is facing ever increasing competition for such investment by other 'high tech' states, notably California and Massachusetts.

CONCLUSIONS

Globalisation has increased the competition among firms, industries, within subnational regions and among rival regions. This four-dimensional dynamism influences the location of economic activity along separate but linked aspects of the value chain. An increasing proportion of economic activity is potentially 'footloose' in its location. The owners of that activity are therefore locationally responsive to changes in the factors of production that influence their costs and revenues.

The eclectic or OLI paradigm (Ownership-specific advantages, Location-specific advantages and Internalisation-incentive advantages: Dunning 1977 and 1993a) maintains that in order to attract (and implicitly retain) foreign direct investment, the recipient economy must offer some particular location-specific advantage(s). The state of New Jersey can be viewed, therefore, as a landlord with various location-specific advantages within a regional context, to be exploited and enhanced by the ownership-specific advantages of individual firms. Firms, in choosing a particular state within the USA in which to invest, weigh the pros and cons of locating in each state the platform on which to build a national or international strategy (Wallace 1995). Compared with other states, New Jersey is losing position with respect to its net stock of inbound FDI (tables 15.1 and 15.2).

There are two main reasons why New Jersey's inbound FDI position may have fallen in the last two decades, at a time when the stock of FDI in the USA rose sixfold, and faster than at any other period since the turn of the last century. The first is that FDI is being increasingly attracted to economic activities in which US states *other* than New Jersey have a comparative advantage. This reflects the changing sectoral structure of FDI, which is less favourable to New Jersey than that of past days. The second is that New Jersey is losing ground to other US states in sectors in which it currently has, or has had, a comparative advantage, or in those which it is well suited to develop (and sustain) such an advantage.

Governments influence the relative advantages and disadvantages of regions and the actions of firms. The globalising economy increases the costs of misinformed or inappropriate government action (Dunning 1993b). Policy-making, investment-generating bodies must understand clearly the specific and unique attributes of their own region or subregion. Rather than *ad hoc* 'carrot' increases (for example, tax incentives to attract any and all FDI) in response to political pressure or perceived opportunism, New Jersey must increase the focus of its economic development on a strategically systemic government policy, targeted to identifying and upgrading the region's unique resources and capabilities (Wallace 1995). Precious energy and increasingly limited resources should not be spent on projects that do not match the region's existing or potential revealed comparative advantage.

Worthwhile systemic government policies are best developed with a thorough appreciation of the trends, economic significance, concentration and role of FDI in the state as well as the position of the state within the regional and national economy. With this appreciation, priorities can be established and promising industry sectors targeted for economic development policy both in the short run and for the long haul. This requires a shift from New Jersey state government strategies and policies which focus solely on static state competitiveness to ones which revolve around the concept of long-term sustainable advantage.

NOTES

1. The formula for revealed comparative advantage (RCA) is straightforward: it measures the share of inward FDI in a given industry in the state as a percentage of total FDI in that industry in the nation and then "normalises" that ratio by the state's share of national FDI. Any industry with a larger than proportionate state share than that of the state's share of total national FDI (i.e. RCA>1) is one that leans preponderantly towards investing in the state. This definition denies the possibility that a state can have a comparative edge in all industries.

The formula for RCA is based on the 1988 UK case study conducted by John H Dunning. This formula is identical to that used by economic geographers location quotient, who use the term '(LQ)' and that used by Wallace (forthcoming) revealed location advantage, who use the term '(RLA)'.

2. Refer to studies by Bartik 1989; and Papke 1987.

3. The research of Smith and Reinertsen (1991) shows through empirical examples, that, in rapidly changing markets, a delay of six months when bringing a new product to market can reduce its life-time profit yield by a full one-third.

4. Refer to studies by Kieschnich 1981; Hekman 1982; Schmenner 1982; Hake *et al.* 1985; Bartik 1989; and Papke 1987 which show that generally, high energy costs are a disadvantage in attracting manufacturing firms.

5. Not all firms included incentives in their net present value calculations (Gray and Walter, 1983).

6. See studies such as: Barlow and Wender 1955; Walker 1965; Ahroni 1966; Robinson 1961; Dunning 1979; Agarwal 1980; and Guisinger and Associates, 1985; Arpan 1981 (whose research on regional incentives in the United States found that incentives did not have a significant influence on the investment location of MNEs); Morse and Farmer 1986; and Coughlin *et al.* 1991 (whose research found that differences in state taxes were an important locational determinant).

7. Agarwal's (1980) research, showing the general ineffectiveness of incentives, is based primarily on developing countries. In this work he argues that incentives merely compensate for structural disincentives (see page 762). Agarwal does acknowledge that while incentives do not affect the overall FDI flows, they may influence the distribution of FDI in these developing countries.

16 Conclusions: Multinationals and Global-Localisation – some Themes

In this concluding chapter we attempt to draw together some of the main issues and themes which have emerged from the individual contributions to the book, and to emphasise the linkages between them. The discussion is organised according to the sections in the book although several recurring themes cut across these book sections. While the main title of the book is FDI and the Global Economy, the intention was that the collection would embrace aspects of both the corporate and institutional dynamics at several spatial scales implicit within the notion of global-localisation. The fact that certain themes recur throughout the book highlights the difficulty in discussing and analysing issues at global, regional, national and subnational levels in isolation from, and without an understanding of, the context formed at the other territorial scales.

FDI AND THE GLOBAL ECONOMY

Successive UNCTAD World Investment Reports (UNCTAD 1993, 1994, 1995, 1996, 1997) have addressed issues associated with foreign direct investment (FDI) and the global economy. For example, the 1993 report illustrated how greater openness in the world economy has intensified international competition and expanded the potential role of FDI. Transnational corporations have responded to these changes and adopted new structures and strategies to locate and govern their activities at a variety of spatial scales from global to local. The 1994 report focused on transnational corporations, firm competitiveness and FDI.

The interplay between FDI, the growth in international trade and emerging international policy arrangements were the focus of the 1996 UNCTAD report. It also noted that world economic growth and the response of transnational corporations to technological development, international competition and liberalisation had increased FDI flows to unprecedented levels by 1995. Following the end of the FDI recession in 1993, investment flows rose by 9 per cent in 1994 and by another 40 per cent in 1995. It is not surprising, therefore, that the phenomena of FDI within the context of a global economy has attracted so much attention and interest.

The contributions by Young and Brewer, Hine and Phelps have all commented on the importance of globalisation and regionalisation as powerful forces which have shaped the world economic system in recent years. Globalisation focuses on the increasing integration of the world economy through the growth in international trade and FDI. Regionalisation has focused particularly on regional trade arrangements and closer integration among neighbouring economies. Chapters 2, 3 and 4 by the above contributors therefore link well with chapter 5 by Raines and Wishlade, with the EU being one of the best examples of regionalisation and the development of policy and regulation of FDI.

These contributors asked whether globalisation and regionalisation are contradictory or complementary processes. Although on the one hand both globalisation and regionalisation have driven economies in the direction of increased trans-border interaction, these may have been opposing forces if this closer regional integration has been at the expense of links with the rest of the world (Hine chapter 3). Young and Brewer in chapter 2 also noted that progress in liberalising investment policies at all levels has been influential in providing a stable and supportive environment for FDI, while the existing patchwork of investment policies is a deterrent to transnational corporations' global integration strategies. Any shift in focus on regionalisation rather than multilateralism in the future could also inhibit global strategies. There is clearly tension here between globalisation and regionalisation in the processes of trade liberalisation and regulation. Hine even suggests that to the extent that regional integration arrangements are necessarily inward-looking and protectionist then they may well be on a collision course with globalisation. However, he tempers this view by reminding us that the evidence points generally in the opposite direction, that is regionalism and globalisation have been initially reinforcing. Overall, perhaps regionalism may have a mediating role to play in the influence of globalisation.

The questioning of the concept of globalisation, and the observation of a number of commentators that there has been a retreat from corporate strategies of global integration towards integration centred on major regional trade blocs and markets, was highlighted by Phelps (chapter 4). He too has discussed the contradictory and complementary aspects of global and regional corporate integration when exploring their impact at a subnational scale.

The increasing complexity of the global economy and the operations of multinational corporations has been agreed and discussed by all of the contributors to the section on FDI and the global economy. Phelps reviewed evidence which suggests that recent multinational investments are more disposed to engaging with their local environments, although the relationship between affiliates and their parent company organisations remains complex. Young and Brewer noted that while economic analysis suggests that, as with international trade, international flows of FDI should be encouraged since they generate both global and local benefits, the present overall investment policy context is not only complex but also characterised by fragmentation, confusion and conflict, with a wide range of FDI policies at national, bilateral, regional and multilateral levels. Hine came to a similar conclusion, where the upsurge in regionalism over the past decade may be matched in the future by an increasingly complex web of trade preferences.

The issue of regulation is an important theme to emerge from these contributions on FDI and the global economy. Indeed, it might be suggested, based on many chapters of the book, that there is not a level playing field here for nations, regions of a country or localities in terms of regulatory mechanisms, let alone at the global or trade bloc level. The development of investment rules at an international and global level will continue to be a dominant issue for FDI. A number of contributors have emphasised that while a feature of FDI in the 1990s has been a strong movement in favour of liberalisation at the national level, many barriers still exist. Furthermore, as Young and Brewer have reminded us, the issue of multilateral investment rules has not just suddenly appeared on the international policy agenda in the mid-1990s. Interest in the development of a multilateral framework for investment has taken place over a period of some fifty years, from the Havana Charter for an International Trade Organisation in 1948 to the creation of the World Trade Organisation in 1995, and intervening initiatives of NAFTA, the EU and the GATT. These, together with the series of multilateral negotiations (illustrated by the Kennedy Round of the 1980s and 1990s), recognised the interrelatedness of trade and FDI in the global economy. The link between trade and FDI is underlined by Hine with his reference to the extent of intra-firm trade, with about one-third of world trade involving transactions between parts of the same MNE. This, of course, highlights the growing complementarity of FDI and trade within increasingly complex forms of corporate integration practiced by MNEs (UNCTAD 1994).

In the section on FDI and the global economy, reference was made in chapter 2 (Young and Brewer) to investment incentives, an aspect of competition policy which has important implications for FDI and economic development at the national and subnational levels, as illustrated in later chapters. It was also identified by Raines and Wishlade (chapter 5) as an important issue facing FDI at a regional, that is EU, level. Investment incentives have been identified as another area where very few policy initiatives have been taken to date. There do seem to be as many non-regulatory spaces within the FDI debates as regulatory ones. Considerable controversy has arisen over the extent to which many investment incentives may represent inefficient and inequitable government intervention and bidding within and between regions of a nation. For example, in the UK in 1997, the UK government, represented by the Department of Trade and Industry, although concerned over competitive bidding between Scotland, Wales and the English regions, was forced to abandon its plans to reclaim central control over inward investment subsidies throughout the UK. The interested parties concerned did, however, agree to try and avoid excessive bidding wars. The devolution and spread of more powers and governance to regions might be expected to exacerbate these problems. This is not, of course, an issue facing just the UK.

While investment incentives, competition policy and regulation were issues discussed in this section at the global level, a good example of its reality at local level is the example quoted by Alden (chapter 12) of the attraction of the South Korean firm LG (Electronics and Semiconductors) to south Wales. LG's decision in 1996 to invest £1.7 billion in the two plants made it the largest FDI project ever to come to the UK or Europe. The Welsh Development Agency offered LG their most prestigious site, and government grants and land to the value of £247 million, a deal which required agreement with the European Commission. The attraction of LG was a coup for the WDA, but raised questions of how much financial support should be given to attract inward investment projects, as there are important opportunity costs involved for the development agencies concerned.

FDI AND REGIONAL ECONOMIC INTEGRATION

One of the emerging tensions in the FDI debates is highlighted by the contributors to the section on FDI and regional economic integration, with reference to the regulation of multinational companies. How much regulation is there, and at what spatial level does this regulation and governance take place? Raines and Wishlade have discussed (chapter 5) the challenge of FDI for EC policy-making in two particular areas, namely the use of anti-dumping and trade protection measures in external trade policy, and the regulation of financial incentives through competition policy. It is clear from their contribution that the regulation of MNEs at the EU level has been incomplete and very much an iterative process. However, the emergence of a more protectionist policy by the EC, for example to prevent anti-dumping measures, has been clearly observable, particularly in relation to certain industrial sectors. Jung emphasised, in chapter 6, the extent to which a main motivation for South Korean FDI in the EU has centred on trade policies such as anti-dumping tariffs and quotas imposed by the EC rather than by individual member states. There are signs here in the FDI debate at a regional level which add weight to the assertion that the nation-state as an entity may be dead, or at least in severe retreat as a regulatory force. However, both Jung and Aoyama refer to the importance of the global–local interplay, and the practice of Korea and Japan to target specific countries. This might suggest that the EU cannot be viewed as a homogeneous single market, a point developed further below.

While the relationship between trade policy and FDI has been concerned with the regulation of firms, the operation of competition policy has focused upon regulating the behaviour of governments. Of particular interest here is the regulation of restrictive practices, abuse of monopoly position and, more recently, increasing trends towards mergers/acquisitions. The EC has been actively involved, of course, in the development framework of global investment rules (discussed in chapter 2 by Young and Brewer) as well as developing its own policies. While there are no specific policies for FDI at EU level, the EC has increasingly adapted existing policies to address FDI issues. The EC has also had to react to the fierce competition between member states to attract FDI.

The existence and importance of the Single Market is discussed by a number of contributors. Is there a homogeneous single market? Chapman, in chapter 8, not only identifies the importance of merger/acquisition activity in the FDI debate but also the impetus provided by the Single Market for the recent trends which have occurred. Chapman does recognise, however, that several factors have contributed to the growth of merger/acquisition activity, and it is difficult to isolate European from global influences. However, the making of economic efficiency gains was one of the main objectives underlying the creation of the SEM.

Also linked to the SEM is the controversy within the FDI debate surrounding state aid, an issue discussed by both Raines and Wishlade (chapter 5) and Chapman (chapter 8). With the completion of the Single Market in 1992, state aid became one of the few measures of protectionism at the disposal of member states. While under Article 92 state aids are banned, the notion of state aid has been difficult to define. It is important to note that there are no EC rules relating specifically to state aids for FDI or mobile investment within the EC. There are significant issues arising here for the operation of regional and subregional aids by member states of the EU as well as for the European Commission itself. These issues are illustrated in a number of contributions to this book.

The concentration of recent Korean FDI in Europe rather than in North America is discussed by Jung. This concentration on the EU in particular has been the result of push and pull factors. These factors have been examined by Raines and Wishlade (chapter 5), Jung (chapter 6), and Aoyama (chapter 7), and have been the subject of much interest in the FDI debate. The main push factors mentioned by Raines and Wishlade were anti-dumping tariffs, non-tariff barriers and quotas. In terms of pull factors, Jung, in his coverage of the main locational requirements for Korean firms in the EU, identifies the importance of relative wage levels in certain EU countries, flexible employment legislation and grants from central and local government. The UK has been the main host country for its outward investment in Europe. However, as successive United Nations' World Investment Reports have emphasised, multinational firms and FDI do not only operate in low-cost locations. They are more concerned with high productivity and efficiency than with mere low-wage/low-cost locations. This aspect of FDI is addressed by Aoyama with reference to the Japanese electronics industry in Europe. The focus of her concern is the competitive advantages that multinationals gain by having some kind of local presence. This again reinforces the view that local or country-specific dimensions are as important for FDI as the regional dimension of the trade bloc or SEM. Her chapter highlights the current interest in learning regions and intelligent regions, and that multinationals are concerned with using global strategies to remain competitive through continuous innovation. Aoyama's conclusion is that Japanese firms have been moving operations to overseas markets, despite the cost of operations, in an attempt to circumvent protectionist measures. Japanese firms in the electronics industry, like many others, are facing a much tougher market in Europe in the 1990s than previously, and the competitive advantage of firms is not just a price but also product differentiation which again emphasises the importance of technology and innovation. As competition shifts from cost-based competition to technology (innovation) knowledge-based competition, then these changes will need to be reflected in regional and subregional strategies for inward investment by member states of the EU. These points resonate with those made by several contributors to the section of the book on FDI and subnational economic development, including those made by Dunning and Wallace in chapter 15 in relation to American experience.

The growing trend of mergers and acquisitions within FDI is attracting growing interest at all spatial scales. This is another controversial area within the FDI debate, especially in relation to the assertion that FDI in recent years has often been associated with fewer new openings and job creation and a much larger effect on ownership through mergers/acquisitions. The increasing importance of mergers/acquisitions in FDI was identified by Raines and Wishlade (chapter 5) and developed further by Chapman (chapter 8). While mergers/acquisitions are most commonly associated with industrial and competition policies, they also have important implications for transnational policies associated with globalisation or cross-border transactions. Agenda 2000 (EC 1997) has stressed the growing importance being attached by the EC to cross-national transactions.

As mergers/acquisitions involve changes in ownership, and therefore in corporate control, these changes can take on significant geographical dimensions, particularly in terms of multilevel governance, one of the underlying themes of this book. The undesirable consequences of external control for countries and communities have attracted attention in the economic development literature. The fact that mergers/acquisitions have replaced greenfield investment as the main mechanism of FDI in many cases is a point raised by Chapman and discussed by other contributors. As Chapman and other contributors have noted, there is a need for more research on the nature of corporate restructuring and its impact on places. Two emerging trends in the geography of mergers and acquisitions appear to be the concentration of production within industries and companies at fewer sites, and the development in the largest companies of corporate locational hierarchies across Europe. The significance of this shift is a matter of debate as illustrated by Phelps (1997) and recognised by Chapman himself in chapter 8.

FDI AND NATIONAL ECONOMIC DEVELOPMENT

As the 1994 World Investment Report emphasised, despite the operation of powerful forces creating a higher degree of global integration of economic activities, it should not be assumed that there is a smooth or inevitable process towards a uniform system of integrated international production. To those commentators who suggest that the nation-state as an entity may be dead, there is considerable evidence that technological developments have not removed the influence of space – that is, geography still matters. Furthermore, MNEs continue to operate on a regulatory surface which is highly uneven and complex; the actions of governmental and non-governmental organisations at various territorial scales still matter. Both the sections on FDI and national/subnational economic development illustrate the relevance of both geography and government in influencing the potential for, and manner in which, the activities of global corporations may be tied to particular territories. Many firm and industry-specific advantages remain tied to regional, national or subnational territories. As much of the recent economic geography literature has reminded us, concentration remains a persistent feature of the geography of production (for example Storper and Walker 1989).

Munday and Peel (chapter 10) have challenged the conventional view that multinational companies, as illustrated by the Japanese transplant sector in the UK, necessarily represent a means of improving the competitiveness of domestic UK manufacturing, for example through technological transfer or through increased competitive pressure. If Japanese firms are found to be performing at a similar (or lower) level to their domestic counterparts, in terms of employment, investment growth and financial performance, then the potential of the domestic sector benefiting from Japanese investment may be reduced. This is particularly relevant in policy terms since technology and knowledge transfer is one objective underpinning UK government aid to foreign companies, as Munday and Peel point out.

Following a critical review of the development of the Japanese manufacturing sector in the UK, Munday and Peel used cross-sectional corporate data to examine changes in the performance of foreign-owned companies in the UK and concluded that domestic companies actually grew faster than their Japanese counterparts in terms of both sales and assets over the period 1991–4. While Japanese subsidiaries scored comparatively badly on indicators of profitability, they did much better on productivity and efficiency variables. Their results also showed that Japanese firms paid their employees significantly more than their domestic counterparts, an important finding bearing in mind the concerns about low pay levels in FDI subsidiaries. Moreover, although over twice as many Japanese subsidiaries experienced financial losses than did domestic firms, the Japanese failure rates were lower than for domestic firms. The explanation given by Munday and Peel is that while Japanese subsidiaries are prima facie more failure prone, they receive more support from their parent company. In view of the more competitive European market of the latter 1990s, this may not be the case in the future. It is perhaps worth bearing in mind the authors' own comments regarding the limitations of their study in terms of the short time period used and the need to compare performance over several points in the trade cycle. Munday and Peel noted, as have other contributors, the trend for Japanese firms increasingly to turn to acquisitions and joint ventures as a means of UK entry, although not on such a scale as practised by European firms.

The relevance of national policies and contexts is also illustrated by Legewie (chapter 11). The scale of the losses in Japanese domestic manufacturing employment have been dramatic, with a loss of one million jobs between 1991 and 1995. Although this trend must be partially attributable to a number of domestic and global factors in the 1990s, Japanese FDI (particularly in Asia) has been quoted as a major reason for the marked decline in domestic manufacturing employment. The impact of FDI on domestic employment in terms of the phenomena of industrial hollowing-out in Japan is an issue of considerable relevance and significance to a number of South-east Asian and other economies at the present time. The conclusion reached by Legewie in his chapter is an important one. Japan is very concerned over its poorly performing domestic industry in terms of international competitiveness. These issues raised by Legewie also resonate with those discussed by Munday and Peel on the performance of Japanese subsidiaries abroad. Within this process the relocation of industries that have lost their competitive edge to developing countries serves as an important means of enabling a shift to newer, higher value-added sectors that can keep production, employment and wages high in Japan. To this extent Japanese FDI may be seen as a positive instrument of industrial restructuring. Notwithstanding this, however, Legewie is doubtful whether FDI can solve the structural problems that hinder the growth of new industries and provide a revitalisation of the Japanese economy.

The importance of national space and infrastructure/governance to multinational corporations is further illustrated by Collis, Berkeley and Noon (chapter 9) in relation to FDI in the emerging markets of the East European Economies (EEEs). The authors have shown that although globally the level of FDI flows into EEEs is still relatively small, there has been significant growth in such investment since 1990. There is perhaps a temptation to overestimate the dominance of Western Europe in FDI, and the authors have reminded us that between 1990 and 1995 the global share of annual FDI inflows accounted for by Western Europe and North America declined from

78 per cent to 59 per cent. At the same time, the developing regions of Latin America, Asia/Pacific, Central and Eastern Europe and Africa have increased their global share of annual FDI inflows from 17 per cent to 35 per cent. As might be expected, most FDI flows in the EEEs originate from the EU, and there has been a concentration in three EEC countries, – Hungary, the Czech Republic and Poland.

Collis, Berkeley and Noon identified some of the reasons why multinational companies have been selective in targeting certain EEEs. They point to a number of deterrents to FDI in some EEEs, associated with risk and uncertainty, the poor legal framework and weak infrastructure, and a lack of reliable information about the region. While Hungary, the Czech Republic and Poland have all strengthened their organisation and governance at a national level in the 1990s to promote and manage FDI more effectively, on the other hand, it is at the regional and local levels of government and governance that policies towards the attraction of inward investment are most developed in the UK. To date, as might be expected, the EEEs have concentrated on more traditional approaches to FDI, such as fiscal policies in the form of tax rates and capital investment allowances, whereas factors such as the provision of better information and knowledge to investors may be more useful.

FDI AND SUBNATIONAL ECONOMIC DEVELOPMENT

While the importance of both global and regional levels of governance and regulation cannot be overestimated for the operation of FDI, the local and subnational dimension has also attracted an increasing amount of interest, particularly in terms of the institutions and policies involved in the attraction and regulation of global corporations. This increasing interest in the local level of influence reinforces the view that geography and government/governance certainly do matter in shaping patterns and trends in FDI.

Dunning and Wallace's contribution (chapter 15) helps to fill a gap in the literature on FDI, as they emphasise that FDI in the USA has rarely been rigorously analysed at the subnational level. Their analysis of the ongoing globalisation on the economy of the state of New Jersey (a subnational region within the USA) has implications for state governments in identifying areas or industries for strategic priority setting and policies to improve their resources and capabilities. It also has implications for identifying the particular role of an individual state, as opposed to that of the federal government, in attracting and retaining desirable mobile investment.

Given the absolute decline in employment in foreign-owned companies in the state of New Jersey since 1991, Dunning and Wallace illustrate the challenge facing policy-makers in respect of FDI. The authors' survey of selected corporations and practitioners revealed a wide range of motivations for FDI tied to New Jersey, including the regulatory environment, labour availability (which had replaced labour cost minimisation), incentives, infrastructure, state information, quality of life and clusters of firm activities. This subnational example of the regulatory environment complements nicely the references made by earlier contributors (for example Young and Brewer, Hine, and Raines and Wishlade) to the regulatory framework at broader spatial scales.

The way in which multinational companies engage with regulatory organisations, particularly at a subnational or local level, has raised the question of who gains from FDI. The issue of 'planning gain' reflects the interest and role of the statutory planning framework in the global–local dimension of FDI. Alden's analysis of FDI in Wales (chapter 12) provides evidence which suggests that while local planning authorities have been active in seeking planning gain from large residential, retail or mixed-use developments, they have been reluctant to negotiate planning gain agreements with large, high-profile FDI projects. The general view of the development agencies and local authorities in Wales is that the job creation associated with FDI projects equates to planning gain achieved. With international competition for FDI projects being so intense, a point stressed by many contributors to this book, the planning process – local regulatory framework – is often seen as a hurdle to overcome for inward investors. While Alden concludes that Wales has been very successful in recent years in attracting FDI projects which have created new jobs, he expresses some caution in so far as a significant number of jobs have involved mergers/acquisitions rather than new openings (a point also noted by Raines and Wishlade in chapter 5 and Chapman in chapter 8). FDI has, therefore, had a large effect on the ownership of Welsh manufacturing as well as on the provision of jobs.

The phenomena of ownership within the FDI debate has a long tradition in the regional development literature in relation to the branch plant economy. Pike (chapter 13) has examined the impact of FDI in terms of the emergence of a new type of branch plant with more progressive implications for local and regional economic development. Pike uses an in-depth study of the automobile industry in an old industrial region of England to review critically the assertion that the alleged change in the branch-plant economy, with the emergence of 'performance plants', has heightened local economic development potential. His focus on the automobile industry (again referred to by other contributors) is particularly relevant, and it has historically been associated with the creation of branch-plant economies. The conclusion reached by Pike is that the changes in the type of plant which have emerged appear partial, revealing the overlap of both old and new practices. The implications for local economic development also appear limited and contingent upon the ability of local institutions to exploit the more positive developments. Even if the changes are only partial, and the benefits for local economic development only limited, the contribution by Pike has further enhanced the debate between the traditional and revisionist schools of thought on this longstanding theme within the local and regional economic development debate.

While the phenomena of ownership and the branch-plant economy has had a long tradition in the regional development and FDI debate, the role and influence of institutions in local economic development has been the subject of more recent debate in the literature, particularly in the 1990s. The contribution by Peck and Durnin (chapter 14) illustrates that while local institutional support has always been critical in the process of attracting inward investment, the agencies concerned have needed to become increasingly sophisticated in their approach to winning new projects, particularly as the field has become highly competitive. Inward investment agencies have been under increasing pressure to demonstrate their region's willingness and capacity to provide a range of services and access to public resources over a time period beyond the initial set-up period. While the attraction of new greenfield investment from overseas has become increasingly difficult, Peck and Durnin cite Cumbria as an example of a marginalised local economy which has secured a number of new investments through local initiatives.

The marginalisation facing Cumbria, and no doubt many other local economies, is of an institutional nature, and particularly in relation to the role of insititutions in regional development. Cumbria has experienced the effects of various forms of institutional marginalisation, described by Peck and Durnin, due partly to a lack of clarity regarding its formal regional place that has only recently been resolved. Local economies have needed to compete for inward investment through an insitutional structure that has not been set up primarily to serve their particular needs. The focus of the institutional framework for FDI has evolved mainly at a national and regional level in the UK. This again emphasises the importance of the local–regional–national interplay within global FDI.

CONCLUSION

A number of scholars have pointed to novel forms of corporate organisation being adopted by MNEs in the 1980s and 1990s. These new forms of corporate organisation have been variously captured in terms such as 'alliance capitalism' (Dunning 1997c), and the 'embedded' (Dicken et al. 1994) multinational. In part, these embedded forms of organisation embody responses to 'natural' processes of competition which have drawn firms closer to their host economy contexts as sources of input- and output-related external economies. However, increasingly they revolve around institutionally constructed market regimes and business systems (for example see Ruigrok and Van Tulder 1996). The increasing efforts being made to regulate both investment and trade and hence the operations of multinationals at the global or multilateral level also, in theory at least, mean that institutions at narrower geographical scales are becoming more constrained in their relationships with multinationals. Yet, irrespective of this, the attitudes of many supranational, national and subnational institutions have changed in favour of less interventionist stances over the actions and performance of multinationals. One could say that despite the drift toward the greater regulation of trade and investment activities of multinationals, especially at the global and regional levels, there remain many largely unregulated spaces in which multinationals can operate at the national and subnational levels. The novel, embedded, forms of corporate organisation being instituted by multinationals are as much an adaptation to the opportunities presented by such unregulated spaces as they are to the regulation of trade and investment at global and regional scales.

There is clearly room for further research to address a variety of claims and assertions within debates surrounding FDI, many of which have been touched on in the contributions to this book. The role of multinationals in economic development at various geographical scales will continue to be a rich and fruitful subject of study for researchers in this field for many years to come. Hopefully, the contributions to this book have offered some further points of departure for research on multinationals in the global economy.

REFERENCES

Acocella, N (1992) 'Trade and direct investment within the EC: the impact of strategic considerations', in J Cantwell (ed.) *Multinational Investment in Modern Europe.* Aldershot: Edward Elgar, 192–213.

Adam, G (1975) 'Multinational companies and worldwide sourcing', in H Radice (ed.) *International Firms and Modern Imperialism.* Harmondsworth: Penguin.

Agarwal, JP (1980) 'Determinants of foreign direct investment: a survey' *Weltwirtschaftliches, Archiv* 739, 761–2.

Aharoni, Y (1996) *The Foreign Investment Decision Process.* Boston, MA: Harvard Graduate School of Administration.

Alden, J (1996) 'The transfer from a problem to powerful region: the experience of Wales', in J Alden and P Boland (eds) *Regional Development Strategies: A European Perspective,* London: Jessica Kingsley Publishers, 129–58.

Alden, J (1997a) 'The impact of foreign direct investment on job creation : who gains? the experience of Wales.' Paper presented at European Regional Frontiers Conference, 20–3 September 1997, Frankfurt-on-Oder, Germany.

Alden, J (1997b) *The British Planning Approach to Planning Obligations and Planning Gain.* Proceedings of an International Workshop on Planning Obligations and Industrial Development. National Taiwan University, Taipei, 3 June.

Allen, J and Thompson, G (1997) 'Think global, then think again – economic globalization in context' *Area* 29, 213–27.

Amin, A, Charles, D R and Howells, J (1992) 'Corporate restructuring and cohesion in the new Europe,' *Regional Studies* 26, 319–31.

Amin, A, Bradley, D, Howells, J, Tomaney, J and Gentle, C (1994) 'Regional incentives and the quality of mobile investment in the less favoured regions of the EC', *Progress in Planning* 41, 1–112.

Amin, A and Thrift, N (1994) *Globalization, Institutions and Regional Development in Europe.* Oxford: Oxford University Press.

Amin, A and Thrift, N (1995) 'Globalisation, institutional "thickness" and the local economy', in P Healey, S Cameron, S Davoudi, S Graham, and A Modani-Pour (eds) *Managing Cities: the New Urban Context.* London: Wiley, 91–108.

Amin, A and Tomaney, J (1995) 'The regional dilemma in a neo-liberal Europe', *European Urban and Regional Studies* 2, 171–88.

Anderson, JC and Narus, JA (1991) 'Partnering as a focused market strategy', *California Management Review* 33, 3, 95–113.

Anderson, K and Norheim, H (1993), 'History, geography and regional integration', in Anderson and Blackhurst (eds) *op. cit.*

Anderson, K and Blackhurst, R (eds) (1993), *Regional Integration and the Global Trading System.* Hemel Hempstead: Harvester Wheatsheaf.

Aoyama, Y (1996) From Fortress Japan to Global Networks: Locational Specificity of Globalization for the Japanese Electronics Industry in the 1990s. PhD dissertation, Department of City and Regional Planning, University of California at Berkeley, unpublished.

Archibugi, D and Michie, J (1995) 'The globalisation of technology: a new taxonomy', *Cambridge Journal of Economics* 19, 121–40.

Arpan, J (1977) 'Regulation of foreign direct investments in the United States: quo vasit quo vadit', *The Journal of Contemporary Business* 6, 4, Autumn, 99–119 (reprinted in *CFA Digest* 9, 1, 1979).

Atik, J (1992) 'Investment contests and subsidy limitations in the EC', *Virginia Journal of International Law* 32, 4, Summer, 838–69.

Aydalot, P (1986) *Milieux innovateurs en Europe.* Paris: GREMI.

Baldwin, RE (1993) 'A Domino theory of regionalism', NBER Working Paper 4465.

Baldwin, RE (1997) *The Causes of Regionalism,* CEPR Discussion Paper 1599.

Baldwin, RE, Forslid, R and Haaland, J I (1996), 'Investment creation and diversion in Europe', *The World Economy* 19, 635–59.

Ball, R and Pratt, A (1994) *Industrial Property: Policy and Economic Development.* London: Routledge.

Barnes, I and Barnes, P (1995) *The Enlarged European Union.* London: Longman.

Barnet, RJ and Müller, RE (1974) *Global Reach : The Power of the Multinational Corporations.* New York: Simon and Schuster.

Barrell, R and Pain, N (1993) *Trade Restraints and Japanese Direct Investment Flows.* Discussion Paper, 43. London: National Institute of Economic and Social Research.

Bartik, TJ (1988) 'The effects of environmental regulation on business location in the United States', *Growth and Change* 19, 22–44.

Bartik, TJ (1989) 'Small business start-ups in the United States: estimates of the effects of characteristics of states', *Southern Economic Journal,* 55, 1004–18.

Bartlett, CA. and Ghoshal, S(1989) *Managing Across Borders: The Transnational Solution.* Boston: Harvard Business School Press.

Bartlett, CA and Ghoshal, S (1990) 'Managing innovation in the transnational corporation', in CA Bartlett, Y Doz and G Hedlund (eds) *Managing the Global Firm.* London: Routledge.

Beardwell, I (1992) 'The "new industrial relations"? a review of the debate', *Human Resource Management Journal* 2, 2, 1–7.

Belderbos, R (1997) 'Antidumping and tariff jumping: Japanese firms' DFI in the European Union and the United States', *Weltwirtschaftliches Archiv.* 133, 3, 419–57.

Bennett, RJ (1997) 'Administrative systems and economic spaces', *Regional Studies* 31, 3, 323–36.

Berggren, C (1995) 'The fate of branch plants – performance versus power', in Å Sandberg (ed) *Enriching Production: Perspectives on Volvo's Uddevalla Plant as an Alternative to Lean Production*. Aldershot: Avebury, 105–6.

Bergsten, CF and Graham, EM (1992) 'Needed : new international rules for foreign direct investment', *International Trade Journal* 7, 1, 15–44.

Beyfuss, J and Kitterer, B (1990) Direktinvestitionen im Ausland. Exportkonkurrenz oder Marktsicherung. Köln.

Beynon, H (1984) *Working for Ford (2nd edition),* Harmondsworth: Penguin.

Beynon, H, Hudson, R and Sadler, D (1991) '*A Tale of Two Industries: the Contraction of Coal and Steel in the Northeast of England*', Milton Keynes and Philadelphia: Open University Press.

Bhagwati, J (1993), 'Regionalism and multilateralism: an overview', in Anderson and Blackhurst, *op. cit.*

Biehl, D (1991) 'The role of infrastructure in regional development', in R W Vickerman (ed) *European Research in Regional Science 1, Infrastructure and Regional Development.* London: Pion, 9–35.

Bilal, S (1998), 'Political economy considerations on the supply of trade protection in regional integration arrangements', *Journal of Common Market Studies,* 36, 1–31.

Birkinshaw, J (1996) 'How multinational subsidiary mandates are gained and lost', *Journal of International Business Studies* 27, 467–95.

Bishop, M and Kay, J (1993) *European Mergers and Merger Policy.* Oxford: Oxford University Press.

Boutruri, M and Fukusaku, K (1993) 'Globalisation and intra-firm trade: an empirical note', *OECD Economic Studies* 20, 145–59.

Breathnach, P (1993) 'Women's employment and peripheralisation: the case of Ireland's branch plant economy', *Geoforum* 24, 19–29.

Brech, M and Sharp, M (1984) *Inward Investment: Policy Options for the UK,* Chatham House Papers 21, London: Routledge.

Brewer, TL and Young, S (1995) 'European Union policies and the problems of multinational enterprises', *Journal of World Trade Law* 29, 1, 33–52.

Brewer, TL and Young, S (1997) 'Investment incentives and the international agenda', *The World Economy,* 20, 2, 175–98.

Brewer, TL and Young, S (1998) *The Multilateral Investment System and Multinational Enterprise.* Oxford: Oxford University Press.

Bromwich, M and Inoue, S (1994) *Management Practices and Cost Management Problems in Japanese Affiliated Companies in the UK.* London: CIMA.

Brown, AJ (1949) *Applied Economics, Aspects of the World Economy in War and Peace.* London: George Allen and Unwin.

Browne, M (1993) 'Logistics strategies in the Single European Market and their spatial consequences', *Journal of Transport Geography* 1, 75–85.

Buckley, P and Artisien, P (1988) 'Policy issues of intra-EC direct investment: British, French and German multinationals in Greece, Portugal and Spain, with special reference to employment effects', in J Dunning, and P Robson, (eds) *Multinationals and the European Community.* Oxford: Blackwell.

Buckley, P and Casson, M (1976) *The Future of the Multinational Enterprise.* London: Macmillan.

Buckley, P and Hughes, J (1997) 'Japanese transfer pricing policy: a note', *Applied Economic Letters* 4, 3–17.

Burge, K (1996) 'Korean investment in the UK', *Business Review North* 18, 1, 13–17.

Burge, K (1997) 'Japanese manufacturing investment in Europe – recent history and future prospects', *Business Review North* 18, 4, 14–19.

Business Monitor (1995) *UK Census of Production Summary Tables (1992).* London: HMSO .

Business Monitor (1997) *Overseas Transactions (1993), MA4.* London: HMSO.

Calzonetti, FJ and Walker, Robert T (1991) 'Factors affecting industrial location decisions: a survey approach', in H W Herzog and A M Scholttman (eds) *Industry Location and Public Policy.* Knoxville: The University of Tennessee Press, 221–40.

Campbell, D (1994) 'Foreign investment, labour immobility and the quality of employment', International Labour Review 133, 185–204.

Cantwell, J (ed) (1992) *Multinational Investment in Modern Europe.* Aldershot: Edward Elgar.

Cantwell, J (1995) 'The globalisation of technology: what remains of the product cycle model', *Cambridge Journal of Economics* 19, 155–74.

Carlino, GA and Mills, ES (1987) 'The determinants of country growth', *Journal of Regional Science* 27, 39–54.

Castells, M (1989) *The Informational City; Information Technology, Economic Restructuring and the Urban–Regional Process.* Oxford: Basil Blackwell.

Castells, M and Henderson, J (1987) 'Techno-economic restructuring, socio-political processes and spatial transformation: a global perspective', in J Henderson and M Castells (eds) *Global Restructuring and Territorial Development.* London: Sage.

Caves, RE (1996) *Multinational Enterprise and Economic Analysis,* 2nd edition. Cambridge University Press.

CEC (1994a) 'Competition and integration: community merger control policy', *European Economy* 57.

CEC (1994b) *Competitiveness and Cohesion: Trends in the Regions.* Fifth Periodic Report on the Social and Economic Situation and the Development of the Regions in the Community. Luxembourg: Commission of the European Communities.

CEC (1994c) *Europe 2000+ Cooperation of European Territorial Development.* Luxembourg: Commission of the European Communities.

CEC (1995) 'Mergers and acquisitions', *European Economy Supplement A3.*

CEC (1996a) 'Economic evaluation of the internal market', *European Economy* 3.

CEC (1996b) *First Report on Economic and Social Cohesion.* Luxembourg: Commission of the European Communities, OOPEC.

CEC (1996c) *An Industrial Competitiveness Policy for the European Chemical Industry: An Example.* Communication from the Commission of The European Communities, Brussels.

CEC (1996d) *Taxation in the European Union: Report on the Development of Tax Systems.* Commission of the European Communities, COM(96) 546 final, 22 October.

CEC (1997a) *Agenda 2000: For a Stronger and Wider Union.* Bulletin of the European Union Supplement 5/97. Luxembourg: Commission of the European Communities.

CEC (1997b) *Foreign Direct Investment,* Single Market Review IV/1. OPEC/ Kogan Page/ Earthscan.

Cecchini, P (1988) *The European Challenge 1992: The Benefits of a Single European Market.* Aldershot: Wildwood House,

Central Statistical Office (1997) *Economic Trends,* No. 519 January/February No. 521 April and No. 523 June, London.

Chandler, AD, Jr (1977) *The Visible Hand: The Managerial Revolution in American Business.* Cambridge, Mass: The Belknap Press.

Chapman, K (1991) *The International Petrochemicals Industry: Evolution and Location.*Oxford: Basil Blackwell.

Chôgin Sôgô Kenkyûsho (ed.) (1996) Zenkaibô kûdôka suru sangyô shinai sangyô [Complete Analysis of Industries that Do Hollow Out and of Those that Do Not]. Tokyo: Tôyô Keizai Shinhôsha.

Christodoulou, P (1996) *Inward Investment : an Overview and Guide to the Literature.* London: The British Library.

Clark, GL (1990) 'Piercing the corporate veil: the closure of Wisconsin Steel in South Chicago', *Regional Studies* 24, 405–20.

Clark, GL and Wrigley, N (1997) 'Exit, the firm and sunk costs : reconceptualising the corporate geography of disinvestment and plant closure', *Progress in Human Geography,* 21, 3, 338–58.

Clarke, T and Beaney, P (1993) 'Between autonomy and dependence: corporate strategy, plant status, and local agglomeration in the Scottish electronics industry', *Environment and Planning* A 25, 213–32.

Clegg, J (1995), 'The determinants of United States foreign direct investment in the European Community: a critical appraisal'. Bath: University of Bath, mimeo.

Coen, D (1997) 'The evolution of the large firm as a political actor in the European Union', *Journal of European Public Policy* 4, 91–108.

Collis, C and Noon, D (1994) 'Foreign direct investment in the UK regions : recent trends and policy issues', *Regional Studies* 28, 843–8.

Connell, R (1996) 'Navigating the Internet: Site selection', *Area Development* 31, March, 57–60.

Contractor, F J (1990) 'Ownership patterns of U.S. joint ventures abroad and the liberalization of foreign government regulations in the 1980s: evidence from benchmark surveys', *Journal of International Business Studies* 1, 1, 55–73.

Cooke, P (1989) (ed.) *Localities: The Changing Face of Urban Britain.* London: Unwin Hyman.

Cooke, P (1993) (ed.) *Global Localisation.* London: UCL Press,

Cooke, P (1995) 'Introduction', in P Cooke (ed.) *The Rise of the Rustbelt.* London: UCL Press, 1–19.

Cooke, P and Morgan, K (1993) 'The network paradigm: new departures in corporate and regional development', *Environment and Planning D: Society and Space* 11, 543–64.

Cooke, P and Morgan, K (1998) 'The Institutions of Innovation', in *The Associational Economy: Firms, Regions and Innovation.* Oxford: Oxford University Press.

Cooke, TE (1988) *International Mergers and Acquisitions.* Oxford: Basil Blackwell.

Cornish, S (1997) 'Product innovation and the spatial dynamics of market intelligence: does proximity to markets matter?', *Economic Geography* 73, 2, 143–65.

Coughlin, CC, Terza, JV and Arromdee, V (1991) 'State characteristics and the location of foreign direct investment within the United States', *Review of Economics and Statistics,* 73, 675–81.

Cowles, MG (1996) 'The EU committee of AmCham: the powerful voice of American firms in Brussels', *Journal of European Public Policy* 3, 339–58.

Cowling, K and Sugden, R (1996) 'Capacity, transnationals, and industrial strategy', in J Michie, and Grieve-Smith, J (eds) *Creating Industrial Capacity: Towards Full Employment.* Oxford: Oxford University Press, 289–307.

Cox, A and Watson, G (1995) 'The European Community and the restructuring of Europe's national champions', in J Hayward (ed.) *Industrial Enterprise and European Integration: From National to International Champions in Western Europe.* Oxford: Oxford University Press. 304–33.

Crone, TM (1997) 'Where have all the factory jobs gone – and why?', *Business Review* May/June, 3–18.

Cumbria County Council (1995) *Economic Development Statement.* Carlisle: Cumbria County Council.

Curbelo, JL and Albuqurque, F (1994) 'The lagging regions of the EC in the face of economic and monetary union', *European Planning Studies* 1, 275–97.

Cyert, RM and March, JG (1963) *A Behavioural Theory of the Firm.* New York: Wiley.

Czech Invest (1995) *Ten Good Reasons to Invest in the Czech Republic*: Business Briefing Publishing.

Czech Invest (1997a) *Foreign Direct Investment in the Czech Republic*: Business Briefing Publishing.

Czech Invest (1997b) *Establishing a Business in the Czech Republic.* Business Briefing Publishing.

Davies, S and Lyons, B (1991) 'Characterising relative performance: the productivity advantage of foreign owned firms in the UK', *Oxford Economic Papers* 43, 4, 584–95.

Davies, S and Lyons, B (1996) 'Conclusions and applications', in S Davies, and B Lyons (eds) *Industrial Organisation in the European Union: Structure, Strategy and the Competitive Mechanism.* Oxford: Clarendon Press, 233–8.

Davis, E (1990) 'Synergies and the motivations for cross border mergers', in Centre for Business Strategy, *Continental Mergers are Different.* London Business School, 47–63.

Dawkins, W (1989) 'Some original ideas on the limits to free trade', *Financial Times,* 10 February, 13.

De Jonquieres, G (1995) 'Japan's overseas plants fly the nest', *Financial Times,* 8 June, 7.

De Smidt, M (1992) 'International investments and the European challenge', *Environment and Planning A.* 24, 83–4.

Deardorff, AV (1998) 'Determinants of bilateral trade: does gravity work in a neoclassical world?' in Frankel, *op. cit.*

Dent, C (1997) *The European Economy: The Global Context.* London: Routledge.

Dent, CM and Randerson, C (1996) 'Korean foreign direct investment in Europe : the determining forces', *The Pacific Review* 9, 4, 531–52.

Department of the Environment (1992) Research Report: *The Use of Planning Agreements.* HMSO.

Devlin, G and Bleakley, M (1988) 'Strategic alliances: guidelines for success.' *Long-Range Planning* 21, 5, 18–23.

Department of the Environment (1995) Circular 11/95. *The Use of Conditions in Planning Permissions,* July, HMSO.

Department of the Environment (1997a) PPG (Revised), *Planning Policy guidance: General Policy and Principles.* February, HMSO.

Department of the Environment (1997b). Circular 1/97. *Planning Obligations.* January, HMSO.

Deutsches Institut für Japanstudien (ed) (1998) *Die Wirtschaft Japans – Strukturen zwischen Kontinuität und Wandel.* Berlin *et al.* Springer Verlag.

Diamond, D and Spence, N (1984) 'Infrastructure and regional development: theories.' *Built Environment* 10, 262–9.

Dicken, P (1976) 'The multiplant business enterprise and geographical space: some issues in the study of external control and regional development'. *Regional Studies* 10, 401–12.

Dicken, P (1988) 'The changing geofigurey of Japanese foreign direct investment in manufacturing industry: a global perspective', *Environment and Planning A* 20, 633–53.

Dicken, P (1992a) 'Europe 1992 and strategic change in the international automobile industry', *Environment and Planning A* 24, 11–31.

Dicken, P (1992b) *Global Shift: The Internationalization of Economic Activity,* 2nd edition. London: Paul Chapman Publishing Ltd.

Dicken, P (1994) 'Global–local tensions; forms and states in the global space-economy', *Economic Geography* 70, 2, 101–28.

Dicken, P, Forsgren, M and Malmberg, A (1994) 'The local embeddedness of transnational corporations', in A Amin and N Thrift (eds) *Globalisation, Institutions and Regional Development.* Oxford: Blackwell, 23–48.

Dicken, P and Öberg, S (1996) 'The global context: Europe in a world of dynamic economic and population change', *European Urban and Regional Studies* 3, 101–20.

Dicken, P and Quevit, M (eds) (1994) *Transnational Corporations and European Regional Restructuring.* Utrecht: Netherlands Geographical Studies.

Dicken, P and Thrift, N (1992) 'The organisation of production and the production of organisation: why business enterprises matter in the study of geographical industrialisation', *Transactions of the Institute of British Geographers* 17, 279–91.

Dicken, P and Tickell, A (1992) 'Competitors or collaborators? The structure of inward investment promotion in Northern England', *Regional Studies* 26, 1, 99–105.

Dillow, C (1989) *A Return to the Trade Surplus? The Impact of Japanese Investment in the UK.* London: Nomura.

Donahue, J (1997) *Subnational business-attraction policies in the United States.* Paris: Report for the OECD Development Centre, mimeo.

Doyle, P, Saunders, J and Wong, V (1992) 'Competition in global markets: a case study of American and Japanese competition in the British market', *Journal of International Business Studies* 3, 419–42.

Duffy-Deno, KT (1992) 'Pollution abatement expenditures and regional manufacturing activity', *Journal of Regional Science* 32, 419–36.

Duncan, S and Goodwin, M (1988) *Local State and Uneven Development.* Cambridge: Polity Press.

Dunford, M (1996) 'Disparities in employment, productivity and output in the EU: the roles of labour market governance and welfare regimes', *Regional Studies* 30, 339–58.

Dunford, M (1993) 'Regional Disparities in the European Community: evidence from the REGIO databank', *Regional Studies* 27, 8, 727–43.

Dunford, M (1994) 'Winners and losers : the new map of economic inequality in the European Union', *European Urban and Regional Studies* 1, 2, 95–114.
Dunning, JH (1977) 'Trade, location of economic activity and the multinational enterprise: a search for an eclectic approach', in B Ohlin, P O Hesselborn and P J Wijkman (eds) *The International Allocation of Economic Activity*. London: Macmillan, 395–418.
Dunning, J (1979) 'Explaining changing patterns of international production : in defence of the eclectic theory', *Oxford Bulletin of Economics and Statistics*. Volume 41, 269–95.
Dunning, JH (1981) *International Production and the Multinational Enterprise*. London: George Allen and Unwin.
Dunning, J (1986) *Japanese Participation in British Industry*. London: Croom Helm.
Dunning, JH (1988) *Multinationals, Technology and Competitiveness*. London: Allen and Unwin.
Dunning, JH (1993a) *Multinational Enterprises and the Global Economy*. Addison-Wesley: Wokingham, Berkshire.
Dunning, JH (1993b) *Globalisation: The Challenge for National Economic Regimes*. Dublin Economic and Social Research Institute, The 24th Geary Lecture, 1993.
Dunning, JH (1996) *Multinational Enterprises and the Global Economy*. Harlow: Addison-Wesley.
Dunning, J (1997a) 'The European internal market programme and inbound foreign direct investment, part I', *Journal of Common Market Studies* 35, 1–35.
Dunning, J (1997b) 'The European Internal Market Programme and inbound foreign direct investment, part II', *Journal of Common Market Studies* 35, 189–223.
Dunning, J (1997c) *Alliance Capitalism and Global Business*. London and New York: Routledge.
Dunning, J (1998) 'Location and the multinational enterprise: a neglected factor?' *Journal of International Business Studies* 29, 45–66.
Dunning, J and Narula, R (1995) 'The R&D activities of foreign firms in the United States', *International Studies of Management and Organization* 25, Spring/Summer, 39–75.
Durnin, J, Hind, D and Stokes, B (1995) *Cumbria in the Pink?* Northumbria University of Northumbria in association with Cumbria Training & Enterprise Council.
Economic Planning Agency (ed.) (1996) *Economic Survey of Japan (1995–1996)*. Tokyo: Printing Bureau, Ministry of Finance.
The Economist (1989), 'Set up or stay out'. 18 February, 56.
Economist Intelligence Unit (1996) *International Mergers and Acquisitions*. New York: Economist Intelligence Unit.
Egan, C and McKiernan, P (1994) *Inside Fortress Europe: Strategies for the Single Market*. The Economist Intelligence Unit (EIU) Series. Wokingham: Addison-Wesley.
Electronics Industries Association (EIA) (1995) *Consumer Electronics Products Offer Outstanding Value*. Speech by Joseph P Clayton, Executive Vice- President of Marketing & Sales, Thomson Consumer Electronics.
Electronics Industries Association of Japan (EIAJ) (1993) *'93 kaigai hojin risuto*. Tokyo: Nihon denshi kikai kogyokai. Chosabu.
Electronics Industries Association of Japan (EIAJ) (1995) *'95 kaigai hojin risuto*. Tokyo: Nihon denshi kikai kogyokai. Chosabu.
Eltis, W and Fraser, D (1992) 'The contribution of Japanese industrial success to Britain and Europe', *National Westminster Quarterly Review*, November, 2–19.
Ernst and Young (1995) *West Cumbria Partnership: Review of Economic Development Strategy*. Workington: West Cumbria Partnership.
Estrin, S, Hughes, K and Todd, S (1997) *Foreign Direct Investment in Central and Eastern Europe: Multinationals in Transition*. London: Pinter.
Ethier, WJ (1996), 'Theories about trade liberalisation and migration: are they substitutes or complements?' in L Williams, and PJ Lloyd (eds) *International Trade and Migration in the APEC Region*. Melbourne: Oxford University Press.

European Commission (1995) *Competition Policy in the New Trade Order: Strengthening International Cooperation and Rules.* Luxembourg: Office for Official Publication of the European Communities, July.

European Commission (1996) 'Draft horizontal framework on regional aid for larger investment projects.' Directorate-General XVI Regional Policy and Cohesion, Brussels, mimeo.

European Council (1998) *'Conclusion of the ECOFIN Council Meeting on 1 December 1997 concerning taxation policy'*, *Official Journal of the European Communities,* C2, 6 January.

Eurostat (1995) *European Union Direct Investment 1984–1993.* Brussels/Luxembourg: Office for Official Publications of the European Communities.

Evans, A (1997) *EC Law of State Aid.* Oxford: Clarendon Press.

Evans, R and Harding, A (1997) 'Regionalisation, regional institutions and economic development', *Policy & Politics* 25, 19–30.

EXIM Export–Import Bank of Japan (ed.) (1997) 1996 nendo kaigai chokusetsu tôshi ankêto chôsa kekka hôkoku [1996 Survey: The Outlook on Japanese Foreign Direct Investment]. *Kaigai tôshi kenkyûjô hô* 23, 1 January 1997, 4–79.

Feldman, M and Schreuder, Y (1996) 'Initial advantage: the origins of the geographic concentration of the pharmaceutical industry in the mid-Atlantic region', *Industrial and Corporate Change* 5, 3, 839–62.

Fielding, AJ (1994) 'Industrial change and regional development in Western Europe', *Urban Studies* 31, 679–704.

Financial Times (1997) Supplement on 'International banking in London', 27 November, 42.

Findlay, AM (1995) 'The future skills exchanges within the European Union', in P White and R Hall, (eds) *Europe's Population: Towards the Next Century.* London: UCL Press. 130-141.

Firn, JR (1975) 'External control and regional development: the case of Scotland', *Environment and Planning A* 7, 393–414.

Fisher, LM (1996) 'Sony set to introduce personal computer line; an electronic giant jumps into a growth market', *New York Times,* Section C, 6.

Flam, H (1994) 'EC members fighting about surplus, VERS, FDI and Japanese cars', *Journal of International Economics* 36, 117–31.

Florida, R (1995) 'Toward the learning region', *Futures* 27, 5, 527–36.

Forester, T (1993) *Silicon Samurai: How Japan Conquered the World's IT Industry.* Cambridge, Mass.: Blackwell Business.

Frank, R and Freeman R (1978) *Distributional Consequences of Direct Foreign Investment.* New York: Academic Press.

Frankel, JA (ed) (1998) *The Regionalization of the World Economy,* Chicago: University of Chicago Press.

Frankel, JA, Stein, E and Wei, S-J (1998), 'Continental trading blocs: are they natural or supernatural?', in Frankel, *op. cit.*

Freeman, C (1990) 'Networks of innovators: a synthesis of research issues', *Research Policy* 20, 5, 499–514.

Fröbel, F, Heinrichs, J and Kreye, O (1980) *The New International Division of Labour: Structural Unemployment in Industrialised Countries and Industrialisation in Developing Countries.* Cambridge: Cambridge University Press.

Fuchs, VR (1968) *The Service Economy.* New York: National Bureau of Economic Research, Columbia University Press.

Fujita, K, Child Hill, RC (1995) 'Global toyotaism and local development', *International Journal of Urban and Regional Research* 19, 1, 7–22.

Fujitake, Kikuharu (1990) 'The transition and future of marketing research: a changing industrial and social structure', *Journal of Advertising Research* 30, 2, 58–67.

Fukushima, Kiyohiko and Chi Hung Kwan (1995) 'Foreign direct investment and regional restructuring in Asia,' in Institute for Southeast Asian Studies (ed) *The New Wave of Foreign Direct Investment in Asia.* Tokyo: Tokyo Club Foundation for Global Studies.

Furness Enterprise (1992) *Technology and People in the Right Environment.* Barrow-in-Furness: Furness Enterprise.
Furness Enterprise (1996) *Assisting Companies to Create Jobs: The First Four Years 1992–1995.* Barrow-in-Furness: Furness Enterprise.
Furness Enterprise (1997) *Towards Two Thousand and Ten*. Annual Reports and Accounts 1995–6. Barrow-in-Furness: Furness Enterprise.
Garofalo, GA and Malhotra, DM (1995) 'Effect of environmental regulations on state-level manufacturing capital formation', *Journal of Regional Science* 35, 201–16.
Gertler, MS 1995 ' "Being There": Proximity, organization, and culture in the development and adoption of advanced manufacturing technologies', *Economic Geography* 71, 1, 1–26.
Gestrin, M and Rugman, AM (1996) 'The NAFTA Investment Provisions : Prototype for Multilateral Investment Rules' in Organisation for Economic Cooperation and Development', in *Market Access After the Uruguay Round.* Paris: OECD, 63–78.
Gibb, R and Michalak, W (1994) 'The European Community and East-Central Europe', *Tijdschrift voor Economische en Sociale Geographie* 85, 401–16.
Gibb, R and Michalak, W (1996) 'Regionalism in the world economy', *Area* 28, 446–58.
Gittelman, M (1997) 'Foreign direct investment in the triad: a framework for understanding regionalisation in the 1990's', *The International Executive* 39, 67–81.
Glickman, N and Woodward, D (1989) *The New Competitors, How Foreign Investors are Changing the United States Economy.* New York: Basic Books.
Goldberg, PM and Kindleberger, CP (1970) 'Toward a GATT for Investment', *Law and Policy in International Business* 2, 4, 295–325.
Gomes-Casseres, B (1985) *Multinational Ownership Strategies.* PhD dissertation, Harvard University, Graduate School of Business Administration, unpublished.
Goodwin, M and Painter, J (1996) 'Local governance, the crises of Fordism and the changing geographies of regulation', *Transactions of the Institute of British Geographers* 17, 292–305.
Gordon, D (1990) 'The global economy: new edifice or crumbling foundations', *New Left Review* 168, 24–64.
Graham, EM (1996) *Global Corporations and National Governments.* Washington, DC: Institute for International Economics.
Graham, EM and Krugman, PR (1995) *Foreign Direct Investment in the United States.* Washington, DC: Institute for International Economics.
Graham, EM and Richardson, JD (1997) *Global Competition Policy.* Washington, DC: Institute for International Economics.
Granovetter, M (1985) 'Economic action and social structure: the problem of embeddedness', *American Journal of Sociology* 91, 3, 481–510.
Grant, W (1991) 'The overcapacity crisis in the West European petrochemicals industry', in A Martinelli (ed.) *International Markets and Global Firms: A Comparative Study of Organised Business in the Chemical Industry.* London: Sage 249–71.
Grossman, GM (1998), 'Comment on Deardorff', in Frankel, *op. cit.*
Guisinger, SE and Associates (1985) *Investment Incentives and Performance Requirements.* New York: Praeger.
Hague, R and Wylie, R (1994) *Perceptions of West Cumbria as a Destination for Leisure Travel and Inward Investment.* Government Enterprise Communications Unit, University of Newcastle upon Tyne.
Hague, R and Wylie, R (1996) 'Place and politics in West Cumbria: the place process, political attitudes and place promotion policies', *Westlakes Research Monographs No 2.* Government Enterprise Communication Unit, University of Newcastle upon Tyne.
Hake, DA, Ploch, DR, and Fox, WF (1985) 'Business location determinants in Tennessee', Knoxville: University of Tennessee Working Paper.
Halkier, H and Danson, M (1997) 'Regional development agencies in Western Europe: a survey of key characteristics and trends', *European Urban and Regional Studies* 4, 243–56.

Hamill, J (1994) 'Cross-border mergers, acquisitions and strategic alliances', in P Bailey, A Parisotto and G Renshaw (eds) *Multinationals and Employment: the Global Economy of the 1990s.* Vienna: International Labour Office.

Hamill, J and Castledine, P (1992) 'Foreign acquisitions in the UK: impact and policy issues'. *Strathclyde International Business Unit Working Paper* 92/15.

Hany, C (1995) 'Foreign direct investment in Central Eastern Europe: some lessons for Poland and Hungary', *Intereconomics* 30, 36–43.

Haslam, C, Williams, K, Adcroft, A, Johal, J and Williams, J (1995) *Learning from Japan.* Paper presented at The Japan and the Periphery Regions of Europe Conference, Queens, Belfast, April.

Healey, P (1997) *Collaborative Planning: Shaping Places in Fragmented Societies.* London: Macmillan,

Hedlund, G and Rolander, D (1990) 'Action in heterarchies: new approaches to managing the MNC', in CA Bartlett, Y Doz and G Hedlund (eds) *Managing the Global Firm.* London: Routledge.

Heitger, B and Stehn, J (1990) 'Japanese direct investment in the EC: response to the internal market 1993?', *Journal of Common Market Studies* XXIX, 1 1–15.

Hekman, JS (1982) 'Survey of location decisions in the South', *Economic Review,* Federal Reserve Bank of Atlanta, June, 6–19.

Helleiner, G (1973) 'Manufactured exports from less developed countries and multinational firms', *Economic Journal,* 83, 21–47.

Hepworth, M (1989) *Geography of the Information Economy.* London: Belhaven.

Hill, S and Munday, M (1994) *The Regional Distribution of Foreign Manufacturing Investment in the UK.* Basingstoke: Macmillan.

Hill, S and Roberts, A (1993) 'Why Wales? The Competitive Advantage', *Welsh Economic Review,* June 18–22. Special issue on Inward Investment in Wales.

Hine, RC (1992), 'Regionalism and the integration of the world economy', *Journal of Common Market Studies,*30, 115–23.

Hirst, P and Thompson, G (1996) *Globalisation in Question.* Cambridge: Polity Press.

Holmes, P (1989) 'Economies of scale, expectations and Europe 1992', *The World Economy* 12, 525–37.

Holmes, P and Kempton, J (1996) 'EU anti-dumping policy : a regulatory perspective', *Journal of European Public Policy* 3, 4, 647–64.

Hood, N and Young, S (1997) *The Economics of Multinational Enterprise.* London: Longman.

Houston, DT Jr (1995) 'Is New Jersey a good place to do business?' *Profiles,* 7–8.

Howells, J (1990) 'The internationalisation of R&D and the development of global research networks', *Regional Studies* 24, 495–512.

Howells, JR (1992) 'Pharmaceuticals and Europe 1992: the dynamic of industrial change', *Environment and Planning* A24, 33–48.

Howells, J and Wood, M (1993) *The Globalisation of Production and Technology.* London: Bellhaven Press.

Hudson, R (1989) *Wrecking a Region : State Policies, Party Politics, and Regional Change in North East England.* London: Pion.

Hudson, R (1997) 'Regional futures: industrial restructuring, new high volume production concepts and spatial development strategies in the new Europe', Regional Studies 31, 5, 467–78.

Hudson, R and Sadler, D (1986) 'Contesting works closures in Europe's old industrial regions: defending place or betraying class?', in AJ Scott, M Storper (eds) *Production, Work and Territory.* New York: Unwin Hyman, 172–93.

Hufbauer, G and Schott, G (1994) *Western Hemisphere Economic Integration.* Washington DC: Institute for International Economics.

Hufbauer, GC, Lakdawalla, D and Malani, A (1994), 'Determinants of foreign direct investment and its connection to trade', *UNCTAD Review*, 39–51.

Hummel, M *et al.* (1996) Stärken und Schwächen Deutschlands im internationalen Wettbewerb um Einkommen und Arbeitsplätze = Schriftenreihe des ifo Instituts für Wirtschaftsforschung Nr. 143. Berlin/München: Duncker & Humboldt.

Hunya, G (1992) 'Foreign direct investment and privatisation in Central and Eastern Europe', *Communist Economies and Economic Transformation*. 4, 501–11.

Hymer, S (1960) 'The international operations of international firms: a study of direct foreign investment', Unpublished PhD dissertation. Massachusetts Institute of Technology.

Imai, K (ed.) (1992) 21-*seiki gata kigyo to nettowaku* (21st-Century Oriented Form of Firms and Networking). Sogo Kenkyu Kaihatsu Kiko. Tokyo: NTT Shuppan.

Institute of Welsh Affairs (1996) *Wales 2010: Three Years On*. Cardiff: Institute of Welsh Affairs.

INWARD (1995–6) *Annual Report: from Vision to Growth*, Warrington.

Ipsen, E (1997) 'In Wales, doubts on foreign investment', *The International Herald Tribune* 29 January, 1 and 10. New York.

Jacquemin, A, Buigues, P and Ilzkovitz, (1989) 'Horizontal mergers and competition policy in the European Community', *European Economy* 40.

Jacquemin, A and Sapir, A (1988) 'European integration or world integration?' *Weltwirtschaftliches Archiv* 124, 127–39.

Jensen-Moran, J (1996) 'Trade battles as investment wars: the coming rules of origin debate', in B Roberts (ed.) *New Forces in the World Economy: A Washington Quarterly Reader*. Cambridge, Mass: MIT Press, 193–205.

Jessop, R (1994) 'Post-fordism and the state', in A Amin (ed.) *Post-Fordism: A Reader*.Oxford: Basil Blackwell,

Jessop, R (1997) 'The future of the national state: erosion or reorganisation? General reflections on the West European case', Department of Sociology, University of Lancaster, mimeo.

JETRO (1996a) *The 12th Survey of European Operations of Japanese Companies in the Manufacturing Sector*, London: JETRO:

JETRO (1996b): Nihon no seihin un'yu 1995 (Japanese Merchandise Import 1995). Tokyo: Kanpô Toriatsukaisho.

Julius, D (1997) 'Globalisation and stakeholder conflicts: a corporate perspective', *International Affairs* 73, 453–68.

Jung, S-H (1996) 'South Korean foreign direct investment in the European Union', Paper presented to the international conference on Local Productive Systems and European Integration organised by Sviluppo Economico Comparato ICP 1266/14 and the International Training Centre of the International Labour Office, Turin, Italy, 4–12 July 1996.

Jung, S-H (1997a) 'Regional and sectoral distribution of Korean foreign direct investment in the United Kingdom', Paper presented to the Regional Science Association 28th International Conference : British & Irish Section, Falmouth, Cornwall, UK, 10–12 September 1997.

Jung, S-H (1997b) 'The global–local interplay of Korean foreign direct investment in the European Union', Paper presented to the European Regional Frontiers Conference, 20–23 September 1997, Frankfurt-on-Oder, Germany.

Kang, YC (1994) 'Globalisation of Korean capital.' Globalisation and Korean Society, the 7th Conference of the Korean Academic Association, Seoul : Nanam, 103–41 (in Korean).

Karatsu, Hajime (1986) Kûdôka suru amerika sangyô e no chokuzen (Just before the hollowing-out of American Industry). Tokyo: PHP Kenkyûjo.

Keating, M (1997) 'The invention of regions: political restructuring and territorial government in Western Europe', *Environment & Planning C, Government & Policy* 15, 383–98.

Keizai Kikakuchô Chôsakyoku (ed.) (1996): Chiiki keizai repôto '96 (Report on the regional economy '96). Tokyo: Ôkurashô Insatsukyoku.

Kemp, MC and Wan, H (1976), 'An elementary proposition concerning the formation of customs unions', *Journal of International Economics*, 6, 95–7.

Kieschnich, M (1981) 'Taxes and growth: business incentives and economic development', in *Studies in Development Policy.* Washington, DC: Council of State Planning Agencies.

Kikai Shinkô Kyôkai (ed.) (1996): Kaigai seisan shifuto no eikyô to sono taiô, kikai sangyô o chûshin toshite (The influence of a production shift abroad and its counter measurements, concentration on machinery industries). Tokyo: Keizai Shinkô Kyôkai Keizai Kenkyûjo.

Killick, T (1982) 'Employment in Foreign Owned Plants', *British Business,* November.

Kline, SJ and Rosenberg, N (1986) 'An overview of innovation', in R Landam and N Rosenberg (eds) *The Positive Sum Strategy.* Washington, DC: National Academy Press.

Knickerbocker, FT (1973) *Oligopolistic Reaction and the Multinational Enterprise.* Cambridge, MA: Harvard University Press.

Kobayashi, N (1990) 'Comparison of Japanese and Western multinationals – Part 1', *Tokyo Business Today* 58 (October), 50.

Kobrin, S (1991) 'An empirical analysis of the determinants of global integration', *Strategic Management Journal* 12, 17–31.

Kobrin, SJ (1995) 'Regional integration in a globally networked economy', *Transnational Corporations* 4, 2, 15–33.

Kojima, K (1964) 'The pattern of international trade among advanced countries', *Hitotsubashi Journal of Economics* 5.

Kokko, A (1993) *Home Country Effects of FDI: Some Evidence from Sweden.* Stockholm: School of Economics.

Kolz, AC (1995) 'Quality of life: is it essential to consider in the site selection process?', *Area Development* 30, (July) 27–8.

Korean Foreign Trade Association (1993) Case studies of Korean foreign direct investment (in Korean).

Korean Export and Import Bank (1992) *Trends of Korean foreign direct investment overseas and reports on Korean overseas operations* (in Korean) Seoul: KEIP.

Kravis, Irving and Lipsey, R (1988) *The Effect of Multinational Firms' Foreign Operations on the Domestic Employment.* Washington, DC: National Bureau of Economic Research, Working Paper No. 2760.

Krugman, PR (1991) 'Is bilateralism bad?, in E Helpman and A Razin (eds) *International Trade and Trade Policy* Cambridge Mass: MIT Press.

Krugman, PR (1993) 'Regionalism versus multilateralism: analytic notes', in de Melo and Panagariya, *op. cit.*

Krugman, PR (1995) 'Growing world trade: causes and consequences' *Brookings Papers on Economic Activity,* 1, 327–77.

Krugman, PR, and AJ Venables (1990) 'Integration and the competitiveness of peripheral industry', in C Bliss and J Braga de Macedo (eds) *Unity with Diversity in the European Economy.* Cambridge: Cambridge University Press.

Kwan, Chi Hung (1997) 'The rise of Asia and Japan's "Hollowing Out" problem'. *NRI Quarterly,* Spring, 58–75.

Lane, S (1994) 'The pattern of foreign direct investment and joint ventures in Hungary', *Communist Economies and Economic Transformation* 6 , 341–65.

Lansbury, M, Pain, N and Smidkova, K (1996) 'Foreign direct investment in Central Europe since 1990: an econometric study', *National Institute Economic Review* 56, 104–14.

Lawrence, RZ (1991) 'Emerging regional arrangements: building blocks or stumbling blocks?', in R O'Brien (ed.) *Amex Bank Review Prize Essays.* Oxford: Oxford University Press.

Lawton, TC (1996) 'Industrial policy partners: explaining the European firm–Commission interplay for electronics', *Policy & Politics* 24, 425–36.

Legewie, J (1998) Außenwirtschaftliche Verflechtungen. In: Deutsches Institut für Japanstudien (ed.) Die Wirtschaft Japans – Strukturen zwischen Kontinuität and Wandel. Berlin: Springer Verlag, 293–316.

Lewis, C (1938) *America's Stake in International Investments.* Washington, DC: The Brookings Institution.

Li, J and Guisinger, S (1991) 'Comparative business failures of foreign controlled firms in the United States', *Journal of International Business Studies* 22, 209-24.
Lloyd, PJ (1992), 'Regionalisation and world trade', *OECD Economic Studies* no. 18, 8–42.
Lloyd, PJ (1998), 'Globalisation, international factor movements and market adjustments', University of Nottingham, mimeo.
Love, JH (1989) 'External takeover and regional economic development: a survey and critique', *Regional Studies* 23, 417–29.
Love, JH (1994) 'EC mergers regulation and regional economic cohesion', *Environment and Planning A* 26, 137–52.
Lovering, J (1989) 'The restructuring debate', in R Peet & N Thrift, (eds), *New Models in Geography.* London: Unwin Hyman.
Lovering, J (1996) 'New myths of the Welsh economy', *Planet 116*, (April/May) 6–16.
Lovering, J (1997) 'We need a new pattern of economic development', *Agenda*, Journal of the Institute of Welsh Affairs, Summer, Cardiff, 29–32.
Lundvall, B (1985) *Product Innovation and User–Producer Interaction.* Industrial Development Research Series, 31. Aalborg: Aalborg University Press.
Lundvall, B (1992) *National Systems of Innovation: Towards a Theory of Innovation and Interactive Learning.* London: Francis Pinter.
Mackay, R (1997) *The Economies of North Wales and Wales – The Nature of Regeneration.* Research Paper Series RP97/21. Bangor: School of Accounting, Banking and Economics. University of Wales.
Madeuf, B (1995): Foreign direct investment, trade and employment delocalisation, in: OECD, op. cit., 41–65.
Maillat, D (1995) 'Territorial dynamic, innovative milieux and regional policy', *Entrepreneurship and Regional Development* 7, 157–65.
Mair, A (1993) 'New growth poles? Just-in-time manufacturing and local economic development strategy', *Regional Studies* 27, 3, 207–21.
Makino, N (ed.) (1992) *Nihon kigyo no gurobaru senryaku* (The global strategy of Japanese corporations). Tokyo: Daiyamondosha.
Malmberg, A, Solvell, O and Zander, I (1996) 'Spatial clustering, local accumulation of knowledge and firm competitiveness', *Geografiska Annaler* 78, B, 85–97.
Marks, G, Hooghe, L and Blank, K (1996) 'European integration from the 1980s: state-centric v. multi-level governance', *Journal of Common Market Studies* 34, 341–78.
Markusen, A R (1994) *Sticky Places in Slippery Space: The Political Economy of Postwar Fast-Growth Regions.* Rutgers University, Project on Regional and Industrial Economics, Dept. Of Urban Planning and Policy Development, Working Paper No. 79.
Marshall, A (1920) *Principles of Economics. An Introductory Volume,* 8th edition. London: Macmillan.
Martin, R (1994) 'Economic theory and human geography', D Gregory, R Martin, G Smith (eds) in *Human Geography: Society, Space and Social Science.* Basingstoke: Macmillan.
Marton, K (1993) 'Foreign direct investment in Hungary.' *Transnational Corporations* 2, 111–34.
Mason, M (1994) 'Elements of consensus: Europe's response to the Japanese automotive challenge', *Journal of Common Market Studies* 32, 4, 433–53.
Mason, M (1994), 'Historical perspectives', in M Mason and D Encarnation (eds) *Does Ownership Matter? Japanese Multinationals in Europe.* Oxford: Clarendon Press.
Massey, D (1984) *Spatial Divisions of Labour.* London Macmillan.
Massey, D (1995) *Spatial Divisions of Labour: Social Structures and the Geography of Production,* (2nd edition) New York: Methuen.
Maturi, RJ (1995) 'The skilled labor imperative', *Area Development* 30, (November) 89–90.
Matyas, L (1997), 'Proper econometric specification of the gravity model', *The World Economy,* 20, 363–8.

Matzner, E and Streeck, W (1991) *Beyond Keynesianism: The Socioeconomics of Production and Full Employment.* Aldershot: Edward Elgar.

Mayes, D (1991) *The European Challenge*: Harvester Wheatsheaf.

McAleese, D and Counahan, M (1979) 'Stickers or snatchers? Employment in multinational corporations during the recession', *Oxford Bulletin of Economics and Statistics* 41 November 345–58.

McConnell, VD and Schwab, RM (1990) 'The impact of environmental regulation on industry location decisions: the motor vehicle industry', *Land Economics* 66, 67–81.

McKinsey Global Institute (1993) Manufacturing Productivity. Washington DC: McKinsey and Company.

Melo, J de and Panagariya, A (1993), 'Introduction', in J de Melo and A Panagariya (eds) *New Dimensions in Regional Integration.* Cambridge: Cambridge University Press.

Merck Archives (1992) *Merck Sharp & Dohme: A Brief History.* Rahway, New Jersey: Business History Group.

Middlemas (1995) *Orchestrating Europe: The Informal Politics of European Union 1973–95.* London: Fontana.

Miles, Raymond and Snow, Charles (1986) 'Network organizations: new concepts for new forms', *California Management Review* 28, 62–73.

Ministry of Finance (ed.) (1997) Direct Overseas Investment Recorded FY 1996. Tokyo: Ministry of Finance.

Mitsubishi Sôgô Kenkyûjo (ed.) (1992): Nihon kigyô no gurôbaru senryaku (Globalisation strategies of Japanese firms). Tokyo: Daiyamondosha.

MITT (1997a) *Foreign Direct Investments.* Hungarian Ministry of Industry, Trade and Tourism.

MITT (1997b) *Incentives for the Inflow of Foreign Direct Investment in Hungary in 1997.* Hungarian Ministry of Industry, Trade and Tourism.

Mofidi, A and Stone, JA (1990) 'Do state and local taxes affect economic growth?', *Review of Economics and Statistics* 72, 686–91.

Moore, L (1997) 'Developments in trade and trade policy', in M Artis and N Lee (eds) *The Economics of the European Union,* 2nd edition. Oxford: Oxford University Press, 292–329.

Morgan, K and Sayer, A (1988) *Microcircuits of Capital.* Cambridge: Polity Press.

Morgan, K (1995) *Institutions, Innovation and Regional Renewal: The Development Agency as Animateur.* Paper for Regional Studies Association Conference, Gothenburg, March, 6–9 May.

Morgan, K (1996) 'State of the Welsh economy' *Planet* 117 (June/July) 94–6.

Morgan, K (1997) 'The learning region: institutions, innovation and regional renewal', *Regional Studies* 31, 5, 491–504.

Morris, J (1988) 'The Japanese are here: for better or worse?', *Welsh Economic Review* 1, 1, 45–7.

Morris, J, Munday, M and Wilkinson, B (1993) *Working for the Japanese.* London: Athlone.

Morse, GW and Farmer, MC (1986) 'Location and investment effects of a tax abatement program', *National Tax Journal,* 34.

Munday, M (1995) 'The regional consequences of the Japanese second wave : a case study', *Local Economy* 10, 1, 4–20.

Munday, M, Morris, J and Wilkinson, B (1995) 'Factories or warehouses – a Welsh perspective on Japanese transplant manufacturing', *Regional Studies* 29, 1, 1–17.

Munday, M and Peel, M (1997) 'The Japanese manufacturing sector in the UK: a performance appraisal', *Accounting and Business Research* 28, 1, 1–21.

Mundell, R (1957) 'International trade and factor mobility', *American Economic Review,* 67, 321–35.

Mytelka, LK (1996) *Locational Tournaments, Strategic Partnerships and the State.* Ottawa: Carleton University, mimeo.

Negandhi, Anant and Serapio, Manuel (eds) (1995): *Research in International Business and International Relations: Japanese Direct Investment in the United States: Trends, Developments, and Issues – 1.* Greenwich: Jai Press.

Netherlands Economic Institute and Ernst and Young (1993) *New Location Factors for Mobile Investment in Europe* (final report for European Commission, Directorate-General for Regional Policies). Luxembourg: Office for Official Publications for the European Commission.

Nicolaides, P and Thomsen, S (1991) 'Can protectionism explain direct investment?', *Journal of Common Market Studies* XXIX, 6, 635–43.

Nilsson, JE and Schamp, EN (1996) 'Restructuring of the European production system: processes and consequences', *European Urban and Regional Studies* 3, 121–32.

Nonaka, I (1991) 'The knowledge-creating company', *Harvard Business Review* 69 (November–December) 96–104.

Nonaka, I (1993) 'Kigyo to chishiki sozo: soshiki-teki chishiki sozo no riron', in H Itami, T Kagono and M Ito (eds) *Nihon no kigyo shisutemu: Kigyo towa nanika* 1. Tokyo: Yuhikaku.

Norcliffe, G (1995) 'The regulation of restructuring: Corner Brook 1984', *Environment and Planning* C13, 315–34.

Norimoto, M (1996) *How Japanese Business is Developing Internationally.* Paper given at the AJEI/WDA Conference, Cardiff University, March.

North West Partnership (1996) *Learning for Earning.* Wigan: North West Partnership.

Northern Development Company (1997) *Profitable Business in the North: Programme & Budget.* Newcastle: NDC.

O'Brien, R (1992) *Global Financial Integration: The End of Geography.* London: Pinter.

O'Dowd, L (1985) 'Car manufacturing at Linwood: the regional policy issues – Sims D, Wood M & Industrial development in Merseyside: motor vehicle assembly and the port of Liverpool – Stoney P J M, Bourn M'. (Book Review) *International Journal for Urban and Regional Research* 9, 1, 149–51.

OECD (1976) *Guidelines for Multinational Enterprises.* Paris: OECD.

OECD (1992) *International Direct Investment: Policies and Trends in the 1980s.* Paris: OECD.

OECD (1993) *Territorial Development and Structural Change: A New Perspective on Adjustment and Reform.* Paris: OECD.

OECD (1994) *Globalisation and Local and Regional Competitiveness.* OECD Working Papers, II, 16, Paris: OECD

OECD (1995) *Foreign Direct Investment, Trade and Employment.* Paris: OECD Publications Service.

OECD (1996) *Globalisation of Industry. Overview and Sector Reports.* Paris: OECD Publications Service.

OECD (1997) 'MAI : The Multilateral Agreement on Investment', *OECD Policy Brief* 2, Paris: OECD.

Ohmae, K (1995) *The End of the Nation State: The Rise of Regional Economies.* New York: The Free Press.

Oinas, P (1997) 'On the socio-spatial embeddedness of business firms', *Erdkunde,* Band 51, 23–32.

Okajima, Akira (1996): Nihon keizai no shinro o tou (Ask for the course of the Japanese economy). Tokyo: Gakushû no tomosha.

Oman, C (1997) 'The policy challenges of globalisation and regionalisation', *Development* 40, 43–53.

Owens, P. (1980) 'Direct foreign investment – some spatial implications for the Source Economy', *Tijdschrift voor Economische en Sociale Geografie* 71, 1, 50–62.

Oxelheim', L (ed.) *The Global Race for Foreign Direct Investment.* Berlin: Springer-Verlag, 151–76.

Oyelere, P and Emmanuel, C (1996), *Seeking Evidence of International Transfer Pricing Abuse.* Working Paper 96/3, Department of Accounting and Finance, University of Glasgow.

Padoa-Schioppa, T *et al.* (1987) *Efficiency, Stability and Equity: A Strategy for the Evolution of the Economic System of the European Community.* Paris: Economica.

Painter, J and Goodwin, M (1996) 'Local governance, the crises of Fordism and the changing geographies of regulation', *Transactions of the Institute of British Geographers.* NS 21, 635–48.

Panic, M and Vacic, A (1995) 'International economic integration and disintegration: an overview', in M Panic and A Vacic (eds) *Economic Integration in Europe and North America.* Geneva: United Nations Economic Commission for Europe, Economic Studies No. 5.

Papke, LE (1987) 'Subnational taxation and capital mobility: estimates of tax–price elasticities', *National Tax Journal,* 40, 191–203.

Partridge, C (1994) 'Discover the joy of intimacy', *Sunday Times* Supplement, 15 May, 5.

Patel, P and Pavitt, K (1991) 'Large firms in the production of the world's technology: an important case of "non–globalisation" ', *Journal of International Business Studies* 22, 1–21.

Pearce, R and Papanastassiou, M (1997) 'European markets and the strategic roles of multinational enterprise subsidiaries in the UK', *Journal of Common Market Studies* 35, 243–66.

Peck, F (1995) 'The infrastructure and economic growth chapter', in Evans, L Johnson and Thomas (eds) *The Northern Regional Economy.* Mansell.

Peck, FW (1996) 'Regional development and the production of space: the role of infrastructure in the attraction of new inward investment', *Environment and Planning A* 28, 327–39.

Peck, F and Burdis, C (1996) 'After–care for inward investors: implications for regional development in the EU', in C Collis and Peck (eds) *Industrial Restructuring: FDI and Regional Development.* London: Regional Studies Association, 67–83.

Peck, F, Durnin, J and Stokes, B (1997a) *Industrial Change and Regional Development in Cumbria.* Barometer Series No.1, Centre for Regional Economic Development, University of Northumbria at Carlisle.

Peck, F, Durnin, J and Stokes, B (1997b) 'Cumbria vs the North East: industrial change and contrasting experiences in the northern region, 1973 to 1995', *Northern Economic Review* Autumn, 26, 47–62.

Peck, F and Stone, I (1991) 'Inward investment in the north-east of England: impact on the market for skills and training', *Planning Outlook* 34, 2, 96–101.

Peck, J (1996) *Workplace: The Social Regulation of Labour Markets,* New York: Guilford Press.

Phelps, N (1993) 'Branch plants and the evolving spatial division of labour: a study of material linkage change in the northern region of England', *Regional Studies* 27, 87–102.

Phelps, N (1995) *Post-structuralist location theory.* Papers in Planning Research No 146. Department of City and Regional Planning, Cardiff University.

Phelps, N (1997) *Multinationals and European Integration: Trade, Investment and Regional Development.* Regional Policy and Development Series No. 14. London: Jessica Kingsley Publishers.

PIEDA (1991) *Sellafield Redundancies: Labour Market Effects.* Report for Training Agency and Cumbria TEC.

PIEDA (1992a) *Research into Redundancies at VSEL, Barrow.* Report for Department of Employment and Cumbria TEC.

PIEDA (1992b) *A Strategic Framework for Economic Development Policy in Carlisle.* Main Report for Carlisle City Council.

Pike, A (1996) 'Greenfields, brownfields and industrial policy for the automobile industry in the UK', *Regional Studies* 30, 1, 69–77.

Pike, A and Tomaney, J (1996) 'A regional industrial strategy for the North', *Business Review North* 7, 4, 13–16.

Pine, BJ, II, Victor, B and Boynton, AC (1993) 'Making mass customization work', *Harvard Business Review* 71, 5, 108–11.

Piore, M and Sabel, C (1984) *The Second Industrial Divide.* New York: Basic Books.

Pitelis, C and Sugden, R (1991) *The Nature of the Transnational Firm,* London: Routledge.

Porter, M (1985) *Competitive Advantage: Creating and Sustaining Superior Performance.* New York: The Free Press.

Porter, M (1990) *The Competitive Advantage of Nations.* New York: The Free Press.
Porter, M (1994) 'The role of location in competition', *Journal of Economics and Business* 1, 1, 35–9.
Porter, M (1996) 'Competitive advantage, agglomerative economies and regional policy', *International Regional Science Review* 19, 1 and 2, 85–94.
Potter, JG (1995) 'Manufacturing plants as sources of new job creation: evidence from Devon and Cornwall', *Geoforum* 26, 2, 139–52.
Powell, WW (1990) 'Neither Market nor hierarchy: network forms of organisation', *Research in Organizational Behaviour,* 12, 295–336.
Prahalad, CK and Doz, Y (1987) *The Multinational Mission – Balancing Local Demands and Global Vision.* New York: The Free Press.
Price, A, Cooke, P and Morgan, K (1994) *The Welsh Renaissance: Inward Investment and Industrial Innovation.* Regional Industrial research Report No. 14. Centre for Advanced Studies, Cardiff University.
Raines, P and Brown, R (eds) (1998) *Policy Competition and Foreign Direct Investment in Europe.* Paris: OECD.
Raines, P and Wishlade, F (1997) 'Cross-European perspectives on the use and control of financial incentives in foreign investment promotion', In M Danson, S Hill and G Lloyd (eds) *Regional Governance and Economic Development.* London: Pion, 155–72.
Randolph, RS (1997) 'Central Europe – still a promising market', *Journal of Commerce* 28 *August,* Reuters News Service.
RAPID (1997a) IP/97/1005 *The Commission intends to refine its criteria for applying the state aids rules to tax measures.* 18 November, Brussels.
RAPID (1997b) IP/97/1138 *Commission to propose a three year test for new rules to refocus aid on job creation.* 17 December, Brussels.
Rees, G and Thomas, M (1994) 'Inward investment, labour market adjustment and skills development: recent experience in south Wales', *Local Economy* 9, 48–61.
Reich, R (1990) 'Who is us?', *Harvard Business Review* 68, 53–64.
Reuters Ltd (1997a) 'Foreign direct investment in Poland' to 30 June 1997, Reuters News Service, 28 August.
Reuters Ltd (1997b) 'Slovak government mulls tax breaks for foreign investors'. Reuters News Service, 23 June.
Rheault, DN (1996) 'War of the consumer electronics worlds', *Upside* 8, 7, 28.
Richet, A (1996) 'Transnational corporations, direct foreign investment and attractiveness of East European economies in transition', in M Dimitrov and K Todorov (eds) *Industrial Organisation and Entrepreneurship in Transition.* Sofia: Informa Intellect Ltd, 59–67.
Ridderstrale, J (1997) *Global Innovation – Managing International Innovation Projects in ABB and Electrolux.* PhD dissertation, Institute of International Business, Stockholm School of Economics, Stockholm, unpublished.
Roberts, K and Corcoran Nantes, Y (1992) *Training and Skill Formation in Large Companies: Management and Workforce Perspectives.* Report for Employment Department. Department of Sociology, University of Liverpool.
Roberts, P and Noon, D (1987) 'The role of industrial promotion and inward investment in the process of regional development', *Regional Studies* 21, 167–73.
Robinson, A (1997) *Investing in Central and Eastern Europe. Financial Times* Survey, 11 April.
Robinson, HJ (1961) *The Motivation and Flow of Private Foreign Investment.* Stanford, CA: Stanford Research Institute.
Rôdôsha Kyôiku Kyôkai (ed.) (1988) Sangyô kûdôka to koyô shitsugyô mondai. (The hollowing out of industry and the problem of employment and unemployment). Tokyo: Gakushû no Tomosha.
Rodrik, D (1997) *Has Globalization Gone Too Far?* Washington DC: Institute for International Economics.

Roth, K and Morrison, AJ (1992) 'Implementing global strategy: characteristics of global subsidiary mandates', *Journal of International Business Studies* 23, 715–35.

Rozenblat, C and Pumain, D (1993) 'The location of multinational firms in the European urban system', *Urban Studies* 30, 1691–709.

Rubery, J (1992) 'Productive systems, international integration and the single market', in A Castro, P Mehaut and J Rubery (eds) *International Integration and Labour Market Organisation.* London: Academic Press.

Ruigrok, W and Van Tulder, R (1996) *The Logic of International Restructuring.* London: Routledge.

Rutherford, TD (1994) 'From "sitting by Nellie" to the classroom factory? The restructuring of skills, recruitment and training in a South Wales motor components plant', *International Journal of Urban and Regional Research* 18, 3, 470–90.

Sachwald, F (ed.) (1994) *European Integration and Competitiveness.* Aldershot: Edward Elgar.

Sadler, D (1992) *The Global Region: Production, State Policies and Uneven Development.* Oxford: Pergamon Press.

Sadler, D, Swain, A and Hudson, R (1993) 'The automobile industry and Eastern Europe: new production strategies or old solutions?', *Area* 25, 339–49.

Safarian, AE (1993) *Multinational Enterprise and Public Policy: A Study of the Industrial Countries.* Aldershot: Edward Elgar.

Saitô, Takeshi (1996): Nihon sangyô daitenkan. (The big change in Japanese industry) Tokyo: Tôyô Keizai Shinhôsha.

Salt, J (1967) 'The impact of the Ford and Vauxhall plants on the employment situation of Merseyside, 1962 – 65', *Tijdschrift Voor Econ. En Soc. Geografie* (Sept./Okt.) 255–64

Salt, J (1988) 'Highly skilled international migrants, careers and internal labour markets', *Geoforum* 19, 387–400.

Sapir, A (1997), *Domino Effects in West European Trade, 1960–92.* CEPR Discussion Paper 1576.

Saxenian, AL (1994) *Regional Advantage; Culture and competition in Silicon Valley and Route 128.* Cambridge, MA: Harvard University Press.

Sayer, A (1985) 'Industry and space: a sympathetic critique of radical research', *Environment and Planning D* 3, 3–29.

Sayer, A (1995) *Radical Political Economy: A Critique*, Oxford: Basil Blackwell.

Sayer, A (1989) 'Dualistic thinking and rhetoric in geography', *Area* 21, 301–5.

Schamp, E (1991) 'Towards a spatial reorganisation of the German car industry?: the implications of new production concepts', in G Benko, M Dunford (eds) *Industrial Change and Regional Development: The Transformation of New Industrial Space.* London: Belhaven Press.

Scherer, FM (1994) *Competition Policies for an Integrated World Economy.* Washington, DC: The Brookings Institution.

Schmenner, RW (1982) *Making Business Location Decisions.* New Jersey: Prentice–Hall.

Schmidt, VA (1995) 'The new world order, incorporated: the rise of business and the decline of the nation-state', *Daedalus*, 124, 75–106.

Schoenberger, EJ (1984) *Foreign Manufacturing Investment in the United States: Investment Strategy and International Location.* Unpublished PhD dissertation. University of California at Berkeley.

Schoenberger, EJ (1988) 'Multinational corporations and the new international division of labour: a critical appraisal', *International Regional Science Review* 11, 2, 105–19 .

Schoenberger, EJ (1990) 'United States-manufacturing investment in Western Europe: markets, corporate strategy, and the competitive environment', *Annals of the Association of American Geographers* 80, 3, 379–93.

Schoenberger, EJ (1997) *The Cultural Crisis of the Firm.* Oxford: Blackwell.

Scott, AJ (1983) 'Industrial organisation and the logic of intra-metropolitan location i', *Economic Geography* 59, 233–50.

Scott, AJ (1986) 'Industrial organisation and location: division of labour, the firm and spatial process', *Economic Geography* 62, 215–31.
Scott, AJ (1988a) 'Flexible production systems and regional development: the rise of new industrial spaces in North America and Western Europe', *International Journal of Urban and Regional Research* 12, 171–86 .
Scott, AJ (1988b) *New Industrial Spaces: Flexible Production Organization and Regional Development in North America and Western Europe*. London: Pion.
Scott, AJ (1996) 'Regional motors of the global economy', *Futures* 28, 5, 391–411.
Seideman, A (1994) 'Getting to know you: developing electronics intimacy with customers', *Potentials in Marketing* 27, 32–9.
Seki, Mitsuhiro (1997) Kûdôka o koete – gijutsu to chiiki no saikôchiku. (Overcoming hollowing out – the reorganisation of technique and regions). Tokyo: Nihon Keizai Shinbunsha.
Servan-Schreiber, JJ (1968) *The American Challenge*. New York: Athenaeum.
Shaiken, H (1994) 'Advanced manufacturing and Mexico: a new international division of labour?', *Latin American Research Review* 29, 2, 1–34.
Shapiro, D (1983) 'The comparative profitability of Canadian and foreign controlled firms', *Managerial and Decision Economics* 4, 2, 97–106.
Shibata, Takashi (1993) 'Sony's successful strategy for compact discs', *Long Range Planning* 26, 4, 16–21.
Shin, YH and Lee, Y-I (1995) 'Korean direct investment in Southeast Asia', *Journal of Contemporary Asia* 25, 2, 179–96.
Simon, HA (1947) *Administrative Behavior: A study of decision-making processes in administrative organization*. New York: Macmillan.
Sklair, L (1997) 'Social movements for global capaitalism: the transnational capitalist class in action', *Review of International Political Economy* 4, 514–38.
Slocum, JW Jr, McGill, M and Lei, D (1994) 'The new learning strategy: anytime, anything, anywhere', *Organizational Dynamics* 23, 2, 33–47.
Smith, and Reinertsen, D (1991) *Developing Products in Half the Time*. New York: Van Nostrand.
Sômuchô Tôkeikyoku (ed.) (1994) Nihon tôkei nenkan 1995. (Japan Statistical Yearbook 1995). Tokyo: Ôkurashô Insatsukyoku.
Sômuchô Tôkeikyoku (ed.) (1996) Nihon tôkei nenkan 1997 (Japan Statistical Yearbook 1997). Tokyo: Ôkurashô Insatsukyoku.
Sômuchô Tôkeikyoku (ed.) (1998) Nihon tôkei geppô dai 439–gô. (Monthly statistics of Japan No. 439) Tokyo: Nihon Tôkei Kyôkai.
Sony (1995) 'Sony in Europe Towards a New Age'. Company Brochure.
Spence, N (1992) 'Impact of infrastructure investment policy', in P Townroi and R Martin (eds) *Regional Development in the 1990s: The British Isles in Transition*. London: Jessica Kingsley.
Srinivasan, K and Mody, A (1998) 'Japanese and US firms as foreign investors: do they work to the same time?' *Canadian Journal of Economics*, 31, 778–99.
Srinivasan, TN, Whalley, J and Wooton, I (1993) 'Measuring the effects of regionalism on trade and welfare', in Anderson and Blackhurst (eds), *op. cit.*
SSKK Sangyô Seisakukyoku Kokusai Kigyôka (ed.) (1996) Kaigai tenkai senryaku ni kakaru kigyô chôsa hôkoku. (Survey of firm strategies towards overseas development strategies). Tokyo: Sangyô Seisakukyoku Kokusai Kigyôka (MITI).
Stafford, HA (1985) 'Environmental protection and industrial location', *Annals of the Association of American Geographers* 75, 227–40.
Stafford, HA. (1991) 'Manufacturing plant closure selections within firms', *Annals of the Association of American Geographers* 81, 1, 51–65.
Stalk, G and Hout, T (1990) *Competing Against Time*. New York: The Free Press.
Stone, I and Peck, F (1996) 'The foreign-owned manufacturing sector in the UK peripheral regions, 1978–1993: restructuring and comparative performance', *Regional Studies* 30, 55–68.

Storper, M (1995) 'The resurgence of regional economies, ten years later: the region as a nexus of untraded dependencies', *European Urban and Regional Studies* 2, 3, 191–221.

Storper, M and Walker, R (1989) *The Capitalist Imperative: Territory, Technology, and Industrial Growth.* Oxford: Basil Blackwell.

Strange, R (1993) *Japanese Manufacturing Investment in Europe: Its Impact on the UK Economy.* London: Routledge.

Strange, S (1996) *The Retreat of the Nation State: The Diffusion of Power in the World economy.* Cambridge: Cambridge University Press.

Styczek, D (1996) 'A slightly wider (green)field of vision', *Warsaw Voice* 5 (4 February) 380.

Sunley, P (1996) 'Context in economic-geography – the relevance of pragmatism', *Progress in Human Geography* 20, 338–55.

Swyngedouw, E (1992) 'The mammon quest. "Glocalisation", interspatial competition and the monetary order: the construction of new spatial scales', in M Dunford and G Kafkals (eds) *Cities and Regions in the New Europe: the Global–Local Interplay and Spatial Development Strategies.* London: Belhaven.

Takagi, Takenori and Tatsunori Tsuchiya (1995) Kokunai seizôgyô no kûdôka to chûshô kigyô (The hollowing out of the domestic industry and the small and medium enterprises), Shôkô Kin'yu 45, 4, 16–38.

Taylor, J (1993) 'An analysis of the factors determining the geographical distribution of Japanese manufacturing investment in the UK 1984–1991', *Urban Studies* 30, 7, 1209–24.

Teague, P (1994) 'Governance structures and economic performance: the case of Northern Ireland', *International Journal of Urban and Regional Research* 18, 275–92.

The Bank of Korea (1993) The current aspects and the future directions of Korean foreign direct investment : its linkage to industrial restructuring (in Korean).

The Bank of Korea (1994) Regulations on Korean foreign direct investment (in Korean).

The Bank of Korea (1997) Evaluations and future tasks of Korean foreign direct investment (in Korean).

Thomas, K (1997) *Competing for Capital: European and North American Responses.* St. Louis: University of Missouri, mimeo.

Thomsen, S and Woolcock, S (1993) *Direct investment and EuropeanIntegration : Competition Among Firms and Governments.* London: Pinter.

Tickell, A and Peck, J (1995) 'Social regulation after Fordism: regulation theory, neo-liberalism and the global-land nexus', *Economy and Society* 24, 357–86.

Tomaney, J, Pike, A and Cornford, J (1999) 'Plant closure and the local economy: the case of Swan Hunter on Tyneside', *Regional Studies*, 33, 401–12.

Tomizawa, Kenji (1989) Sangyô kûdôka to koyô mondai. (The hollowing out of industry and the employment problem). Tokyo: Ochonomizu no Shobô.

Toshiba (1994) *Toshiba Today: Corporate Profile.* Tokyo: Toshiba Corporation.

Townroe, TM (1975) 'Branch plants and regional development', *Town Planning Review* 446, 47–62.

Toyo, K (1992) *Kaigai shinshutsu kigyo soran 1992/93.* Tokyo: Toyo Keizai Shuppan.

Toyo, K (1995) *Kaigai shinshutsu kigyo soran 1995.* Tokyo: Toyo Keizai Shuppan.

Treacy, M and Wiersema, F (1993) 'A customer intimacy and other value disciplines', *Harvard Business Review* 71, 4, 84–93.

Trevor, M (1985) *Japanese Industrial Knowledge: Can it Help British Industry?* Aldershot: Gower.

TSDKCT (Tsûshô Sangyô Daijin Kanbô Chôsa Tôkeibu) (ed.) (1993) Heisei 3-nen kôgyô tôkeihyô, sangyôhen. (Census of manufactures 1991, report by industries), Tokyo: Tsûshô Sangyô Chôsakai.

TSDKCT Tsûshô Sangyô Daijin Kanbô Chôsa Tôkeibu (ed.) (1997) Heisei 7-nen kôgyô tôkeihyô, sangyôhen. (Census of manufactures 1995, report by industries), Tokyo: Tsûshô Sangyô Chôsakai.

Tsûshô Sangyôshô (ed.) (1991) Dai 4-kai kaigai tôshi tôkei sôran. (Basic statistical survey of overseas investment, vol. 4) Tokyo: Ôkurashô Insatsukyoku.

Tsûshô Sangyôshô (ed.) (1992) Dai 21-kai wagakuni kigyô no kaigai jigyô katsudô. (Overseas activities of domestic firms, vol. 21) Tokyo: Ôkurashô Insatsukyoku.

Tsûshô Sangyôshô (ed.) (1993) Dai 22-kai wagakuni kigyô no kaigai jigyô katsudô. (Overseas activities of domestic firms, vol. 22) Tokyo: Ôkurashô Insatsukyoku.

Tsûshô Sangyôshô (ed.) (1994) Dai 5-kai kaigai tôshi tôkei sôran. (Basic statistical survey of overseas investment, vol. 5) Tokyo: Ôkurashô Insatsukyoku.

Tsûshô Sangyôshô (ed.) (1995) Dai 24-kai wagakuni kigyô no kaigai jigyô katsudô. (Overseas activities of domestic firms, vol. 24) Tokyo: Ôkurashô Insatsukyoku.

Tsûshô Sangyôshô (ed.) (1996) Dai 25-kai wagakuni kigyô no kaigai jigyô katsudô. (Overseas activities of domestic firms, vol. 25) Tokyo: Ôkurashô Insatsukyoku.

Tsûshô Sangyôshô (ed.) (1997a) Dai 6-kai kaigai jigyô katsudô kihon chôsa sokuhô. (Basic survey of overseas business activities of domestic firms, vol. 6, preliminary report) Tokyo: Tsûshô Sangyôshô – Sangyô Seisakukyoku Kokusai Kigyôka.

Tsûshô Sangyôshô (ed.) (1997b) Tsûshô Hakusho, sôron, 1997. (White Paper of international trade – general overview 1997) Tokyo: Ôkurashô Insatsukyoku.

UNCTAD (1989) *The Process of Transnationalization and Transnational Mergers.* New York: United Nations.

UNCTAD (1993) *World Investment Report: Transnational Corporations and Integrated International Production.* Geneva: United Nations.

UNCTAD (1994) *World Investment Report: Transnational Corporations, Employment and the Workplace.* Geneva: United Nations.

UNCTAD (1995) *World Investment Report: Transnational Corporations and Competitiveness.* Geneva: United Nations.

UNCTAD (1996a) *Incentives and Foreign Direct Investment* UNCTAD/DTCI/28 Current Studies, Series A, 30. New York: United Nations.

UNCTAD (1996b) *World Investment Report: Trade and Investment Policy.* Geneva: United Nations.

UNCTAD *World Investment Report, Transnational Corporations and Competitiveness,* Annual Reports 1993, 1994, 1995, 1996 and 1997. New York and Geneva: United Nations

Venable, T (1995) 'Incentive lures: firmly embedded in the location equation', *Site Selection* 40 (April) 254–71.

Vermulst, E and Waer, P (1990) 'European Community rules of origin as commercial policy instruments', *Journal of World Trade* 24, 3, 55–99.

Vernon, R (1966) 'International investment and international trade in the product cycle', *Quarterly Journal of Economics* 80, 190–207.

Vernon, R (1979) 'The product cycle hypothesis in a new international environment', *Oxford Bulletin of Economics and Statistics* 41, 4, 255–67.

Voisey, CJ (1993) The International Organizational Network as Core Capability: Global Product Development in Fujitsu Limited. Cambridge, MA: MIT Japan Program.

Walker, R (1989) 'A requiem for corporate geography: new directions in industrial organisation, the production of place and uneven development', *Geografiska Annaler* 71 (B), 1, 43 – 68.

Wall Street Journal (1996) 'Sony's first PC due today, priced at $2,000 to $3,000' B7(W), col 1, section 13, 17 June, 7.

Wallace, LH (1995) 'Foreign Direct Investment Into the State of New Jersey' in Conference Proceedings: *International Firms: The New York Experience.* New York City: Sept., New York: Baruch.

Walter, I (1994) 'The role of mergers and acquisition in foreign direct investment' in Oxelheim, L (ed.) *The Global Race for Foreign Direct Investment.* Berlin: Springer-Verlag, 151–76.

Warsaw Voice (1996) 'Not so risky business'. 48 (1 December) 423.

Warsaw Voice (1997) 'Europe's Open Secret'. Polish Agency for Foreign Investment, 8 (23 February) 435.

Watts, HD (1980) *The Branch Plant Economy.* London: Macmillan.

Watts, HD (1981) *The Branch Plant Economy: A Study of External Control.* Harlow: Longman.

Waverman, L (ed.) (1991) *Corporate Globalization through Mergers and Acquisitions.* Ottawa: Ministry of Supply and Services.

Webster, FE, Jr (1992) 'The changing role of marketing in the corporation', *Journal of Marketing* 56, 4, 1–17.

Wells, LT Jr and Wint, AG (1990) 'Marketing a country: promotion as a tool for attracting foreign investment', in *Foreign Investment Advisory Service,* Occasional Paper No. 1. Washington, DC: International Finance Corporation Multilateral Guarantee Agency.

Welsh Affairs Committee (1995) *Wales in Europe Volume 2.* London: HMSO.

Welsh Development Agency (1995) *Working for Wales.* WDA Three Year Corporate Plan. Cardiff.

Welsh Office (1995) *Welsh Economic Trends, 1995 Edition.* Cardiff: Welsh Office.

Welsh Office (1997) *An Economic Strategy for Wales: A Welsh Office Consultative Document.* October 1997.

West Cumbria Development Agency (1994) *Annual Reports and Accounts.* Carlisle: WCDA.

West Cumbria Partnership (1994) *Economic Development Strategy for West Cumbria.* Carlisle: WCP.

West Cumbria Partnership (1996) *Economic Development Strategy for West Cumbria.* Carlisle: WCP.

Whalley, J (1993), 'Regional trade arrangements in North America: CUSTA and NAFTA', in de Melo and Panagariya, *op. cit.*

Whalley, J (1998), 'Why do countries seek regional trade agreements?', in Frankel, *op. cit.*

Wheeler, D and Mody, A (1992) 'International investment locational decisions – the case of U.S. firms', *Journal of International Economics* 33, 57–76.

Whitley, R (1992) 'The comparative study of business systems in Europe: issues and choices', in R Whitley (ed.) *European Business Systems: Firms and Markets in Their National Contexts.* London: Sage.

Whittington, D (1995) 'The name of the game is incentives', *Area Development* 30 (July) 24–6.

Wilkins, M (1989) *Foreign Investment in the United States to 1914.* Cambridge, MA: Harvard University Press.

Wilkinson, B (1995) 'The free trade agreement between Canada and the United States', in M Panic and A Vacic (eds) *Economic Integration in Europe and North America.* United Nations Economic Commission for Europe, Economic Studies No. 5. Geneva: United Nations.

Williams, K, Williams, J and Haslam, C (1991) 'The hollowing out of British manufacturing and its implications for policy', *Economy and Society* 19,56–90.

Williams, K, Williams, J, and Haslam,C (1992) 'Against lean production', *Economy and Society* 21, 3, 321–54.

Williams, K, Williams, J, Haslam, C, Adcroft, A and Sukhdev, L (1992) *Factories or Warehouses? Japanese Manufacturing FDI in Britain and the US.* Occasional Papers on Business Economy and Society, No.6. Polytechnic of East London.

Wint, AG (1992) 'Public marketing of foreign investment: successful international offices stand alone', *International Journal of Public Sector Management* 5, 5, 27–39.

Winters, LA (1994), *The EC and World Protectionism: Dimensions of the Political Economy.* CEPR Discussion Paper 897.

Wishlade, F (1997) *When are Tax Advantages State Aids and When are They General Measures?* Regional and Industrial Research Paper Series 20. Glasgow: European Policies Research Centre, University of Strathclyde.

Wishlade, F (1998) 'EC competition policy: the poor relation of EC regional policy?' *European Planning Studies,* 6, 573–598.

Wishlade, F *et al.* (1998) *Economic and Social Cohesion in the European Union: the Impact of Member States' Own Policies.* Luxembourg: Regional Development Studies, Commission of the European Communities.

Wolf, M (1997) 'The global company: the heart of the new world economy', *Financial Times,* 1 October, 1b.

World Economic Forum (1995) *The World Competitiveness Report, 1995.* Geneva and Lausanne: The World Economic Forum and IMEDE.

World Trade Organisation (WTO) (1995) *Regionalism and the World Trading System.* Geneva.

World Trade Organisation (WTO) (1997) 'The Growing Impact of Investment on Trade', *WTO Focus,* June–July.

World Trade Organisation (WTO) (1996) *Annual Report 1996, Volume 1.* Geneva: WTO.

Wyatt-Walker, A (1995) 'Regionalism, globalisation and world economic order', in L Fawcett and A Hurrell (eds) *Regionalism in World Politics: Regional Organisation and International Order.* Oxford: Oxford University Press, 74–121.

Yamamoto, Y (1997) 'Weaker yen strengthens fiscal 1997 profit projections', *Nikkei Weekly* 10 March, 1, 19.

Yannopoulos, GN (1990) 'Foreign direct investment and European integration: the evidence from the formative years of the European Community', *Journal of Common Market Studies* 28, 235–59.

Young, S and Hood, N (1993) 'Inward investment policy in the European Community in the 1990s', *Transnational Corporations* 12, 2, 35–62.

Young, S, Hood, N and Dunlop, S (1988) 'Global strategies, multinational subsidiary roles and economic impact in Scotland', *Regional Studies* 22, 487–98.

Young, S, Hood, N and Peters, E (1994) 'Multinational enterprises and regional development', *Regional Studies* 28, 7, 657–77.

Young, S, McDermott, M and Dunlop, S (1991) 'The challenge of the single market', in B Burgenmeier and JL Mucchielli (eds) *Multinationals and Europe 1992 : Strategies for the future.* London and New York: Routledge, 3–2.

Yuill, D, Bachtler, J and Wishlade, F (1997) *European Regional Incentives 1997–8,* 17th edition. London: Bowker–Saur.

Zemplinerova, A (1997) *The Role of Foreign Enterprises in the Privatisation and Restructuring of the Czech Economy.* Vienna: Vienna Institute for Comparative Economic Studies.

INDEX

Page numbers in italic indicate reference to a table or figure.